Echoes of the Sixties

Marti Smiley Childs
and Jeff March

BILLBOARD BOOKS
An imprint of Watson-Gu

Senior editor: Bob Nirkind

Editor: Sylvia Warren

Production manager: Ellen Greene

Book and cover design: Areta Buk/Thumb Print

First published in 1999 by Watson-Guptill Publications

1515 Broadway, New York, NY 10036

Library of Congress Cataloging-in-Publication Data

Childs, Marti Smiley.

    Echoes of the sixties / Marti Smiley Childs and Jeff March.

      p. cm.

    Includes index.

    ISBN 0-8230-8316-0

    1. Rock Musicians—Biography. 2. Composers—Biography. 3. Rock
music—1961–1970—History and criticism. I. March, Jeff. II. Title.

    ML394.C53 1999

    781.66'09—dc21   99-049826

Manufactured in the United States of America

First printing, 1999

1 2 3 4 5 6 7 8 9 / 07 06 05 04 03 02 01 00 99

CONTENTS

Acknowledgments IV

Preface V

CHAPTER 1 **SUGAR SHACK** 1
THE FIREBALLS, featuring vocalists
Chuck Tharp and Jimmy Gilmer

CHAPTER 2 **QUARTER TO THREE** 37
GARY "U.S" BONDS

CHAPTER 3 **THE LION SLEEPS TONIGHT** 49
THE TOKENS

CHAPTER 4 **MY BOYFRIEND'S BACK** 77
THE ANGELS

CHAPTER 5 **A WORLD WITHOUT LOVE** 97
PETER & GORDON

CHAPTER 6 **NIGHTS IN WHITE SATIN** 115
MOODY BLUES / MIKE PINDER

CHAPTER 7 **LAUGH, LAUGH** 129
THE BEAU BRUMMELS

CHAPTER 8 **WOOLY BULLY** 161
SAM THE SHAM AND THE PHARAOHS

CHAPTER 9 **SUMMER IN THE CITY** 197
THE LOVIN' SPOONFUL

CHAPTER 10 **LADY WILLPOWER** 225
GARY PUCKETT AND THE UNION GAP

CHAPTER 11 **I FEEL LIKE I'M FIXIN' TO DIE** 255
COUNTRY JOE AND THE FISH

CHAPTER 12 **IN-A-GADDA-DA-VIDA** 283
IRON BUTTERFLY

Index 310

ACKNOWLEDGMENTS

This book is the result of the assistance and participation of dozens of individuals—performers, composers, producers, recording company executives, administrative aides, booking agents, personal managers, and others who offered us their suggestions, their assistance, and their time. While all contributed in significant ways, a few were particularly important in the development of this project.

We appreciatively acknowledge the gracious participation of Peter Asher and Gordon Waller, who were the first artists to agree to speak with us and who entrusted us with details of their professional and personal lives. Their involvement helped reassure other performers about the worthiness of the project. We likewise are indebted to entertainer Donnie Brooks, a packager of oldies shows, who helped open many doors for us.

We extend sincere thanks as well to Bill Belmont, Bob Birk, Gerry Boehme, Steve Brigati, Gary Cape, Joel Denver, Jim Dotson, Michael Gracy, Bill Hathaway, Larry Lauzon, Rick Levy, Tim Livingston, Danny Loria, Steve Meloan, Eric Olsen, Stephen Peeples, Alan Redstone, and Kenny Schreiber, as well as to each of the photographers who generously granted us permission to publish their photos.

We acknowledge Record Research Inc. as our source of historical *Billboard* Hot 100 chart information.

And of course, we are deeply grateful to all 43 musical performers and the members of their families for sharing their aspirations, fears, triumphs, tragedies, disappointments, and dreams. We will always value their candor, trust, and kindness, and are proud to now call them friends.

PREFACE

As the 1960s recede ever further away in our recollective rearview mirror, the overwhelming influence of those watershed years on American culture has never been more apparent. Today, 54 million Americans who call themselves children of the '60s, people who lived their formative years during that decade, find a common bond in the events, sights, and sounds of that remarkable era of change.

Ushered in under the strong but conventional leadership of Dwight David Eisenhower, the 1960s soon took an abrupt idealistic turn skyward as charismatic John Fitzgerald Kennedy unfolded his vision of the "New Frontier" that included a promise to land an American astronaut on the moon by the end of the decade. We had no idea how wild the ride would be through that jubilant, chaotic, angry decade, a blur of sights and sounds through which we hung on for dear life. And pop music provided the soundtrack that accompanied—and reflected—the era's tumultuous political and sociological changes.

At the dawn of the decade, the pop charts were dominated by doo-wop and innocuous puppy-love ballads by teen idols Frankie Avalon, Brenda Lee, Fabian, and others of the bouffant-hair set. Yet already there were signs of things to come. One of the first indications of a new kind of potency for pop came in January 1962, when Chubby Checker's *The Twist,* capitalizing on the popularity of a dance craze that had already swept the country, heralded a string of dance-inciting hits by Checker, Dee Dee Sharp, the Dovells, Gary "U.S." Bonds, Little Eva, and Joey Dee and the Starliters—the stomp, the hucklebuck, the watusi, the fly, the limbo, the slop, the pony, the mashed potatoes, and others that not only were immensely popular among teenagers, but captivated adults as well. While dancers were gyrating, however, the groundwork for profound societal changes was under way. Sit-ins began February 1, 1960, in Greensboro, North Carolina, in protest of the treatment of four black college students who were refused service at a lunch counter in a Woolworth's store. At the University of Mississippi, 3,000 troops quelled an October 1962 riot that was provoked by the admission of James Meredith as the first black student at the campus. The following August, 200,000 civil rights demonstrators gathered in Washington, D.C., where the Rev. Martin Luther King delivered his stirring "I Have a Dream" speech.

Meanwhile, international tensions were building between the United States and communist nations. On May 1, 1960, the Soviet Union shot down an American U-2 reconnaissance plane over Russia. The United States severed relations in January 1961 with Soviet ally Cuba after that island nation commandeered American business properties in Cuba, and three months later a CIA-engineered military attempt to overthrow Cuban premier Fidel Castro failed. Halfway around the world, American military personnel had been dispatched in South Vietnam since the mid-'50s as advisers to help train South Vietnamese troops for combat with communist North Vietnam. But America's role in the conflict changed irrevocably in February 1962, when President John Kennedy authorized American military "advisers" to return fire if attacked by enemy troops. The discovery of a buildup of Soviet missiles in Cuba aimed toward the United States led to an American naval and air blockade that brought the world to the brink of war in October 1962. Meanwhile, mainstream America was paying little attention to the growing intensity of the civil rights movement and the escalation of the Vietnam conflict. Hit recordings by the Beach Boys, Jan and Dean, Dick Dale and the Del-Tones, the Fireballs, and the Angels reflected the preoccupation of American kids with surfing, cars, and dating. The undercurrents of folk music that the Tokens rode with "The Lion Sleeps Tonight" in early 1962 surfaced prominently in 1963, when the college-based, hand-clapping hootenanny fad thrust the Kingston Trio, the New Christy Minstrels, the Rooftop Singers, and Peter Paul and Mary into the top 20. Even though their success at the time was based more on musical than on lyrical content, the folk-flavored hits of the early '60s—particularly those by Peter, Paul and Mary—helped elevate the social consciousness of pop music and hastened the acceptance of acoustic folk music artists such as Pete Seeger, Joan Baez, and Bob Dylan. Peter, Paul and Mary first popularized the music of Dylan, whose composition "Blowin' In The Wind" became an anthem for the civil rights movement and whose influence on pop music was monumental. The assassination of President Kennedy in Dallas on November 22, 1963, rocked America to its foundations. The U.S. involvement in Vietnam, which had begun with 700 military advisers in 1956, had increased to 15,000 troops by the time of Kennedy's death. In those confused times, American kids were ripe for a change. And in those closing days of 1963, disc jockeys at a few radio stations complied by spinning a record called "From Me To You" by an English band calling itself the Beatles. After the Beatles' "I Want To Hold Your Hand" captured the No. 1 position on the *Billboard* Hot 100, where it remained for seven weeks in February and March 1964, American kids embraced everyone and everything British. Peter and Gordon, Chad and Jeremy, the Moody Blues, the Rolling Stones, Marianne Faithfull, Herman's Hermits, Dusty Springfield, Gerry and the Pacemakers, the Animals, Petula Clark, the Dave Clark Five, the Kinks, Cilla Black, Billy J. Kramer and the Dakotas, and other British performers catapulted onto the American charts—and into the repertoire of American bands. British influences were assimilated successfully by a number of American bands, including the Beau Brummels and the Sir Douglas Quintet. And because the Beatles played so well to television audiences, a number of bands—including Sam the Sham and the Pharaohs, Paul Revere and the Raiders, and, later, Gary Puckett and the Union Gap—achieved prominence not only on the basis of their musical talents but also by virtue of the visual impact of their costumed personas.

Midway through the decade, the nation found itself deep in turmoil. American involvement in the Vietnam War increased dramatically after passage of the Tonkin Resolution in August 1964 led to President Lyndon Johnson's authorization of bombing raids over North Vietnam. A year later, the first of a series of major race riots in the United States during the 1960s erupted when a routine arrest in the predominantly African American Watts section of Los Angeles caused the smoldering resentment of the residents to burst into flame—both figuratively and literally. Antiwar protests that had begun on college campuses spread to the streets as well. And when folksinger Bob Dylan shocked acoustic folk aficionados by appearing on stage backed by an amplified blues-rock band in 1965, he energized popular music as a tool of social protest. Barry McGuire's "The Eve Of Destruction," Donovan's "Universal Soldier," Buffalo Springfield's "For What It's Worth," the Byrds' "Chimes Of Freedom," and other songs protesting war and discrimination altered the vernacular of pop music, defined the genre of folk-rock perfected by groups such as the Lovin' Spoonful, the Mamas and the Papas, and the Turtles, and helped galvanize the youth movement.

As the Vietnam War dragged on and escalated despite public outcry, many young people sought respite in the escapism offered by hallucinogenic drugs—inspired by the vivid musical imagery present in post-1965 Beatles albums and by the preachings of psychologist Timothy Leary, who after experimenting with hallucinogenic drugs urged his followers to "tune in, turn on, and drop out." Intertwined with the peace movement, the "hippie" bohemian counterculture that flowered in San Francisco's Haight-Ashbury district in 1966 and 1967 gave rise to "psychedelic" music, heavily laden with drug references and mind-numbing acoustic feedback. A scant five years after adolescent boys with crew cuts and girls with ponytails were digging Bobby Rydell, the Four Seasons, and the Shirelles, many teenagers had grown long, shaggy hair, distanced themselves from their family's values, and embraced the wildly soaring and often dark and brooding music of Jefferson Airplane, Iron Butterfly, Cream, Steppenwolf, Country Joe and the Fish, the Doors, Big Brother and the Holding Company, Spirit, and the Jimi Hendrix Experience, all of whom remained popular through the end of the decade. Now, three decades later, echoes of the '60s reverberate throughout the contemporary cultural scene. We hear them on oldies radio stations, in motion pictures, in television commercials. Oldies remain touchstones for a generation of adults who call themselves children of the '60s. The music lives on. But what happened to the artists who recorded, and often wrote, those golden oldies? Perhaps not surprisingly, many of the singers, songwriters, and musicians who had their greatest success during the 1960s remained in the recording industry, moving into production, talent management, background singing, commercial jingle recording, concert booking, or executive positions. But many others moved on to other fields, taking advantage of new opportunities and discovering new abilities. *Echoes of the Sixties* shares the aspirations, trials and triumphs, and life lessons of artists from both groups.

Each of the 12 chapters is devoted to one vocal group, soloist, or band. The sequence is roughly chronological, beginning with the Fireballs, who first broke onto the Hot 100 in September 1959, and ending with Iron Butterfly, whose multi-platinum album *In-A-Gadda-Da-Vida* was released in 1968. All of the chapters open with a short essay chronicling the key events in the artists' (or artist's) rise to fame, followed by a "Then and Now" section which supplies, for each performer, further details from the past as well as an account of what has happened to them over the last 30 years.

Several bands underwent personnel changes, and we decided to concentrate on the individuals who were present during the principal hit-making years of the 1960s. Although we contacted all surviving members of each band, a few declined to participate in the project. In the end, 43 artists agreed to speak with us. Through deeply personal and revealing conversations with these 43 people, we have created illuminating profiles of some of the musical pied pipers who influenced the styles, thoughts, and attitudes of a generation of Americans and helped in many ways to shape the course of history.

It is a privilege to introduce you to musicians whose most famous songs may be as familiar to you as old friends but whose lives you probably never really knew anything about—until now. These artists share their aspirations and fears, triumphs and tragedies, and dreams and disappointments. Through their stories, we learn something about ourselves.

—MARTI SMILEY CHILDS AND JEFF MARCH

CHAPTER 1

Sugar Shack

The Fireballs

FEATURING VOCALISTS
CHUCK THARP AND
JIMMY GILMER

The Fireballs in 1958, at their first photo session. Left to right: Lead guitarist George Tomsco, singer Chuck Tharp, drummer Eric Budd, bassist Stan Lark, and rhythm guitarist Danny Trammell.

PHOTO BY CLYDE WILLISTON.

mark

FROM THE TIME CAPSULE

JUNE 1961: The fourth Fireballs hit single, "Quite A Party," reaches No. 27.

- JUNE 16: NBC-TV's *Today* show closes for the first time in a decade without Dave Garroway's "Peace" sign. (Garroway was replaced by John Chancellor after he resigned following a dispute with NBC programming executives.) Rudolf Nureyev defects to the West in Paris.
- JUNE 18: The *Gunsmoke* western series starring William Conrad ends its run on the CBS radio network.

SEPTEMBER 1963: Jimmy Gilmer and the Fireballs release what was to be the top single of the year, "Sugar Shack."

- SEPTEMBER 2: Alabama Gov. George C. Wallace orders Tuskegee High School encircled by state troopers to prevent black students from entering the school. Eight days later, President Kennedy dispatches National Guard troops to enforce the order of integration.
- SEPTEMBER 17: First episode of *The Fugitive,* starring David Janssen, airs on ABC-TV.

DECEMBER 1967: Fireballs release "Bottle Of Wine," which climbs to the No. 9 spot.

- DECEMBER 3: Dr. Christiaan Barnard and a team of surgeons from South Africa perform the world's first successful heart transplant on a human, who lived for 18 days following the groundbreaking procedure.
- DECEMBER 10: Singer Otis Redding dies in a plane crash in Wisconsin at the age of 26.
- DECEMBER 18: The Spaghetti Western era begins in earnest with the release of Sergio Leone's film *A Fistful Of Dollars,* starring Clint Eastwood.

Although the hit-making era of the Fireballs spanned just nine years, the band that first glowed at the close of the innocent '50s weathered one of the most tumultuous periods in musical and cultural history, one which smothered the careers of many other artists. Formed in 1958, the band—consisting of lead guitarist George Tomsco, singer-guitarist Chuck Tharp, drummer Eric Budd, rhythm guitarist Dan Trammell, and country music bass player Stan Lark—drew a measure of inspiration by recording in the same New Mexico studio in which the legendary Buddy Holly and the Crickets cut their hits.

The Fireballs, who first achieved notoriety with a cluster of guitar-driven instrumentals in a style also characteristic of Duane Eddy, Jorgen Ingmann, Ernie Freeman, Link Wray, and the Ventures, were chameleon-like in their ability to change style in step with the times. The musical charts in 1963 were populated by hits from an eclectic assemblage of artists, including Japanese vocalist Kyu Sakamoto, the Singing Nun from Belgium, doo-woppers-turned-surfers Jan and Dean, crooner Steve Lawrence, the folksinging Kingston Trio and Peter, Paul and Mary, balladeer Bobby Vinton, and 13-year-old Little Stevie Wonder, who made his stunning debut with the chart-topping "Fingertips, Part II." But the record that remained the longest time in the No. 1 position that year—five weeks—came from a group that hadn't scored a hit for two years: the Fireballs.

The Fireballs, all from the tiny town of Raton, New Mexico, initially came to the national forefront in 1959 through the production genius of Norman Petty, whose studio in the New Mexico town of Clovis produced hit recordings for Buddy Holly, Roy Orbison, Jimmy Bowen, Buddy Knox, and the String-A-Longs. Acting as the Fireballs' manager, Petty began sending their tapes to record companies, including Kapp Records. In early 1959, when *Gunsmoke* was the highest-rated prime-time television program, Domenico Modugno's "Nel Blu Dipinto Di Blu (Volare)" captured top honors in the first-ever Grammy awards, and Alaska became the 49th state, Kapp released "Fireball." The song landed on local charts in the Southwest, and the Fireballs took to the road.

Touring was anything but glamorous. "I wouldn't want to go through again what we did those years," says George. "During our first tour we sold tools out of our tool box to buy hamburgers. Sometimes our meals were crackers and water. We usually had no money for motels, so we slept in our cars. We spent the summer of 1959 on the road in the Midwest with no air conditioning in our cars. We had no way to clean up or get our laundry done. We'd pull into service stations and they'd look at us and ask, 'You boys following the harvest?' That burning desire to be in the music business kept us going."

Danny Trammell, in particular, found touring disheartening. "We lived on peanuts. We were popular but didn't have any money. I remember one time we wanted to take a disc jockey out to dinner but we didn't have enough cash to order hamburgers for everybody. The disc jockey got fed but I didn't," Trammell sardonically recalls.

Despite the problems, the camaraderie among the boys strengthened on the road, and they took on nicknames they gave each other: Shirsk (Tomsco), Dumbo (Lark), and Trampy (Trammell). Some days on tour were more uncomfortable than others. For Dan, one stands out. "On the way to a tour date we were driving by a bunch of plum trees. We pulled over on the side of the road, picked up a bunch of plums and put them in our T-shirts. As we drove on down the road we ate all those plums. Let me tell you what, when we were on stage playing at about 9 that night, I looked at Stan and his fingers were strumming his bass guitar but he was not moving otherwise. And I looked back at poor Eric and he had this pained look on his face. Well, in about 10 more minutes, I realized what they were going through. Man, we all had the runs. We were suffering on stage. I don't know how many intermissions we had to have that night," he laughs.

Life on the road gave the Fireballs grander experiences as well. At a Massachusetts performance on which the band appeared on the bill with the Everly Brothers, Eric Budd found himself sitting in the dressing room with Don and Phil Everly. "They sang 'Bye Bye Love' to me back there. Two years earlier I was listening to that song every morning on the radio, and here I was backstage with them. To this day, I hear an Everly Brothers song and I stop what I'm doing to listen. They were just two damn swell guys. They didn't have a big head and they had time to talk. I was as impressed with them as individuals as I was with their harmonizing and musicianship."

Eric also speaks fondly of "country gentleman" Sonny James, with whom the Fireballs toured for a month in the early fall of 1959. "We were his backup band on a Midwest tour. He was a fabulous gentleman. When Sonny James was on the stage, the bar was closed. He was a very religious person and his contract specified that no alcoholic beverages could be served when he was performing. I remember traveling down the road with everyone asleep except Sonny James, who was sitting in the back seat with his guitar, softly singing religious songs." During that tour with Sonny James the Fireballs experienced their first change in personnel: Dan Trammell's asthma forced him to leave the group.

To their discredit, producers at Kapp Records became ambivalent about the band's potential and thought little of a new song called "Curious," which George had written in 1959. So Petty approached Norman Wienstroer, executive with a new record company called Top Rank, where he sold "Curious" within an hour. (Weinstroer signed the band in part because "Curious" evoked a feeling that reminded him of a coastal resort town in England he had recently visited. With the blessing of George and Norm Petty, Top Rank renamed the song after the town—"Torquay.") In October 1959, "Torquay" cracked the *Billboard* top 40 and solidified the popularity of the group.

In February 1960, just four months after "Torquay" made the charts, another driving instrumental, "Bulldog," brought the Fireballs back into the top 40 as Top Rank prepared to release the group's first album. But the band was soon to undergo the second of three personnel changes within two years. Singer Chuck Tharp, who had filled in on rhythm guitar after Danny's departure, himself left the group in August of 1960, at first working on a ranch and later enlisting in the Army. Eric Budd was first to hear about his resignation, and played a hand in hiring his replacement. "During a break I had gone back to Raton and while we were there Chuck told me he was tired and was going to quit," recalls Eric. "Years later Chuck told us he was just joking about quitting, but at the time I thought he was serious. So we went back to Clovis, and he told everyone he was going to quit." The band and Petty took him at his word, and began searching for a new singer to take on the road on their next tour, which had already been booked.

It didn't take the group long to think of a young singer from Amarillo, Jimmy Gilmer. The Jimmy Gilmer Combo, in which Jimmy sang and played rhythm guitar, had developed a following in the Texas panhandle and eventually made contact with Norman Petty. Gilmer gives credit to his drummer, Gary Swafford, who began doing session work for Petty and played with the Norman Petty Trio in the late '50s. Swafford introduced Jimmy to Norman. Although Jimmy wrote few songs, one of his compositions, "Look Alive," appealed to Petty, who recorded Gilmer and arranged for the song's release on the Decca label in 1958. "'Look Alive' was big in Amarillo, but that was about it," says Gilmer.

Unable to build success for his group beyond the Amarillo region, Gilmer had decided to abandon his musical ambitions and return to his college engineering studies in the fall of 1960 when Norm Petty phoned to ask if he'd be interested in joining the Fireballs to fill the vacancy created by Tharp's departure. "That offer was exciting because the Fireballs were going to be touring and I hadn't really done any of that," says Gilmer. The Fireballs had previously met Gilmer at Petty's studio, and they knew they'd get along together. Just like that, he joined the band.

After rehearsing for a few weeks with Jimmy, the Fireballs toured extensively throughout the Midwest, backing numerous other acts in performances. "We played for people like Donnie Brooks, the Kalin Twins, and others who had hit records at the time." The early sixties were lean years; the Fireballs continued to release records, but with little success on the charts. Even so, that transitional period provided some time for creative experimentation. In the summer of 1960, the Fireballs set to work on *Blue Fire*. Jerry MacNeish, who later would play bass with the band and who served as historian for the Fireballs, observes that *Blue Fire* was one of the first concept albums ever recorded. All songs on the album, including "Blacksmith Blues," "St. Louis Blues," and "Blues In The Night," contained either the word "blue" or "blues." However, with the collapse of Top Rank Records, the Rank Organisation's ill-fated foray into the record business, the album remained in the vault for more than three decades until 1993, when it was released by Ace Records.

The return of the Fireballs to the charts in 1963 came through a friendship with Keith McCormack of Plainview, Texas, whose band the String-A-Longs had scored an international hit with "Wheels" in early 1961. "Keith was a friend of mine and he always had really neat songs," says Jimmy. "I sat down with him one time when we were looking for some new material to record and one of his songs happened to be 'Sugar Shack.' When we tested 'Sugar Shack' in our live performances, people wanted to hear it again."

The Fireballs recorded "Sugar Shack" during the next break in their tour schedule, but the final production didn't turn out as they had expected. All the band members worked on the song arrangement, but Petty added flutelike electronic Solovox notes after the Fireballs had gone back on the road. "I remember Norman sent us a test pressing, and I thought he had ruined the damn record," says Gilmer. "I was very upset and I tried to stop it, but it was too late. It had already gone to pressing. Of course, had I stopped it, I probably wouldn't be where I am today," Gilmer acknowledges.

Gilmer's crisp vocals and the signature Solovox kept "Sugar Shack" in the national top 40 for 13 weeks and led directly to a second hit, "Daisy Petal Pickin'" in January 1964. The group's resurgence was unfortunately timed, however, coinciding with the emergence of a genuine phenomenon: the British pop music "invasion" of 1964. (In February of '64, the Beatles became the first artists to simultaneously place five songs on the *Billboard* Hot 100: "I Want to Hold Your Hand," "She Loves You," "I Saw Her Standing There," "Please Please Me," and "My Bonnie.") Enchanted with mop-top hair and Liverpool accents, American kids deserted many of their American pop music heroes during that crazed year and a few to follow. The fortunes of Jimmy Gilmer and the Fireballs declined.

By the late '60s, British acts had slipped way down on the American pop music charts. The so-called drug culture was pervasive in many parts of the country, and accepted musical styles were as varied as the "do-your-own-thing" clothing and hair styles through which young people expressed themselves. By 1968, pop music had become a medium of political expression. Otis Redding had come and gone, and the Doors, Cream, Jimi Hendrix, and Big Brother and the Holding Company were making profound changes in the American musical scene. In 1967, a psychedelia-tinged year in which Steppenwolf soared on a "Magic Carpet Ride," the Beatles encouraged "Revolution," and the Chambers Brothers emphatically declared that "Time Has Come Today," the Fireballs scorched their way back onto the charts with Tom Paxton's "Bottle Of Wine." It was a rollicking top 10 hit, but the lyrics, about the ruined life of a wino, conveyed a sobering message. Although the song would be the last significant hit for the Fireballs, "Bottle Of Wine" remained on the *Billboard* Hot 100 for three and a half months in early 1968, leaving behind a powerful statement as the group exited the charts. Even though three decades have passed since the group last scored a hit, the afterglow of the Fireballs still burns warmly.

HIT SINGLES BY THE FIREBALLS

DEBUG	PEAK	TITLE	LABEL
9/59	39	TORQUAY	TOP RANK
1/60	24	BULLDOG	TOP RANK
8/60	99	VAQUERO (COWBOY)	TOP RANK
6/61	27	QUITE A PARTY	WARWICK
9/63	1	SUGAR SHACK* (Certified Gold)[†]	DOT
12/63	15	DAISY PETAL PICKIN'*	DOT
3/64	53	AIN'T GONNA TELL ANYBODY*	DOT
12/67	9	BOTTLE OF WINE	ATCO
4/68	79	GOIN' AWAY	ATCO
11/68	63	COME ON, REACT!	ATCO
2/69	73	LONG GREEN	ATCO

* JIMMY GILMER AND THE FIREBALLS
† THE RECORDING INDUSTRY OF AMERICA (RIAA) CERTIFIES GOLD AND PLATINUM RECORDS ACCORDING TO SALES. BETWEEN 1958 AND 1988, SINGLES THAT REACHED 1 MILLION IN SALES AT THE WHOLESALE LEVEL WERE AWARDED GOLD RECORDS. HISTORICALLY, RIAA AWARDED A GOLD ALBUM FOR $1 MILLION IN SALES; IN 1975, AN ADDITIONAL PROVISO OF 500,000 COPIES SOLD WAS ADDED. IN 1976, RIAA INTRODUCED A PLATINUM AWARD FOR SINGLES SELLING 2 MILLION COPIES AND FOR ALBUMS SELLING 1 MILLION COPIES AND REACHING $2 MILLION IN WHOLESALE RECEIPTS. IN 1984, RIAA INTRODUCED THE MULTIPLATINUM AWARD TO ACCOMMODATE SALES OF 2 MILLION OR MORE ALBUMS. FIVE YEARS LATER, RIAA REDUCED THE PLATEAU FOR GOLD SINGLES TO 500,000 COPIES AND THE PLATEAU FOR PLATINUM SINGLES TO 1 MILLION.

THEN AND NOW
GEORGE TOMSCO

For three days George Tomsco and the four other Fireballs had been killing time in Clovis, New Mexico, having driven 235 miles from their hometown Raton, in the state's hilly northeastern region, to audition and to buy some recording studio time to cut their first record. They had arrived in town on a Sunday, the last day of August 1958, only to learn that the studio was booked the first two days of the week, and now they were trying to stretch the $200 they had pooled for the journey and the session.

When Wednesday finally arrived, they set up their gear in the studio in the late afternoon in preparation for their night session. George unpacked his brand-new Fender Stratocaster guitar and plugged it into his brand-new Fender Tremolux amplifier. [*Editor's note:* The Fender Stratocaster line, introduced in 1954, is arguably the most famous brand of electric guitars ever, and played an integral part in the evolution of pop/rock during the fifties and sixties.] As evening approached, they went to a local diner for burgers,

PHOTO BY DAWN LARK.

then drove back on Seventh Street to the studio. Parked at the door was a pink Cadillac. George and the boys went inside. Through the double-paned glass separating the reception area from the studio, George saw a stranger plucking on his brand-new guitar. George angrily marched into the control room.

"Hey, who's that playing my guitar?" George demanded. "I don't know that guy, and I never said he could touch my guitar."

Norman Petty, the recording studio owner, smiled. "That's Buddy Holly," he replied. The pink Cadillac belonged to Holly, who with his band the Crickets had spent the previous two days in what would be one of his last recording sessions. Petty produced the sessions and guided the brilliant career of Holly, who only five months later died along with pop stars Richie Valens and J. P. Richardson—the "Big Bopper"—in a plane crash during a concert tour in Iowa.

The demise of Holly, Valens, and Richardson coincided with the emergence of the Fireballs, a group whose pursuit of stardom had begun a year earlier in a PTA talent show in Raton, a sleepy town at the 7,000-foot level along the old Santa Fe Trail off U.S. 85 near the Colorado border, where most folks earned their living in ranching or coal mining. George's father, Albert, had been a coal miner before he and his brother opened a service station in Raton in 1945, at the close of World War II. They also operated a local taxicab service. George's mother, Mary, a homemaker, battled ill health much of her life. Albert and Mary hoped that George would take an interest in business, put on a coat and tie, and go to work for a bank or some other solid institution. George had something else in mind.

George, born April 24, 1940, was 5 years old when the lively music of the Harmonicats caught his ear. During the waning years of the big band era, he also liked the smooth harmonies of the Mills Brothers, the Andrews Sisters, and the McGuire Sisters, and country standards by Lefty Frizzell, Jimmie Rodgers, and Carl Smith. When he was 9, George took a few guitar lessons, but soon became bored and put his guitar and the chord diagrams written by his teacher away in a closet. There they remained until 1951, when George heard Les Paul and Mary Ford's electrifying recording of "The World Is Waiting For The Sunrise." At about the same time, a couple of local guitar-playing brothers performing in an assembly at George's elementary school played "Guitar Boogie," a tune that had been recorded by Arthur Smith and the Crackerjacks in 1948. "It was so cool. It was rock and roll, but nobody knew that yet," says George, who retrieved his guitar and his teacher's notes. In his short stint as a guitar student he hadn't learned to read music, but he was still able to read those chord diagrams.

Playing a Gibson "cutaway" acoustic guitar equipped with an electric pickup, George began rehearsing with his accordion-playing sister, Alberta. In 1952 they played their first professional job—a Saturday night dance at the Yankee Dance Hall in Yankee, New Mexico, about 10 miles up the canyon from Raton.

"I made two bucks and I loved it," laughs George. Alberta, who was already playing regularly with a country music band, asked George to fill in. That experience led George to decide he wanted to be more than an accompanist. He wanted to play lead.

George's musical horizons broadened one day in 1956 when a friend invited him to listen to a couple of new records he had just bought: "Rock Around The Clock" by Bill Haley and the Comets and "Mystery Train" by Elvis Presley. "I could not believe my ears. We sat there all afternoon and listened to those records over and over." Gradually, radio stations began playing the new rock and roll music, and George tuned in to songs by Chuck Berry, Little Richard, the Moonglows, and other bright new stars of the day.

George paired with a school acquaintance of his, Chuck Tharp, who had a good singing voice. They persuaded three friends—Trammell, Budd, and Lark—to join them in starting a rock and roll band. The group began rehearsing in December 1957 and appeared for the first time in late January 1958 at a talent contest sponsored by the Raton PTA. Contest rules allowed them to perform only one song, so it had to be a good one. They chose the hottest record in the country at the time, Jerry Lee Lewis's "Great Balls Of Fire," and christened themselves the Fireballs. As Budd recalls, "I'm pretty sure it was George's cousin Ed Tomsco who suggested reversing the two words to get the name Fireballs." Their rocking performance captured the first-place trophy, and that was all the encouragement they needed. They rehearsed songs by Johnny Cash and Carl Perkins, learned to play the hot new "Tequila" by the Champs, and mastered "Guitar Boogie," the tune that had first caught George's ear as a sixth-grader.

Although the band performed vocals as well as instrumentals, Chuck was the sole singer. "When we started out we had only one microphone," George explains. As the Fireballs began to work steadily at the Yankee Dance Hall and other nightspots in the region, George sold his Harley-Davidson motorcycle in order to buy his first solid-body Fender Stratocaster electric guitar and a new Tremolux amplifier. Pat Chavez, the high school band director, took notice of the group. He had a record lathe that he used for recording the high school band, and in the spring of 1958 he invited the boys to cut a record for the fun of it. They watched the cutter churning up curly black ringlets as it etched grooves in the smooth lacquer disc. But the Fireballs had no record contract, and no hopes of getting one.

When June came, and with it George's graduation, the band dissolved. George's parents persuaded him to enroll in the New Mexico Institute of Mining Technologies in Socorro, along the Rio Grande about 40 miles from the Trinity site, where the first atomic bomb was detonated. "I really didn't want to go to college," George admits. "I wanted to pursue music, but I didn't know how to do it."

His immediate future appeared settled, however, when he won a "working schol-arship" that he would use to subsidize his education by working half days and attending school half days.

George's job—setting up equipment for experiments measuring patterns of explosives—wasn't entirely without interest, but music remained on his mind. And in his dreams. One of those dreams was to change his life. He awoke in his dorm room in the middle of one night with a melody in his head. "It was a song that literally came to me in a dream. I reached under my bunk and got my guitar out, and figured out how to play that tune that I was hearing. [He still didn't know how to read or write music.] I had to play it and remember how to play it. I stayed up a couple of hours that night just playing that song over and over again." He called the song "Fireball."

The next day, George's dream prompted him to dig through his belongings and pull out his copy of the homemade acetate disc he and his buddies had recorded a few months earlier. He was playing the record when a fellow student from Clovis named Chuck Townsend overheard it and walked into George's room. "Man, that's pretty good music," said Chuck. "Who is that?" George replied, "That's our little band up in Raton." Surprised, Chuck said, "You guys sound good. You should go and record over at Norm Petty's studio in Clovis, where Buddy Holly records." George called his fellow Fireballs and together they decided they want-ed to make a record at Petty's recording studio. George phoned Petty, who asked to hear a tape. Too embarrassed to admit he didn't have a tape recorder, George persisted, "No. We would rather play for you in person." Petty relented, and told George and the boys to drop by on a Sunday afternoon two weeks later.

George hung up the phone, promptly quit his job, and withdrew from school. "I'm going into the music business," he proudly announced. Realizing the need for material, George and Chuck Tharp set to work and together improvised an up-tempo vocal tune they called "I Don't Know." Down to Clovis they went with Stan, Eric, and Dan, taking with them a repertoire of two original songs: "I Don't Know" and the dream-inspired "Fireball."

After the audition, Petty agreed to record the group, charging his usual $75-per-side studio fee. Petty had previously booked sessions for Buddy Holly and the Crickets for Monday and Tuesday, but studio time was available Wednesday afternoon. On Sunday afternoon, the boys had the $150 to cover the cost of recording their two songs. But by Wednesday afternoon, meals and motel bills had eroded their stash to $95. Petty agreed to let them cut both songs for an advance of $75, with the remaining half of the money to be paid later.

Because a fill-up cost only about $5 in those days, the $20 the boys had left was enough to make the trip back to Raton in the two cars they had driven. The next weekend, they played a gig at a little dance hall in Springer, not far from Raton. "We made $80, sent $75 of that to Norman the very next week, and we split $5 among the five guys," George laughs. Desperate as those times were, the boys were propelled by the exuberance of youth. They were on their way. And although the Fireballs released their last top 100 single in 1969, their spark, ignited by George Tomsco, was to remain aglow for three more decades, through successes and struggles, through enormous popularity and decline, through dissolution and reemergence as a popular touring group in the 1990s.

The Fireballs rode the momentum generated by "Bottle Of Wine" into 1969, but were unable to duplicate that level of success again. In 1969 the band severed its relationship with Norm Petty and began working with producer Glen Pace in North Hollywood, California. Incompatibly packaged in tours with other Atlantic-Atco artists of the time, including Vanilla Fudge, Sonny and Cher, the Bee Gees, Iron Butterfly, Buffalo Springfield, the Allman Brothers Band, and the Rascals, the Fireballs seemed out of place. Stan and George wanted to keep trying, but Jimmy and drummer Doug, who had replaced Eric Budd in 1961, definitely wanted out. The band made a mutual decision to dissolve after fulfilling a dance club date in Colorado Springs on New Year's Eve 1970.

Doug Roberts became an insurance salesman while pursuing his dream of owning a club, but found nightclub management more difficult than he anticipated. He died in November 1981, after a long illness.

Without Doug and Jimmy, George and Stan set about rebuilding the Fireballs. They recruited a new lead singer, "Sugar Shack" composer Keith McCormack of the String-A-Longs, whose 1961 hit "Wheels" was produced by Norman Petty. The reconstituted Fireballs, now a trio, became the house band in a club in Springfield, Missouri, where they remained for two years. When the band was hired in 1973 for another steady gig in Kansas City, Keith decided to remain in Springfield, where he planned to start his own band. In 1974 Stan returned to Raton to run a nightclub. Alone, but unwilling to abandon the Fireballs, George recruited some musicians in Kansas City.

While he kept the band active, playing local gigs, George developed a lucrative sideline. Based in the Kansas City suburb of Independence, Missouri, he began composing and recording jingles for Kansas City advertising agencies in the late '70s. When interest in country music and line dancing surged in the early '80s, George, moving with the times, changed the name of the Fireballs to George Tomsco and the Sugar Canyon Band. But it all soured in 1984. "I got tired of beating my head against the wall. I was tired of music, and I set my guitar down."

After 25 years as a professional musician, he enrolled in courses in investments and the insurance business, passed his exams, and became an agent for an insurance and investment firm. "I really liked what I learned, but I just wasn't a good salesman. I began looking for an excuse to get back into the music business."

In 1989 George found his excuse. He received a phone call in his Kansas City office asking if he could get as many Fireballs as possible to appear at a Clovis Music Festival. Without hesitation, George abandoned the insurance business. The resurrected Fireballs, again based in Clovis, consisted of George, Eric Budd, Chuck Tharp, and Jerry MacNeish, who substituted on bass because Stan was initially unavailable. "It was a lot of fun," George says.

Since then, the Fireballs have gone through many changes, but have continued to work steadily, appearing at oldies shows, casinos, private parties, and one-nighters in clubs with George, Stan, drummer Dan Aguilar, and keyboardist-guitarist Ron Cardenas, all from Raton.

When he's not on the road, George enjoys life in his hometown. "Raton has not changed a whole lot since 1959," says George. He's back at the "old homestead," the childhood home in which he and his sister, Alberta, grew up. "That house was the birthplace of the Fireballs," George says fondly. When their parents died, they left the property to George and Alberta. George bought out Alberta's share, and he's been working on the home, which had fallen into disrepair. Down the road, the Yankee Dance Hall, vacant for years, is now someone's home, but George has heard rumors that the place has been bought by a local entrepreneur who is thinking about turning the place back into a dance hall.

Once married but childless, George is now divorced, as is his sister Alberta, the mother of five children. "My sister and I have a very close relationship. We live near each other and there's nothing we wouldn't do for each other. That's a blessing I have."

These days, George views his life in terms of what he says God has done for him. "I'm really starting to be conscious about my fellowship with Him. He's blessed my life and blessed me in music in a lot of ways. You don't realize the dimension of what God is and will do for you in your life until sometime later on, down the road. The most important thing in my life right now is Jesus Christ and my fellowship with God through Christ. He's given me music, and even though I don't read music, I've written a lot of songs. And that's a gift."

George has resumed songwriting, and he's been thinking of recording once again. He'd like to record some vocals and instrumentals with the Fireballs in California and in Clovis—if possible at the original Norman Petty studio site and if possible with vacuum tube recording equipment. "I still prefer the sound of that era," says George.

THEN AND NOW
STAN LARK

Only two of the dozen musicians who called themselves Fireballs over the past four decades maintained their association with the band throughout its recording history: lead guitarist George Tomsco and bassist Stan Lark.

The parity is fitting and poignant. Lark, like Tomsco, was born and raised in the small northern New Mexico town of Raton. Their kinship developed in 1951 when both were in elementary school. As they were growing up they periodically played in the same country music combo together, and Stan played an integral role in the formation of the Fireballs in 1957. Stan was there when singer-guitarist Jimmy Gilmer replaced Chuck Tharp in 1960, and he remained after Jimmy and drummer Doug Roberts left in 1970.

After taking a 15-year hiatus from performing, he returned to the stage in 1989 with the Fireballs, and has continued to perform with the group since. And like George, after living in a half-dozen states in the 1970s and '80s, Stan has returned

Stan Lark (standing, second from left) with family members. Front row, left to right: Shibil, Brittany, Chelsea with dog Sophy, and Barbi; back row: Christy, Stan, Dawn, Justin, and Shannon.
PHOTO BY JOHN VINCENT.

to Raton to live. In his new home six miles out of town, he thinks back to the days when he used to ride his horse from his parents' ranch to George's home. Today, Stan's mother still lives in the house in which Stan grew up, and George now lives in his parents' house.

"George has been one of my closest friends since I was in sixth grade," Stan says. "George and I are on all the Fireballs recordings. He and I are the only two who are on everything that's been released." And now, after enduring a devastating personal loss and surviving a near-fatal accident, Stan says he's learned something important about life: enjoy it. And he has.

Stan, the oldest of 11 children, was born July 27, 1940. His parents ran a working ranch, but his dad, Richard "Floyd" Lark, also owned school buses, taught, and played music at local venues. "He had to do all of that to feed 11 children," Stan laughs.

Floyd strongly encouraged his children's interest in music. He had been a saxophonist who led a jazz sextet in Denver from 1932 to 1938. After moving to Raton upon his marriage in 1930, he became choir director at the church the family attended. (One of Stan's four brothers plays violin and another plays cello. Three of Stan's six sisters play piano, as does Stan's mother.) Floyd wanted Stan to become a concert pianist. "But of course, I am not," says Stan, who took piano lessons from age 4 until he turned 12, when his piano teacher died. By that time young Stan was tired of piano, and jumped at the chance to play upright bass when the school orchestra needed a player.

Stan took to the bass easily. For five straight years he and his cellist and violinist brothers, also orchestra members, were selected to be in the New Mexico all-state competition. Within a year of joining the orchestra Stan had turned professional, playing a style of music quite distinct from classical. "I had an aunt who played honky-tonk piano and a cousin who played lead guitar in a country music group called the Night Riders, and by the time I was 14 years old, they had convinced my parents to let me go and play country music at dances with them." Stan sang and played with the Night Riders for four years, but when his buddy George Tomsco asked Stan to be part of a rock and roll band he was forming, Stan unhesitatingly said yes.

The decision to join the Fireballs took Stan far from the course he had been pursuing. As a high school student, Stan was interested in a career in petroleum engineering, in which he demonstrated a spark of ingenuity that earned recognition. He had won several scholarships and had already enrolled at New Mexico State University in Las Cruces when he and the other Fireballs first recorded at Norman Petty's studio in Clovis. "When I finished recording in the studio, I was supposed to go straight to New Mexico State, but I didn't, even though everything was already paid for." Stan's father, who had several academic degrees, was terribly upset. But Stan knew that the decision to follow his passion rather than sit in a classroom was right for him. "My life would have been very different had I stayed in school, but I don't regret anything," Stan says resolutely.

After the Fireballs began regularly playing the ballroom circuit in the Midwest in the summer of 1959, they moved to Minneapolis. It was there in 1960 that they first met singer Donnie Brooks, who was on the road promoting his single "Mission Bell," which was making its way up the pop charts. Brooks had been invited to stay in the home in which the Fireballs were rooming, and he asked the group to come fishing with him. The Fireballs said no, they needed to rest for a concert appearance that night. Brooks went without them, but interpreted the Fireballs' decline of his invitation as a snub that merited retaliation. By the time the Fireballs returned from their concert, Brooks was gone. But he had left a souvenir.

"When we got into bed we found out he had short-sheeted us and wrapped these dead fish in paper and put them in our beds," laughs Stan. Attached to one fish Brooks had left a note: "Screw you, Fireballs. 'Mission Bell' made the top 10." The next time Brooks and the Fireballs met on the road, they all shared a good laugh about the "fish incident." Over the years, the Fireballs have remained good friends with Brooks, who has been a prominent producer of oldies shows for three decades now.

The band worked regularly on tour with the Champs, Sonny James, Jimmy Bowen, and Bobby Vee from 1959 into the early '60s, and even during difficult times, in the latter part of the decade, Stan stayed with the group.

By 1973 the Fireballs, with Keith McCormack singing lead, were based in Kansas City. "We were doing harmonies like the Eagles, but we weren't going any-place. I got tired of looking up and seeing the same drunk falling off the same barstool every night. I was closer to George than to my own family because we grew up together. But it just burned out for me, and I decided I wanted to do something different."

In 1974, after 16 years with the Fireballs, Stan left and returned to Raton, where he bought a nightclub, the Carriage House. There, he formed a six-piece country music house band that he called Willow Springs, after the original name of the town of Raton. Five years later, Stan sold the club but kept the band, which he took on the road. But on November 13, 1979, the road almost did him in. On an icy stretch of Interstate 25 about 40 miles northeast of Albuquerque, Stan was a passenger in a Jaguar XKE that veered and smashed into a bridge abutment at highway speed. Stan's head was split open in the crash, but the injury was not life-threatening. Stan's wife, Charlotte Day, however, suffered massive injuries, including four spinal fractures, and remained unconscious in intensive care for 21 days. When she finally regained consciousness, she needed extensive physical therapy before she could walk again.

As soon as he was able, Stan returned to the stage with Willow Springs, but in an effort to get off the road, the band headed west to Las Vegas, Nevada, where lounges abound. "I had three kids in the band who had degrees in music. That was one of the times that I was really pleased with the music I was doing. It was an incredible group, and we did very well. We got some really nice write-ups and the band was named Entertainer of the Year for the Nevada circuit. Unfortunately, we took only two weeks off in nearly two years playing the show club circuit, and the band fell apart."

Stan decided to leave music and chose a radically different professional field: the mining business. He had developed an interest in geology in high school and, had he stayed in school at the University of New Mexico, would have studied engineering and geology in preparation for a career in the petroleum industry. Even during his time with the Fireballs, Stan continued his education through correspondence courses. Over time, he earned an associate of arts degree in architectural design and engineering from California's North American School of Architectural Design and Drafting. After Willow Springs dissolved, Stan enrolled in mining engineering and chemistry courses at the University of Nevada, Las Vegas. In 1981, the same year his 14-year marriage ended in divorce, Stan began a new phase of his life as a lab technician for a minerals research firm in the small southern Nevada desert outpost of Pahrump. After joining Mill Creek Mining in Carson Sink near Fallon, Nevada, he was promoted to lab supervisor, and in 1985 he became a vice president at Knox Research, which operated laboratories that conducted research and development in precious metals. Stan remained a mining executive until the spring of 1997, when he resigned to set up shop as an independent consultant.

Although his years in the mining industry brought Stan professional satisfaction and achievement, he endured an agonizing personal tragedy that spanned a decade. In 1982 Stan's eldest son, Bobby, received a transfusion of contaminated blood. "It took 10 years to get him, but it got him," Stan says quietly. "Bobby had a double master's from Texas Tech and had everything in the world going for him. He was 6-foot-6 and trim at 280 pounds, but dwindled down to about 90 pounds. I eventually had to carry him every place."

Following Bobby's death in 1992, the bonds strengthened between Stan and his old friend George Tomsco, who asked Stan to join Chuck Tharp's current country music group, Phoenix. Sensing he needed that diversion, he agreed. During his second appearance with Chuck's band at the Portales Country Club in Portales, New Mexico, Stan spotted Dawn Vincent, who had been a drink server in Stan's nightclub in Raton. Although Stan had thought about Dawn from time to time, he hadn't seen her for 15 years. Dawn, like Stan, was divorced, and the two were happy to renew their friendship. They married in 1994, after a two-year courtship, and Stan—the father of two grown daughters—became the stepfather of Dawn's four school-age children: 5-year-old Brittany, 10-year-old Shibil, 12-year-old Chelsea, and 18-year-old Justin.

"Dawn has been my best friend for a long time," Stan says lovingly. "She used to baby-sit my girls (Shannon, born in 1969, and Christy, born in 1974) when I had the nightclub. When they were little, her son Justin and my daughter Christy used to sleep in the same bed. They would never admit that, though." Of their chance meeting, Stan says, "It's just one of those things that's worked out very well. We have a beautiful home about six miles outside of town. We live right next to a state park and we have deer and turkeys and bears in our yard. And our rottweiler."

Currently, Stan is involved in an emerging business that has developed an Environmental Protection Agency–approved technology to detoxify tailings (waste from the processing of ground ores) from played-out gold mines so that they can be used in the manufacture of road surface material or building blocks. "I had been a chemist on the other side developing ways to extract metals from ore, so this is my way of giving something back." He is working with a nuclear physicist to design the equipment and physical plant necessary for practical application of the new process.

Despite his immersion in mining, chemistry, new technologies, and EPA regulations, Stan leaves room in his life for music. George Tomsco counts on him for occasional appearances with the Fireballs, including the annual Buddy Holly Days program in Lubbock, and Norman and Vi Petty Days in Clovis. Stan's sustained interest in performing is rooted in his simple but essential theory about life. "Enjoy it," he says simply. "I've learned you can't take anything for granted. A lot of people for whatever reason are dealt hands that aren't too wonderful and they have to live with them. But I believe that people have the potential to be anything that they want to be. Even after losing a son, I still feel that way. There are things you wish never happened, but it also makes you realize how good and wonderful life can be and be thankful that you have it."

Given the opportunity, Stan says he wouldn't have altered the course of his life. "There are some things that I'm not really proud of, but I don't know if I would change them because then I wouldn't be where I am right now. And right now, I'm exactly where I want to be."

THEN AND NOW

ERIC BUDD

The subscribers on Eric Budd's newspaper route knew when their paper was going to land on their porch. They'd hear the whistling first. As a boy, Eric was always whistling country music tunes, and when he delivered papers on his route in Raton, New Mexico, residents could hear him coming. As a kid in the late '40s and early '50s, Eric liked the music of Webb Pierce, Faron Young, Jim Reeves, Slim Whitman, and Hank Thompson. And he became proficient at whistling their songs. "I still can't carry a tune in a wet paper sack, but I've always been able to whistle on key," grins Eric.

Eric and fellow Fireball George Tomsco have been friends for more than 55 years, ever since both were toddlers. "I've known George since we were neighbors back when he was about 3 and I was 4. We grew up together and went to school together. He used to go to grade school dragging a guitar with him, even though he didn't have a case for it."

Eric's musical development didn't proceed past whistling until the fifth grade, when he began playing the tonette, a simple wind instrument with eight finger holes and a thumb hole. Eric, born October 23, 1938, was the youngest in a family of three boys. They lived with their parents, Tom and Irma Budd, on the family's ranch on Johnson Mesa, 20 miles from Raton. "But after the war, they closed the schools out there, so we moved into town and my father became a cabinetmaker and carpenter. My mom raised three boys, which was a full-time job."

Eric's oldest brother, Nelson, played the violin for a while, so Eric decided to try that in sixth grade. Eric might have become a violinist were it not for a class scheduling error when he entered junior high school. "I got my schedule mixed up and ended up in the band class instead of orchestra class. So there I was carrying my violin into a band class. I very discreetly laid it down and hid it behind a partition, and walked over to the drums that were set up. And that's how I started playing drums. I just watched what the other kids did and stayed after class to practice. We played the regular Sousa marches, and the first time I had a chance to sit down to a trap set that a friend had, I was very lost, because I could play only march songs."

PHOTO BY JOSH BUDD.

But Eric was intrigued, and soon bought an old set of trap drums. "It consisted of a bass drum, snare, and two little cymbals about the size of pie pans."

Eric recalls that his drumming technique was not learned in band class. He received an important tip at a dance sponsored by the Raton Chamber of Commerce. "For one dance, the chamber hired a New York group called the Tony Pastor Orchestra, an eight-piece rhythm band. Their drummer had a big drum set and I sat behind him all during their concert. After their performance I asked him why he didn't swing his whole arm and he told me you have to develop your speed and power with your wrist. A lot of drummers are just elbow thumpers who bang from their elbow down. I remembered what he had told me, and I taught myself to use my wrists to get my speed."

Eric had practiced with other local musicians, but had no professional experience before Tomsco, Tharp, and Lark persuaded him and rhythm guitarist Danny Trammell to enter that PTA talent contest in 1958. Like the others, Eric had a strong interest in rock and roll, even though he had grown up on country music and Sousa marches. "I'd wake up to this radio station from Trinidad, Colorado, that played 'Bye Bye Love' by the Everly Brothers every morning, and I became an Everly Brothers fan from day one."

At the time of the contest, Chuck was a high school sophomore, and George, Stan, and Dan Trammell were seniors. Eric, who had already graduated from high school, was working for Elco Metal Products as a frame welder, a skill he had learned on the job.

Although he had begun taking engineering drafting courses at a local junior college Eric admits now that his ambitions were less than academic. "I wanted to chase girls and have fun," he grins. "I had no goals. I did eventually work as a draftsman and I'm mechanically minded—probably more gifted at that than I am in music." At any rate, Eric unhesitatingly interrupted his early career with Elco when stardom beckoned in the spring of 1959. Eric paid a local automobile pinstriping artist to paint "Fireballs" on his bass drum. "And then we took off on a gamble on a tour of Minnesota. George had heard about this booking agent in Minneapolis. We called and they said, 'Send a demo so we can hear what you sound like.' We said, 'Heck, we'll just come up and audition for ya.' So we all quit our jobs, loaded up two old junk cars with our clothes and instruments and away we went. We auditioned for him and he said, 'I like your sound. Do you have a place to stay?' He made arrangements for us to room in a house with an older couple and got us a booking about two days later in some lakeshore ballroom." During a break in performances, the five band members drove back to Clovis, New Mexico, to record some more tracks, including "Torquay."

Eric remained with the Fireballs until November 1961, when he was drafted into the U.S. Army. After basic training at Fort Ord in California, he was transferred the following spring to Ft. Bliss near El Paso. In September 1962 he was shipped out to Korea, where he spent 13 months as launcher crew chief in a Hawk ground-to-air missile unit. After Eric's discharge in October 1963 he met with Tomsco and Gilmer about rejoining the Fireballs, who were then riding high with "Sugar Shack." But the touring life, doing one-nighters throughout the country, no longer appealed to Eric. "I had been living out of a suitcase and a shaving kit for four years, and I decided I wanted something else." He parted company with the Fireballs for good.

Eric bummed around Albuquerque for a month, hoping to hook up with a music group offering steady work at a club. Two months later, he was still searching. "From October 1963 to February 1964 I just goofed off and lived off my soldier's retirement. By February I was hungry." That's when he decided to phone his old boss at Elco, who gladly took him back. This time around Eric stayed at Elco until 1970, when an Albuquerque lumber company hired him to set up a "stick shop," a fabrication facility for metal door frames used in commercial buildings. In 1975, Elco, which was closing its Raton shop due to labor relations difficulties, asked Eric if he would be interested in going to Harper, Kansas, with them to set up a new plant. "I thought about it for about five minutes, and here I am," says Eric. When Elco temporarily closed its Kansas plant in the late '70s, Eric was transferred to an Oklahoma facility, where he stayed for eight years, until the company, now Elco Manufacturing Company, reopened the Harper plant and hired Eric as an engineer in the hardware department. While in Oklahoma, he met Jeanette Smarsh, whom he married on Valentine's Day 1980. The Budds have two children, 18-year-old Josh and 16-year-old Jesse.

These days, Eric and his family are enjoying life in Harper, population 1,400, out on the flat Kansas prairie. "We're 45 miles southwest of Wichita, close to the Oklahoma border. We live in a double-wide mobile home on some land we bought. We're in tornado alley. I've seen them go by and heard the sirens blowing," he says matter-of-factly. "We've gone down into the shelter, but we haven't ever had any damage."

Eric enjoys the simple life, and says his greatest preoccupation is watching his boys grow. Despite growing up in Denver Broncos country seven miles south of the Colorado border, Eric is, with his son Jesse, a devoted Dallas Cowboys fan. Out in the garage, Eric and his son Josh tinker with an older model Chevy pickup they bought.

For a while Eric kept his drums set up in the garage, the same Slingerland Gene Krupa model drums he'd bought in Trinidad, Colorado, in 1958. He'd go out and play them from time to time, and he'd think back to the time that he met drumming greats Gene Krupa and Cozy Cole at the Metropole Cafe in New York. But by 1997 the drums had so deteriorated due to the effects of weather that Eric packed them up in their case, where they have remained. He doesn't think about drumming much anymore, but still enjoys country music, as his co-workers and neighbors know. They hear him whistling while he works.

THEN AND NOW

DAN TRAMMELL

For two days, Dan Trammell had been riding in a cramped bus on the way from North Dakota to his parents' home in Raton, New Mexico. After traveling steadily for 48 hours, with only a brief stop in Denver to change buses, Dan stiffly stood as the bus rolled to a stop and he stepped off as the air brakes released a sigh. Drawing in a deep breath of the crisp air that fall morning in 1959, Dan picked up the two heavy suitcases out of which he had lived during the previous three months. Because his parents had no telephone, he hadn't let them know he was coming home now. He began walking.

As his house came into view, Dan saw his father, Joe Trammell, sawing lumber in the garage.

"Dad, I'm home," Dan announced as he approached.

"I knew you would be home today," replied his father without looking up from his work.

Dan replied, "There's no way you knew I'd be home."

"Dan, I had a dream last night," said Joe. "The Lord gave me a dream that you would be home at 12 o'clock today." Dan looked at the clock. Not only were the hour and minute hands on the 12, but so was the second hand. His father continued, "I've been praying to the Lord to jerk you out of that band. Now tell me how He did it."

Dan said he'd been having trouble breathing in the humid air and that he'd had an asthma attack that landed him in the hospital while on tour with the Fireballs in the Midwest. Singer Sonny James had convinced Trammell to quit the tour and had paid for his bus ticket home. Dan's father said, "I wondered how the Lord was going to get your attention. You know you don't have asthma. You were raised to play in a church and this rock and roll is not edifying your Heavenly Father. So if you

PHOTO BY GEORGEANN ALBRECHT TRAMMELL.

return to this band, I'm through praying for you and you'll just have to deal with the Lord any way you can."

Dan went to work for a construction company, where he took a lot of ribbing from the other guys on the job. "Hey Fireball, how about autographing my shovel for me?" they'd jeer. When the Fireballs finished their tour with Chuck Tharp playing rhythm guitar in Dan's place, they returned to Raton hoping that Dan would rejoin them on the circuit out of Minneapolis. Tomsco pleaded, "Danny, we need you, we want you. You're one of us, you started with us and we want to finish with you." But Dan was resolute. "I could not make them understand that it was a higher power that determined I couldn't go," he says. Even though he left early in the recording career of the Fireballs, his remarkable musicianship helped define the distinctive sound of the band. Dan Trammell played rhythm guitar like no one else.

Trammell, born on July 20, 1940, grew up in the mountains of northern New Mexico with his younger brother, Johnny, his father, Joe, and his mother, Agnes. They lived in a remote settlement called Black Lake, 25 miles from Taos through Palo Flechado Pass at the 9,100-foot level. "We didn't have electricity half the time and we had no running water. We got our water from a well." His father, the son of a minister, was a minister as well. "My daddy had such a way with the Lord that I have never seen anyone come close. He was the kind of person who refused to take an offering, and as a result, I grew up in a very poor family." Dan earned $5 per month hauling spring water to his school, and gave most of it to his parents. "Back then," recalls Dan, "you could buy a pair of cowboy boots for $2.50 and a pair of blue jeans cost a couple of bucks. We kept ourselves clothed just on that $5 a month."

Danny got his first taste of music at age 8 when his father, who had been a fiddle player in his own youth, pulled out an old guitar and showed him how to tune it and play a few chords. But Joe demonstrated an unconventional tuning method. "It was the way Spanish people tune a guitar, by octaves. He taught me to play chords in C, F, and G, but I picked up the rhythm on my own. You can't teach anybody rhythm—you're either born with it or you don't have it," says Dan. Since his church couldn't afford an organ or piano, Danny played guitar at services. "If you could sing in C, F, or G, that was fine. If you couldn't, I couldn't find your key."

Dan realized he needed to learn more, and tantalized by an offer he heard on the radio, began saving for a guitar instruction book offered for $2.95 by a mail order house in Clint, Texas. "I don't know how long it took me to save $2.95, but I eventually set it aside, sent it to them, and in the mail I got a guitar book that taught how to play using pictures. I can't read a note of music to this day, but I can sure tear up a guitar," laughs Danny, whose inspired playing propelled the Fireballs recordings of "Fireball," "Torquay," and "Bulldog."

When Dan entered his junior year in high school, his family came out of the wilderness and moved 65 miles to Raton, where his father established a nondenominational church. Eager to advance his musicianship as well as his contributions in support of his family, he took two jobs in Raton—as a janitor at the J.J. Newberry department store and on the production line at the local Coca-Cola bottling plant. With the money he earned he purchased a Kay electric guitar and Magnatone amplifier, on which he played hymns at church.

Dan kept to himself in school. In addition to his ministry, Joe operated a second-hand store in Raton called the Bargain House. "Kids at school nicknamed me Bargain House. It shamed me a little bit. I didn't have the money to buy the best of clothes. Most of the money I got, I gave to my parents. I treasured them."

Despite Dan's rather solitary ways, word of his musical talent got around. "Ol' George found out that I played a little rhythm guitar, and he asked me to come and jam with him," Dan recalls. "I can't play no rock and roll," Dan told George. "Man, if my daddy found out, he'd kill me." George reassured him, "We're just going to jam." Dan cautiously agreed. He snuck his guitar out of the house and slipped over to George's house. "George was awesome. He could pick when he was a teenager. There was nothing he couldn't do on a Fender guitar. I was so taken in. He was just great! And I didn't know Stan Lark, Chuck Tharp, and Eric Budd were going to be there. We knew each other in high school but I didn't know that they played instruments." It wasn't long after that first impromptu session that the group decided to enter the PTA talent contest.

"Oh my God," Danny said. "I can't tell my dad I'm going to play for the PTA." Dan managed to get out of the house with his guitar the day of the concert, but that was only the beginning. "After we played for the PTA, darn if they didn't want us to play for the prom. Well, we played for the prom and all of the other schools wanted us to play for their proms. I finally had to come clean." Danny cautiously approached his father and said, "Look Dad, I've got a problem." His father replied, "Yeah, I know you've got a problem. I don't like the music you're playing. It doesn't edify the Almighty. But you're at the age where you're going to do what you want to do, and I'm going to have to let you do it."

Despite his growing interest in music, Danny took no music courses in school. His time in high school was aimless. "I never knew what I wanted to be. All I knew was I had to finish high school," says Dan. So when George set up the first recording session at Norman Petty's studio in Clovis, New Mexico, that was fine with Dan, who had no other particular plans. To avoid picking up the rumble of passing traffic, Petty preferred recording after dark. "Back then everybody had glass-pack mufflers and gunned it down the street. So I remember recording all night long and sleeping the next day," says Trammell.

Trammell has high praise for Norman Petty. "Norman was not only a great pianist, he was also a genius in imagining and creating different sounds." At one recording session Petty told Trammell to unplug his electric guitar, and he close-miked the instrument. "I couldn't even hear myself playing, but the microphone was picking up the sound." The result was an ethereal "whack-whack" palpitation that gave the Fireballs a sound like no other band.

The severe asthma attack that ultimately led to Trammell's departure from the Fireballs happened on an oppressively humid night in North Dakota. "I remember finishing the show, but when I woke up in the hospital I didn't remember how I got there," says Dan, who had no previous episodes of asthma. "I remember them giving me adrenaline shots." After his release from the hospital, Dan was resolute about continuing on the tour. A few days later, Sonny James called Dan aside. "I've got to tell you something," Sonny said. "I've been watching you on and off stage. Son, you're losing your health, and I'm going to buy your ticket home." When Dan objected, Sonny calmly replied, "At your age, you don't have the brains to think about your health. All you're thinking about is music." Dan finally agreed to accept Sonny's offer. After one more recording session in Clovis, Dan walked away from the Fireballs for the last time.

After briefly working in construction, Dan landed a job in the signal depart-ment of the Santa Fe Railroad, climbing poles to install glass insulators and wires. And he chased storms throughout the prairie states, repairing and rewiring lines felled by wind-driven rains and tornadoes. In 1961 he wed Mary Dobbs, with whom he had three children: Debbie, born in 1965; Jonie, born in 1968; and David, born in 1972. Through those years, Dan was content to live in quiet anonymity. "I concentrated on giving my life to the Lord. I never told anyone that I used to be a Fireball. I just worked on the railroad."

In 1962 Mary's father, Harvey Dobbs, asked Dan to join him in his retail tire business, Tyler Tire Exchange of Tyler, Texas (about 95 miles east of Dallas). Dan was initially reluctant, considering the salary, benefits, and opportunities his job in the railroad had brought him. But he didn't like all the traveling associated with his job, and he was still feeling wounded after losing seniority through a consoli-dation of the railroad's Eastern and Western divisions. So he accepted his father-in-law's offer and began work as a tire changer. "My daddy-in-law and I got along fabulously," says Dan, who dutifully dismounted and mounted tires, balanced wheels, and did other automotive work in the shop. After six months Dan's father-in-law told him that he had uncovered cash inequities and management problems at his other shop in Longview, about 40 miles to the east, and asked Dan to take over that store. Dan refused at first, flatly stating, "I'm not a manager." His father-in-law replied, "I'll make you a deal. You go to Longview and run that store. If you succeed, we'll leave it open. If you don't succeed, we'll close it." Feeling responsible for saving the jobs of the employees in the Longview store, Dan reluctantly agreed. On his first day in the Longview location, he told the employees that they needed to work together as a team to keep the store open. Apparently they listened, because the bottom line began to improve almost immediately.

In 1980, Dan and Mary were divorced, after nearly 20 years of marriage. Not long after the divorce, Dan's working relationship with his father-in-law also ended. Dan had been looking forward to the day when he would inherit the business, but instead, his father-in-law sold Tyler Tire Exchange to a friend, V.C. Tharp. Dan decided to stay with the company, and Tharp promptly paid him a substantial raise and increased his benefits. In 1992, Tharp decided to sell. Dan bought the company, has since paid off his debt, and now runs a highly successful business.

"But it all goes back to a man who prayed for me," says Dan, referring to his father, who died in 1985 at the age of 79. "I gave up my popularity, and I gave up a life of glamour and a road tour, but I've since been terrifically rewarded professionally and spiritually, and that's where I'm at right now, as I'm getting ready to retire."

In 1981 Dan married Georgeann Albrecht, who now works with Dan in the office at Texas Tire Exchange. The couple have three children, but only one is a musician: Jonie, who sings with a pop-country music band in San Antonio.

Dan sends the occasional small royalty checks for Fireballs recordings on which he played to his mother, Agnes, who is living in Seattle. "I have not kept a royalty check yet," he says. "I've always figured my mom had to put up with my sorry tail, and I'm going to pay her back."

Although the guitar that Dan played with the Fireballs was broken and discarded, a casualty of road life, he still plays on occasion for family members, friends, and for himself. "Although George and Stan have kept their youth pretty well, I'm an ol' coot," he laughs. "The problem with an old musician is you still sound good, but you don't look real good on stage."

Dan is resolute that he took the right road that day he accepted the ticket from Sonny James and boarded the bus in North Dakota. "I never had a doubt. I never looked back. I'm healthy, my children are healthy, my wife's healthy. We haven't been to a doctor in a long time. It's always better to retire with your health than with your wealth, and I'm blessed with health. I feel very fortunate to be where I'm at. I always give the Almighty credit, for without him we cannot do anything. The nicest thing about the boys is that they never did hold it against me when I quit. There's a bond there that will never break among me and George, Stan, Eric, and Chuck. They're still my heroes—all of them. We had a terrific understanding among each other and still do. When they're sad, I'm sad. And when they're happy, I'm happy." And Dan Trammell is happy.

THEN AND NOW
CHUCK THARP

Chuck Tharp has spent his life doing things that most guys can only imagine, surviving dangers that most guys can't possibly imagine. As a young man, he earned his living in a saddle, "gentling" untrained horses, and herding cattle on open range. After two U.S. Army tours of duty with ground forces in Vietnam, he enlisted in the Navy and became a radar operator aboard an aircraft that was shredded by enemy fire over the Tonkin Gulf. He studied marine biology in college, became a music publishing administrator, and worked as a staff songwriter in Nashville, and has performed not only with the Fireballs, but with jazz-flavored and country music bands as well. And now Chuck Tharp has a new passion: settling down in suburbia.

Chuck was born February 3, 1941, along the banks of the Rio Grande in the southwest Texas settlement of Ysleta. His father, James Will Tharp, died when Chuck was 2 years old, and his mother, Willie, subsequently married Eugene Thwaits, a cowboy who went where the work was, so the family was always on the move. When Chuck was still a toddler his folks moved to Anthony, New Mexico, then up the road to a town named Hatch, and on to Modesto, California, where Chuck started grade school. They remained in California only until Eugene

PHOTO BY JOAN THARP.

took a job at an open-pit copper mine near Silver City, New Mexico. Referring to his stepfather, Chuck says, "Daddy worked as a brakeman on the train that carried ore from the bottom of the mine. During a rain, he was killed when his foot slipped and the train ran over him. From that point, Momma raised us all."

After completing third grade, Chuck moved with his mother, his sister, and his five brothers back to Hatch, where they remained until Chuck was 12 years old. Then they moved to Seguin, Texas, before settling in Waco. "I went to seven schools in one year. Like my Dad, all the boys in my family became ranch cowboys. I was in the saddle by the time I was 13 and drawing a man's wage. We took care of horses and cattle, rode fence, and did brandings and ropings."

During his high school years, Chuck moved with his family to Raton, New Mexico, where he found work at the 1.5-million-acre CS Ranch near Cimarron, about 25 miles southwest of Raton along the route of the old Santa Fe Trail. He sandwiched school between work, and he roomed with other cowboys in bunkhouses. "I'd get up an hour before sunup and ride out to the pasture, round up the catch horses, and drive them back into the corral so the cowboys could pick up their mount for the day. After that, I'd have breakfast and I'd go to school. After school, I'd go back to work until sundown. During the summer I worked sunup to sundown. I tell ya, though, I enjoyed that life." Still, when the time came the choice between life as a cowboy and life as a musician wasn't a hard one. "Back then I was making $125 a month as a cowboy, but shoot, I'd make that much money in a couple of hours playing a gig with the Fireballs."

Chuck had first shown interest in music at age 3, when he entertained the neighbors by singing "The Old Lamplighter" and other wartime-era songs. Chuck's mother and stepfather both played guitar and sang, and his brothers and sister sang as well. Chuck, who developed a liking for country music artists, taught himself to play guitar and bass. He studied music at Raton High School, and his acquaintances in the school choir included guitarist George Tomsco and bass player Stan Lark. When the Fireballs briefly went their separate ways following high school graduation in June 1958, Chuck became assistant manager of a record store in Las Vegas, Nevada, where his mother had moved while he was in high school. When George phoned in August 1958 and said, "Get your butt back here, we're going to make a record," Chuck packed his bags and spent every dime he had to take the bus to New Mexico to audition at Norman Petty's studio.

Tharp recorded "Fireball," "Torquay," "Cry Baby," and "Bulldog" with the Fireballs. He recalls that Top Rank Records released "Torquay"/ "Cry Baby" while the group was on the road in the Midwest. "We woke up in Minneapolis one morning and 'Cry Baby' was on the radio, and that was the side picked by the radio station in that area. But *Billboard* magazine picked 'Torquay,' so 'Torquay' became the hit side of the record because *Billboard* was the bible of the industry."

But before the Fireballs scored their next top 40 hit, "Quite A Party," Chuck left the group—unintentionally, he says.

"It's a long story," he drawls. "It started out as a joke and wound up being serious. We were in between gigs and we were recording all night and sleeping all day. When we took a break and went to Raton for a couple of days in August 1960, everybody was acting bored. So I decided I'd spruce things up a bit and I said, 'Guys, I've got a flash for ya. I'm quitting the band.' They looked at me like I had just gone nuts. I was just kickin' up a little dust and havin' fun. Unfortunately, George called Norman that night and before I knew it, I had been replaced by Jimmy Gilmer. So I went and cowboyed for a couple of years, and then I went to meet Uncle Sam."

Along with his brother Gene, Chuck enlisted in the Army in 1961 and shipped out for Vietnam. He was stationed at fire support bases in the Golden Triangle and the A Shau Valley. "I was a grunt, and I did a lot of assignments with the [Green] Berets," says Chuck, who, after promotion to sergeant, was named a squad leader. "I took my people out into the bush. Our mission generally was to make contact with the enemy, inflict as much damage as we could, and get the hell out." Chuck was in line to come home after a year there, but elected to remain. "I had 12 really good guys, and I decided to extend because they were like my family," says Chuck, whose men called him "Pop" because he was the oldest among them.

After he left the Army in 1966, Chuck met and married his first wife, Roma Mason, and took a job as yard clerk with the Southern Pacific Railroad in Santa Cruz, California, a coastal resort town about 70 miles south of San Francisco. The railroad handled shipments of lettuce and other produce from the nearby Salinas Valley. At the same time, Chuck enrolled at Hartnell College in Salinas, then at California State University, Hayward, where he studied marine biology. After Chuck and Roma's first baby arrived (they were to have two more), Chuck found it increasingly difficult to make a 7:30 a.m. class and dropped out of school, two classes short of his degree. All the while, he worked for the railroad, checking rolling stock in the yards. "I was so bored, but I didn't have the confidence to play music anymore," says Chuck. "The only other thing I liked was the military, so I went and joined the Navy."

That was in the fall of 1967. Chuck requested assignment to an antisubmarine squadron, believing that the Tonkin Gulf was too shallow for submarines. Chuck's unit was attached to the U.S.S. *Kearsarge,* and as he reported for duty in San Diego his greeting wasn't quite as he expected. "Welcome aboard," he was told. "We leave for Vietnam in 90 days." For the next year, he roamed the Tonkin Gulf and skirted the Vietnamese coast as a radar operator aboard a Grumman S2 tracker aircraft. "We would watch for anything moving south along the roads or in the water, and we'd call in gunfire from ships. They hung 250-pound Bullpup missiles on us. There wasn't a plane slow enough for us to bomb with those things, but they weren't going to throw them away, so they hung them on us." His job was to line up targets on his radar scope, then to call for fire when his aircraft was within three miles of the target. "We made an easy target," he said.

In 1968, Tharp's plane was ripped by enemy fire. "As we blew up two barges we went in too close to the beach, and we had to pull out over the jungle. We knew there were guns in there, and they got us." When rounds of 50-caliber bullets tore through the fuselage, Tharp was thrown through the air and landed in the console of the co-pilot, who had been killed. Tharp suffered severe spinal injuries, for which he was hospitalized, unable to walk, in a Veteran's Administration hospital in Vancouver, Washington, where he remained for 18 months. "The VA didn't know exactly what my injury was or how to treat it. So I said, 'Aw hell, check me out of here.' My mother took care of me at her house, and my brothers would come over and carry me into the bath." Finally Chuck agreed to see a chiropractor. "He took an X-ray and said my spine looked like a snake." The chiropractor told Chuck, "I can fix it, but it's going to hurt like hell." It did hurt like hell. And he did fix it.

Chuck, then single following his divorce from Roma in February 1970, enrolled in a community college in Vancouver with no particular goal in mind. "Come summertime in 1971 I flipped a coin. I was going to either buy a Harley and go visit a bunch of friends, or I was going to start a band. Two out of three spins later, I decided to start a band."

Chuck contacted some musicians he had met in a music appreciation class at Cal State Hayward and with them formed a seven-piece jazz-oriented rock group called Open Road, with which Chuck sang and played bass. The band went on the road, playing clubs in nine states before arriving in Las Vegas, where the group eventually broke up in 1972. Open Road must have made an impression, because Chuck was immediately hired as a director of publishing for Hollywood-based Oak Records. He found the corporate environment stifling and was irritated that some of his song recommendations—including "Midnight Train To Georgia" and "Neither One Of Us (Wants To Be The First To Say Goodbye)"—were ignored. "Hell, if you ain't going to listen to me, you don't need me," Chuck told them as he quit.

After marrying his second wife, Lanie Desica, in Las Vegas in 1973, Chuck went to Nashville on the strength of a song he co-wrote called "Sweet Country Woman," which had become a hit for Johnny Duncan and for the Stampeders. Tharp worked in Nashville from 1974 to 1976 with Frank and Nancy Music, owned in part by Frank and Nancy Sinatra and managed by producer-arranger Billy Strange. But Chuck always felt like an outsider in Nashville, and never gave up the idea of returning to California. Lanie and Chuck were divorced in 1975, and that same year he married Yuli Liu. During a trip to the Bay Area to visit his brother Gene, Chuck and Yuli decided to move to San Jose, where they bought a house in 1976. Chuck returned to performing as a solo act. Accompanied only by guitar, he booked himself into local clubs singing pop tunes by James Taylor, Billy Joel, and Neil Diamond. "I was bringing home $800 to $900 per week and back then that was damn good money," says Chuck. "I had a lot of fun doing that."

He was content in that role until 1989, when George Tomsco called to ask about putting the Fireballs back together. "Once a Fireball, always a Fireball," declared Chuck, by then a single man again. "I told George, 'Hell yeah.' I threw everything into the car and I left California." Back in New Mexico, Chuck reunited with George, drummer Eric Budd, and Jerry MacNeish on bass and began touring through the Southwest and Midwest, their old stomping grounds. Chuck remained with the reconstituted Fireballs until April 1997, when an old friend of Chuck's asked him to join a country band called Cold Country. Chuck was tired of living on the road, and agreed. In Cold Country, Chuck switches off playing rhythm and bass, and sings lead. The band plays tunes by popular country artists as well as new compositions by Chuck. And he's having a great time. "I'm better at country singing than I am at most anything," he says.

Chuck always remained close to his brothers and sisters, several of whom were also musically inclined. Jimmy Tharp, who played steel guitar and sang, performed with a number of prominent artists, including country swing greats Spade Cooley and Bob Wills. Sister Dorothy and brother Gene were both singers, and Gene also played guitar. Marty Tharp, who plays guitar and bass and sings well, travels with a singing ministry.

Chuck is now married to his fourth wife, nee Belinda Munn, but she goes by her middle name, JoAn. Like JoAn, Tharp isn't known by his birth certificate name, which is Charly. "I didn't know my name had that spelling until I applied for a passport in 1995," says Tharp. "I had to get my birth certificate and I looked at it and said, 'Hello?' I called my mom and asked, 'Momma, why did you give my name Charly that unusual spelling?' She said, 'I don't remember spelling it that way.' But then I decided I kind of like it," Chuck decided.

Chuck readily admits that he's not perfect. "I've done a lot of things wrong in my life, but I'm most proud of all of my kids." He has four daughters. Three of them—Jamie, Shellie, and Christie—were born during the late '60s to Chuck and Roma. The fourth, Sulin, was born in 1979 to Chuck and Yuli.

Chuck and Jo have bought a house in Clovis, on a block on which they know all their neighbors. "In San Jose I had only one good friend across the street, and I never even learned the names of any other neighbors. In Clovis, we have cookouts with everyone on the block. It's just great. A couple of my friends come over with guitars and we'll sit around and entertain the neighbors." Along with Jo, Chuck lives with his stepdaughter Gina and stepson Sean.

Chuck still hopes to complete his degree in marine biology. "I love that field," he says. But in any case, he'll need to balance that against his prevailing interest in music. "I also love to play music. I'll do that until I'm too old to do it, which I hope never happens."

THEN AND NOW

JIMMY GILMER

Nine years before radio stations across the nation turned Jimmy Gilmer into a household name with the 1963 hit "Sugar Shack," Gilmer was on the radio, but with a different identity: K5CCQ. At age 14, Jimmy was licensed as a ham radio operator, and had interest in becoming an electrical engineer—even though he had only the vaguest notion of what electrical engineers did. Although he periodically used voice transmission, he communicated mostly through his hands using the dots and dashes of Morse code, in which he had to become proficient enough to pass the difficult general-class amateur license test. When asked how he managed to pass the advanced electronics theory portion of the exam, Gilmer jokes, "I was smarter then than I am now." Because pulsed code transmissions typically cover far greater distances than the amplitude modulation used for voice, Jimmy applied his Morse skills in competitions in which the objective was logging as many contacts with other distant ham operators as possible within a defined time period. "I got to where I was pretty dad-gum good," says Gilmer in his soft Texas accent.

Gilmer's speech pattern belies his origin. Despite a widely held misconception, he is not a native Texan, but was born in Chicago and spent his toddler years in

Jimmy Gilmer in 1996.

Wichita, Kansas. Even though he came from the Windy City, he intensely disliked the stiff prairie winds that blew regularly through Amarillo, where he grew up. Another false rumor is that he was a conservatory-trained pianist. He did, however, strongly oppose inserting the electronically generated flutelike sounds into "Sugar Shack," which he initially thought ruined the song. And although he was never attracted to country music, he's now managing the careers of a couple of country music artists.

Jimmy Gilmer might well have become an engineer were it not for the lure of the new rock and roll music in the late '50s. "Elvis came to Amarillo around 1956, and *Life* magazine took photographs showing girls in the audience reaching up for him." Gilmer was in the audience at that appearance and remembers the excitement Elvis generated. Inspired, Gilmer got a guitar, taught himself to play, and in his senior year formed a band composed of fellow high school students. After graduating from Amarillo High School in 1958, Gilmer enrolled at Amarillo Junior College, but the evening club dates that his band played began to compromise his performance in his 8 a.m. trigonometry class. "And my engineering ambitions started to fade away," he says.

Jimmy, who was born September 15, 1940, remembers frequent family sing-alongs with songs like "You Are My Sunshine" and "Birmingham Jail." Jimmy's father, an Oklahoman, worked in sales and credit management for Phillips Petroleum Co. in Chicago and Wichita before being named to manage a new division that opened in Amarillo. For relaxation, Jimmy's father sang in choirs, glee clubs, and barbershop quartets. Jimmy did take some private piano lessons for a couple of years beginning at age 8, but disliked the instrument and quit playing. Music meant little to him until the advent of rock and roll. And rock and roll led to his 10-year tenure with the Fireballs.

During that time, the band sputtered as well as sparked. After the success of "Sugar Shack" and "Daisy Petal Pickin'" in early 1964, the popularity of the Fireballs and many other American groups withered as British acts overran the pop charts. After a top 50 hit called "Ain't Gonna Tell Anybody" in 1964, the Fireballs all but disappeared from radio playlists and took a self-imposed hiatus. Jimmy, who said he could read music only well enough to just get by, enrolled in Eastern New Mexico University to increase his understanding of music and explore the possibility of entering law school. But his return to school lasted less than a year. The Fireballs went back into the studio in 1967 and cut some hot new material, including "Bottle Of Wine." Misinterpreting the intent of the song's lyrics, which *did not* romanticize alcohol abuse, label owner Randy Wood labeled the song offensive and refused to allow its release on Dot, a label of primarily traditional artists including Pat Boone, Debbie Reynolds, and bandleaders Billy Vaughn and Lawrence Welk. Likewise, ABC-owned radio stations in key markets, including New York, Detroit, and Chicago, unthinkingly banned the record.

"It was absurd," says Gilmer. "When Dot passed on the record we let Randy know we felt very strongly about it because it had tested really well on our previous tour. Randy told us that if we felt that strongly about it, he wasn't going to hold us back, and he gave us a release from our contract. So we shopped the record, Atco picked it up, released it and Bam! The dang thing started up the charts. I remember I was in school and here come the booking agents from William Morris and I had to drop out of school again. I never went back after that time."

Gilmer recalls when the band split up, in 1970. "I was so burned out, I was ready. I hated the last six months. I was tired of the road and although I loved the music business, I needed a change. My original idea was to go to California and put a new band together, get a new manager, and start over."

But instead of going west to L.A., he went east, to Nashville, at the invitation of an old school pal, Eddie Reeves. For a time Reeves had run a New York office for the Fireballs and was involved with Norman Petty's publishing interests. Reeves, who would in the 1990s become senior vice president and general manager of Warner Brothers in Nashville, was working for United Artists Music when he called Gilmer in early 1971. Reeves knew that Gilmer had been dabbling in production and management and had signed an act to Atlantic. Eddie asked Jimmy if he'd like to be involved in establishing a United Artists publishing operation in Nashville. Gilmer replied, "Nashville? That's country music. What do I know about country music?" But with encouragement from Reeves and other United Artists executives, Gilmer joined United Artists Music that February.

"It was me and a secretary, and my job was to find some writers and build this company. I knew nothing about publishing. I remember my boss at that time said, 'As a performer, you knew good songs when you heard them. Just find good songs and go get them cut.' That was my mandate." Gilmer was to remain with that publishing operation for 26 years. At the time he joined the firm it was called United Artists Music, a division of United Artists films. The United Artists stable of artists brought Gilmer into contact with numerous old friends, including Bobby Goldsboro, with whom he and the Fireballs had toured. In his new position Gilmer published Goldsboro's songs.

Over the years United Artists underwent several mergers and acquisitions, and was known at various times as CBS Songs, SBK Songs, and EMI Music Publishing. In differing capacities, Gilmer worked with songwriter Alex Harvey and country singer-songwriters Billy Edd Wheeler, Billie Jo Spears, and Del Reeves. He is particularly proud of signing country artist Mary Chapin Carpenter to a publishing contract. At times, Gilmer supervised up to 40 songwriters.

When the company was known as SBK, Gilmer was vice president of the southern region, supervising pop and country music product. The acquisition by EMI in 1989 led to establishment of SBK Records, where Gilmer was in charge of discovering and signing composer-artists to the label. Although the pop market was doing well for the label, the company grew impatient and decided to collapse its country music effort in Nashville. Gilmer returned to publishing for the company until his departure in April 1997 to launch his own artist management firm, JAG Management. Although pronounced to rhyme with "bag," JAG was derived from the initials of his name—James Axley Gilmer. Within his first few months of operation, he had already signed three country music acts—Cactus Choir, Brad Paisley, and Melodie Crittenden—and had secured major recording agreements for each. Since 1980 his assistant has been Susan Sherrill. Her husband, Billy Sherrill, is one of the leading recording engineers in Nashville. In the corporate environment, Gilmer worked with artists only during certain phases of their careers. He started JAG management to enable him to more fully guide the careers of artists.

Jimmy, who originally married in 1966 but divorced eight years later, raised his son Drew, who was born in 1970. In 1976 Jimmy married Carolyn Downey, and together they raised her two children, Carla and Bobby Baker, from a previous marriage. Both Drew and Carla are in the music business: Drew works in the songwriter relations department at BMI in Nashville and Carla has been a road crew member for various singers, including Brian White and Billy Dean.

Jimmy is proud of his extended family. "I had a good spiritual foundation built by my parents. I was singing in church choirs from a very early age. During my wandering years I was about as far away from the church as you can get, and I think there were some times in my career that I really could have taken a wrong turn, but somehow I was given divine direction and I pulled myself through that," says Jimmy, who recalled his own youth experiences when raising the three kids. "Those years between 18 and 28 are risky times, but somehow I made it through that tunnel and now they've all made it through. Today you see so many families with kids who are just kind of lost. I've tried to maintain good, honest principles in this business," he adds. "I've turned down many deals in which I would have made lots of money under the table. Somehow I've been blessed with a lot of success. I hope that the kids will carry this foundation on with them and raise their families the same way."

Quarter To Three

CHAPTER 2

Gary "U.S." Bonds

FROM THE TIME CAPSULE

OCTOBER 1960: Frank Guida's Legrand label releases "New Orleans," the first single by Gary "U.S" Bonds.

- OCTOBER 7: Corvette-driving Martin Milner and George Maharis star in the debut of the *Route 66* television series on CBS.
- OCTOBER 12: Soviet Premier Nikita Khrushchev pounds a desk with his shoe during a United Nations General Assembly session.
- OCTOBER 14: John F. Kennedy first proposes the Peace Corps, asking 10,000 students if they would be willing to serve the cause of peace by living and working in the developing world.
- OCTOBER 19: The United States imposes an embargo on exports to Cuba.

MAY 1961: "Quarter To Three" begins its climb on the charts to No. 1 and stays on the top 100 throughout the summer.

- MAY 5: Navy Commander Alan B. Shepard Jr. becomes the first American in space on a 116-mile-high suborbital flight aboard the *Freedom 7* space capsule.
- MAY 9: Addressing the National Association of Broadcasters, Federal Communications Commission Chairman Newton Minow declares television programming a "vast wasteland."
- MAY 13: American film star Gary Cooper dies at age 60.

MARCH 1962: "Twist, Twist, Señora" is released.

- MARCH 2: Wilt Chamberlain scores 100 points for the Philadelphia Warriors in a National Basketball Association game against the New York Knicks.
- MARCH 22: The musical *I Can Get It For You Wholesale* opens on Broadway starring Elliott Gould and 19-year-old Barbra Streisand.
- MARCH 29: Jack Paar hosts NBC's *Tonight* show for the last time.

OPPOSITE: Gary "U.S." Bonds in a 1961 photo promoting "Quarter To Three." FROM PHOTOFEST ARCHIVES, NEW YORK.

In the early '60s era of high school sock hops and college fraternity beer bashes, no artist did more to define the genre of party music than Gary "U.S." Bonds. In a soulful rasp overdubbed multiple times and layered over a raucously throbbing beat, Bonds perfected a penetrating vocal style that drove him into the national top 10 with his very first release, produced a No. 1 hit on the *Billboard* Hot 100, and eventually brought him nine top 40 hits spanning three decades.

But seven years before he became known to the world as Gary "U.S." Bonds, he was a 14-year-old boy named Gary Anderson who was looking for something to do with his friends. It was 1953, and while the Korean War raged in its final months and the Soviet Union detonated its first hydrogen bomb, life droned on in sleepy Norfolk, Virginia, where young Gary lived. The emergence of early rhythm and blues artists inspired Gary and several friends to try a capella singing and they chose a street corner—the corner of Granville Avenue and Park in the Brambleton section of Norfolk—for their stage.

"There was not that much to do in Norfolk so my friends and I just said, 'Well let's sing.' None of us knew how, but we'd practice songs on the radio by the Flamingos, the Drifters, and the Mills Brothers until we actually started sounding pretty good," recalls Gary. "We'd just stand on the street corner, what we'd call our street corner, at night, in front of Mr. Boone's Market. We'd get out there and just keep all the neighbors awake, into the wee hours of the night, until they'd run us away, and then we'd go home and go to bed." Gary and his friends, Melvin "D.D." McNair, Hollis "Frizell" Coleman, and Thomas "Moose" High, formed a group called the Turks. Raymond Haskins and Hermione Gross later replaced McNair and High.

Night after night they gathered to sing on the same corner, and as the months stretched into years, they honed their harmonizing skills into near perfection. One night in 1957 local record store owner Frank Guida stopped to listen to the boys. He told them they sounded pretty good. He also said he was planning to open his own studio and record company and asked if they would be interested in recording for him a few years down the road. But by the time Guida actually opened his recording studio, the other members of the street corner singers had joined the service and Anderson was the only one left.

Guida had achieved initial success in 1959 with "High School U.S.A," a novelty record that became a national hit through the aggregate sales of 28 different regional versions, on each of which singer Tommy Facenda revised lyrics to mention local high schools.

Anderson recalls, "Guida came by and he said, 'OK, I'll take you.' And we went down to his studio and he gave me a song called 'New Orleans,' which was a country and western song written by Joe Royster, a guy who worked in the shoe department in one of the major department stores in Norfolk. Joe eventually became the staff engineer and songwriter, and I guess everything else around the studio. It really wasn't hard to be an engineer back then; the recording equipment was only two-track. All you had to do was find some tape and turn it on and, bingo, you were an engineer."

His spirited recording of "New Orleans," issued on Guida's tiny Legrand label, hit the pop charts in the fall of 1960, driving to No. 6 on the *Billboard* Hot 100. Seeking a gimmick to attract the attention of disc jockeys, Guida credited the vocal to Gary "U.S." Bonds and inscribed the message "Buy U.S. Bonds" on the sleeves of promotional copies that were sent to the radio stations. So at the age of 19, Gary Anderson became Gary "U.S." Bonds.

After "New Orleans" concluded its run on the charts, Bonds wrote and recorded a song called "Not Me," which bubbled under at No. 116 in 1961. Reportedly, Dick Clark found a line containing the words "punch you in the lip" objectionable, and many radio stations refused to play the song. In 1963, the female vocal group the Orlons recorded "Not Me," with the offending lyrics excised; their version garnered significant airplay and became a No. 1 hit.

Bonds worked magic for his second hit, turning a prosaic instrumental into one of the most rollicking party records of the rock and roll era. In 1961, Guida employed a studio band called Daddy G and the Church Street Five, which recorded an instrumental called "A Night With Daddy G." When the song failed to attract much attention, Guida asked Gary to come up with some lyrics for it. "I went into his little office, sat down for about 15 or 20 minutes, came back and said, 'I've got something.' And Guida said, 'Well, let's record it.' And we recorded 'Quarter To Three' based on 'A Night With Daddy G.'" The song became Gary's strongest record, a No. 1 hit that remained on the charts throughout the summer of '61.

Following the success of "New Orleans" and "Quarter To Three," Gary joined the premier summer stage show, the Dick Clark Caravan of Stars. That traveling entourage toured much of the nation, beginning in Atlantic City, New Jersey, on July 29, 1961, and ending in Detroit, Michigan, that September 4. He toured the country by bus, appearing with Chubby Checker, Freddy Cannon, the Shirelles, Bobby Rydell, Fabian, and other top artists of the time. While he was on tour, Gary's single "School Is Out" climbed to fifth position on the charts and by October 23, the follow-up, "School Is In," reached 28.

While many of the 1960s dance crazes—the locomotion, the pony, the mashed potatoes—were short-lived, the popularity of the twist, which had spawned them, lasted over two years. From late 1960 through 1962 the twist inspired numerous song titles, including Chubby Checker's "The Twist," "Let's Twist Again," "Slow Twistin," and "Twist It Up"; Joey Dee and the Starliters' "Peppermint Twist"; Sam Cooke's "Twistin' The Night Away"; and King Curtis's "Soul Twist." In early 1962, Gary "U.S." Bonds managed to keep the craze going with a twist style of his own in "Dear Lady Twist," and on March 18, 1962, Gary appeared on *The Ed Sullivan Show* to perform his newest hit, "Twist, Twist Señora." Both songs on the Legrand label peaked at No. 9 on *Billboard*'s Hot 100 pop chart.

Gary enjoys telling the story about firing his backup band, which had been known as the Silver Beatles. "During my first trip to Europe, I was on the bill with Gene McDaniels, who had the 1961 hits 'A Hundred Pounds Of Clay' and 'Tower Of Strength.' Our backup band, which people would later know as the Beatles, was just not cutting it. At that time they really didn't know the feel of rock and roll," recalls Gary, grinning. "So we hired another band when we got back to home base in London. That band was worse than the Beatles! So we had to rehire them."

Some of Gary's fondest memories include meeting idols Sam Cooke, Jackie Wilson, and B.B. King for the first time on a bus tour in 1960. He recalls, "They really wanted to turn me around because I was very rigid on stage, since I had no training. I was from Norfolk, Virginia. What the hell did I know? I had a hit record, I went out on stage and I sang. I didn't move, I didn't talk, I didn't dance. So one afternoon, after we left one of the venues, Sam Cooke said to me, 'B.B. and I have a limousine, and we want you to ride with us in the limousine to the next gig. We want to talk to you.' So I said, 'Oh, OK.' And I got in there and they started telling me, 'You talk to us backstage and you're mouth almighty but when you get on stage you don't say nuthin', you don't move. We've gotta loosen you up a little bit.' And they started showing me a few things and telling me some things to say. They said, 'So the next gig you go out and you do that, OK?' And I said, 'Oh, yessir, OK.' And the next gig I didn't do it. And they put me back in the limousine again and they talked to me, and they said, 'At the next gig you do it,' and I didn't do it. The third gig, when I was coming off the stage, after I didn't do it again, Sam Cooke slapped the shit out of me. As soon as I hit the side of the stage, BAM!, and he says, 'The next time you go out there, dammit, do it, or I'm gonna punch you.' I've been a dancing fool ever since."

On another early '60s bus tour through the South and into Texas that included the pop duo Dick and Dee Dee, who were promoting their hit "The Mountain's High," Bonds was the only black performer. "I remember they used to smuggle me into the hotels because, you know, blacks weren't allowed. But they got me through it. Dick and all the guys. They'd say, just hang here for a minute, we'll make sure you're in. I'd go to the side door and run."

Bonds also toured with some legendary rhythm and blues performers, including the Shirelles, the Cadillacs, the Flamingos, Bobby Lewis, and Bo Diddley. "I remember Bo Diddley cooking chicken in the back of the bus. Being young I didn't mind sitting in that bus for 20 hours. Everybody was playing cards and gambling. Oh, God, and no mothers and fathers. We were drinking and smoking cigarettes. Man, I thought it was great." Bonds laughs. "A lot of times we wouldn't get to a hotel, and it got pretty funky in there for a couple of days. We'd just do our gig, get back on the bus, stop at a truck stop or whatever and kinda wash up a little bit, get to the next gig and perform. Then maybe we got to a hotel room, took a shower and cleaned our clothes up a little bit. I think the bus tours were the most memorable things I can remember doing. I got to see the world, make money, *and* chase the girls."

In addition to bus tours, Bonds occasionally played theaters during the '60s, including the Apollo, the Regal, and the Royal. "I also went down South and got into the chitlin' circuit, they called it, the chicken shacks. We all did those with James Brown and whoever else. They were fun. A little rough, but fun. We were young so we could run real fast."

In 1962 Gary introduced the late Jimmy Soul to Guida, who produced Soul's recording "If You Wanna Be Happy," a No. 1 hit in 1963. "Jimmy and I used to sing together in Suffolk. This was before either of us had a hit record. Jimmy was 'wonder boy' and I was 'nature boy.' We didn't wear many clothes back then. The place we were working was really strange so we tried to find a gimmick. It was like a long corridor with the bandstand in the middle, so we'd come swinging in on ropes from both ends wearing little loincloths. Thank God I don't have to wear that damn loincloth anymore," he says, erupting into laughter.

HIT SINGLES BY GARY "U.S." BONDS

DEBUT	PEAK	TITLE	LABEL
10/60	6	NEW ORLEANS	LEGRAND
5/61	1	QUARTER TO THREE	LEGRAND
7/61	5	SCHOOL IS OUT	LEGRAND
10/61	28	SCHOOL IS IN	LEGRAND
12/61	9	DEAR LADY TWIST	LEGRAND
3/62	9	TWIST, TWIST SEÑORA	LEGRAND
6/62	27	SEVEN DAY WEEKEND	LEGRAND
8/62	92	COPY CAT	LEGRAND
4/81	11	THIS LITTLE GIRL	EMI AMERICA
7/81	65	JOLE BLON	EMI AMERICA
6/82	21	OUT OF WORK	EMI AMERICA

GARY ANDERSON

Gary "U.S." Bonds is as fun-loving and full of life as his music. His light-hearted humor and infectious laughter reveal his enjoyment of life. With nine top 40 hits under his belt, Gary hasn't let any grass grow under his feet. He continues to electrify audiences with lively performances while pursuing a newfound career in a food products company and serving as a goodwill ambassador to Third World countries.

Born to Gary and Irene Anderson in Jacksonville, Florida, on June 6, 1939, Gary carved out a career for himself beginning in high school and spanning more than four decades. His father was a professor at Hampton Institute

Gary Anderson flanked by his wife, Laurie (at left), and his daughter, Laurie.

PHOTO COURTESY OF GARY "U.S." BONDS.

(now Hampton University), a college in southeastern Virginia, and his mother was a piano teacher. In the mid '40s, Anderson's family moved to Norfolk, Virginia, where Gary was first introduced to theater when he was 8 years old. He recalls his mother taking him to the Booker T. Washington Theater in Norfolk, which featured musical performers such as Bullmoose Jackson, Pigmeat Markham, and Ivory Joe Hunter. "The first time I saw Bullmoose Jackson with all the lights, stage, and sound, I thought 'this is what I want to do,'" says Anderson.

Anderson attended Booker T. Washington High School, but when he landed his first record deal with Guida he dropped out of school. "It was a choice between going to school or going out and making money. My mom was all for me going out and making money, but my dad didn't like it because he was a university professor."

Gary's father had taught math and science at Florida State University for many years before joining Hampton, where he taught science and woodwork. "He always loved to do woodwork and when he was getting ready to retire, he said 'I want to teach woodwork,' so he did," says Anderson. "There's a man who went to school all of his life. He had every degree there was, and he didn't take too kindly to me quitting school."

Gary recalls one time his father agreed to attend one of his performances. "He sat in the back and watched the show, and on the way home I didn't say anything. He didn't either. He just shook his head. Finally, he said, 'I don't understand it. I don't know how you make money doing that.' He didn't understand it 'til the day he died."

In 1962 Gary met his wife-to-be, Laurie Cedeno, in Atlantic City. She was a member of a doo-wop vocal group called the Love Notes, who recorded the hit single "United" in the late '50s. At the time Laurie, whose stage name was Laurie Davis, was performing solo at the Bamboo Club on the boardwalk and Gary was performing at the Hialeah Club four blocks away.

"I stopped by to have a drink. I saw her and said to myself, 'Wow. She looks pretty good.' After the show, she came around to see me and we went out to breakfast. We've been seeing each other ever since."

Married since 1963, Gary and Laurie tour throughout the country with their daughter, also named Laurie, and a five-piece band. They have set up a recording studio in their Long Island home, where daughter Laurie writes and produces music with her father. "Our show is based around good times. We go out and create a party," says Gary. "We try to create a 'Come on! Let's dance, let's sing atmosphere. So I guess I'm perceived as some old good-time, happy guy." Since the late 1980s, Gary and Laurie have been managing their own musical engagements. "Now when the money's missing, I know who's got it. It's either me or my wife," he laughs.

Gary is regarded in the music industry as an accomplished songwriter as well as a singer. His song, "Friend Don't Take Her, She's All I've Got," recorded by Johnny Paycheck in 1971, was nominated for a Grammy Award and earned Gary a nomination for the Country Music Association's Songwriter of the Year. In 1971 Freddie North's recording of the same song reached No. 1 on the R&B charts, and in 1997 the song became a top 10 hit for country artist Tracy Byrd.

Anderson regards his association with Frank Guida and Bruce Springsteen as his two biggest breaks. He met Springsteen in 1979 while working at a club in New Jersey. At the time Springsteen was involved in a lawsuit and wasn't recording. "He saw me and said, 'Maybe I'll just work with you until this court thing is over with.' And that's what he did." With a sterling roster of backup singers and musicians, including Ben E. King and Chuck Jackson, Springsteen produced the 1981 Gary "U.S." Bonds album *Dedication* released on EMI. That was followed a year later by another successful album, *On The Line.* "And then we had two kids and Bruce left. And I'm still upset over that," Anderson jokes. The Springsteen-produced "This Little Girl" and "Out Of Work" rose to the No. 11 and No. 21 positions on the charts in 1981 and 1982, respectively.

Anderson maintains his friendship with Springsteen, although he says, "Bruce is mostly out in California now, so I don't get a chance to see him that much. He's a married man now. We talk every now and then." Springsteen and Miami Steve Van Zandt presented Anderson with the Pioneer Award for achievement in the music industry at the 1997 Rhythm and Blues Foundation awards ceremony at the New York Hilton.

Anderson continues to perform from 55 to 60 dates a year. "I still do what I like to call 'legend shows,' but thanks to 'This Little Girl' with Bruce Springsteen and that album, I get to do a lot of contemporary venues also." Gary "U.S." Bonds played a role with Bo Diddley cast as a member of the Louisiana Gator Boys in the 1998 movie *Blues Brothers 2000.* "I performed 'New Orleans' and I also sang backup for B.B. King in the movie."

In 1973 and again in 1983, Anderson met Yank Barry, former lead singer of the traveling Kingsmen, at a benefit golf tournament that Barry was sponsoring. "I love golf, man, I'll fly anywhere," says Anderson. "We met each other in Myrtle Beach, South Carolina, and struck up a friendship. One day Yank came back from South Africa, where he had been doing some recording with a philharmonic orchestra. At that time he was producing Engelbert Humperdinck and Tom Jones. He had met a scientist over there, who had an idea for a high-protein, soy bean–based food product, and he asked me if I would be interested in joining him in it, and investing some money. I said, 'This sounds like a good idea. I don't know anything about food, and I don't know anything about investing, but I trust you. Let's go with it.' And thank God, it's been a great thing for me."

The products, under the Vita Pro name, are low in fat and calories and high in protein. Distributed through a network marketing company called Global Village Market, Vita Pro is a line of meat substitutes created from soy isolate with the taste and texture of meat. Because it's dehydrated and requires no refrigeration, the food is ideal for famine relief. Barry, who was involved with the "We Are The World" relief project, believes strongly in donating a percentage of Global Village Market's revenue to hunger relief in the United States and throughout the world. In August 1997, Anderson joined Barry, former world heavyweight boxing champion Muhammad Ali, singer Celine Dion, and other celebrities, as well as numerous Global Village supporters, in a relief mission to the Ivory Coast in western Africa. The project, funded completely by Global Village Market, provided food, medicine, wheelchairs, toys, and writing materials to a rehabilitation center there that houses and cares for 480 disabled, orphaned, and abandoned children who fled civil strife in Liberia.

"We took *Entertainment Tonight, Life* magazine, and our own camera crew. In all there were 67 people, including a number of African reporters that we picked up in Abidjan. The president of the Ivory Coast gave us his plane to fly around in, and that was cool." Following the trip, Anderson appeared on *Entertainment Tonight* with Muhammad Ali and Yank Barry. "When you've got Muhammad there, you become background. So I became background, and I was glad to be there."

The trip was an eye-opener for Anderson. He said, "Some of the children have malaria, cholera, polio, one leg, one eye. It was really, really cruel. When I think about it, I feel really bad, but it was the greatest thing that ever happened to me in life. And I didn't get paid for it. People can't understand that I would do that. It was fantastic. It really was."

Anderson says he's happy with his career and life. Driven by his love of golf, Gary has been involved in several PGA celebrity golf tournaments. He also enjoys recording, performing, and throwing parties for his neighbors. "I would have moved out of this neighborhood years ago, but our neighbors are fantastic. We all look out for each other and there's no problems within a half-mile radius of here," said Gary. "I never work New Year's Eve so I can throw a party at my house. Since about 1985 we've invited all of our neighbors to walk to our house for a party so that no one has to drive, and we have about 60 people here. It's a lot of fun."

Communicating with people is one of Gary's greatest strengths, but he says singing is not. "I'm not that great a singer. Even though I've learned a lot over the past 40 years. I haven't quite reached the stature of singer that I would like to be, like a Sam Cooke or Jackie Wilson. But I can hold my own. With Sam Cooke slapping me and Jackie Wilson showing me things, I learned how to do it."

Anderson's greatest pleasure is spending time with his family. "We have the greatest time together. That's why we're always here alone. Me and my wife and daughter. We sing and dance and watch movies. I also like working around the house. I'm one of those fix-it guys. Even though I can't fix it that good, I like doing it."

It's very important to Anderson how people remember him. "I like to feel that I made some impact on somebody's life. That's why it gives me such a thrill that I'm doing something with the Champions for Children with Muhammad Ali and Yank. Not only for self-gratification, but also for people to know that the family I'm involved with, my family, is part of something that may change something for somebody in this world. When I'm gone, I don't want people to say 'This guy was here, and he didn't do shit.' Especially for my daughter, I want them to say, 'Her father made a meaningful contribution to society.'"

CHAPTER 3

The Lion Sleeps Tonight

The Tokens

FROM THE TIME CAPSULE

NOVEMBER 1961: "The Lion Sleeps Tonight" begins its rise to the top of the charts.

- NOVEMBER 11: Izzy Young books Bob Dylan at Carnegie Recital Hall in New York City. Only 53 people attend.
- NOVEMBER 11: Dean Rusk and Robert McNamara send a White Paper to President John F. Kennedy strongly supporting the use of United States forces in Vietnam if necessary in the future "to prevent the fall of South Vietnam to Communism."

MARCH 1966: The B.T. Puppy label releases the Tokens' "I Hear Trumpets Blow," the group's third song to reach at least the top 30 on the pop charts.

- MARCH 6: A British magazine quotes John Lennon as saying the Beatles "are more popular than Jesus," arousing furious anti-Beatles sentiment worldwide.
- MARCH 6: Barry Sadler's "Ballad Of The Green Berets" hits No. 1 on the charts (and stays for 13 weeks).
- MARCH 15: A second wave of riots in the Watts section of Los Angeles erupts, causing 2 deaths and 25 injuries.

DECEMBER 1969: "She Lets Her Hair Down (Early In The Morning)" (Buddah), the last Tokens single to reach the top 100 (No. 61) during the sixties, is released.

- DECEMBER 6: In front of 300,000 fans attending a free rock concert at Altamont Speedway in Livermore, California, a Hell's Angels' security guard stabs 18-year-old Meredith Hunter to death while the Rolling Stones play "Under My Thumb."
- DECEMBER 17: Falsetto-pitched singer Tiny Tim (Herbert Khaury) marries "Miss Vicky" Budinger on NBC's *Tonight Show* starring Johnny Carson.
- DECEMBER 18: Great Britain abolishes the death penalty.

OPPOSITE: The Tokens in 1967. Top, left to right: Jay Siegel, Hank Medress; bottom: Phil Margo, Mitch Margo. FROM PHOTOFEST ARCHIVES, NEW YORK.

In the summer of 1961 four guys from Brooklyn walked into the RCA Victor recording studio for what might have been the last time. The oldest among them was not quite 23. The youngest was 14. Known initially as Those Guys, they had changed their name to the Tokens. They'd previously scored one national hit, "Tonight I Fell In Love," on another label, Warwick. But when the boss at Warwick told them they wouldn't be paid because their record hadn't cleared a profit, they took their songs and brought them to RCA, which offered them a three-record contract.

Their first two sessions for the RCA label in the spring of 1961 yielded two releases, "When I Go To Sleep At Night"/"Dry Your Eyes" and "Sincerely," neither of which registered on the *Billboard* Hot 100. At the next recording session, which was likely to be their last, the producers huddled with the quartet members to review the songs they'd brought. The RCA execs weren't impressed by what they heard. They asked the Tokens if they had any other songs.

Well, yes, there was one other song. An African-style folk melody they'd been singing at music gigs and adapted to their own style. It was called "Mbube," and it was also known as "Wimoweh." The producers at RCA loved it. With English lyrics added by a team consisting of George Weiss and session producers Hugo Peretti and Luigi Creatore, the Tokens recorded the song and released it under a new name: "The Lion Sleeps Tonight."

The public loved it as well. At the close of 1961, it became the first African song to top the American pop charts. And while other African melodies, including Miriam Makeba's pulsating "Pata Pata," have found success, none has so endeared itself to pop fans as "The Lion Sleeps Tonight," performed by Jay Siegel, Hank Medress, and Phil and Mitch Margo: the Tokens. But the Tokens ultimately proved to be more prolific behind the controls than they were in front of the microphone. Making an overwhelmingly successful transition to production work, the Tokens became the first group to produce a No. 1 record by another group: "He's So Fine" by the Chiffons.

Hank Medress first began harmonizing with drummer Phil Margo and his piano-playing brother Mitch in December 1959. Needing a lead singer, they recruited Jay Siegel, who sang with Hank in two other neighborhood vocal groups. The four began writing songs, then bought some time in Allegro Recording Studios on Broadway in Manhattan. They recorded a demo of a song called "Please Write" and started knocking on doors in Tin Pan Alley, midtown Manhattan's famous music publishing district. While "Please Write" didn't convince anyone to sign on the bottom line, the owner of Warwick Records liked the Tokens' composition "Tonight I Fell In Love." The label signed the group, and recorded and released the song in February 1961, just after John F. Kennedy took office as president.

In less than two months "Tonight I Fell In Love" brought the group into the national top 20 and onto *American Bandstand*. "At that time, to us, you didn't get any bigger than that," remembers Hank. The Tokens took to the road. Pittsburgh. Cleveland. Detroit. "In those days groups promoted records by lip-synching at record hops. Back then, we didn't perform live. We'd do seven record hops in one night."

None of the group members really gave serious thought to careers as musicians, and Hank Medress, Phil Margo, and Jay Siegel all enrolled in Brooklyn College after graduating from high school.

Hank entered college in 1956 with thoughts of becoming a teacher. He began studying elementary education, but couldn't really see himself teaching school the rest of his life. After "Tonight I Fell In Love" became a hit, it was easier for Medress to switch directions, and he left college during his junior year. "I had a better perspective then of where I was going," Hank says.

Phil, who graduated from high school in 1959, began working in a stock brokerage firm while attending college. His brother, Mitch, five years his junior, was still in junior high school.

Jay transferred from Brooklyn College to New York City Community College, where he obtained a degree in retail market research. He entered the trade as a merchandise buyer for Rainbow Shops, a retail chain. "I never thought that music would be my career, because people I knew who had jobs didn't really enjoy what they did. So it never occurred to me that I could have a career and make money doing something that's so much fun," said Jay. By the fall of 1961, Jay had married Judy Fischer and had a back-office job doing cost analysis for Lerner Shops, a chain of women's apparel stores. When "The Lion Sleeps Tonight" began its four-week climb to the top of the charts in mid-November 1961, the attorney handling financial affairs for the Tokens advised Jay to quit his job. Jay's parents, wife, and in-laws all had the same reaction to that suggestion: "Quit your job? What are you, crazy?" Jay considered their pleas. Then he quit his job.

The Tokens returned to *American Bandstand* when "The Lion Sleeps Tonight" returned them to the charts. "That was difficult for us to lip-synch because 'The Lion Sleeps Tonight' doesn't have an instrumental introduction. It begins with my falsetto," says Jay. "So I held my head down so my lips couldn't be seen, until I heard the first note come through the speakers, and then I looked up and lip-synched with the song."

As stunning a success as "The Lion Sleeps Tonight" was, it proved problematic when it came to booking engagements. "We just didn't fit in anywhere. We weren't folk, we weren't rock. We had this wonderful record, but nobody knew what it was," says Phil. "After doing some college gigs we found that we needed to accompany ourselves. That's what inspired us to learn how to play our own instruments. Hank played bass, I played the drums, Mitch played the guitar, and Jay sang lead and occasionally played guitar."

On the record hop circuit, the Tokens became friends with the Angels, the Marcels, Dion and the Belmonts, and Del Shannon. They also met Tony Orlando, who as a solo artist was out on the road promoting his records "Halfway To Paradise" and "Bless You." A decade later, the Tokens would produce Orlando's hits with Dawn and resurrect his flagging career.

Although they continued recording and releasing songs that generated some chart action, the Tokens were unable to crack the national top 40 for four more years. While the public may have thought that the group was suffering from a creative drought, quite the opposite was true. The four Tokens, who had always played a large role in the production of their own records, were still writing songs and producing sessions for other artists. "It was a natural progression," observes Hank. "I didn't think we were that great as a performance group. I didn't see any real longevity, but we made really terrific records." Top executives at Capitol Records agreed, and Capitol signed the Tokens as producers.

The association between the Tokens and Capitol was short-lived but fruitful. There, the Tokens produced a record by a then-unknown vocal group that had come their way, a female quartet called the Chiffons. The song, "He's So Fine," was by a songwriter named Ronnie Mack, who had walked into the Tokens' office off the street and persuaded them to listen to the Chiffons do the tune. Capitol, which had first right of refusal, didn't think much of the track. After shopping the recording without success at a number of New York City–based labels, including MGM and Columbia, Hank and Phil finally emerged with a deal at a smaller company, Laurie Records. The royalty deal with Laurie included an advance, which the Tokens used to buy out of the contract with Capitol. The gamble on "He's So Fine" paid handsomely, as the song quickly rose to No. 1 and stayed there for four weeks. Jay recalls, "With 'He's So Fine,' we became the first group to produce a No. 1 record by another group." On the strength of that musical coup and their business acumen, the Tokens leapt from the ranks of doo-wop vocal groups to become top producers.

Their record production credits mounted with "Denise" by Randy and the Rainbows (No. 10) and all of the Chiffons' top singles: "One Fine Day" (No. 5), "A Love So Fine" and "I Have A Boyfriend" (both top 40), and "Sweet Talkin' Guy" (No. 10). Working both sides of the glass, the Tokens threw themselves fully into every phase of music production work: songwriting, instrumentation, background singing, arranging, producing, and mixing. "We were having more success as producers than we were having as artists," says Phil with characteristic candor. "Right from the beginning, we produced our own demos. You see, a career in entertainment at that time for rock and roll groups was very short. Who knew that 35 years later we'd still be working? I never could have imagined that, because 10 weeks after 'The Lion Sleeps Tonight' was no longer No. 1 we were forgotten. So if we wanted to remain in the business, we had to do something else. We seemed to have a natural ability for producing—we all had good ears, we all had solid music backgrounds, we all knew what a good song was."

Hank Medress concurs. "I remember one period during the 1960s when we had five or six records on the charts at the same time. And we continued to perform even after we had begun producing records and had formed corporations with our lawyer and business manager, Seymour Barash." The corporations the Tokens formed included Bright Tunes Music—their publishing firm named in honor of their Brighton Beach home—and B.T. Puppy Records, their own label established in 1964. The "Puppy" portion of the name was a satirical reference to Nipper, the dog that appears on the RCA logo. The Tokens themselves returned to the charts with "I Hear Trumpets Blow," a top 30 hit released on B.T. Puppy in the spring of 1966. They followed that with "Portrait Of My Love," issued on the Warner Brothers label, which made the top 40.

Meanwhile, the Tokens also became deeply involved in producing music for television and radio commercials, including spots for airlines, cigarettes, beer, and other products. "We spent a good four or five years writing and producing jingles. It was a very lucrative business," says Siegel.

Even so, lion tracks would follow them throughout the remainder of their career. "The Lion Sleeps Tonight," heard on the soundtrack of 11 motion pictures, emerged once again with the June 1994 release of the Disney animated feature *The Lion King*. That megahit film, and the Tony Award–winnning musical of the same name, which looks like it may stay on Broadway for years to come, have introduced the captivating song to an appreciative new generation.

Today's oldies music radio stations typically obtain their music in packages from broadcast production firms. Even though "I Hear Trumpets Blow," "Portrait Of My Love," and "Tonight I Fell In Love" all cracked the national top 40, they're often excluded from the packages that radio stations acquire. But no oldies station worthy of its title would be without a copy of "The Lion Sleeps Tonight." Their listeners still love that record—a token of their esteem for Hank Medress, Phil Margo, Mitch Margo, and Jay Siegel: the four guys from Brooklyn with a huge passion for music—finding it, making it, and producing it.

HIT SINGLES BY THE TOKENS

DEBUT	PEAK	TITLE	LABEL
3/61	15	TONIGHT I FELL IN LOVE	WARWICK
11/61	1	THE LION SLEEPS TONIGHT (Certified Gold)	RCA
2/62	55	B'WA NINA (PRETTY GIRL)	RCA
6/62	85	LA BAMBA	RCA
8/63	94	HEAR THE BELLS	RCA
8/64	43	HE'S IN TOWN	B.T. PUPPY
3/66	30	I HEAR TRUMPETS BLOW	B.T. PUPPY
4/67	36	PORTRAIT OF MY LOVE	WARNER BROTHERS
7/67	69	IT'S A HAPPENING WORLD	WARNER BROTHERS
12/69	61	SHE LETS HER HAIR DOWN (EARLY IN THE MORNING)	BUDDAH
3/70	95	DON'T WORRY BABY	BUDDAH
8/73	30	IN THE MIDNIGHT HOUR*	ATCO
8/94	51	THE LION SLEEPS TONIGHT	RCA

* RELEASED UNDER THE GROUP NAME CROSS COUNTRY.

HANK MEDRESS

From its northern terminal in the Bronx, the subway D train burrows its way down the Upper West Side of Manhattan under Central Park West and clatters beneath Broadway at 53rd Street before traversing the Manhattan Bridge and drilling underground once again in Brooklyn. The train finally emerges from the darkness and roars past the backyards of houses in the neighborhoods of Flatbush, Millwood, and Sheepshead Bay. Three stations before the other end of the line, the train veers in a wide sweep to the right and squeals to a stop on the elevated steel platform atop the intersection of Coney Island and Brighton Beach avenues.

The grimy streets below are lined with luncheonettes, laundries, shoe repair shops, small appliance stores, newsstands, sawdust-floored butcher shops, pizzerias, Chinese restaurants, Jewish delicatessens, and open-front produce markets. Seven-story brownstone apartment buildings shadow the narrow side streets leading to the boardwalk and beach a block away. Farther from the beach, the apartments yield to brick duplexes and modest clapboard cottages built around courtyard enclaves that turn their backs on the streets.

Back in 1955, Brighton 5th Place, Brighton 8th Place, and other courtyards were tight-knit communities. Hank Medress, who was only 2 years old when his father died, lived in a Brighton Beach apartment building with his mother, who worked as a bookkeeper. Hank and Neil Sedaka, then teenagers, lived on the same block. From his bedroom, Hank could

PHOTO BY JANE MEDRESS/ARTEXTURES DESIGN.

hear Neil practicing classical music on his piano each day after school until 5 p.m. That's when Hank would dash across the courtyard, Neil would start pounding forbidden boogie-woogie on his keyboard, and the two would harmonize doo-wop tunes.

Hank—an only child who enjoyed shooting hoops with other kids in the court-yard—played basketball and ran track at Lincoln High School, which Neil also attended. Hank was a talented athlete, and could have won a sports scholarship from any of several small colleges. But he loved music too much. In 1954 he and Neil decided to form a musical group, the Linc-Tones, with three other Lincoln High School friends, Eddie Rabkin, Cynthia Zolitin, and Jay Siegel. Renamed the Tokens, the group performed during their junior and senior years and recorded a few tunes, including a Sedaka-penned song called "I Love My Baby" for the small Melba label, before disbanding in 1956.

Hank Medress, born November 19, 1938, was first drawn to music when he began listening in the early '50s to pioneering disc jockey Martin Block's "Make-Believe Ballroom" on New York radio station WNEW. In an era of live big band broadcasts, Block played phonograph records and counted down the most popu-lar songs of the day by Patti Page, Don Cornell, Eddie Fisher, and Perry Como.

Then came Alan Freed in the fall of 1954, broadcasting a steady diet of doo-wop and rock and roll on WINS. Freed played "Earth Angel" by the Penguins, "Goodnight, Sweetheart, Goodnight" by the Spaniels, "Tweedle Dee" by LaVern Baker, and "Sh-Boom" by the Chords. Medress loved the new sound and began going to the Brooklyn Fox and the Brooklyn Paramount to see the Moonglows, the Harptones, the Flamingos, and other groups.

When the first Tokens combo dissolved, Hank joined a group called Darryl and the Oxfords, but remained with them only long enough to record one tune, a Roulette release called "Picture In My Wallet" that became a local hit. Preoccupied with the idea of forming a new group of his own, he wasn't concerned about the Oxfords' lack of momentum. It didn't take long for Hank to convince the Margo brothers to join, and Hank, the Margos, and Jay Siegel formed a new Tokens group, an association that would last more than a decade.

The Tokens remained intact until the early '70s, but Hank began drifting away to pursue his own production interests. "We ran the Tokens as a partnership. If I wrote a song, all four of us were credited with writing it. If another one of the guys wrote a song, we all divided the credit equally. If I produced a record, all of our names went on it. And I left the group partly because I felt there was an inequity to that arrangement." Pivotal in Medress's decision to make a break was the association that the group began with producer Dave Appell, who operated the Tokens' publishing firm.

Appell had worked at Cameo Parkway, where he had considerable success as a songwriter and producer working with Chubby Checker, Dee Dee Sharp, and Bobby Rydell. "He found the song 'Candida,' played it for me, and I knew it was a hit," remembers Hank. In the original session in 1970, Phil Margo and Jay Siegel played instruments and Frankie Paris, a blues singer in the B.T. Puppy fold, performed the lead vocal. After the mix, it seemed the vocals needed a different treatment. Hank thought of Tony Orlando, who'd enjoyed a solo singing career in the early '60s but who by then had gone on to work for April Blackwood Music as a music publisher. So at lunch Medress met with Orlando and asked him to try to think of a singer who could record the track. Orlando had no suggestions, but Medress had one. "Tony, you do it," Medress finally said. "Hank, I can't do it," sputtered Orlando. "I've got a job." Medress replied, "Look, I'll tell you what. We'll use a group name and nobody will ever know that it's you." Orlando finally relented and he cut the lead vocal track, with backgrounds provided by Jay and two female singers, Toni Wine of the Archies and jingle singer Leslie Miller. "Only Dave Appell and the engineer and I knew that Tony's voice was on 'Candida' by Dawn. We kept it a secret. And after 'Knock Three Times,' same thing. And, finally, I said, 'Tony, this is insane. You're losing all kinds of money you could be making.' Eventually he agreed to change the group name to Tony Orlando and Dawn."

In early 1972 Medress and the other Tokens produced a remake of "The Lion Sleeps Tonight" by Robert John, a version for Atlantic Records that returned the song back to the charts and captured another gold record. Medress and Dave Appell continued collaborating in record production through the 1970s.

Together they worked with Frankie Valli, Melissa Manchester, Mac Davis, and other popular artists. Medress also began producing on his own in the early '80s, at first inauspiciously. "I started feeling like maybe life was passing me by a bit," Medress acknowledges. "I wasn't a kid anymore and the phone wasn't ringing. I didn't think that I had lost anything but when I was approached to become a staff producer I went to work in my first corporate job." Medress was hired in 1986 by a firm called the Entertainment Company, which was later to become SBK Entertainment World, Inc. (SBK was gobbled up in 1989 by the much bigger EMI Music.) At SBK, Medress worked with Olivia Newton-John and produced albums for Buster Poindexter, the Nylons, the Weather Girls, and Dan Hill, including "Never Thought (That I Could Love)" and the No. 1 hit "Can't We Try" in collaboration with John Capek.

Medress was content—for a while. "In 1990 I woke up one day and decided I needed to do something else. Recalling how much he'd enjoyed Toronto while recording the tracks for Canadian Dan Hill's album, he wrote a memo to EMI executives observing that the company's lack of an EMI music publishing office in Canada was detrimental because Canada's treaty with China was better than that of the United States. EMI liked the idea and asked Medress to open a Canadian office, of which he was named president. "I spent the next two and a half years in Toronto, started the company and within two years we were voted publisher of the year. But the business was totally insane."

He likens his role to that of the character played by Peter Sellers in the 1979 motion picture *Being There*. Sellers, playing a gardener named Chance whose mental age is that of a child, wanders away after his employers die and is catapulted to fame when the people he meets interpret his occasional terse statements—all gleaned from television programs—as deep insights. "I was equally out of position with EMI in Canada," Medress says. "I was wearing Armani suits, attending board meetings, preparing economic forecasts, and doing other functions that had no relationship with what I had done my whole life until then. I was a creative music person, yet there I was doing that rhetoric bullshit. I hated it." Medress endured that job for more than two years before resigning in 1992. "I was 54 years old, still feeling good, I ran marathons, I was still playing basketball, didn't look my age, had tons of energy, and I didn't know what I was going to do. And the phone didn't ring," says Medress.

For two years, he concentrated on family life with his wife, Jane, an interior designer, and his youngest son, Zach, born in 1986. He also strengthened his relationship with Danny (born in 1976), Sarah (1972), and Julie (1964), children from two previous marriages.

In November 1992 Hank ran into Allan Pepper, a friend of his who owns the Bottom Line, a famous nightclub on West 4th Street in lower Manhattan. Knowing that the club had regularly recorded the performances of the legendary artists who appeared on its stage, Hank replied, "Allan, it's the 20th anniversary of the club. It would be great to document these past two decades of performances, maybe in a PBS special or something." Allan said, "I don't have the time to do it, but if you want to, you have my blessings."

Applying some of what he'd learned at EMI, Medress developed a business plan and started making phone calls. Among the people he contacted was former Sony Music executive Walter Yetnikoff, subject of the book *The Hitman*. Together, Hank, Walter, Allan, and Bottom Line associate Stanley Snadowski decided to launch an independent record company on which to sign new artists as well as draw from archival recordings made during performances at the Bottom Line. With the assistance of other investors, they opened Bottom Line Records in October 1996. "It's a dream come true," says Medress, a partner in the venture. "I get to nurture artists and do what I came here to do 35 years ago."

On its first anniversary the label issued the first release in the Bottom Line Encore Collection: a double CD of a performance by Harry Chapin recorded live at the Bottom Line. The club's vault of archival recordings includes an eclectic selection of artists encompassing Jerry Garcia, Merle Saunders, Bruce Springsteen, Gary "U.S." Bonds, Carla Bonoff, Canned Heat, Eric Carmen, Jim Carroll, the Chambers Brothers, John Cougar, the Chieftains, John Hammond, Kiki Dee, Rick Derringer, Dion, Flo and Eddie, the Turtles, the Four Tops, Hall and Oates, John Hartford, Richie Havens, and Hiroshima.

"When I wake up in the morning I can't wait to get to work. I think I'm where I belong at last," says Medress. "This is a business in which people ask, 'What have you done lately?' and windows of opportunity close quickly. I wasn't blessed with great musical ability or great tools," Medress admits with honest humility, "and consequently I'm very proud of what I've been able to accomplish." Yet he acknowledges he remains a work in progress. "I think even at my age, I'm very judgmental and because I expect too much from people I become disappointed. I'm beginning to think that the disappointment I feel when someone fails to live up to my expectations may often result from my own misjudgment."

As he works on that personality trait, Hank says he now intends to grow old gracefully. "At this point my priorities have really changed. I don't have to impress anybody anymore. As a result, I was able to show up for my daughter's wedding in San Francisco and was with her again when my granddaughter was a few months old. I missed those kinds of special times in the earlier part of my life when I was too wrapped up in my career. So now," Medress said in a 1997 conversation, "I'm 58 years old and I'm going to go out and run tomorrow. I'm going to wake up in the morning and kiss my son hello. I've gone from riding in limousines and cabs to riding in subways, and I like the subways now."

THEN AND NOW

JAY SIEGEL

Jay Siegel admits he is a worrier. On the road he worries about getting to the next musical gig on time. As manager of a recording studio he worried about attracting new clients. As a marketing executive for a music publishing firm he succeeded in persuading Perry Como to record John Lennon's "Imagine" but worried that the Beatles songs for which his firm held copyright intimidated most artists. He declined an invitation to join the Lettermen because he worried that their road concert schedule might harm his family relationship. At production sessions during the peak popularity of the Tokens, Siegel quietly worried about what songs to record next and how to arrange them.

Lead singer of the Tokens throughout their hit recording era of the 1960s, Jay Siegel gave the group its characteristic falsetto sound epitomized by the soaring a cappella introduction of "The Lion Sleeps Tonight." Although the group bisected when members Phil and Mitch Margo took root in Los Angeles, Siegel remains the emblematic persona of the East Coast branch of the Tokens.

Jay sang for the fun of it. His musical talent became apparent by age 10, when he began singing in his neighborhood community choir for the holidays. "I soon

PHOTO BY CHUCK GOEHRIG.

gained an appreciation for harmony," says Siegel. "I was a boy alto, and my voice was really high. I sang in a 12-person choir in which I was one of only two kids, yet the choirmaster gave me a lot of solos." In high school, Jay joined the chorus, where he was taught how to breathe and form words but was given only minimal individual voice training. Choir music was OK, but the rock and roll music the Linc-Tones performed was much more fun for Jay. Although he studied guitar for a year when he was about 15, singing remained his primary interest.

Jay and his brother, Jerry, were the sons of hardworking parents. Their father Louis came to the United States from Austria when he was 16 years old.

"He found work as a furrier in a sweatshop in New York City. It was a terrible, terrible job, and my heart breaks every time I think about it," says Siegel. "He rode the subway and when it was 95 degrees he sat in a factory that was not air-conditioned and worked on furs on his lap, sewing fur coats together. My mother, Yetta, stayed home and made dinner and cleaned the house and took care of the kids."

As a young man, Jay was most pleased by the success of the Tokens in recording and production because it enabled him to buy things for his parents: a color television, a stereo system, a new couch, a washing machine. "My ability to help them out gave me the biggest joy in my life. My mother was one who thought the sun rose and set on whatever my brother or I did. When I would bring them to see me perform, it was the same thing as handing them 10 million dollars. It was just as important for them to see the people applaud me—their son. But my father was always worried. He'd urge me, 'Get a real job.' My mother was just as worried as he was, but she always encouraged me to stick with the music. They were always very supportive."

Siegel, who was born October 20, 1939, treasures the years of his youth. "I had the greatest childhood growing up in Brighton Beach. There was a singing group on every corner and a lot of talent in Brooklyn," says Siegel, noting that former Lincoln High School students include flutist Herbie Mann, actors Harvey Keitel and Lou Gossett Jr., and playwright Arthur Miller. "It was great growing up in the summer by the beach. We used to hang out on the beach and we were singing all of the time. That's how we attracted girls."

Siegel describes his old neighborhood as a mosaic of cultures. "But we were similar in financial status, which ranged from medium to poor. All of our mothers stayed home and took care of the kids. I have only happy memories. We used to climb over the rooftops to get from one street to the next. When I tell my kids these things they just don't understand. We used to walk from Brighton Beach to Coney Island, but we didn't hang out at Coney Island because of the tough kids, who used to ride their motorcycles to the Cyclone roller coaster. We went to Coney Island only to go to Nathan's to eat the best frankfurters. For 25 cents you'd get a frankfurter, a drink, and french fries. The aromas from Nathan's— there was nothing like it in the world. We used to love to go on all of the rides, have a frozen custard at Nathan's, and then leave to avoid the tough kids."

Another favorite haunt of Jay's was Mrs. Stahl's Knishes, a tiny stand of Jewish delicacies tucked in under the elevated train on Brighton Beach Avenue. "In the summertime it was probably 120 degrees in there but that didn't matter because no place else had potato knishes like Mrs. Stahl's. We'd hang out on the Boardwalk in Brighton, or we'd go down to Manhattan Beach. There was a delineation. Manhattan Beach kids had money and cars, Coney Island had the tough guys, and Brighton Beach was in the middle. I remember playing football on the beach in the fall, and I remember the clean ocean breezes. Every Tuesday night during the summer, fireworks would shoot from a barge off Brighton Beach. We used to meet every Tuesday night on the Boardwalk and that's where we'd get together and sing."

The kids in Jay's neighborhood, like city kids all over the country in the forties and fifties, played street games like kick the can, stoopball, and stickball. Stoopball was a game of points played by throwing a rubber ball at a stoop (front-entry stairway) with the hope of hitting the lip of a step to achieve maximum bounce. In stickball an old broom handle typically served as a bat; home and second were usually manhole covers, and first and third bases could be any two objects directly across from each other, like a parked car and a street light. "There were storm sewers down the street and if you stood on one sewer and you hit the ball down the block past three more sewers, it was a home run," Siegel recalls. "Our kids have no idea what we're talking about."

Inspired by his culturally vibrant surroundings, Siegel developed an interest in folk music as a high school student. "I would listen to music that most other people never heard of." He became a fan of the pioneering folk music group the Weavers, whose repertoire included an intriguing African melody. He discovered that the same song had been captured on tape by a folklorist named Alan Lomax who, beginning in the 1930s, spent six decades recording indigenous music throughout the world. His documentary collection includes songs of Appalachia, of the rural South, and of Africa, Australia, the Caribbean, and South America. A label called Rounder Records cataloged and distributed the recordings Lomax made of work songs, blues, spirituals, ballads, and nursery rhymes. One of those tracks, a rhythmic chant called "Wimoweh," fascinated Siegel. He rearranged the Weavers' adaptation of the chant to emphasize the falsetto line and sang it to the other members of the Linc-Tones, and later to his fellow members of the Tokens.

"We rehearsed it and every time we'd sing it for our friends or to an audience, they loved it," says Jay. So did producers at RCA Victor, who thought the song needed lyrics to achieve commercial potential. "Hank, Phil, Mitch, and I were very much opposed to that idea initially." But he determined that if lyrics had to be written, they must be appropriate. He visited the South African consulate in New York, where he learned that "Wimoweh" was a traditional African hunting song. "The chant 'Wimoweh' had meaning about a lion hunt, and said that if everybody remained quiet, the lion would sleep and they would be able to make their kill." The group had their title, and the rest is history.

Although they functioned as a team, each of the four Tokens assumed specific roles in the production process. Mitch and Phil worked on instrumentation, Hank oversaw mixing and other technical functions in the booth, and Jay worked on vocal arrangements. "The result was a kind of magic that we worked together," Jay reminisces.

But then the magic wore off. "When the Tokens disbanded, it wasn't the result of dislike or disharmony," says Jay. "Nobody ever had a fight. We're all very good friends. We just weren't having any success after a while, and it was getting stale." Hank began his collaboration with Dave Appell. Phil and Mitch moved to California. And in 1974 Don Kirshner Productions hired Jay as music coordinator for all the firm's television productions, including the syndicated *Rock Concert* television series, beginning an 11-year association. Jay also served as a backup singer and in-house producer for Kirshner's music production firm, for which he coproduced sessions by Kansas and other groups.

After Kirshner left the business, Siegel joined a British company called ATV Music, which owned copyrights to the Beatles music catalog. As manager of the company's American operation, Jay was responsible for persuading record producers to choose songs that ATV owned. That proved more difficult than it seemed. "I encountered a lot of resistance to recording Beatles songs because performers believed their rendition would be measured against what the Beatles had done," says Jay. Consequently, he attributes his only success in that effort to Perry Como, who had the courage to record John Lennon's "Imagine." Siegel remained in that position for about a year until Michael Jackson purchased the company in September 1985. Jackson released all ATV executives and staff members because he already had his own organizational structure in place.

In 1986, Jay was hired to manage Mayfair Recording Studio on 47th Street in midtown Manhattan. About 80 percent of the studio's business came from advertising agencies that used Mayfair to produce commercials for Coca-Cola, Miller Brewing, and other national accounts. The studio also produced music for the *Bill Cosby Show* for about a year, as well as some session work, notably for Blondie and Ian Hunter. Jay sang on numerous commercials he produced for Häagen Dazs Ice Cream, Quaker Crunchy Granola, and Wendy's Hamburgers, for which he sang "Only Wendy's," based on "Only You" by the Platters. But running the business monopolized his time. "I had to wine and dine advertising executives to try to get them to use our studio instead of the hundreds of other studios around New York. It was a tremendously competitive business and I didn't enjoy it at all. In fact, I hated it." Siegel remained in that high-pressure business for about five years until the studio's landlord gave notice that the monthly rent would triple to $12,000. Mayfair shut its doors.

At that point Siegel declined another tempting offer. In their version of Steve Lawrence's "Portrait Of My Love," the Tokens blended their voices in a style somewhat reminiscent of the Lettermen, who also recorded the song. Perhaps that's what led Hank Medress to produce the Lettermen in the 1980s and prompted Lettermen member Tony Butala to invite Jay Siegel to join the group. "I had to decline because the Lettermen stay on the road so much and I didn't think I was ready to do that, considering my family and kids."

He instead decided to resurrect the Tokens in New York, as Phil and Mitch Margo had done in California. He put together an East Coast version of the group that began performing, at first on a modest scale. "Demand increased until it became a full-time job," says Siegel, whose Tokens perform about 100 dates per year. Their audiences often include families with children who want to hear what they call the "jungle song." For them, "The Lion Sleeps Tonight" is fresh and new, and Jay says that knowledge energizes his performances. The East Coast Tokens include Bill Reid, Ed Rezzonico, Jay, and Jay's son, Jared, who plays keyboards and serves as musical director of the band. When he's not singing with Jay's Tokens, Ed Rezzonico is a drug and alcohol counselor for young people. He previously sang with a number of New York groups, including the Passions. Bill Reid's performing career dates to the early '60s, when he sang background on Curtis Lee's "Pretty Little Angel Eyes" and Barry Mann's "Who Put The Bomp." In recent years Reid has moved into record production.

Even today, after all the shows in which he's performed over four decades, Jay says no feeling rivals the exhilaration that a standing ovation gives him. And he still agonizes over the rigors of the road. "Traveling to concert dates is very stressful because we want to make sure things are the way they're supposed to be when we get there. And like other performers, I worry about when the next job is going to come. I guess I'm the group worrier. That's my job. Even if this year looks good, I find myself hoping next year is going to be as good."

Jay Siegel shouldn't worry. Today he still enjoys producing sessions by new artists, but his jingle writing and recording talents are heavily in demand as well. "With jingles you don't have to worry about dealing with record promotion or radio airplay. And we're paid," grins Siegel.

He says he's preserved his voice by living a normal life. "I get up at 9 a.m. and I go to sleep at midnight. I have a family. I have three kids. When I'm on tour and I've finished working at night I go back to my hotel room. I don't hang out and I don't smoke. I live the same type of life that an accountant would live."

Jay and his wife, Judy Fischer Siegel, who met while they were students at New York City Community College and married in 1961, have two daughters and a son. Their oldest daughter, Stacy Dawn, born in 1963, is an elementary school teacher and has two children of her own. Her middle name inspired the name for the group Dawn, whose records the Tokens produced. Jay and Judy's younger daughter Jamie, born two years after Stacy, is in the advertising business and has one child. Their son Jared, born in 1975, is employed by Arista Records and has a specific career goal. "He wants to run Sony Records one day," says Jay.

"One day I'll retire and watch my grandchildren grow," Jay muses, "but in the meantime I'll keep on performing as long as it makes people happy."

MITCH MARGO

Mitch Margo tried to treat May 25, 1997, like an ordinary day. But it was a difficult day for Hank Medress, Jay Siegel, and Mitch's brother, Phil. On that day Mitch turned 50. He handled it gracefully, but his fellow Tokens were suffering disbelief. Mitch, after all, had always been the "baby" of the group. He was 13 years old when the Tokens recorded "Tonight I Fell In Love." The group achieved international stardom when he was 14. By his mid-teens he was a partner in the group's own label, B.T. Puppy. And he was but 24 years old when the Tokens dissolved. "When Phil, Hank, and Jay showed up for my 50th birthday party in New York, they kept looking at me and saying, 'This is not right. It's just not right.' The baby was not supposed to be 50."

Being the kid of the group had its advantages and its disadvantages. "I got treated special by the kids in my regular high school to a certain degree," says Mitch. "I tried to remain a regular guy as much as I could. But after a couple of years in regular high school my parents enrolled me in Quintano High School for Young Professionals in Manhattan, where I attended class for a few hours each morning before going to the office the rest of the day." Young actors and actresses populated the student body at Quintano, which enabled students to juggle

PHOTO BY JEFF MARCH.

school and work schedules. Patty Duke is an alumna of the school, and Bernadette Peters was one of Mitch's classmates. "Luke Halpin, the kid from *Flipper,* also went to that school," adds Mitch. The office where Mitch spent his afternoons was Bright Tunes Productions, at 1697 Broadway in the heart of Tin Pan Alley. At Bright Tunes, Mitch was still in school in a sense because he had no specific role with the company at that time. "I was a kid. I didn't know nothin'. I composed songs and wrote lyrics and contributed in that way."

Mitch remembers that his role in the Tokens' best-known production work of the mid-'60s, on the Chiffons' "One Fine Day," was minimal. "We used the piano from the original demo track recorded by Carol King, who wrote the song. In the studio the guys added a bass and a saxophone, and my brother came up with the idea for the 'shoo-bee-doo-bee-doo-wah-wah' thing. The Tokens sang background in the bridge, but actually, my job on that record was when I got home from school one day, they called me up and played it for me on the phone. I said, 'Yeah, that sounds good.' That was my job on that record." Mitch still loves that recording. "It's just a wonderful piece. Carol was a big inspiration to me, and she and Gerry Goffin greatly influenced my writing."

Carol King's piano artistry particularly captivated Mitch, who has been playing piano since age 5. When his parents, Leon and Ruth Margulies, realized his uncanny ability to play songs by ear, they enrolled him in lessons under the tutelage of their rabbi's wife, a piano teacher. The piano teacher observed that Mitch had a talent for musical notation and encouraged him to compose. And he began to sing. "I knew I had an ear for singing, though I wasn't too crazy about my voice. I didn't have much warmth or trill in my voice, but I developed a very good ear for harmony by singing along with Everly Brothers records on the radio, and I could blend well with background parts. The first song that my brother Phil and I ever sang together in person was 'All I Have To Do Is Dream.' And we still perform that in person sometimes."

Phil and Mitch still pride themselves on their rich harmonies, which they perform these days at the drop of a hat. Or mask. Or cap. After perfecting their richly harmonized rendition of the National Anthem at sporting events throughout Southern California, including Anaheim Ducks hockey and Los Angeles Dodgers baseball games, they took their show on the road in 1998. Out of their love of baseball, their country, and performing, they paid their own way in an "Anthem Tour" in which they sang the national anthem before games at all 30 major league baseball parks—setting a record for a singing group the same year in which Mark McGwire set his 70-home-run record. "We do a nice chime-off at the end: 'the land of the free-free-free-free-freeee.' It's a good moment," says Mitch.

He has come a long way since the spring of 1964 after he had tumbled to the bottom of a cruel slide from ovation to dejection. At 17, an age when most teenagers are contemplating career paths to follow, Mitch thought he'd reached the end of his, the victim of changing musical tastes. Mop-tops, Merseybeat,* and Britain were in. Preppies, doo-wop, and Brooklyn were out. "I had written 'I Hear Trumpets Blow,' which gave our recording careers a boost, but by the time I was 17, I was the most depressed I've ever been in my life," says Mitch. He had become aware that the music business that had once been so much fun was not as it appeared.

---

*THE TERM "MERSEYBEAT" IS GENERALLY USED TO REFER TO A MUSICAL STYLE, SKIFFLE, BORN IN THE LATE 1950S IN LIVERPOOL, WHICH IS ON THE MERSEY RIVER. THE QUARRY MEN, WHICH EVOLVED INTO THE BEATLES, WERE A SKIFFLE GROUP.

"I was confronted by the realization that people you trust are not always honest. That's why I wrote the songs for the *Intercourse* album," says Mitch, referring to a 1968 recording that remained in the vaults for three decades.

After the Tokens finally slipped off the charts in 1971 and Hank headed out on his own, Mitch, Phil, and Jay signed a production deal with Don Kirshner for a few years, but ultimately the Margo brothers split off from that arrangement, leaving Jay behind. Phil and Mitch signed a production contract with RCA and moved to the West Coast, where their projects included production of an album by Kristy and Jimmy McNichol. In 1981, Hank, Jay, Phil, and Mitch took to the stage at Radio City Music Hall in New York for a reunion concert. That was the last time they performed together. Mitch quietly walked away from the spotlight. "There were a few years in the early 1980s when I didn't know what I was doing. A few bad years," says Mitch. "I became a house-husband while my wife was supporting the family. I say it with pride, even though society doesn't really accept it. I was delighted to be home with my little boy Ari. I remember dancing around the living room with him in my arms to the *Thriller* album by Michael Jackson. He was a little baby. It was great."

As a result of the alienation that set in when he was 17, Mitch has remained cautious, like a pup abused by the master who feeds him. "I basically spent most of my adult life avoiding the music business. I've been staying on the outskirts. I don't jump in. I don't make a lot of calls. It's really almost a crime. I'm sure there are some nice people out there, but I've been that frightened off by it. Although I have scored the music for several TV movies, I was never one to peddle my wares, and I never got good at that, to this day. So I write songs that I seldom play for people."

Still, ask Mitch what he fills in on the blank line next to "occupation" and he'll tell you "entertainer and composer." With the Tokens group based in Los Angeles, he performs at casinos, fairs, corporate parties, conventions, clubs, concerts, and stage shows. "Our live show has become very good. We've learned what audiences enjoy, and it's a lot of fun to do. Even when we don't perform it as well as we can, it still works really well. It's better than we are," Mitch laughs. In addition to Mitch, who plays guitar, bass, drums, and keyboards, and drummer Phil, the group includes Phil's son Noah on drums as well, and Mike Johnson on keyboards, along with saxophone virtuoso Jay Leslie, a former member of the Sha Na Na retro doo-wop vocal group of the '70s. Mitch can sub for Mike on keyboards, Phil and Noah alternate on drums, and all the members of the group sing. All the members of the audience sing, as well. After four decades in show business, Phil and Mitch have perfected an infectious blend of music and comedy. Tokens performances are joyous celebrations that encourage laughter and invite enthusiastic audience participation.

Although they often reserve "The Lion Sleeps Tonight" or a dance medley for their show closer, they've begun performing "Only In My Dreams," a new song that Mitch composed. He wrote the song, reminiscent of the music of another era, when he heard that production had begun for the 1996 Tom Hanks motion picture *That Thing You Do,* about a fictional one-hit 1960s rock band. "Only In My Dreams" just missed the cut for inclusion in the movie soundtrack, but the Tokens liked it so much they included it on a new album they released in 1997 on their resurrected B.T. Puppy label. Several cuts from that album were used on the daytime television drama *The Young And The Restless.* The album is titled *Tonight The Lion Dances (Esta Noche El León Baila).* "It's an album of Latin doo-wop—Latin and oldies," grins Mitch. "When Phil was a kid, he used to go to dances at the community center on weekends, where they would play a mix of styles—some Latin, some old rock and roll, some Sinatra, this and that. Phil and his friends would hang out and listen to records like that, and I guess that had an effect on me as well. We wanted to recall those feelings and re-create them in this album. And it's a delightful album. It might be our best production to date."

Mitch says the new album reflects his musical preferences as well. "I have eclectic tastes. I like all kinds of music." His music collection at home encompasses Bartok, Bach, Zappa, the Beatles, the Beach Boys, Ladysmith Black Mambazo, and the King's Singers. Now divorced from his wife, Sherry, Mitch lives alone. Their 19-year-old son Damien, who is a computer animation artist by trade, also enjoys drumming and sits in with the Tokens when Noah is unavailable. Although interested in video game design and testing, Ari hasn't decided upon a career, and Mitch has not tried to influence his decision. "I want him to follow his bliss," says Mitch, borrowing a sentiment from author Joseph Campbell. "I take that to mean find whatever your heart is telling you and follow it."

Mitch counts his children and the creation of "The Lion Sleeps Tonight" among his proudest achievements. "It seems to be loved by the world as a whole, and it's likely that it's being played on the radio somewhere right now. And that amazes me," Mitch says with sincere humility. "I feel very fortunate to be a part of it."

Although he says he still loves performing and finds entertainment a joy, he also has talent in another medium of artistic expression: painting, which he has enjoyed since the age of 16. He's created the cover art for two Tokens albums, *Oldies Are Now* from 1994 and *Tonight The Lion Dances.* "The second cover I designed so that it would look good on a cassette as well as on a CD. For the first one I did just a square painting, and it didn't fit a cassette box very nicely," explains Mitch, who works in watercolors, acrylics, and oils. "You live, you learn." Mitch has already had a couple of showings in galleries, and has sold some of his paintings. He's also dabbled in animation, using images he created in watercolor. His first effort was an eight-minute short called *It's Okay To Laugh,* which was broadcast on the USA Network. He used a technique called cutout animation, photographed the images with friend Ray Templin, and transferred them to video. (Cutout animation is a stop-motion technique in which foreground figures are placed atop a backdrop, then photographed frame by frame as they are moved ever so slightly in relation to the background.) "It was an interesting project and a fun way to do animation. Something tells me I should have been doing more of that in my life."

The current B.T. Puppy catalog also includes *Intercourse,* an album recorded in 1968 during Mitch's era of deep depression. "Writing the songs for the *Intercourse* album was my therapy," Mitch said in liner notes for the album. *Intercourse* had been gathering dust for nearly three decades because Warner Brothers, for which they were recording in the late '60s, declined to release it. Mitch considered the album, on which the Tokens played all their own instrumental accompaniment, an artistic triumph. "I was crushed when Warner Brothers didn't release it," he says. Mitch also laments the disappointing response to *Cross Country,* an early '70s album with a country music flavor that Atlantic-Atco released without the benefit of enthusiastic promotion. The album, in which he, Phil, and Jay displayed their singing virtuosity as well as their ability to cast familiar songs in a new light, was distinguished by a ballad treatment of Wilson Pickett's raucous 1965 hit "In The Midnight Hour."

Although Mitch's artistic and musical talents both emerged in his youth, he doesn't ascribe much of his present persona to his family environment. "Although I see I have certain traits from my parents, I don't think my lifestyle has turned out to be much like theirs at all." His parents, Leon and Ruth, operated Ruthy's Clothes Closet, a clothing store in Brighton Beach for a time. Leon also held various jobs over the years, including work as a presser for a dress manufacturer. "My dad passed away a while back. He was a good man, a humble man, and I was close with him. My mom, thank God, is still around, and she's great."

Mitch's mother, who is now living in retirement in Fort Lauderdale, Florida, often cautioned him, "Love many, trust few, always paddle your own canoe," words that Mitch has taken to heart. Those were among the words that Mitch was able to understand. "My parents used Yiddish as a code language, so they could say things we wouldn't understand as kids, which I kinda wish they hadn't. I would like to have been able to speak Yiddish." Still, he says he managed to learn "a bissel"—a little—of the language. "I love Yiddish. It's a very expressive language, and plenty of Yiddish sayings are rich in wisdom. And a lot of people don't realize how much Yiddish has become common usage. If you say you saw a *schmaltzy* performance, you're talking Yiddish."

As he turned 50, Mitch reflected on his life. He regards himself as a good person, a principal ingredient of which is respect, he says. "It's essential to have respect for life—respect for your own life, and respect for the lives of others, in that order. I think that by and large people are inclined to take life for granted, to forget that they're alive. And that's why I often remind myself that every second is a miracle. *Every second is a miracle.* I say that because I happened to notice that is true. I truly go through life astonished that I exist."

THEN AND NOW
PHIL MARGO

In 1967, with a new recording contract from Warner Brothers and a Tokens single, "Portrait Of My Love," climbing the charts, Phil Margo bought a new Oldsmobile convertible. The record has long faded from the airwaves, but Phil is still driving that Oldsmobile. That's not to suggest that Phil hasn't done well for himself in the ensuing years. Quite the contrary. He lives in Beverly Hills and has established himself in the tightly knit television production circle in Hollywood. But Phil is governed by a sense of reserve that appears to be the product of an oddly disparate set of guiding influences: frugality, humility, savvy, artistic creativity, and adventurousness, strongly laced with Brighton Beach brashness.

Phil Margo is a self-sufficient man. Not only can he sing for his supper, he can also drum, play guitar and piano, compose songs, write screenplays, pilot his own plane to concert dates, and, in a pinch, manage the careers of other performers.

Phil never had designs on a musical career. "My dad played the violin a bit, and my grandfather played the clarinet, but I had no reason to expect that I had any talent," Phil claims. "I was just a kid growing up. The whole thing was an accident. It was just a set of circumstances that led me from one thing to another. I guess life is like that. Some people know what they want to be when they're 3 years old and pursue that course right until they get there. I never knew what I wanted to be. I still don't. That's why I got into producing movies, writing

PHOTO BY JEFF MARCH.

for television, all kinds of things—because they interest me and I don't feel that you have to be locked into one thing for your whole life."

At age 6 or 7, Phil happened to like the 78-rpm records by Frankie Laine, Xavier Cougat, and Dinah Shore that his parents had in their collection. He'd sit in the living room and listen to those songs on the record player. Born Phil Margulies on April 1, 1942, he went all the way through his elementary school years with nary an indication that he had any musical talents of his own. But entering his sophomore year at Abraham Lincoln High School in the fall of 1956, he participated in the mandatory tryouts for chorus. "We had to go up on the stage and as the music teacher played notes on the piano we would have to sing along," Phil recalls. "I was able to sing all of the notes. I really had no clue that I would be able to do that. The piano teacher said to me, 'Very good. You're in the chorus.' Who wanted to be in the chorus? Yuck! But that was it. I had no choice." At some point, he remembers, he wanted to become an aeronautical engineer. "But in high school I confronted math and decided I didn't really want to do that."

Meanwhile, his musical interest and abilities had begun to develop. By the spring of his junior year, in 1958, he had decided he wanted to be a musician in the Catskill Mountains, a resort area in southeastern New York State about 75 miles from Manhattan. "It was cool to be a musician in the Catskills. Only problem was I didn't play anything. So I decided to learn how to play the piano. I tried lessons for about two weeks and I asked when I would start playing songs." The piano teacher replied, "That's not for six months yet." Phil said, "Six months is too late. I could already have a job by then." So at age 16 he taught himself to play piano using a "fake" book that had the chords of the songs and notations for the right hand. "The book didn't have both staffs of the sheet music—bass and treble. It just had the notes of the song, with the chords written on top of the bar line. So I learned how to play chords. Now they teach that way, but back then they didn't," says Phil. "That summer I learned how to play and by fall I had a little band with a trumpet player, a drummer, a guy who played saxophone and clarinet, and me on piano. We got gigs like sweet sixteens and stuff like that, where we made about $10 each per night, which was pretty good for a kid in 1958."

Phil made it to the Catskills in the summer of '59 following his graduation from high school, then settled back in New York City where his uncle Mal helped him land a job with Steiner, Rouse and Company, a stock brokerage firm. Meanwhile he enrolled in Brooklyn College as his band continued to play gigs around town. Phil's drummer, Lenny Budnick, heard that Lincoln High alumnus Hank Medress wanted to produce an instrumental for Roulette Records, the label for which his group, Darryl and the Oxfords, recorded. Phil, then 17, brought his 12-year-old brother, Mitch, along to record a demo. They played a boogie-woogie version of "Chopsticks." The demo session itself was disappointing, but it led to development of a relationship with Hank. "Hank just saw something in us and we started writing together. In December of 1959 we sang the background part of 'Teenager In Love' together for the first time, and we recognized that we sounded good. I knew I could sing harmony because I had sung it in chorus." They were particularly pleased with their three-part harmony that complemented the lead vocals of Jay Siegel.

Following the formation of B.T. Puppy Records, Phil set about fulfilling another dream: getting his college degree. In the late '60s he began attending night classes at Kingsboro Community College in Brooklyn and Rockland Community College in Suffern, New York, about 25 miles northwest of Manhattan. He earned his bachelor's degree from Empire State College, an alternative liberal arts adult education program of the State University of New York, in 1977.

Around that time he'd begun participating in production of an album for Kristy McNichol, who was then starring in the ABC television dramatic series *Family*. At one point Phil met with Kristy at the Osmond Brothers' studio in Orem, Utah, where she was filming a special for ABC. In an adjacent studio, production was under way on an episode of the *Donna Fargo Show* in which actor Robert Guillaume was making a guest appearance. Margo and Guillaume met and started talking. Guillaume was between managers. He and Margo found they got along well, and that began a 10-year business relationship during which Phil served as Robert's personal manager. "Robert didn't have any reason in the world to think that I'd be any good as a manager, but yet he had a certain degree of faith in me."

Phil quickly learned what it took to be successful in management. "Balls. You need a set of balls, you need to be able to ask people for ridiculous things, you need to be able to say, 'Robert doesn't like this, Robert should be in first class,' and you need to be able to take advantage of opportunities. And you need to have a brain to figure out how soon to stop negotiations. You need to know when you've pushed them as far as they can go. You also learn to never take the first offer." That axiom is true, he says, when managing a star. "It's different when you're first starting out. Then the rule is 'tread marks on your back.' We didn't get paid for our first hit record. They never paid us a cent in royalties. We don't know to this day how many copies of 'Tonight I Fell In Love' sold. And even RCA tried to screw us out of the money for usages in movies. They used 'The Lion Sleeps Tonight' in five or six movies and when I told them they never accounted for that, they told us it's not in our contract. I said, 'What do you mean it's not in my contract? If it's not in my contract, you're allowed to use it?' Finally after two years, we settled it, but it was a nightmare."

Margo continued managing Guillaume until 1988. "It was time for both of us to move on. We just went our separate ways. It was amicable," says Phil. "Afterward he appeared on 'The Lion Sleeps Tonight' video that is still broadcast as a staple on the Learning Channel. He's a good guy, he's a good friend, and I love him very much. He gave me some of the most joyous times of my life. We were at the White House twice. We did some wonderful things together."

Exposure to Guillaume's projects convinced Phil that he should take a shot at writing and producing movies for television. He conceived the idea for *The Kid From Left Field,* a 1979 movie starring Guillaume and Gary Coleman. After that Phil wrote and produced two other movies starring Coleman, *The Kid With The 200 IQ* and *The Fantastic World Of D.C. Collins;* another movie for ABC in 1985 called *This Wife For Hire* starring Pam Dawber; *Goddess Of Love,* a 1988 TV film starring Vanna White; and 1997's sensational *Asteroid* for NBC. All the while he's writing scripts and producing films, Phil continues performing with the Tokens.

"I was off shooting *Asteroid* in Denver, and I get a call saying I had to be in L.A. the next day because we're doing the *Tonight Show.* So I'm on the plane, doing the *Tonight Show* the next day with the Tokens. We did a Jay Leno version of 'The Lion Sleeps Tonight.' We had written it because a guy who sometimes does publicity for us said, 'Look, if you want to do the Jay Leno show, do a parody.' So I wrote a parody of 'The Lion Sleeps Tonight' and I sent it to them and that was all forgotten. Then seven months later, the *Tonight Show* people said, 'We have a parody of 'The Lion Sleeps Tonight.' I said, 'Good, I'm glad you thought of it.' I didn't care. As long as it got on the show. It was a very nice spot for us."

Phil married Abbie Dimond in 1966. Their son Noah, who was born in 1969, is the Tokens' road drummer. Noah's twin brother, Joshua, is completing his doctoral studies at UCLA in East Asian languages and cultures. Phil and Abbie also have a daughter, Neely, born in 1974. Phil and Mitch and their sister, Maxine Margo, along with Paula "Rusti" Wolintz, are partners in B.T. Puppy Records. The label, resurrected in 1993, now operates out of an office in the small town of Millwood, New York, about 20 miles north of Manhattan.

Phil shuns flamboyance and lives modestly. "I don't go on vacations often, I don't go to the track, I don't spend big bucks, I don't have expensive clothes. I do have some nice old cars: a 1967 Oldsmobile convertible, which I've had since it was new, and a 1966 Mustang convertible. And I teach kung fu with my son Noah. I started taking the course with my sons when I was 44 years old. It was something I could do with them and it was a good outlet for exercise. Now we're high-degree black belts, which has given me a great deal of confidence."

Phil sometimes flies his Varga Kachina, which looks like a little fighter plane, to gigs, and he periodically covers air shows for *In Flight* magazine. "If I wasn't doing what I'm doing, I would be working in the aircraft industry—flying, preferably," says Phil, who has been a pilot since 1963. He takes to heart the old song "Fly Me To The Moon"—and beyond. "If somebody said to me, 'Phil, we're going to Mars tomorrow, you want to come?' I'm gone, man. I try to make my life an adventure. But I can also be very reclusive. I can disappear in my room for days at a time and watch television and smoke cigars. I'm as shy or as bold as anybody else. You just have to pull on a particular trait when you need it. You take a circumstance and turn it into something."

Mitch Margo enjoys telling a story about his multitalented brother. "Phil was originally a drummer. He plays percussion now with us when we perform. He also played drums on hit records. He was the drummer on 'He's So Fine,' 'Denise,' and 'Candida.' As a matter of fact, Max Weinberg, the drummer on NBC's *Late Night With Conan O'Brien,* once said that one of his favorite drum parts was the drumming on 'Denise,' but said that he didn't know who the drummer was. And I'm not sure if he knows to this day that it was my brother, Phil."

Perhaps he knows now.

My Boyfriend's Back

The Angels*

* THE ANGELS™ GROUP NAME IS A FEDERALLY REGISTERED TRADEMARK.

FROM THE TIME CAPSULE

OCTOBER 1961: The first of the Angels' five songs to hit the top 50, "Til," is released on Caprice.

- OCTOBER 1: In the final game of the baseball season, New York Yankees slugger Roger Maris clobbers a fastball by Boston Red Sox pitcher Tracy Stallard into the right field stands and surpasses Babe Ruth's 34-year-old single-season home run record with his 61st homer of the year, a record which stood for the next 37 years.
- OCTOBER 19: The film *West Side Story,* starring Natalie Wood, George Chakiris, Russ Tamblyn, and Rita Moreno, opens in theaters.

AUGUST 1963: The Angels release "My Boyfriend's Back," which hits No. 1 the week of August 31, in front of Allan Sherman's "Hello Mudduh, Hello Fadduh (Here I Am, In Camp Granada)."

- AUGUST 7: The motion picture *Beach Party,* starring Annette Funicello and Frankie Avalon, introduces a new film genre.
- AUGUST 9: The British Broadcasting Corp. premieres its new rock and roll television program *Ready, Steady, Go!*
- AUGUST 24: Little Stevie Wonder becomes the first artist to top the American pop singles, pop albums, and rhythm and blues singles charts simultaneously.
- AUGUST 28: The Rev. Martin Luther King Jr. delivers his immortal "I Have a Dream" speech from the steps of the Lincoln Memorial in Washington, D.C., before 200,000 people attending a massive civil rights rally. Joan Baez, Odetta, Mahalia Jackson, Bob Dylan, and Peter, Paul and Mary lead the masses in song.

JANUARY 1964: The last of the Angels hit singles, "Wow Wow Wee (He's The Boy For Me)," rises to No. 41.

- JANUARY 3: *Time* magazine names the Rev. Martin Luther King Jr. the 1963 Man of the Year.
- JANUARY 11: The U.S. Surgeon General issues a report linking cigarette smoking with lung disease.
- JANUARY 18: The Beatles' single "I Want To Hold Your Hand" makes its debut on the *Billboard* Hot 100.

OPPOSITE: The Angels in 1963. Left to right: Barbara Allbut, Peggy Santiglia, and Jiggs Allbut. FROM PHOTOFEST ARCHIVES, NEW YORK.

I t was the late '50s, a time when films and TV programs tended to show teenage girls curled up on the sofa painting their nails bright red in anticipation of a boy calling to ask them out to the weekend sock hop. Three who definitely did not fit that image were friendly rivals Peggy Santiglia of the Delicates and Barbara and Jiggs Allbut of the Starlets, determined and multi-talented New Jersey teens who spent a lot of their spare time writing songs and planning their weekend musical performances. The girls had been performing for years at dances and local events and singing professionally as session group artists before joining forces as the Angels and unleashing their wildly popular denouncement of male boorishness, the million-selling "My Boyfriend's Back."

The first all-white female rock and roll group, the Angels first hit the charts with a cover of a Tony Bennett ballad, "'Til," which reached No. 14 on the charts after Caprice Records released it in 1961. At that time the group consisted of Barbara, Jiggs, and Linda Jankowski. By early 1962, the trio had scored again with "Cry Baby Cry," which peaked at No. 35 on the pop charts, but performed even better on the R&B charts. After lead singer Linda Jankowski left the group to pursue other interests, Peggy stepped in and provided the tough-girl attitude that "My Boyfriend's Back" needed. The song, written and produced for the group by Bob Feldman, Richard Gottehrer, and Gerald Goldstein (FGG), was just what they'd been searching for. The single, released by Smash Records, unseated Stevie Wonder's "Fingertips" from the No. 1 position in the summer of '63 and remained at the top of the charts for four weeks.

Barbara and Jiggs had known Peggy for a few years before she joined them. "We had met Peggy when our group, the Starlets, and Peggy's group, the Delicates, played local record hops. In fact, we all did a New York TV show together," says Jiggs. The show's producer instructed the girls to assume an unanimated pose while their record was being played. "We didn't know what was going on, so we just kind of stood there. As the record was playing we saw this guy off-camera wildly gesturing and saying, 'Come on, do something, sing, move!' So we started lip-synching, doing our little routine, swinging and playing to our beautiful ballad. When we finished, the program producers were furious with us and told us, 'Well, now we have to pay you because you performed.' The girls did get paid, but only because the guy who had been waving and gesturing was from AFTRA (American Federation of Television and Radio Artists). Later, someone from the show called and asked them to give back the check, but, says Jiggs, "We called Peggy and asked her what the Delicates were going to do. We all agreed to keep the money."

Right from the beginning, the Angels were insightful enough to know how to manage their own career and money. They signed with managers from time to time, but didn't allow them to monopolize their livelihoods. "In getting out of our Caprice Records contract, we did get involved a little bit with people some might characterize as unsavory. However, I think that brought us some of our very best, most prestigious jobs. There was never any problem connected with it in any way," says Jiggs. "We did a lot of really cool stuff with them. We always got our money, things were done for us. As far as how I think a manager is supposed to perform, that possibly was the best of them. And there were many bad ones out there."

Peggy, Barbara, and Jiggs were dulcet harmonizers, but they were looking to transform their image from a trio of respectable, submissive females singing innocuous, albeit beautiful ballads, to a group with a more fun, aggressive style. "We were looking for a song that was really different—something you could dance to," Peggy explains. "And we found it in 'My Boyfriend's Back.'"

The album version of "My Boyfriend's Back," published by Blackwood Music, had an extra chorus that was deleted for the 45-rpm pressing to comply with the preference of radio programmers for records of about two and a half minutes. "One time we did a TV show lip-synching 'My Boyfriend's Back' and they had the wrong version of the song. We didn't know what to do because we didn't really remember the extra chorus at all. We had been doing it the short way for so many years, it was a shock," remembers Jiggs.

Although they had been performing professionally for years, Peggy, Jiggs, and Barbara were still kids when "Boyfriend" went national on the Smash label. "At the time, it was a bit more difficult for females in rock and roll groups, I think, because it was sort of unheard-of, and it was a bit frowned upon, that nice girls would want to be traveling with rock and roll bands," recalls Peggy. "It was a little scary at times. I can remember in some situations people trying to pull us off the stage, and security personnel on the stage grabbing one leg and somebody in the audience pulling the other."

One of the highlights of Peggy's career was her first visit to Europe. The group was part of a musical entourage assigned to entertain the American troops at various Army and Air Force bases there. "We were shocked but thrilled with all of the attention we were getting," admits Peggy. "But don't forget, here's all these young American guys, without their wives or girlfriends. They just wanted to see women. It really spoiled us. We got back to the United States after one of the extended tours and wondered, "Gee, why aren't people falling at our feet any more?"

In addition to military shows, the group performed in a few nightclubs in Europe, becoming wildly popular with the Germans. Philips Records, the German parent company of Mercury and Smash at the time, recorded an album featuring the Angels singing their songs phonetically in German. In the 1970s Peggy recorded another foreign LP, a Brazilian Latin-charged album called *Fantasia Carnivale.*

A good part of the trio's career involved singing background for other artists— either individually or collectively. Between Angels appearances Barbara, Jiggs, and Peggy began recording together as background singers for other musical entertainers, including Neil Diamond, Anthony Newley, Bob Gaudio and Frankie Valli of the Four Seasons, Quincy Jones, Don Costa, Alan Lorber, Lee Holdridge, Steve Lawrence and Eydie Gorme, Patty Duke, David Geddes, and Frank Sinatra.

"We had breaks all the way along. Our first break was finding our first record deal, because that led to the second record deal. After 'Til' and 'Cry Baby Cry,' we spent a lot of time in New York singing backgrounds and doing demos for various artists and that led to our meeting the producers and writers who wrote 'My Boyfriend's Back.' We had done some demos for them and they wrote the song specifically for us," says Barbara. "So I think we had good luck all the way through. One thing led to another and to another."

When "My Boyfriend's Back" was released, Peggy had been vacationing with her parents, and Barbara and Jiggs telephoned her, saying, "Come back now! It's a giant hit!" The record remained No. 1 on the charts for four weeks and in the top 40 for three months. This national recognition earned them spots on the *Ed Sullivan Show, Bill Dana's Las Vegas Show, American Bandstand* with Dick Clark, the *Merv Griffin Show,* the *Tonight Show* with Johnny Carson, *Shindig,* and numerous local TV shows. "We played at Madison Square Garden, the Apollo Theater, the Copacabana, Nassau Coliseum in New York, at Army and Air Force bases in the United States, Germany, and France, and many, many other places," remembers Barbara. "We went from rock and roll to the nightclub act and finally to the oldies shows."

Contributing to their long-lasting friendship and success was the mutual agreement that each individual member could accept other assignments throughout the trio's career. That creative freedom allowed Jiggs to pursue acting, and she has also sung in numerous commercials over the years, including spots for Caravelle watches, Thom McAn Shoes, and a Money Store advertisement with former New York Yankees shortstop Phil Rizzuto. Barbara did a lot of commercial spots and jingles. During the late '60s Jiggs and Barbara continued performing as the Angels with another lead singer, while Peggy toured and recorded with the Serendipity Singers. Peggy recorded one album called *Love Is A State Of Mind* with the "Dips," as the Serendipity Singers jokingly referred to themselves. She then went on to record as a member of Dusk, the female counterpart to Dawn, for former Token member Hank Medress, producer for Tony Orlando and Dawn. With Dusk, Peggy had two chart records, "Angel Baby" and "I Hear Those Church Bells Ringing," which neared the top 40 nationally and reached top 10 in some secondary markets. She later rejoined the Angels and began playing the oldies circuit.

Barbara, who was responsible for taking care of the business end of the trio, left the group in 1978. It was an amicable departure and the three singers remain very close to this day. Jiggs recalls, "After we were all older and we married, being away that much became tough on us. Barbara was the one who started the whole thing. And she was just so much more entwined in the business end than I ever was. She finally came to a point where she just couldn't do it anymore. She said, 'I can't just halfheartedly continue and if I pursue the music career the way I really need to do it, then I'm not going to have anything else.' I shouldn't speak for her, but this is how I saw it."

Jiggs and Peggy tried to replace Barbara twice but it wasn't meant to be. "Both replacements were great singers, but it just wasn't us. They just didn't have the background that we had, they didn't begin their careers during the time we did," observes Jiggs. One of Barbara's replacements had a Broadway singing style. Jiggs and Peggy agreed she was an excellent singer and had a compatible personality, but she didn't fit their musical style. "We performed with her in an HBO special with Robert Klein, and I think maybe that was the point at which we said, 'Oh, my goodness, listen to us.' We had never really realized we were having to sing more in her style because she couldn't bend to ours. So we said, 'This is not going to work at all,'" recalls Jiggs. The duo then signed Jiggs's husband, Stan Sirico, a multitalented conductor and guitar player, to complete the ensemble.

But with only two Angels on the bill, Jiggs and Peggy got a lot of flack from agents. "They said to us, 'Oh, no one's going to book you, they want three girls, blah, blah, blah.' But the first job Peggy and I did without Barbara was a New Year's Eve party in Brooklyn," says Jiggs. "The worst part was that our guitar player, Stan Sirico, who now sings our third part, had already taken another gig that evening. But the band that we worked with was fabulous. They rehearsed with us a couple of times and did some background singing with us. Once we got that under our belt we were OK and we didn't have much trouble getting booked."

The number of Angels' performances varies from year to year. Since each has other careers, Jiggs and Peggy can be selective about their gigs. "One year we toured for a month on the West Coast, including a week in Alaska," say Jiggs. "So we usually do some kind of tour every year as well as weekend jobs, one-nighters, whatever comes up."

Enthusiastic audience response led to the decision by the original trio to record once again. "Jiggs, Barbara, and I are recording together again," says Peggy. "Barbara is involved as producer and has written several of the songs. We're also including a song that Jiggs's husband, Stan, and I wrote together. It's a joy working together again, and we all feel great about our new arrangement."

And while audiences appreciate their musical versatility displayed with varying styles, arrangements, and tempos on familiar as well as new material, fans invariably break out in wild applause at the smoldering spoken recitation that introduces "My Boyfriend's Back."

While superficially "My Boyfriend's Back" was a bouncy ode to teenage indignation, it presaged a new, assertive attitude for females in rock music that ultimately gave rise to numerous other dynamic female performers.

Pretty good for a group of high school kids who decided they had more to do than just wait for the phone to ring.

HIT SINGLES BY THE ANGELS

DEBUT	PEAK	TITLE	LABEL
10/61	14	'TIL	CAPRICE
2/62	38	CRY BABY CRY	CAPRICE
8/63	1	MY BOYFRIEND'S BACK	SMASH
10/63	25	I ADORE HIM	SMASH
12/63	84	THANK YOU AND GOODNIGHT	SMASH
1/64	41	WOW WOW WEE (HE'S THE BOY FOR ME)	SMASH

THEN AND NOW

PEGGY SANTIGLIA

A performer since the age of 11, Peggy Santiglia spent almost every weekend of her early teen years singing at record hops and at the Brooklyn Fox and the Brooklyn Paramount. Although she loved school and had a great interest in learning, landing a hit record immediately out of high school kept her on a musical career track for the next three decades. It wasn't until the '80s that Peggy's yearn to learn sent her back to school.

In 1990 she graduated from the prestigious Goucher College, originally affiliated with Johns Hopkins University, in Baltimore, Maryland, when women were not permitted to attend Johns Hopkins. Five years later she had earned a master's degree in clinical psychology from Loyola College in Baltimore.

Now a full-time psychotherapist, Peggy owns a small clinical practice in Baltimore called Positive Approach that serves a dual clientele—those in need of comfort for life-threatening illnesses and those who require psychological coaching to help them face an audience. Peggy's challenge is to give her critically ill patients the strength to face their treatments and hope in facing the future. Although professionally trained to detach herself from her clients, Peggy admits to going home with her stomach in knots at times. The lighter side of her practice involves seminars and workshops for people nervous about performing or speaking in front of groups. Using a lot of the same techniques she learned to combat her own stage fright in show business, Peggy works with a variety of people, from the business executive who must speak to a corporate board of directors, to a mother who wants to talk in front of her local PTA.

Peggy Santiglia Davison

"I mostly work with 'worried wells,' not people who have serious psychological problems," explains Peggy. "And I do get a lot of gratification working with people who are undergoing treatment for a life-threatening illness. I've grown a lot from helping people and learning about and living life's most important moments."

Raised in Belleville, New Jersey, Peggy grew up in a musical household. As far back as she can remember, Peggy's father played woodwind instruments, guitar, and mandolin, and everyone in the family sang well. During holidays and family get-togethers, aunts, uncles, and cousins would all sing and play together. Her mother wrote an early singing commercial that a department store in New York used for its promotion, and one of her sisters, Ann, attended Juilliard School of Music and sang opera. "I guess I recorded professionally the first time in seventh grade," recalls Peggy. The year before, she and two school chums had formed her first trio, the Delicates. "We would write songs just about our friends and not being able to date. We kept all these songs in our heads. We made up the tune and the words, and we also harmonized. One of our songs was called 'Too Young To Date,' which we later recorded, and it became a regional hit on the United Artists label." The Delicates sang at many public events in Belleville, and Peggy wrote a song about the mayor that the Delicates performed at his victory party.

It was also while she was in the seventh grade that Peggy made the daring move of trekking to radio station WINS in New York City to meet influential disc jockey Murray the K, who was later described as the "fifth Beatle" for his involvement in bringing the Beatles to America. "I decided in my naiveté that Murray the K needed me to write a theme song for him. So I got together with my friend and we wrote something called 'Meusurray,' because he used to talk sort of a pig-Latin, based on his name Murray. He also used to joke about watching the submarine races, which really meant making out on the beach or something, because that's what you'd tell your parents: you were watching the submarine races. So we wrote 'The Submarine Race Watcher's Theme.'" One midwinter day in 1957, Peggy and her friend played hooky from school and took the bus to Manhattan to deliver their songs to Murray the K. "We probably had more nerves than brains," laughs Peggy. "But we found the studio in this huge building and pretended we had an appointment with Murray the K. They knew just by looking at us that we were just kids, but they humored us. They introduced us to Murray and we sang our little songs. Not only did they like it, they instantly recorded it right there in the studio. Imagine, I had no idea that people got paid for writing songs, which is something I loved to do." Murray the K recorded the song, and by the time Peggy got back home, her songs were coming over the airwaves.

The Delicates were invited to appear on Murray's show many times after that. During one of the radio sessions, Billy Muir, a well-known studio guitar player for the UnArt subsidiary of United Artists, heard about the Delicates and brought them into a studio to record a demo of their song "Black & White Thunderbird." He brought the demo to arranger Don Costa, then head of A&R (artists and repertoire) for United Artists. Costa had produced hits for Paul Anka and Donny Osmond and was later to produce a megahit for Frank Sinatra, "My Way" (written by Anka). "We went to meet him and we brought our little songs written on school notebooks and paper bags. He was so encouraging and very nice, and booked a recording session. I remember being so innocent thinking the 40-piece orchestra was all for us. In actuality, he had tagged us onto the end of somebody else's session and, since they were still paying for the musicians, the orchestra backed us. Our songs titled 'Too Young To Date' and 'The Kiss' turned out wonderful, and we got quite a lot of regional airplay in three or four states," says Peggy.

Following the Delicates' regional success with "Black & White Thunderbird," Peggy met Barbara and Jiggs Allbut, then singing for the Starlets. (There were four Starlets; one of them was Peggy's distant cousin Linda Malzone.) They, too, had a hit, "P.S. I Love You." Since the Delicates and the Starlets were too young to play in nightclubs, they sang on the same bill at record hops. When they realized their voices and styles blended well together, they became friends and together started singing backgrounds for notable artists such as Neil Diamond, Anthony Newley, Bob Gaudio and Frankie Valli of the Four Seasons, and others.

"The first time I appeared on the Dick Clark show, I was with the Delicates, which was even before the Angels. Maybe I was in ninth grade at the time. The vice principal of my high school didn't want to announce that I was going to be on Dick Clark, because, you know, rock and roll in those days. It's laughable now what people thought was shocking," Peggy says.

Peggy claims she's the type of person who's not content doing just one thing at a time. While she was going to college, Peggy would often fly home from a concert and go directly to school. "It was hard work, but I graduated Phi Beta Kappa." Although Peggy's parents weren't able to share the excitement of receiving her bachelor's and master's degrees in psychology and her induction into a brand-new career—both died in the early '90s—they were always very proud of her achievements.

"While my parents were thrilled about me going back to school because they knew that's what I wanted to do, they wouldn't be any less proud if I didn't. My family was just so down to earth, not your typical stage mother or stage father. And I'm happy they were the way they were because I never took myself too seriously. I knew at a very young age that we weren't any better than anyone else just because we had some good fortune. There are a lot of very talented people out there who have never performed professionally, and there are also a lot of nontalented individuals who happen to be very famous."

Peggy is the youngest of three children. She has clear memories of listening to her sister Ann sing. "Because my sister was a little bit older, I was very influenced by seeing her sing, but I knew I couldn't sing opera. I can remember being 11 years old, sitting on my front porch—we had this wonderful big, old wooden house, my grandparents' house that I lived in. My grandparents grew everything. We had peach trees, pear trees, and a big garden. Anyway, I remember sitting on the steps and just thinking, 'Well this is what I want to do. I'm going to be a singer' and planning how I was going to do this. My sister still has a beautiful voice, but she didn't like performing in front of an audience."

Peggy also enjoyed listening to '50s R&B in her preadolescent years. She recalls a high school teacher, Dr. Peck, who was very encouraging. "I guess he knew I had some natural musical abilities, and he was very encouraging along those lines. I was already singing in the school glee club, and by that time I had already been recording in grade school. But he gave me confidence in myself that I was very musically gifted. He gave me the encouragement that my singing and songwriting was legitimate. Most adults at the time didn't put rock and roll in the same category as 'real' music."

Connie Francis attended the same high school Peggy did in Belleville, although she graduated about six years ahead of Peggy. "A cousin of mine was very good friends with Connie, who influenced some of the very early things that I wrote after the Delicates. We were in the Columbus Day Parade together because I was singing with my little local school group and she had come back to make special appearances. I thought, 'Well, here's another person who not only came from the same cultural background, but also went to the same high school and had hit records. I didn't have a big hit record yet but I was already recording, and it made success more plausible."

After the loss of her parents, Peggy's work as a clinical psychotherapist took on even greater meaning. "Although I do have the education to be able to professionally detach myself, part of the ability to help others stems from genuine caring. But I can't say that it's not stressful if I know my clients are in dire straits and their doctors have sent them to me to cheer them up and, hopefully, give them enough support so that they can face their chemotherapy or other medical challenges. It's something that I can do and should do, and my life certainly has been enriched by it."

Although Peggy says she has also had many happy endings, each case presents its own challenges. "Very strong people cry and very strong people say 'Why me?' There's no expert, especially with things for which we don't know all the answers. So we just try to encourage each other to face the future as bravely as we can and to enjoy and live life to the fullest for whatever time we have left. None of us really knows whether it's a day, or a year, or 10 years. And the singing has helped me in a lot of ways not to sweat the small stuff. I used to envy friends who envied me. They'd say, 'Ooh, traveling all over the country. Ooh, you never know where you're going to be and what you're going to do.' Right. But they had the security of knowing what they were doing. When I'm dealing with people in very serious situations, it has helped me because I've been somebody who has been all over the country and all over the world, and I've been exposed to so many different types of people and cultures. And show business has definitely made me a very nonjudgmental person."

But show business has not been all rosy for Peggy. "I've seen people die from drugs, people who I cared about very much. I haven't been sheltered from life. Nothing anybody can tell me is going to shock me. I just feel very fortunate not only to be alive, but to have these diverse sides to my life and that I've been able to use my brain because my singing came absolutely naturally to me."

Peggy met her husband, Jim Davison, on a blind date. "I had been married many years ago, but I had been single for a long time when I met Jim. I owned a very small cosmetics company called Face Concepts, and earlier was in regional management for a division of Revlon and involved in some projects in Baltimore." A couple of business friends thought Peggy should meet Jim. "I didn't want to meet anybody, and he didn't want to meet me—this crazy rock and roll person. So we just appeased our friends and went on a blind date. We've been married since 1981." Peggy has no children of her own, but is extremely proud of her stepdaughter Diane, who is an entertainment lawyer in Baltimore.

Peggy has no tolerance for promoters making money from "bogus" oldies rock groups. "Unfortunately, I don't think a whole lot of people know the names of individual members of '60s rock groups. There's no other form of show business in which impersonators are not called impersonators, except oldies rock and roll. And that is a little disturbing to those of us who really were the people who sang the songs and grew up in that time period. I'm not blaming the performers; it's the promoters and producers who are being deceitful to people in the audience. Oldies fans, very much like country fans, are very sincere, wonderful people. I can't tell you how lucky we are. People come to see us from all around the country. I love to talk and reminisce with fans. We're usually associated with happy times, so they feel like they know us."

Peggy is justly proud of her achievements, but says that when she decided to return to school as an adult she was worried at first about "going back to school so many years later and never really having been in college." She never expected, she says, to earn a Phi Beta Kappa key at Goucher. "But I did feel really proud to be a Phi Beta Kappa graduate. That is not easy to do. And I was also very proud of my thesis. I worked really long and hard on it, and I'm gratified that I was able to mix real life and my experiences and my educational background and actually see it come to fruition by helping people. That does make me feel very proud. And as for my show business career, at the risk of sounding corny, I guess I'm most proud that I'm able to have gotten through this whole long career without any serious regrets about what could have been. I feel what happened to us and what we achieved was wonderful, especially that we were kids, and I feel very proud that we're still very good friends. We got through all the ups and downs of show business, good and bad. Because for every wonderful thing that happened— all the first big network television appearances, all the singing at famous places all over the world—there were also lots of background problems inherent in that."

In her spare time, Peggy volunteers as a big sister in the Baltimore area's Big Brothers/Big Sisters mentoring program and has recently resumed writing songs, which she says she intends to continue for the rest of her life.

"I didn't ever really feel like I changed careers, because the singing has just been such an important part of my life. I can reach people emotionally with my voice. And in turn, I get a lot of wonderful feeling back."

JIGGS ALLBUT

Through the decades, rock music performers have had a penchant for nicknames. Fats Domino, Ringo Starr, and Boots Randolph all adopted monikers reflective of their adult personas. But Jiggs Allbut earned hers when she was still an infant. Born Phyllis Allbut, Jiggs was given her nickname by her mother, who thought she resembled the monocled character in a long-running comic strip known as "Maggie and Jiggs" in some cities and "Bringing Up Father" in others. "There was this little fat Irish guy who always used to get beat up by his wife, but he did bad things and he deserved it," Jiggs recalls with a grin. "My mother thought I looked like him when I was a baby. I had a big, fat face with a clump of hair sticking up, so she called me Jiggs."

The youngest of two girls, Jiggs grew up in a musical family. Her sister, Barbara, took piano lessons at a very early age, and both girls sang, Jiggs providing harmony. Both wanted to become professional musicians from their early teens on. They had both been born on September 24, two years apart, and one year the girls pooled their birthday cash to finance their first recording. "We found a little recording studio near our home in Orange, New Jersey. Barbara played the piano, and we harmonized some of the songs that she had written. We met some little guy there named Bob Minete, who wrote songs, too. With his guitar accompaniment, we moved on to a larger studio and sang some of his songs for a demo."

Jiggs Allbut Sirico backstage before a performance in Baltimore.
PHOTO COURTESY OF JIGGS SIRICO.

That sparked the beginning of a long and accomplished recording career. Barbara and Jiggs continued singing backgrounds for other artists, moving up to a larger studio in New Jersey where they met the two girls who joined them in becoming the Starlets. The foursome recorded "P.S., I Love You" on a small New Jersey label and it became a regional hit. Peter Tripp, a New York deejay, began regularly playing the Starlets' version of "P.S., I Love You" on his WMGM radio show. "We were getting a lot of airplay and then all of a sudden, we tuned in one day and no more Peter Tripp. He'd been charged with payola," says Jiggs. The small New Jersey recording company tried to make a distribution deal with Canadian American Records in New York once the song began getting some additional airplay, but the deal went sour.

Disappointed but not defeated, Jiggs and Barbara kept on working on new songs. Shortly after the "P.S." deal fell through, Barbara, Jiggs, and lead singer Linda Jankowski adopted the name Blue Angels, later dropping Blue from the name.

For Jiggs, entering into showbiz at such a young age made the adjustment to stardom second nature. "We were young, we were all single at the time, and we were having fun. Although, in those days, the thing that got so many people into trouble was thinking, 'This is fun, this is great, this is what I want to do.' And there were not that many people there to take care of you. Our parents were not showbiz parents by any means. They were normal, middle-class people, and all of a sudden this new kind of rock and roll music was here, and they didn't know what was going on. So we were a little naive, I guess."

In 1976, Jiggs met her husband, Stan Sirico, in Connecticut when the band auditioned for a drummer. Stan hadn't come in to try out himself, but to keep a friend company. But, recalls Jiggs, "We liked Stan's guitar playing so much that we asked him if he wanted a job, too, and he said, 'Yes.'" Stan and Jiggs were married in 1986.

The couple moved to California in 1991 when Stan's employer, AKG Acoustics in Connecticut, offered him a transfer and promotion. AKG Acoustics is a Viennese company that produces microphones and headphones for stage shows, studio work, and the sound reinforcement industry. About a year after the transfer, the company moved to Nashville, Tennessee, and Stan and Jiggs opened their own electronics business in San Leandro called Sirico Instruments. Their company supplies AKG and other companies with electronic components including power supplies for microphones. "We ship stuff all over the place. It's really fun," says Jiggs.

With a long and successful musical career and a track record as business owner as part of her impressive resume, Jiggs still asks herself, "Gee, what am I going to do when I grow up?" She has recently decided to finish her undergraduate degree and obtain a teaching credential from Thomas Edison State College in Trenton, New Jersey. Through the institution's accredited Distance & Independent Adult Learning program, Jiggs is accessing the college's on-line computer classroom to complete her studies. "Teaching was something I never thought was right for me. But then I got involved with Project Literacy at the library, teaching reading as a volunteer, and it was so fabulous. I would come home and say, 'Gee, that was really good.' I'm remembering different teachers in school, and how they taught things, what I thought of them and what I got out of their teaching. And I'm thinking, 'I like this, it's something that I could get into.' So I'll be taking a computer course and probably a music course as an elective. I feel it's a good time to go back to school."

Jiggs says she has never loved performing more than she does now. She enjoys escaping from the routine responsibilities of being home and running a business. "We've met some wonderful people on our tours. We take our CDs and we sell pictures and T-shirts at the shows, we sign autographs, and it's wonderful. Here you are and people are asking you to sign an autograph for them, they're buying your things, and it's just fabulous. Then you have to come home and walk the dog and scoop poop and, you know," laughs Jiggs. "Sometimes when we're out for a while, we get inspired and we start writing. Not me so much, but Stan and Peggy do, and I try to contribute what I can. In fact, they wrote a country-oriented song a while back that's really good and we're thinking of recording it. Things like that happen to us when we're out for a long time and totally into music."

When the Angels go on the road these days, there's a lot of prep work that has to be done to make sure each of their other businesses run smoothly. For example, although Stan and Jiggs don't have permanent employees, they often will hire help to get them through some of the busy times of year. "We have certain things that have to be done at certain times. And when we're going away, we either work real hard before or work real hard after to make sure that tasks are completed by their deadline. And at this point, we can handle all of it."

Jiggs has two daughters: Karalyn, born in 1969, and Sam, born in 1987. "Karalyn is a very good singer and plays piano. In fact, she played piano with us years ago. She was in high school and, to tell you the truth, I never knew how well she could sing because she was shy about singing. But when we realized how well she really sang, we were amazed." Sam, who is the more outgoing of the two daughters, also plays the piano and says she wants to be in show business. "They're both great kids," says Jiggs proudly.

Jiggs describes herself as "adaptable." She says one of her greatest strengths is that she gets along with just about everyone. But on stage she can ham it up with the best of them. "I remember over the years being willing to do just anything on stage. I used to put on a stupid hat and do a drunk act."

A former aerobics and yoga instructor, Jiggs works out at a gym every day. She enjoys weight training and exercise walking and does yoga from time to time. "I also like to watch tennis and baseball. We're big New York Yankees fans. We play a lot of ping pong and a lot of pool, and it's fun, and I'm getting a little bit better, although I don't think I'll ever be a pool shark."

Jiggs listens to all types of music, including jazz, classical, and the oldies. She claims she can sing 99.9 percent of the songs that play on the oldies radio stations. "My husband's always amazed. He wants to put me on *Name That Tune*. I do like to sing along." Growing up, Jiggs says she listened to the early Alan Freed rock and roll and R&B hits by black artists "before they were made hits by the white artists." She also loved to listen to the great harmony groups, including the Four Aces and the Maguire Sisters. "I used to love to go to the movies, too. I did study acting for a while. I never really pursued it because our singing career usually got in the way, but I did voice-overs and things like that. And that's something that someday I'm going to do again."

BARBARA ALLBUT

A multitalented singer, music writer, pianist, and business-woman, Barbara Allbut was instrumental in forming the Angels and overseeing the early business dealings of the group. Her keen business sense has also contributed to the success of Peter Brown Associates, a commercial construction management company she owns with her architect husband Peter Brown. Although she hasn't performed professionally since the late '70s, Barbara has always had music in her blood and continues to satisfy her musical cravings by playing her 1917 Bosendorfer piano in her Santa Barbara home on the flanks of the Santa Ynez Mountains, overlooking the city and the Pacific Ocean 90 miles northwest of Los Angeles.

She insists her interest in music began when she was toddling around at the age of 3. "My mother told me I'd walk around the house humming notes from operas

Barbara Allbut Brown at Pebble Beach.

that I'd heard on the radio. Whenever we would go to a department store—I remember this—I would head for the piano department. They had a whole floor full of pianos and I'd go and sit there and play. I was just crazy about pianos."

When she was 5 years old, Barbara began taking piano lessons, playing mainly classical music. "I studied for 11 years until I was 16, and I just didn't like to practice. A couple of years before that I became interested in rock and roll. So I quit piano lessons, and I started writing songs, singing, and making up harmonies."

That was the beginning of her early performing career and the catalyst for her lifelong close relationship with Jiggs.

Two years to the day older than Jiggs, Barbara formed musical groups with her friends in their Orange, New Jersey, junior high and high schools, performing for classmates and teachers. Barbara played the piano and everyone sang.

Reminiscing about her childhood idols, Barbara recalls, "At age 15 I saw Jo Ann Campbell at the Brooklyn Fox. She was a sexy little rock 'n' roll singer who electrified audiences in the Alan Freed rock 'n' roll concerts in the '50s. She recorded a song called 'Wait A Minute.' When I saw her up there, I was possessed by a powerful feeling that I was going to be a performer."

From her days with the Starlets, Barbara recalls the demise of Peter Tripp vividly. "At that time Peter Tripp was a popular deejay on WMGM in New York, and he just loved 'P.S., I Love You' and was pushing it. But very shortly thereafter he was thrown off the air on payola charges. So that wiped everything out at the time."

Barbara's mother thought that show business was full of dishonest and underhanded people preying on the success of talented performers. "She was right, it really wasn't too nice. People got cheated left and right and we were kids and there were a lot of not very nice people who would take advantage of you. On the other hand, my father was wary but he was secretly proud. He would play our record on the jukebox whenever he went to the diner and he'd tell people, 'Those are my daughters,'" says Barbara with a smile. "When we were on the *Ed Sullivan Show* my mother apparently wouldn't sit in the room to watch it. My father said he was watching the television, and she kind of peeked around the corner and then made her way into the room slowly after she saw that we weren't going to fall on our faces." The girls' father loved to sing bass and his sister was a concert pianist. Their mother also played the piano. Both parents died in the late '70s.

After 21 years on the road with the Angels, Barbara got tired of traveling and decided it was time to do something else. "In 1978 I began singing jingles in New York. I did a commercial for Wendy's, Peter Paul candy, some milk commercials, and stuff like that." She then met Peter Brown, who was an architect at Skidmore, Owings and Merrill, a large architectural firm with offices in Chicago, New York, Washington, San Francisco, and London. Peter and Barbara were married in 1986 in Santa Barbara, California, after Peter was transferred to the firm's Los Angeles office. In 1988 he decided to leave the firm to start his own business, Peter Brown Associates in L.A.

"He's an architect, but this is not an architectural firm," explains Barbara. "We do construction project management for building developers. We do budgeting, scheduling, and assist in hiring project architects as well as advising and making sure everything is done right, on time, and on budget." The company's projects are mainly large commercial buildings, hospitals, and hotels.

"We've done numerous projects for Kaiser Permanente and The Equitable Insurance Company. We're doing Western Digital's new headquarters, projects at

Loma Linda University Medical Center, Childrens Hospital in Los Angeles, Century Plaza Hotel, Nikken North American World Headquarters, the Aventine complex in La Jolla, and a lot of large law firms," she says. "We're currently working on a 25,000-square-foot house in Beverly Hills, and we just finished another one that's just over 30,000 square feet. Those are like commercial buildings."

The successful company has six employees. Most everyone in the firm is an architect by training, but they all function as project managers. Barbara is the business manager, responsible for payroll, billing, financial reports, and supervision of clerical personnel. Although she enjoys running the office, it consumes most of her time. In 1998 she resumed writing music, studying arranging and composing. "I'm working on five songs that I'm very excited about," says Barbara. She spends three and a half to four days a week in her Santa Barbara home. The couple also maintains an apartment in the Bunker Hill area of downtown L.A., within walking distance of their office.

Barbara attended two semesters at the Juilliard School of performing arts in her early twenties. "I took those night courses, and I studied theory, sight singing, and choral music. It was wonderful." But her mother insisted she have something other than music to fall back on and encouraged her to go to secretarial school. "I've done some legal secretarial work here and there in the past. But that's it. I didn't have time to go to college with all of the performing we were doing." Although her company's project managers take care of several multimillion-dollar projects, Barbara says her job is not particularly stressful. "There's a lot of work, but we have somebody wonderful working for us—our project assistant, Jackie. We get along really great. We love to go out to lunch together, to try all the restaurants around here. Everybody in this firm gets along well with everybody else."

Barbara loves to travel, but being on the road and having to perform every night is not the type of traveling she'd like to do these days. "I love traveling on vacation," she says. "Although I do miss performing in a way, especially the interaction with the audience. When it was great it was *so* great. We became high from those performances. The thing I miss most, actually, is the vocal arranging, listening to what it sounds like with the group and hearing the harmonies. I love being in a recording studio, and I'm looking forward to getting back into studio work. I did a lot of work on my own when I was singing jingles. I would practice and tape myself and sing all the parts. And I really loved hearing how it would come out."

Barbara considers herself a quiet person who loves her freedom. "However," she says, "that would change when I'd hit the stage. I felt like I was two different people. When I got up on stage I was a big ham. People would say, 'Wow, you're not at all like you usually are.' I don't mean that I was dull; I think I'm quite interesting. But I did change when I got on stage. I don't like complications, although I have to field some of that in my job. I think I'm a kind person. I'm very fair, fun, hardworking, and smart." Although she has no children of her own, Barbara adores Jiggs's two daughters and visits with them as much as she can. She's also very close to her sister. "Jiggs and I talk all the time. She's the greatest sister ever. Everyone should have a sister like my sister."

In her spare time, Barbara loves tennis and follows the pro tennis tour. "I go to as many matches as possible. I read every result every day. This started about 1985 when I first saw Boris Becker win Wimbledon, and I've just been a total fan ever since. I still play a little bit, but I have a very bad arm and I can't play very much. But I love it, and I love being at home with Peter and puttering around our home."

Barbara is proud of her organizational talents. "I really never thought I would necessarily have any talent in managing financial affairs. It was not something that I ever liked at all. I've sort of had to do it. But because I take care of the administrative end of the business, we don't have to have anybody from the outside doing our bookkeeping. If you'd have told me a few years ago I'd be doing this, I would never have believed you." Barbara also organizes various projects in her Santa Barbara neighborhood. "I live on a private road and we've done a lot of improvements together principally because I got the ball rolling. So I seem to be able to get people to respond."

Barbara is also proud of what the Angels accomplished. "Even though things hadn't necessarily been easy for us, we made it happen. And I think besides luck we also had great drive. I'm very proud that we had our hit records and we stuck with performing for so long, and I'm also proud of myself for what I'm doing now." She does admit that if she could go back in time, she'd satisfy her great longing: continuation of her studies at Juilliard. "I would have probably become a composer-arranger, perhaps for movies. I would have expanded my musical career through personal learning. I would have gone to school and really done something with it. I think of myself first as a musical person. But it's never too late, and I intend to continue with my music."

When Barbara first became interested in performing, she enjoyed listening to the early rhythm and blues music of groups such as the Moonglows, the Harptones, and the Paragons. "I love every kind of music now. I listen to pop music and Alanis Morissette, I'll listen to Mozart, I'll listen to Chick Corea, Manhattan Transfer. And at Christmas, I love Fauré's Requiem, and I love Pavarotti. I guess I like all music, except rap."

When asked how important it is for people to remember her, Barbara seems pensive. "I didn't think it was that important for me to be remembered until a few years ago. Then at one of the Angels shows, Jiggs and Peggy were singing, and I was in the audience. It just struck me that we had really pioneered for the girl groups, and we really made a contribution to the history of music. I was very 'up' that night, and it just dawned on me what we had really done. So I, too, want to be remembered."

A World Without Love

Without

Love

Peter & Gordon

CHAPTER 5

FROM THE TIME CAPSULE

JUNE 1964: Peter & Gordon release "Nobody I Know," which becomes their seond hit single in as many months.
- JUNE 2: The Rolling Stones begin their first U.S. concert tour in Lynn, Massachusetts.
- JUNE 4: The Beatles "World Tour" begins in Copenhagen.
- JUNE 10: The Senate invokes cloture to stop the southern filibuster over the Civil Rights Act after Senator Robert Byrd ends a 14-hour speech. Nine days later, the Senate approves the Act.
- JUNE 12: South Africa sentences apartheid opponent Nelson Mandela to life imprisonment on a charge of attempting to overthrow the government.

JANUARY 1965: Peter & Gordon's "I Go To Pieces" reaches No. 9.
- JANUARY 4: In his State of the Union address, President Lyndon B. Johnson says the U.S. is moving toward a "Great Society," and outlines his plans for getting there.
- JANUARY 12: The pop music program *Hullabaloo* premieres on the NBC television network with appearances by Gerry and the Pacemakers and the Zombies.
- JANUARY 20: Legendary disc jockey Alan Freed, who helped popularize rock and roll on the airwaves in the 1950s and who was prosecuted in the payola scandals, dies, penniless, at the age of 43 in Palm Springs, California.

MARCH 1967: Capitol Records releases "Sunday For Tea," the last of Peter & Gordon's singles to make the top 40.
- MARCH 6: Boxer Muhammad Ali is ordered to be inducted into the U.S. Armed Forces.
- MARCH 18: The Beatles' "Penny Lane" goes from No. 5 to No. 1, ahead of the Turtles' "Happy Together."
- MARCH 25: The Who and Cream both make their U.S. debut on Murray the K's Easter Show.
- MARCH 26: 10,000 people attend the first East Coast "Be In" in New York City's Central Park.

OPPOSITE: Peter Asher (wearing glasses) and Gordon Waller at a south London railway station in early 1965. PHOTO BY CHRIS WALTER, © PHOTOFEATURES.

When the Beatles catapulted to the top
of the American music charts in early 1964, they did so in
sovereign style, scoring four No. 1 singles in rapid succession. So overpowering was their influence that British artists reigned
supreme all but 10 weeks during the first half of the year. While scores
of British recording artists followed in the months to come, the Beatles
shared the top position during the first half of '64 with only one other
British musical act: Peter & Gordon.

The musical success of Peter & Gordon was ordained in a sense. At a time when
anything bearing the Beatles imprint turned to gold, Peter Asher and Gordon Waller
had the distinction of recording a new song by Beatles composers John Lennon and
Paul McCartney. The song, "A World Without Love," helped validate the music composition credentials of the Lennon-McCartney team while giving Peter & Gordon a
career-launching, million-selling record.

Peter Asher and Gordon Waller met as teenagers at Westminster School in London,
where they were students. Westminster, a residential public school founded in the
12th century by the Benedictine monks of the Abbey of St. Peter in Westminster,
counts John Locke, Peter Ustinov, John Gielgud, and Andrew Lloyd-Webber among
its alumni. Waller and Asher discovered early that they shared an appreciation for
the guitar and the silken harmonies of the Everly Brothers, but they had more in
common than that. Both had fathers who were physicians and neither had any
idea of becoming a pop music star. Waller's father wanted Gordon to be a doctor.
Gordon wanted to become a cowboy.

Evidently Gordon had his mind more on riding the range than on education
during his early school years. His recollection of what he was learning? "Nothing!"
Of the three science courses in which he was enrolled—physics, chemistry, and
biology—he passed only physics, and that narrowly. "I wasn't academic and I'm
still not," he insists. Yet on the urging of his mother, who had been a nurse,
and his father, Waller pressed on, transferring from his "junior school" in Pinner,
Middlesex, to Westminster in London.

"I couldn't get into any other school," Waller candidly admits. The "common
entrance exam" required of British schoolchildren tested knowledge in numerous
subjects, including chemistry and physics. The test revealed young Gordon's weak-
ness in the sciences. "I was hopeless," he says. But although Westminster was
considered a difficult "scholarship-level" school, its entrance exam consisted only
of an English paper and a math test. "Those just happened to be subjects that I

found pretty easy. I was a big hero in my junior school when it was announced that I passed into Westminster with flying colors because I got a couple of sports scholarships. I played everything that the school played."

And more. As schoolmates, Asher and Waller developed a repertoire of gentle ballads and folk music, relying heavily upon songs by the Everly Brothers and Joan Baez. Accompanying themselves with acoustic guitars, they played local nightspots including the Pickwick Club, an exclusive dinner club frequented by show business personalities. Harry Seacombe (one of the stars, along with Peter Sellers and Spike Milligan, of the popular British radio series *The Goon Show*), Michael Caine, and Trevor Howard were among the regulars. At the time, Asher had no particular career ambitions.

Following graduation from Westminster School, Peter studied philosophy in his first year at King's College, London University. "I think I chose philosophy because it was the vaguest subject you could choose," he says. Asher thought of music more as a diversion than a potential career. As their audiences grew more appreciative, however, Peter and Gordon began to treat their music more seriously. After Peter made the decision to leave school, Gordon followed suit in July 1963. Then 18 years old, Gordon told his father of his entertainment ambitions.

"I'll give you six months," said Gordon's displeased father. "If you can't make it as a music professional within six months, you'll go back to school."

Gordon protested, saying, "Dad, it's not that easy."

His father left him no choice. "Well, those are your options," he declared.

The clock began ticking.

Up on stage, Peter & Gordon continued singing their ballads and weaving harmonies. Before long, people began to express interest in recording the duo. But despite the fact that Gordon was performing to the rhythm of a six-month metronome that no one else could hear, the duo exercised remarkable discretion. Waller remembers that they were not really interested in the early come-ons because "they weren't the type of people we wanted to work with. I hadn't heard of the record companies they mentioned. I suspect the reason we became successful is that we waited for a decent company."

That company was EMI/Capitol. One night late in 1963 after the two finished a set at a London nightclub, Norman Newell, an A&R specialist with EMI Records, invited them to audition. EMI was a well-respected British label with good recording facilities and resources for strong promotional backing. At the audition Asher and Waller performed a few of the folk songs that constituted their on-stage repertoire. Newell offered them a recording contract, which they signed just as Gordon's six-month grace period was drawing to a close.

As they considered material to record, their thoughts turned to a composition by an acquaintance: Paul McCartney. In early 1964, Paul had started dating Peter's sister, Jane Asher, and Jane introduced Paul to Peter and Gordon. "As we began thinking about material to record in our first session, I remembered a song that Paul said he had been working on but which wasn't finished because John [Lennon] decided he didn't like it," says Asher. "So I asked him if we could have it, and he said we could." The song, "A World Without Love," became Peter & Gordon's first single and soared to No. 1 on the British and American charts.

Instant fame was anything but traumatic to Asher. "I really enjoyed it. I can't pretend there were any huge stresses attached to it. It was all fun at the time." When fame came, Asher's studies ceased. "I went to my 'tutor' at the university—that's like a counselor in the states—and told him that we had a No. 1 hit record and that we'd been invited to travel to America to tour and appear on the *Ed Sullivan Show*. I asked if he or the university would consider giving me a year's leave of absence to go off, and then I'd come back and finish my studies. And to his credit, he consented. Unfortunately," Asher adds, "he's still waiting for me to come back. I never did, and I'm still a dropout."

Whatever fleeting thoughts he may have been entertaining about going back to school must have vanished when 20-year-old Asher stepped off the plane at LAX in the spring of 1964. "Screaming girls at the airport were carrying big signs that said 'We love you, Peter and Gordon,' and tearing at our clothes. That was thoroughly enjoyable."

The live performances turned out to be less so.

"The business was very badly organized back then," recalls Asher. "The gigs were horrible. They were in some awful gym or roller rink. It was a good thing our shows lasted only a half hour because there were no stage monitors and we couldn't hear ourselves. The production aspects of the shows were very amateurish then. It was a complete nightmare," Asher asserts. Well, not a *complete* nightmare.

"The good side was I enjoyed singing with Gordon. He's a terrific singer. We sang very good harmony together. I greatly enjoyed being in America, being in L.A. Here I was, with a No. 1 record, driving down Sunset Boulevard for the first time in my life in a convertible Mustang while girls recognized me and asked if they could jump in the car. Life doesn't get much better than that."

Peter & Gordon produced 11 top 50 American hit singles for Capitol Records during a three-year period, including two other top 10 hits: Del Shannon's "I Go To Pieces" from early 1965 and the whimsical, slightly naughty "Lady Godiva," which hit the charts in October 1966.

Throughout their recording careers, Asher and Waller retained an association with the Beatles and collaborated with Paul McCartney in a celebrated bit of musical subterfuge. When unwavering fan loyalty planted seeds of doubt in Paul's mind about the depth of his songwriting talent (he wondered whether they would just buy *anything* he wrote), he asked Peter and Gordon to consider recording one of his songs, attributing it to a fictitious "Bernard Webb." The song, "Woman," was the seventh hit for Peter & Gordon. McCartney's alias was quickly uncloaked because the publishing company's paper trail wasn't well concealed, but by then "Woman" was already a success. McCartney need have no further doubts about his songwriting talents.

HIT SINGLES° BY PETER & GORDON

DEBUT	PEAK	TITLE	LABEL
5/64	1	A WORLD WITHOUT LOVE	CAPITOL
6/64	12	NOBODY I KNOW	CAPITOL
10/64	16	I DON'T WANT TO SEE YOU AGAIN	CAPITOL
1/65	9	I GO TO PIECES	CAPITOL
4/65	14	TRUE LOVE WAYS	CAPITOL
7/65	24	TO KNOW YOU IS TO LOVE YOU	CAPITOL
11/65	83	DON'T PITY ME	CAPITOL
2/66	14	WOMAN	CAPITOL
5/66	50	THERE'S NO LIVING WITHOUT YOUR LOVING	CAPITOL
7/66	98	TO SHOW YOU I LOVE YOU	CAPITOL
10/66	6	LADY GODIVA	CAPITOL
12/66	15	KNIGHT IN RUSTY ARMOUR	CAPITOL
3/67	31	SUNDAY FOR TEA	CAPITOL
6/67	97	THE JOKERS	CAPITOL

PETER ASHER

Peter Asher is a model of modesty. One of the most artistically prolific and powerful figures in the recording industry, he confesses to being a man without career plans. His career path, he says, was anything but mapped out. To hear him tell it, he simply has a knack for wandering down the right pathway at the right time.

"I don't really have any ambitions. All of the career changes that I've made have been unplanned. They were not the result of ambitions. When I was a university student I had no ambition to be a pop star, when I was a pop star I had no ambition to be a record producer, when I was a record producer I had no ambition to be a manager, and when I was a manager I had no ambition to become a senior record company executive. So it seems almost pointless for me to think of any ambitions at this point. I think I have done a lot by succeeding at whatever I was doing by doing my best at it, but ambition has been more a function of the opportunity that presents itself. When there's an opportunity to jump, I jump."

Peter Asher (left) with Gordon Waller in 1998. PHOTO BY JEFF MARCH.

Asher apparently jumps with impeccable timing. He gracefully leapt from the role of pop star to pop star maker, emerging in the 1970s as a widely sought after producer. The stellar list of musicians Asher produced includes James Taylor, Linda Ronstadt, Neil Diamond, Cher, Randy Newman, Olivia Newton-John, Bonnie Raitt, 10,000 Maniacs, John Stewart, Kenny Loggins, Dan Fogelberg, Billy Joel, Diana Ross, and Ringo Starr.

His success as a music producer is validated by the Record Industry Association of America (RIAA), which has presented him with awards for 31 gold albums and 19 platinum albums. In addition, he has earned many accolades internationally. Eight of the recordings he's produced won Grammy Awards, and he received additional Grammy recognition as producer of the year in both 1977 and 1989.

Although he labels himself a college dropout, Peter approaches record production in a studious, philosophical, thoughtful manner. When considering a song for a particular artist, he proceeds very deliberately. "I'll take the song home, play it a great deal, perhaps program some electronic drum beats, sing along with it, and make a lot of notes. It's a process of thinking and imagining," says Asher. "Then the artist and I sit down and compare notes before eventually going in to the studio, where we try out our ideas. I have found that much of the creativity in the process results from free-ranging conversation between artist and producer." While the musical styles of Asher's productions vary widely, they share at least one quality in common. "My goal is to make records that have a certain kind of catchy quality, such that when you hear the song, you want to hear it again. It hits that right spot in your brain. Songs that make people who hear them say, 'Oh, *yeah!* Turn that up.'"

Born in London June 22, 1944, Asher grew up in a musical household. His mother was a professional oboe player, and young Peter spent the first few years of his life on the road with her as she toured with English orchestras entertaining military troops. When Peter's busy physician father had time, he played the piano to relax. Music filled the household. Even so, Peter's initial musical experience wasn't encouraging. "I was very bad at my piano lessons, and I can't read music properly to this day," he confesses. His affinity for music blossomed when he discovered rock and roll. In school he developed an interest in the guitar. "But it didn't become serious until I started singing in school with Gordon."

Three years after Peter & Gordon arrived in America on the first wave of the British invasion, the ride came to an end. The breakup of the act in 1967 was gradual rather than cataclysmic. "We just became a bit less successful, and began to enjoy each other's company a bit less." By then he had already given thought to developing a career in music production.

Fascinated by the process of record production, Asher mentioned his interest to Paul Jones, lead singer of the Manfred Mann combo. Jones, who had observed

Asher in the studio during Peter & Gordon sessions, asked Asher to produce some tracks for him.

"That was quite brave of him," Asher says. The demands made on a music producer are somewhat analogous to the demands made on the head chef of a fine restaurant. Producers typically help artists choose songs to record, select the musicians, consult on the musical arrangement, oversee technical direction of the mix, direct the pacing and phrasing of vocals and instrumental passages, and more. All the while Asher was testing his wings in the booth with Paul Jones, he was getting encouragement from Paul McCartney. The two frequently hung out together, and McCartney spoke to Asher at length about a conceptual project he and the other Beatles were in the process of developing, the formation of the Beatles' own label, Apple Records. On Apple's launch, in the spring of 1968, Asher was hired as head of A&R. Just four years after he'd been signed to his first recording contract, Asher was given a major role in determining which artists the new Apple label should sign, what kinds of recordings they'd make, and who would produce their sessions. Within the Apple culture, such decisions were a shared responsibility.

"I would have weekly A&R meetings with as many Beatles as wanted to attend, and usually some sort of a 'Beatle quorum' would be present when we made decisions," Asher recalls. One of his first developmental assignments was the signing of Welsh singer Mary Hopkin, whom Paul McCartney had spotted on a local talent show on television. Asher sought her out and promptly signed her to a contract with the intention of recording a specific song, one that Paul had in mind for Hopkin.

"It was a song Paul had heard at a folk nightclub. Although the couple singing it had written English lyrics, it was really a Russian folk song." Asher assisted with arrangements for the hauntingly beautiful "Those Were The Days," which sold a million copies in the fall of 1968.

Shortly after joining Apple, Asher entered into an enduring creative relationship with another artist who would grow to legendary stature, James Taylor. Taylor and Asher had a mutual friend, Danny Kortchmar, who'd been a member of an American band called the King Bees that backed a few Peter & Gordon gigs during a U.S. concert tour. (Asher and Kortchmar had developed a close friendship and stayed in contact through the years.) After the breakup of the King Bees, Taylor and Kortchmar both played in a band called the Flying Machine. In the summer of 1968, Taylor was planning a trip to the United Kingdom and Kortchmar told him to look up Asher when he arrived in London. Taylor did call Asher, who invited Taylor to his home the following evening. Taylor brought his audition tape. "I was blown away when I heard it," says Asher, who signed Taylor to a recording contract. "My job at Apple was to find cool artists, and as soon as I heard James's tape I knew that I had done so."

As it turned out, the self-titled debut James Taylor album, which was moderately successful, was the only record that Asher produced for Apple. Signs of corporate instability began to surface at Apple, and in 1971 Asher followed Taylor back to the states and assumed management of Taylor's career. Although Asher knew nothing of talent management, he received coaching from a friend named Nat Weiss, the Beatles' attorney. Three decades later, Weiss remains Asher's friend and Taylor's attorney.

Under the tutelage of Weiss, Asher learned the ropes quickly and competently.

"Management, as I always thought it was, turned out to be based upon common sense," observes Asher. In short order Asher inked a record deal for Taylor with Warner Brothers, for which he produced Taylor's stunning second album, *Sweet Baby James*. From that success in 1969 Asher's fortunes spiraled. At the same time that Asher was slowly and carefully building Peter Asher Management into a talent powerhouse, he was crafting a brilliant production career as well. He orchestrated a succession of critically acclaimed works not only for James Taylor, but also for Linda Ronstadt, whose chart debut with the Stone Poneys came at about the time the recording career of Peter & Gordon was fading.

Asher began managing Ronstadt in 1973 and produced the albums that propelled her to superstardom, beginning with 1974's country-flavored *Heart Like A Wheel* and encompassing Ronstadt's astonishing musical progression through *Prisoner In Disguise, Hasten Down The Wind, Simple Dreams, Living In The U.S.A., Mad Love, Get Closer,* and *Cry Like A Rainstorm, Howl Like The Wind,* running the gamut from reggae to punk. When Ronstadt collaborated with orchestra leader Nelson Riddle in creating three albums of lush sentimental ballads in the mid-'80s, Asher was at the creative helm.

Beverly Hills–based Peter Asher Management prospered and grew, shepherding the careers of Randy Newman, Warren Zevon, and other artists. Asher was perfectly content overseeing his enterprise until the phone rang one day in early 1995 with an offer too tempting to refuse. Asher accepted, and today he's senior vice president at Sony Music Entertainment, the New York–based arm of the music conglomerate encompassing Columbia, Epic, Legacy, and other labels. Although involved in corporate planning and decision making, Asher remains within the realm of talent development, scouting, and nurturing new acts. He also continues to produce recordings for Sony Music artists.

Asher's role in corporate management is in keeping with his candid view of his performing talents. "I always saw myself as a harmony singer, not a lead singer, so I never wanted to be the guy in front of the band. But I enjoy singing harmony and I still do from time to time, whenever there's a part to which I think I can usefully contribute."

Although Asher has a tiny apartment in Manhattan not far from his office, he's on the East Coast only about a quarter of the year. He travels extensively on behalf of Sony and keeps one foot in London, where he has a flat. He still spends much of his time in Los Angeles, where he prefers to schedule recording sessions. His primary residence is in Malibu, where he and his family own a home. Asher and his wife, Wendy, have a daughter, Victoria, born in 1984.

For a man who in school studied the complex philosophies of ancient scholars, Asher has a disarmingly simple philosophical approach.

"I think my philosophy has always been the same," he muses. "I find myself very uncomfortable with any kind of deceit. I've never been any good at it. My management company developed a reputation of being very straight-ahead and honest. But that shouldn't be the exception upon which to grow a reputation. In my estimation it doesn't do any good to weave a web of confusion and deceit because it makes life too damned complicated. I can't say that I've always told the truth, but one tells as much of the truth as possible without causing anyone tremendous upset or huge social disruption."

In keeping with his philosophy, Asher admits his faults—"impatience and unwillingness to put up with foolishness." But he also sees himself as intelligent and level-headed. "I don't get daunted by problems. I'm convinced that if you think hard enough, everything can be sorted out."

GORDON WALLER

By the time he was 15 years old, Gordon Waller had made an important discovery. "The guitar was a very good vehicle for social attraction by the male species. If you played the guitar you got invited to parties." And so young Gordon set about learning to play the guitar. He'd already become enamored of the rock and roll music of Buddy Holly, Eddie Cochran, Elvis Presley, and the Everly Brothers.

Waller, born June 4, 1945, in the Scottish Highlands town of Braemar, took his guitar with him when he went off to school in London. He learned he was one of very few guitar players at Westminster School, where classical music was emphasized and the guitar was frowned upon. Peter Asher, a year ahead of Gordon, was one of the other guitar players, but Gordon and Peter had different musical tastes. "Peter's tastes were more jazz and folk-oriented than mine," says Gordon. "But when we got together we realized that our voices suited each other, so we started doing a bit of work in local clubs—probably the happiest days of my life."

Those happy days lasted until 1967, when the last Peter & Gordon single to chart, "The Jokers," barely made the top 100 and the two went their separate ways.

Georgiana Steele-Waller and Gordon Waller at their wedding in August 1998. PHOTO BY JEFF MARCH.

Waller wasn't well prepared psychologically for the change. "When it stopped, I carried on trying to live the same way—that was my first mistake," Waller says candidly. "I ran out of money, and that's when it hits you bad. But I survived. I tried different things."

He made an unsuccessful attempt to continue performing on his own.

"The guy we had as a manager thought that I had a very good chance of making it solo, but he had his fingers in too many pies. He was managing too many people. He had a couple of people very similar to me so he didn't concentrate enough. It might have worked if there had been a bit more time and effort put into it, and if someone controlled me a bit more. I was fairly uncontrollable then. Eventually I decided to go off somewhere no one would know where I was, including me."

Gordon found the anonymity he sought in the countryside of Northampton, where he moved into a 17th-century farmhouse and started a landscaping business in which he did the physical labor himself. "It's good work, it keeps you fit," he explains. He dug in the dirt by day and played music in clubs by night. That, he said, kept him out of the pubs. He shared the quiet life in his cottage with his five dogs, a few dozen ducks and geese, a horse, and a parrot named Proby. In the ancient stables he kept both a tractor and an elegant 1936 Austin Seven saloon (that's British for sedan) which he restored himself.

His interest in acting, an ambition Gordon held in his youth, was stirred when he received a call from his friend Tim Rice, lyricist of *Jesus Christ Superstar, Evita,* and other musicals. Rice had collaborated in a new theatrical production with composer Andrew Lloyd Webber, who been a classmate of Gordon's at Westminster School. At Rice's urging, Gordon tried out and won the role of "Pharaoh, The King" in the Webber-Rice musical *Joseph And The Amazing Technicolour Dreamcoat.* Gordon appeared in performances at the 1972 Edinburgh Festival, the Roundhouse, and the Young Vic Theatre in London and in 1973 at the Albery Theatre in the West End of London.

Despite laudatory reviews in which critics praised his performances as "superlative," Waller grew disenchanted after appearing in a couple of other stage musicals and three or four plays. "I didn't like acting much because you have to be there all the way through and you don't get any individual applause afterward, which is something the ego side of me used to love about music—the adoring fans."

In 1975 Gordon traveled to Australia to perform in a run of *Joseph* at the Seymour Centre in Sydney. There, through a mutual friend, he became reacquainted with Gay Robbins, a young woman he had met in Australia in 1964. Gordon and Gay were married in 1975 and settled in Sydney, where their first daughter Natalie was born the following year. Gordon took a job as an ambulance driver and controller (radio dispatch operator) with Deputy Medical Service. "It was fun and the money was great," says Gordon. The young family remained in Sydney until 1978, when they relocated to England, where Gordon set out in search of "proper employment." At the age of 33 he took a bottom-rung sales position with Rank Xerox, a British office equipment firm. During the time he worked there he and Gay celebrated the birth of their second child, Phillippa, who was born in 1980. Gordon stayed with Rank for three years, until one day in 1981 he became angry at his boss and, he says, "slung about a year's paperwork out of the 13th-floor window." Waller spent the next four years with a big Cannon office equipment distributor, where he rose to the position of sales manager before being fired.

"I got sacked from that. I got sacked from most places because I find that I lose respect for people," says Waller. "Some of these guys think they know the ins and outs of everything but they're not quite as cute as they really would like to think they are."

Recognizing the potential of emerging cellular telephone technology, Waller started a cell phone dealership in 1985, but sold out two years later as prices and profits plummeted.

Despite the fact that he was sacked from his sales job, Waller is proud of his move up the ranks to sales manager. "When I was selling office equipment, I worked myself up to a pretty powerful position. Nobody thought I would do it because I was an ex-pop star, but I said, 'Just watch.' And I think that was an achievement, because I really had to work at it. I had to work at being a little bit more polite to people, and I had to learn to control my impatient attitude. I do get very impatient. I hate being late for anything and I hate people being late for me. I do tend to lose my temper about it. Like when I'm with someone and it's quarter to seven and we've got half an hour drive and we're supposed to be there at seven, and they say, 'Oh, don't worry, everyone in California turns up late.' And I say, 'I don't give a shit about people in California being late. If I say I'm going to be somewhere at 7, and it's possible, I'm going to be there at 7.' That's just part of the stubborn Scotsman in me."

Through his wandering years, it took Gordon quite some time to find himself. But he eventually did. "Thinking back on all of the things I should have done and didn't, I should have taken myself a little more seriously instead of being the happy-go-lucky kind of guy I was. I probably would have been bored stiff, working my brains out day in and day out, but making a lot of money. I don't miss a lot of money, but I don't like being absolutely without any. I've never been without any," Gordon adds quickly.

Waller's greatest test of survival did not involve finances, but rather his battle with the bottle. He regards excess drinking as the worst mistake he's made. "I'm just about over that. I do love Guinness, but I used to drink too much bloody whiskey and it made me violent. It doesn't make me violent now; it just makes me silly and I go to sleep. I know Peter used to hate my drinking. It would make him pretty irate. Peter is a very moderate, very clever, easygoing, thoughtful person. He thinks out every move, even from the bad dream in the middle of the night. And, God bless him, we get along far better now than we did when we parted company. We get along great now. He sent me a great big bunch of balloons for my birthday, which arrived in a truck. The message just said, 'from Peter, with love.'"

The balloons arrived at the Los Angeles–area office of Steel Wallet Publishing, a small music publishing firm Waller launched in the early '90s with a business partner, longtime friend Georgiana Steele. Gordon first met Georgiana in April 1966, when she was working with the Gazzari Dancers, who appeared regularly on Dick Clark's television program *Where The Action Is*. The Steel Wallet name was inspired by a friend of Waller's, who has long referred to Gordon as "Mr. Wallet" because he always seemed to have 20 pounds in currency with him, no matter what his true financial state. "Mr. Wallet, this is your round," he'd tell Waller. Most of the songs that Steel Wallet has published were written by acquaintances of Waller's.

Although all of the hits that Peter & Gordon went on to record from 1964 to 1967 were written by other composers, the duo did write several of their B-sides and album tracks. Gordon, who had no formal musical training, composed music on the piano, which he taught himself to play. Gordon still writes songs, even though he has never learned to read or write music. "I don't actually write the notes, but I write down the chord changes. I find that with songwriting, if you can't remember the bloody thing, it probably wasn't worth doing."

In 1997, Gordon composed music for the soundtrack of *James Dean: Race With Destiny,* a motion picture about the later years of James Dean's life. The film, released in video form in 1999 under the title *James Dean: Live Fast, Die Young,* stars Casper Van Dien as James Dean, with Robert Mitchum's granddaughter Carrie Mitchum in a leading role. The late Robert Mitchum also appeared, along with Mike Connors and Connie Stevens. "There's quite a collection in the cast," says Waller. "A whole lot of old rags," he adds, smiling—"like me." To maintain authenticity, music for the film was recorded using techniques common in the 1950s. Waller packaged the motion picture music on a CD that was released in August 1999.

Even though the publishing enterprise remains modest, Waller acknowledges that he's never been at a loss for finding something to do. He has a knack for turning dabblings into dollars. He's shaped model railroad construction, a pursuit he began as a hobby, into a marketable enterprise. He keeps a workshop in the spare bedroom of his house in the Los Angeles area. The shower stall in an adjoining bathroom, equipped with an air compressor, has been converted into a paint spray booth. Soldering irons, drills, and the bits and pieces associated with metal fabrication clutter the sink area. Serious O-gauge hobbyists, lacking the patience and mechanical skills that Waller developed, have commissioned him to hand-build rolling stock for them. Although the locomotives and freight cars he builds are derived from kits, he fashions extensive modifications with exacting precision and historical accuracy.

"Wherever possible I use brass instead of plastic," said Waller. "It's a lot more solid and a lot easier to correct errors. If you make a mistake while you're soldering, you can just re-solder it back to shape. But if you make a mistake with plastic it melts away and so you have to make a new piece. It's time-consuming, but it's also very relaxing. And it requires an analytical approach in finding solutions to problems. I do like a challenge of that sort. I can sit here working for literally a whole day except for slipping out to get a cup of tea or going to the loo."

Waller says he's grateful that his show business career had little effect upon the childhood experiences of either of his daughters, Natalie and Phillippa. While he's supportive of their interests, he has not tried to influence their ambitions the way his own father urged him to pursue a career in medicine. "I have no premeditated ambitions for them. I just hope that whatever they do, they're happy at it. If they're happy with life, that's half the battle. I haven't encouraged them to go into show business because I don't know enough about it to help them. I don't think anybody really does."

Waller's father died in 1981. His mother still lives outside London and the spark of vitality that she shares with Gordon still burns within her. For her 80th birthday party in September 1997, she declared that she wanted a swimming party. "She wanted to have all of her grandchildren splashing around," Gordon explains. "She's still a very good swimmer. If we go anywhere there's a pool, she'll definitely get in. I had to stop her from jumping off my boat once."

Waller, who is at once disarmingly honest, brutally self-critical, hopeful, and pragmatic, developed something of an aversion to fame after the breakup of Peter & Gordon. "I like all the very basic things in life, which is probably why I didn't pursue the music career too damn seriously after Peter and I split up," he reasons. "I really wanted to do what I never had a chance as a teenager to do. For example, I couldn't go down to a local pub and have a couple of pints, because I'd just get lynched. People would say, 'Are you looking at my girlfriend?' And I'd say, 'No, I'm not, I wouldn't bother.' And then they'd hit you because you didn't like their girlfriend."

Waller's ambition today? "To survive. Just to have enough to be going along with. It would be nice if the James Dean soundtrack CD is picked up by a recording company and perhaps if someone wants to invest in my recording another album before it's too late. But if it doesn't happen, it doesn't happen," he says.

Although Waller tends to shun the spotlight, he does occasionally perform when asked. "Whenever I sit in with a band, they say, 'You still have a fantastic voice and it's great that you're here.' I appreciate hearing that because in England, nobody gives a shit about Peter & Gordon, especially Gordon. There's no nostalgia like that. Over here, it's quite embarrassing to me because I'm just a normal person and always have been, apart from the days when I obviously had to act a little bit differently. I'm just a bloke who can play guitar and sing."

Gordon turned in one of his most stirring performances on August 15, 1998, when he sang at his own wedding. After the dissolution of his 22-year marriage to Gay, Gordon exchanged vows with his longtime friend and business partner, Georgiana Steele. As best man, Peter Asher once again stood by Gordon Waller's side during the casual backyard ceremony. Wedding guests included former Monkees member Mickey Dolenz; Spencer Davis and his keyboardist, Jim Blazer; Billy Hinsche of Dino, Desi and Billy; singer Chris Montez; former Byrds member John York; Tom MacLear, who played with the Faces and Rod Stewart; and singer-guitarist Terry Reid. Many of them, along with bassist Don Addee, lead guitarist Dave Perlman, and drummer Jovan, played long into the night.

The evening turned magical when Gordon coaxed the reserved Peter to the microphone. Together, hesitatingly at first, and then bolder, they began singing "A World Without Love." It was the first time they'd sung together in 29 years. Encouraged by the cheers of their guests, they resurrected their characteristic sweet harmonizing with a tender rendition of their 1965 hit "I Go To Pieces," and then mesmerized their guests and musical colleagues with an emotionally powerful performance of "Woman," during which Gordon gazed adoringly at his bride, Georgiana.

"Woman" is the song that for Waller epitomizes Peter & Gordon. It's also the Peter & Gordon song of which Waller remains fondest. "You can sing it without any music, you can sing it with just one guitar, you can sing it with a band, or you can sing it with a bloody orchestra. I think it envelops a lot of our other songs from that period, which were basically all love songs."

Nights In White Satin

Moody Blues/Mike Pinder

CHAPTER 6

Michael Pinder during the 1973–1974 Moody Blues world tour.

FROM THE TIME CAPSULE

FEBRUARY 1965: The first hit single by the Moody Blues, "Go Now," reaches No. 10.

- FEBRUARY 1: The Rev. Martin Luther King Jr. is among 700 African Americans arrested in Selma, Alabama, during demonstrations protesting voter registration restrictions. At age 26, Peter Jennings becomes the anchor of ABC-TV's evening news.

- FEBRUARY 15: Crooner Nat "King" Cole dies at the age of 46 from complications related to lung cancer.

- FEBRUARY 21: Black nationalist leader Malcolm X is shot to death at a rally at the Audubon Ballroom in New York City's Harlem district.

OCTOBER 1968: Deram releases the Moody Blues' fifth hit single, "Ride My Seesaw."

- OCTOBER 7: The Motion Picture Association of America institutes the first rating system for films, which ranges from G to X.

- OCTOBER 14: Wally Schirra, Donn Fulton Eisele, and R. Walter Cunningham aboard *Apollo 7* become the first American astronauts to transmit live television signals from space.

- OCTOBER 20: Former First Lady Jacqueline Kennedy marries Greek maritime tycoon Aristotle Onassis on the island of Skorpios.

JUNE 1969: "Never Comes The Day," the last Moody Blues single to chart during the 1960s, reaches No. 91.

- JUNE 3: NBC broadcasts the last episode of the original *Star Trek* television series.

- JUNE 8: The *Smothers Brothers Comedy Hour* airs for the last time. (CBS canceled the show after Tom and Dick Smothers protested censorship of singer Joan Baez, whose husband David was about to begin a jail term for draft resistance.)

- JUNE 9: Guitarist Brian Jones leaves the Rolling Stones.

- JUNE 20–22: Jimi Hendrix, Jethro Tull, Creedence Clearwater Revival, Joe Cocker, Steppenwolf, Johnny Winter, and other performers attract 150,000 fans to the Newport '69 rock festival at Devonshire Downs in Northridge, California.

- JUNE 25: Guitarist Mick Taylor appears with the Rolling Stones for the first time.

With a clipped, upper-class accent, Mike Pinder recites the signature poem "Breathe Deep . . ." from the Moody Blues' platinum album *Days Of Future Passed*. Each of the band's seven classic albums contains a poem written by drummer Graeme Edge and recited by Pinder or Edge. "I read about 93 percent of the poems," says Pinder. "Graeme read the intro poem on the album *In Search Of The Lost Chord,* and that was his hysterical laughter, which was genuine, by the way. It just happened, it wasn't meant to happen."

First billed as an R&B combo in the days of the British invasion with their first hit "Go Now" debuting in the United States in late 1964, the Moody Blues went on to master an artful sound, blending pop and classical to create a unique genre that garnered them seven gold albums and six platinum albums.

The original Moody Blues, co-founded in early 1964 by Pinder and Ray Thomas, began its history in Birmingham, England. Pinder fondly recalls, "There was a local ballroom called the Carlton where we were rehearsing and playing. The promoter was bringing in current stars. We played on the same bill with Peter and Gordon, who had been touring with their first hit. One afternoon we were at the club rehearsing and Peter and Gordon wanted to know where they could get a bite to eat. I said, 'Why don't you come around and I'll make you an egg and bacon sandwich at my house.' So we all went to my mom's house, had bacon and egg sandwiches and tea, and had a wonderful time. We released our hit, 'Go Now' later that year. Friday, November 13, 1964, it was."

The first Moody Blues band included Pinder (keyboards and vocals) and Thomas (harmonica and vocals) with Denny Laine (guitar and vocals), Graeme Edge (drums), and Clint Warwick (bass and vocals). "Clint was his stage name. His real name is Albert, but he liked Clint Eastwood's rugged image," says Mike with a grin. "We recruited Denny Laine from a group called the Diplomats."

Pinder recalls that the name Moody Blues was inspired by several ideas. One was the fact that Mike's mother worked for a local brewery called Mitchells and Butlers Beer, also known as M&B Beer. "They owned all of the biggest hotels, pubs, and dance halls, so we thought if we named the band with the same initials, we could get a couple of thousand pounds out of M&B to buy some equipment and some outfits," he says. Another inspiration for the name was "Mood Indigo," a piece of music by Duke Ellington that Pinder recalled from his childhood. "I didn't find the tune memorable, but the name stuck with me. I chose Blues because we were playing blues and Moody because of my interest in the mood-changing power of music. So that left the word "Indigo," which I used when I bought a ranch in Malibu in 1975—I called it 'Indigo Ranch.'"

The Moody Blues performed in R&B clubs throughout England, backing blues performers such as Sonny Boy Williamson. "You could grab a handful out of the 20 or so R&B bands that were really happening in England in 1964." Less than six months after their formation, the Moody Blues recorded their first single, "Steal Your Heart Away." Released in September 1964, the song attracted little attention. But when "Go Now," a Bessy Banks song launched two months later, made it to No. 1 on the British charts and No. 10 in America, the band suddenly found itself in demand and on the road with Chuck Berry touring England.

Before "Go Now" climbed the charts, the Moody Blues rented the Richmond Athletic Club in London on Thursday nights and hosted their own dances. "On Tuesday nights the Rolling Stones did the same thing," says Pinder. "Another club, called the Bag O' Nails, was considered a rock musicians' social club because everyone would meet there after recording sessions—the Beatles, the Stones, Jimmy Hendrix. So there was a lot of camaraderie and interaction among the groups."

While the success of "Go Now" propelled the band into the limelight, the band's next singles were not as well received. "From The Bottom Of My Heart," released in May 1965, reached only No. 93 on the *Billboard* Hot 100. The Moodys took nearly a year to chart again, just making the Hot 100 with "Stop!" With that poor showing it appeared that the band's musical output had come to a stop as well, but in fact the Moody Blues were quietly engaged in one of the most intensely creative projects in pop music history. Following the replacement of Laine and Warwick by John Lodge and Justin Hayward in 1966, the Moody Blues were selected by Deram Records to perform the proposed rock version of Dvorak's *New World Symphony* with the London Festival Orchestra. The record company wanted to produce a long-playing record to launch its new "Deramic Stereo" sound. Instead, the band submitted its own material, a rock opera depicting the evolution of a day from morning into night. The staff producer, Tony Clarke, agreed to use the Moody Blues' hauntingly beautiful compositions. Released with little fanfare in 1967, the musical masterwork *Days Of Future Passed* sold more than 2 million copies.

The band went on to produce six more albums, which, with *Days Of Future Passed,* make up what Moody Blues fans call the "classic seven." Titles include *In Search Of The Lost Chord* (1968) and *On The Threshold Of A Dream* (1969), released by Deram Records; and Threshold Records' *To Our Children's Children's Children* (1969), *A Question Of Balance* (1970), *Every Good Boy Deserves Favour* (1971), and *Seventh Sojourn* (1972).

In 1974, after visiting many countries and playing for millions of fans on their World Tour, the members of the Moody Blues parted company to pursue individual recording interests, and Pinder moved to the United States. In 1978, the band reunited to produce the *Octave* album, but disagreements arose during its recording and Pinder declined to tour with the band.

"I had done what I set out to do," explains Pinder. "The group was really successful and by the time we were halfway through the eighth *(Octave)* album, I realized this wasn't meant to be anymore. I caught a vision of a new life, which was to be happily married and have children and 'return to the tribe' as I call it. And that's exactly what I've done."

Even as the Moody Blues continue to compose and perform new works today, the band is cherished most for the songs it recorded between 1964 and 1978—those days that for Mike Pinder were once future and have now passed.

HIT SINGLES BY THE MOODY BLUES WITH MIKE PINDER

DEBUT	PEAK	TITLE	LABEL
2/65	10	GO NOW	LONDON
6/65	93	FROM THE BOTTOM OF MY HEART (I LOVE YOU)	LONDON
4/66	98	STOP!	LONDON
7/68	24	TUESDAY AFTERNOON (FOREVER AFTERNOON)	DERAM
10/68	61	RIDE MY SEE-SAW	DERAM
6/69	91	NEVER COMES THE DAY	DERAM
5/70	21	QUESTION	THRESHOLD
8/71	23	THE STORY IN YOUR EYES	THRESHOLD
4/72	29	ISN'T LIFE STRANGE	THRESHOLD
8/72	2	NIGHTS IN WHITE SATIN (Certified Gold)	DERAM
2/73	12	I'M JUST A SINGER (IN A ROCK AND ROLL BAND)	THRESHOLD
7/78	39	STEPPIN' IN A SLIDE ZONE	LONDON
11/78	59	DRIFTWOOD	LONDON

THEN AND NOW
MIKE PINDER

The poem inside Mike Pinder's first children's story CD, *A Planet With One Mind,* reads:

> Stories and music I heard as a child set me
>   on a path to follow.
> A path of peace, a path of truth, away from
>   fear and sorrow.
> Now my turn has come to scatter good
>   seeds in the meadow.

Michael Pinder in his home studio in the 1990s. PHOTO BY TARA PINDER.

That philosophy, which Mike adheres to today, was also a guiding principle for him throughout the years when the Moody Blues were making their classic albums.

Born December 27, 1941, Mike doesn't remember seeing his father until he was 4 years old. He recalls his mother saying, 'Come in, I want you to meet someone. This is your dad.'" His father, who had served in the British Army, had spent much of his time in France until 1945. Mike fondly recalls VE (Victory in Europe) Day. His family was living in a middle-class housing area in the outskirts of Birmingham. All of the neighbors set out tables draped with white sheets in the middle of the street as well as all of the food and drink that they had been saving during wartime. Mike's parents brought out their upright piano, which his father played, and people danced and partied in the streets all night long. "I was four and a half maybe, and I can see it right now as I speak to you. It made such an impression on me. And then they cleared away all of the tables, went into their houses, and never partied with each other again."

Mike says that the events he experienced as a young child set him on a path that influenced his career as well as his lifestyle. "I listened to the radio a lot and when I was about 5 years old, I heard a song by Jimmy Durante, called 'The Man Who Found the Lost Chord.' I remembered that story 23 years later, after the band's hit album *Days Of Future Passed,* and I coaxed them into calling the next album *In Search Of The Lost Chord.* So you can see that what happened to me as a child had a big effect on my entire life."

Mike followed in his father's footsteps, serving in the Royal Army Service Corps in Germany from 1960 to 1962. "My uncles and my father would tell all of these romantic stories of being in New Delhi, India, and making catapults and actually firing peanuts at the baboons' bottoms that were on the Caliph's castle walls. They talked about throwing a big chunk of meat secured to a meathook on a rope into a river and four guys getting the skin burned off their hands because the fish were so big. We tend to exaggerate the best stories," he says with a chuckle.

The youngest of four children, Mike has an older brother who is retired and living outside of Sydney, Australia, and his two sisters live in England. "My brother was involved a little bit in music but didn't take it beyond the amateur groups that we put together as kids. Together we had a skiffle group that we called the Checkers, which was the first band that I was in."

When Mike was 3 years old, his mother trusted him to open the bottom of the piano and observe the inner workings while pushing down the keys. He would carefully place his hand over the top of the keyboard and play notes and then touch the strings with his fingers. "I realized the lower the note, the slower the vibration of the string. The higher the note the faster the vibration. This was my introduction to science and philosophy."

Although he took a few piano lessons, Mike plays "by ear" and doesn't read music. "People who don't read music wish they could, and people who do read music wish maybe they didn't because it narrows your creative focus," he explains. "Taking the course I did forced me to develop a style of my own, which I may not have done had I taken the academic approach. So I'm rather grateful for that. Even though I can't play wonderful scales, I've developed something that was perfect for me. The music that I create is like a landscape painting—it is visual music."

After completing the required general education in England, 15-year-old Mike decided he'd rather perform music than go on to technical school. From the age of 12 he had been playing piano in the pubs. "My dad played piano down at the big pub that my mother was managing and when he wanted a break, he'd sneak me in and everybody knew about it, and I would play for about 20 minutes. Then he'd take over again. I'd invariably end up with a big pint glass full of coins, and I'd come home with a tidy jug of money."

Mike's father also drove a tour bus on weekends and evenings, escorting tourists to pubs located in remote towns in the scenic English countryside, usually near a river. "The kids would come along and they would have their lemonade and crisps while their parents enjoyed pub specialties. Consequently, there was a piano there and my dad and I would play there, too."

When the Checkers broke up, Mike formed a second band, the Rocking Tuxedos, whose members achieved considerable local notoriety based, in part, on their immaculate attire: white dinner jackets with black satin lapels. The band played mainly Buddy Holly music, which Mike claims had the greatest influence on him. "I liked Elvis in the 'All Shook Up' days, but I weaned myself from him as soon as he started doing country music, as did Tom Jones. I knew Tom because his first hit record was No. 1 [on the U.K. chart] when the Moody Blues came out with "Go Now," which knocked his hit off the top. We were No. 1 for two weeks until a record by the England football team, which had won the World Cup, knocked us off the top. We were knocked off by a bloody football team," he laughs.

After disbanding the Rocking Tuxedos, Mike and Ray Thomas formed a short-lived band called the Krew Kats, which toured Germany for a couple of months. Penniless at the end of the poorly paid tour, Pinder and Thomas struggled to get enough money to return to England. When Mike returned home in 1963, he was searching the newspaper classified ads to find a job when he noticed an ad that read, "Wanted: someone with musical and electronic experience." Intrigued by the prospect, Mike interviewed with a company called Streetly Electronics and got the job. His father's hobby had been electronics. "I grew up with the smell of what Americans call 'SAH-der' and the British call 'SOUL-der,' says Mike, with proper British enunciation. "At Streetly Electronics I was introduced to this machine, and the moment I saw it, I thought, 'This is destiny to me.' It was almost like I knew it was there for me to discover and to use."

The "machine" that Pinder was introduced to was the Mellotron, a tape replay keyboard that produced a warm, haunting, orchestral sound that was to elevate the Moody Blues to unprecedented heights of creativity and musical imagery, distinguishing *Days Of Future Passed* and subsequent work. "The Mellotron is actually a mechanical device, a playback tape recorder with 70 heads and 70 pieces of tape on a giant pinch roller. When you press down a key, you're literally playing a tape recorder," says Pinder. Mike spent a few days in each department at Streetly Electronics, learning all he could about this magnificent new instrument— observing production of the recording heads, the electronics, and the mechanical parts. Soon he was named quality control inspector. "My job was to play the Mellotron to make sure that each machine worked perfectly and that all the tapes were timed correctly." For Mike, landing this job was much like someone who loves ice cream getting a job as ice cream taster.

The experience solidified a philosophy that he recommends to all of the children and adults with whom he comes into contact. "Follow your bliss," he says, pointing to a T-shirt inscribed with his favorite saying by mythologist and author Joseph Campbell. "When you're on the path you're supposed to be on, then all things will come to you. Being who you're supposed to be and not somebody else. That's something that I've always followed."

Mike's introduction to the Mellotron paved the way for the beginning of a successful professional music career, incorporating the unique sound of this versatile new instrument. Mike stayed at Streetly Electronics for about 18 months before leaving to form the Moody Blues.

After seven years of working as a collaborative member of the Moody Blues, Mike got his first taste of individual acclaim in 1971, when the Four Tops recorded his song "A Simple Game." The song became a hit on both sides of the Atlantic. "Motown's box set calls the song 'Maybe the most adult music ever to grace the pop chart,'" says Pinder. He received the Ivor Novello Award for Social Comment for "A Simple Game," and proudly displays the bronze plaque on his desk.

Following a smashingly successful music career with the Moody Blues, Mike began to settle down and bought a piece of property in 1975 overlooking Zuma Beach on the Pacific Coast, west of Malibu. A vacant octagonal Lutheran church sat on the property, and he intended to convert it into an audiovisual workshop to make music videos. But the studio never came about. "That's when I met my wife, Tara Grant, in the summer of 1977. I never actually set up the studio, I just had plans for it." Mike had been previously married to an American woman, the mother of his oldest son, Daniel (born in 1971), but the couple divorced after moving to the United States.

Mike and Tara were married in 1978, moved to Hawaii, and had two sons, Michael (born in 1979) and Matthew (born in 1980). "I became Mr. Mom," says Pinder. "We were in Hawaii for four years but as much as we liked it there, we weren't making friends and in a year or two the children would be going into kindergarten. It was very strange being in the minority on the islands. So we came to Northern California to visit Tara's father. It was November and cold, and the leaves had fallen off the trees. It was the Englishman in me that liked it, so we moved here."

Tara is a real estate agent, although, says Mike, "She took a hiatus for a couple of years in 1994 to help me form my record company, One Step Records, of which she's the CEO." The same year Mike produced his first solo album since *The Promise* (1976) and his departure from the Moody Blues. In *Among The Stars,* Pinder captures the elegance of the Moody Blues' "classic" period of the early '70s. "I hope to make the music, lyrics, and the songs I write make people think. They're not your typical let's get down, let's have fun, shake your booty—that sort of thing. Everybody was doing that and I wanted to do something different. *Among The Stars* is very much in the Moody vein. In the title track is a poem that I wrote."

The name of Mike's production company, One Step Records, was derived from the last song he wrote and performed with the Moody Blues on the *Octave* album. "It's called 'One Step Into The Light,' which was very apt because it was all about humanity taking a step further in our destiny. It's all based on higher consciousness, good principals and good values, without involving the dogma of religion."

Inspired by children's storybooks promoting universal ideas of peace, love, and tolerance, in 1995 Mike released his first album of multicultural children's stories accompanied by music and sound effects. The collection of whimsical tales, called *A Planet With One Mind,* was followed in 1996 by *A People With One Heart* and *An Earth With One Spirit.* He calls the trilogy "One Mind, One Heart, One Spirit." Each CD contains seven stories—one for each night of the week.

"They're all mythological, cosmic stories with wonderful morals," explains Mike. "All of the stories are spiritually uplifting and for everyone aged 4 to 104." Mike travels throughout the country promoting his storybook albums in bookstores and record stores. "When I talk to children and parents, I tell them that I'm a living example of how the events you experience as a child set the pattern for your life. When, as a child at the end of World War II, I saw humanity dancing in the streets, I had a glimpse of something that not too many people were privy to. I had an experience that was soul-shattering. It was an awakening. When you see people doing that, you see the best of humanity and then it goes away. We all have our share to do and we can only teach by example," asserts Pinder.

Mike enjoys meeting people who have been touched by his music. One woman he met at an autograph session rolled up her sleeve to reveal a very large surgical scar and she said to Mike, "I've been using your music for pain for 25 years." A young black man said, "When I heard your line in the song 'One Step Into The Light' that says, 'Find the mission in your life and start to be,' I went out and became a schoolteacher." Mike receives numerous cards, letters, and e-mail messages from people who tell him how his music has enriched and brought focus to their lives. He calls them his "Hall of Fame."

Mike thinks of himself as a fair, well-balanced human being. He explains, "My story is like all of the mythical stories in which the hero goes out in search of something and he sees this magical bird or animal, which he follows to this wonderful place, where he gains knowledge and wisdom. He then goes back to the tribe and shares all of his wisdom and knowledge with the villagers. I experienced and had all of the things I could possibly want and all of the experiences money can buy, and I came back to what really is what I consider to be the most valuable thing in life—raising a family. Having children is the greatest test that any human being can take, without a doubt."

John Lennon was a friend and inspiration to Mike. "I still haven't gotten over the fact that John's not here anymore," says Pinder. "Some of the things that he said and wrote pointed the way and not too many people see it. We're always hearing 'Imagine' but no one really hears the words anymore—Imagine there's no religion. . . . Imagine that we're all one and that we're connected instead of being separated by people's war gods. John said, 'I don't believe in anything except Yoko and me.' All that we need to believe in is ourselves. You don't have to believe in someone else's ideas.

"I have to go to Scripture to make these points. For instance, 'Know thyself.' That means to go within yourself. To know and understand how you work. What makes you emotional? What makes you think? Are they your thoughts, or are you just entertaining them? What makes you tick? Because when you find out what makes you tick, then you find out what makes everyone else tick. Then there's 'Love your neighbor as yourself.' How can you love your neighbor? He or she might be a real jerk. But it's not saying love the character of your neighbor. Love the fact that your neighbor has the same life force within as the life force in you. There's only one life force. People tend to call it God. A personification of something that's a reality. It's within us all. Why are we looking outside of ourselves when the answers are within ourselves? Where is the kingdom of Heaven? The kingdom of Heaven is within you. Location, location, location! All the world's Scriptures contain this same message."

Starting in the '60s, Mike studied all of the religions of the world and read numerous books about physics and philosophy, including works by Stephen Hawkings. In 1968 during the In Search Of The Lost Chord tour, the Moody Blues played at Cambridge University in England. Peter Russell, a well-known author and physicist, and Stephen Hawkings were students at Cambridge at the time. Russell had operated the lights for that particular concert. "Peter and I have since met and become friends. He was influenced by what I was doing musically and lyrically back then, and now it's come full circle, because I read his book *The White Hole In Time* and became interested in his theory about the similarity of the life and death of suns and humanity's possible future."

In the mid-1980s Polygram produced a Moody Blues retrospective videotape called *Legend Of A Band,* which implied that Pinder had left the band because he couldn't handle exposure in front of audiences and had experienced a nervous breakdown. "Funny thing is that I was the one who would invite people backstage, and I was the guy who announced all of the songs, who talked to the audience and recited the poetry," says Pinder. "It's also very interesting that since I left the band, they now have security guards wherever they go—at their hotel, at their shows, backstage. I go out and walk around, and no one knows who I am. So I'm the only free person out of the bunch of us."

Pinder also noted that an encyclopedia of rock produced in the late 1990s repeated the assertion originated in the video that he had to leave the band due to a nervous breakdown. But, he says, "I'm the kind of person who couldn't have a nervous breakdown. I suppose it was difficult for the band to understand that I could walk away from them. They must have thought I was nuts!"

Mike's hopes for his children are their achievement of fulfillment. "If they can attain even half of what I feel I have attained in terms of happiness and achievement, then they will be very happy people." Mike's oldest son, Dan, is a bass player and has his sights on becoming a record producer. Middle son Mike plays rock and jazz guitar and enjoys philosophy. "I said to him, 'If you can find the music in the philosophy and the philosophy in the music, you've got it made, kid.' He's just like me. He said he knew when he was 8 years old that he wanted to play music. Youngest son Matt is also a bass player, so I guess I'm still the keyboard kid in this family. I never overexposed the boys to music. I just put a guitar in the corner of their bedroom, but I never pushed them into anything." The boys learned of their father's fame only after others told them.

"My younger sons didn't know what my career was until they were about 7 or 8 years old. They came home from school one day and said, 'Dad, the parents of my friends at school said that you were in a big rock band. Is that true?' I said, 'Yes. Come with me' and we went into the storage room and opened up some boxes, and I pulled out a bunch of gold and platinum discs. They chose the single gold disc from *Nights In White Satin* to put up on their wall. It was interesting because we had all those wonderful years together while I was Mr. Mom without show business affecting it. I was just Dad. So pulling down the pedestal has been personally satisfying and one of my greatest achievements."

Laugh, Laugh

CHAPTER 7

The Beau Brummels

FROM THE TIME CAPSULE

JULY 1965: Autumn Records releases "You Tell Me Why," the Beau Brummels' third hit single of the year.

- JULY 10: "(I Can't Get No) Satisfaction" becomes the Rolling Stones' first No. 1 hit, ahead of the Four Tops' "I Can't Help Myself (Sugar Pie Honey Bunch)," The Byrds' "Mr. Tambourine Man," Herman's Hermits' "Wonderful World," and Sam the Sham and the Pharaohs' "Wooly Bully."

- JULY 15: U.S. scientists display the first images ever taken by a planetary spacecraft: 22 shots of the surface of Mars photographed the day before by *Mariner IV,* 228 days after it was launched.

- JULY 25: Folk aficionados boo Bob Dylan when he performs on stage at the Newport Folk Festival with amplified accompaniment.

OCTOBER 1965: "Don't Talk To Strangers" reaches No. 52 on the pop charts.

- OCTOBER 4: The Soviet Union launches *Luna 7,* which crashes on the moon. Pope Paul VI addresses the United Nations in New York City, becoming the first Pope to visit the Western Hemisphere (and the first Pope in 150 years to venture outside of Italy).

- OCTOBER 6: The Supremes' "I Hear A Symphony" becomes the sixth of their 1960s tunes to reach the top spot on the pop chart. (The Supremes' total for the decade, 12 No. 1 singles, was surpassed only by the Beatles.)

JUNE 1966: The last Beau Brummels single to chart, "One Too Many Mornings," stalls at No. 95.

- JUNE 5: On the *Gemini 9* mission, American astronaut Eugene A. Cernan takes a record two-hour walk in space.

- JUNE 5: The *Ed Sullivan Show* broadcasts what are arguably the first music videos—motion picture shorts produced by the Beatles to accompany their recordings "Paperback Writer" and "Rain."

- JUNE 11: In San Francisco's Avalon Ballroom, jazz singer Janis Joplin performs on stage with Big Brother and the Holding Company for the first time.

- JUNE 29: American warplanes begin bombing the Hanoi area of North Vietnam.

OPPOSITE: The Beau Brummels in 1965. Left to right, seated in rear: drummer John Petersen and bassist Ron Meagher; standing at left: singer-guitarist Declan Mulligan; seated at right front: composer-guitarist Ron Elliott and singer Sal Valentino (wearing derby). PHOTO BY DICK GILFETHER.

Among American bands of the mid-'60s, the Beau Brummels stood out not only for their melodic hit singles and critically acclaimed albums, but also for the musical trends they pioneered. No city made a more indelible impression on the music of the 1960s than San Francisco. While Jefferson Airplane, the Grateful Dead, We Five, Moby Grape, Quicksilver Messenger Service, Country Joe and the Fish, and other bands solidified the San Francisco sound, the Beau Brummels were responsible for first bringing national attention to the Bay Area music scene of that era.

Contrasting dramatically with many of the chirpy pop tunes of the day, the early releases by the Beau Brummels were rich in texture, with elaborate harmonies and complex arrangements. At the close of the decade, the Brummels, whose music had already contributed to the emergence of folk-rock and presaged the era of psychedelia, fused modern country and rock in a style later echoed by such artists as the Byrds, Bob Dylan, Linda Ronstadt, and the Eagles.

Consisting of vocalist Sal Valentino, composer-guitarist Ron Elliott, Irish-born singer-guitarist Declan Mulligan, bassist Ron Meagher, and drummer John Petersen, the Beau Brummels were a product of San Francisco's eclectic North Beach district. While playing in a bar called the Morocco Room in San Mateo on the peninsula 15 miles south of San Francisco, the Beau Brummels were discovered in 1964 by legendary KYA radio disc jockeys Tom Donahue and Bob Mitchell, partners in the fledgling Autumn Records label. Autumn's staff producer was Sylvester Stewart, a DJ for R&B station KSOL, who later became better known with his own group as Sly and the Family Stone. Looking much like Orson Welles, the bearded Donahue had a voice like distant thunder—booming and somehow soothing at the same time. He had a finely tuned sense for musical talent, and he liked what he heard the first time he saw the Beau Brummels play.

Composer Ron Elliott was the architect of the musical repertoire of the Beau Brummels. Ron's love of light opera and show tunes undoubtedly contributed to the admiration he felt the first time he heard Sal Valentino sing. Like Ron, Sal lived with his family in a North Beach apartment building. Although Sal's junior by two years, Ron attended the same parochial grade school and knew that Sal went to the basement of his building every day after school to sing. "I remember the first time I heard him sing 'Summertime,' I almost fell off my chair because he had a beautiful voice. He didn't have control of it yet, so he would hit a note by sliding up to it. He would sing 'summertiiiiiiiiime' and he'd finally get up there," Elliott fondly recalls. Ron and Sal, who had been singing with other groups, began singing together. And Ron shared with Sal his theories about music. "When Sal listened to advice from other people, he started sounding like Bob Dylan," Elliott asserts. "But when he listened to me, he sang very well because he has a wonderful voice."

Sal shared with Ron an affinity for country music. "Ron was the best guitar player I'd ever heard, and even though he liked country music, too, he was already writing light opera and musicals." The two began performing together at benefits for the local boys' club and for the grammar school they had attended. With Ron strumming and Sal singing, they began to perform at weddings, dances, and other social events. "I just enjoyed singing. But Ron was serious, probably the most serious of all of us. He wanted to do music, and he was a gifted writer. And still is."

Although Ron attended St. Ignatius High School while Sal went to Sacred Heart, they continued to hang out and perform together periodically. During that time Ron remained consumed by his interest in composing, and during his teenage years he wrote several unpublished musical theater and light opera scores. He developed his compositions on the guitar, and as he did he became increasingly proficient on the instrument even though that was not his intention. "Everyone considered me a guitar player, but I was a songwriter who happened to play guitar. That's how I saw myself," says Elliott flatly. "I would have learned piano if we had room for a piano, but you do with what you've got."

Ron was a student at San Francisco State College in the fall of 1963 when he, Sal, and drummer John Petersen began playing gigs together informally. It was at one such performance that they met another singer, Declan Mulligan, at the Irish Cultural Center. Sal, John, and Ron had begun rehearsing with Dec Mulligan and a bass player named Ron Meeker. Although Meeker didn't fit well with the band, his ultimate replacement was a guy with a nearly identical name: Ron Meagher. Through Kay Dane, the girl he was dating, Elliott was introduced to Meagher, who had been a high school classmate of Kay's. "And that's how we put the Brummels together," says Elliott.

Sal is uncertain which member of the quintet suggested the name. But it's likely the inspiration derived from the Beau Brummell Barber Shop in North Beach rather than from early 19th-century British gentleman George Bryan "Beau" Brummell, known for his dapper style of dress. "I didn't know who Beau Brummell was at that time, and I don't think the other guys did, either," Sal grins.

The Brummels' first booking was at a North Beach joint called El Cid, where Sal had previously sung as a soloist. They played there until the club owner learned that Ron Elliott was underage. But word about the band had reached Rich Romanello, owner of the Morocco Room in suburban San Mateo, where the regulatory environment was more relaxed. Billed as the house band at the Morocco Room in the spring of 1964, the Brummels were booked to play each Thursday, Friday, and Saturday night, at $40 per night apiece. Acting as the band's self-appointed manager, Romanello persuaded a rep from Warner Brothers Records to audition the Brummels. They recorded four demo tracks, but the label declined to offer a contract.

While the Brummels were playing the North Beach clubs, Tom Donahue and Bob Mitchell had already become expert in scouting rock music talent. After getting their feet wet conducting record hops, they began staging larger shows in San Francisco's Cow Palace Auditorium, using the profits from those shows to finance Autumn Records. The new label scored a hit with its second release, "C'mon And Swim" by Bobby Freeman, which climbed to No. 5 on the *Billboard* chart in the summer of 1964.

Then Donahue and Mitchell dropped into the Morocco Room. They'd been invited by Romanello and his girlfriend, a nude model named Judy who called herself Judette the Nudette. "She's now a preacher," says John Petersen. When Donahue and Mitchell appeared at the Morocco Room, they were far more serious than were the band members. "Those guys were players. But we were only 18 years old and we didn't care. We were just having fun. It was the funniest scene I've ever seen in my life," says Petersen. "We're jamming away, playing good stuff and in walks this big guy wearing a trench coat. It was Tom Donahue, and with him were Bobby Mitchell, much smaller than Tom, and Carl Scott, who was about the same size as Donahue and is now an executive vice president at Warner Brothers. With them was Sly Stewart, who produced our first couple of albums. He was working for Autumn Records for $80 per week."

Sandwiched between the imposing Donahue and Scott, Bobby Mitchell blurted out, "Look at these guys—Tweedle Dum and Tweedle Dee."

Discovering a mutual interest in cars, Petersen and Mitchell immediately hit it off. "It was 1964 and the Mustang had just come out. So we signed a contract and never made one penny of royalties. Not one cent."

Touring, however, was profitable for Petersen and the other band members. "After a concert tour, we would come home with our preapproved money as well as with gate receipts," Petersen explains. "In those days it probably cost $6 or $7 to get into a concert. We'd each get paid a briefcase full of $1 bills, because that's what the gate took in." Other funds were channeled to pay for the band's per diem expenses, including travel costs, overnight accommodations, and meals. "A lot of that money I never saw. But it sure was fun to get a load of $1 bills, and I bought my parents new furniture and a color TV. I bought myself a 1965 Pontiac Grand Prix. Two-door, hardtop, black leather, navy blue. Everyone bought a car but Sal. He didn't drive. He sort of just hitched a ride. That's Sal. He wasn't into possessions. He's very unpretentious."

Once the Brummels signed with Autumn, their transformation from house band obscurity to national pop stardom occurred with blurring speed. "Laugh, Laugh," their first recording released on Autumn Records, hit the *Billboard* Hot 100 in January 1965 and peaked at No. 15. Their follow-up release, "Just A Little," did even better, reaching No. 8 on the national chart in May of the same year. Their third release, "You Tell Me Why," reached No. 38 that August. The popularity of the Brummels persuaded many radio stations to play the B-sides of their records, including the rousing "Still In Love With You Baby." Other tracks that added to the band's popularity included "Ain't That Lovin' You Baby," "Sad Little Girl," and "Don't Talk To Strangers."

Even before they had a chance to define themselves, they were propelled into the high-profile role of pop style-setters, viewed as one of the first legitimate American challenges to the British pop music invasion. And if composer Ron Elliott was the musical architect of the project, Autumn recording session producer Sly Stone was the general contractor. Sal remembers: "None of us had really wanted to grow up to be rock stars. I wasn't that kind of guy, and neither were the others. We were kind of quiet, and in the recording studio we tried to play and sing as perfectly as we could. Sly was a great help to us because he was loose. He was like a cheerleader who helped loosen us up and get our energy going."

Among the individuals contributing to the success of "Laugh, Laugh" was the late Sonny Bono, who as an independent record promotion man helped generate airplay for the record. The Brummels appeared on stage with Bono as he and Cher launched their own meteoric recording careers. "They appeared with us at the Cow Palace, dressed like prehistoric people. Sonny was a funny guy," Sal fondly recalls.

Donahue and Mitchell deliberately kept from putting the Brummels on tour until "Laugh, Laugh" was a solid national hit. And then they hit the road. "The first place we performed in concert was the Sacramento Memorial Auditorium. We were on the bill with Gary Lewis and the Playboys, who were on the charts with 'This Diamond Ring,' and we closed the show," recalled Sal. The Memorial Auditorium became a favorite stop for the Brummels, who played there several more times with other groups, including the Beach Boys.

In May 1965 the Brummels made a triumphant return to the Bay Area, appearing in a KYA-sponsored concert with the Rolling Stones, the Byrds, Paul Revere and the Raiders, and the Vejtables at San Francisco Civic Auditorium. They played the Cow Palace in the San Francisco suburb of Daly City, the Whisky à Go Go in Hollywood, and on a Murray the K bill at the Brooklyn Fox. "We did a show at the Fox with the Lovin' Spoonful, Marvin Gaye, Martha and the Vandellas, Brenda Holloway, the Temptations, the Four Tops, Stevie Wonder, and Patti LaBelle, who opened the show. Patti LaBelle took the house down every day. Just killed 'em. And the girls went crazy for Marvin. We did all right, too." The Brummels made television appearances on *Action!* and *American Bandstand.* "Dick Clark was special. He either really remembered our names, or he always did his homework," said Sal. "He knew what we were doing, and it was always nice to appear on his show." The Brummels also appeared on *Hullaballoo, The Mike Douglas Show,* and *Shindig.* But touring also aggravated tensions within the band, leading to the departure of Dec Mulligan by the fall of 1965. With Ron Elliott unable to withstand the rigors of the road, Don Irving substituted, leaving only three original members on tour.

The Brummels excelled in the studio, releasing two fine albums on Autumn— *Introducing the Beau Brummels* and *Beau Brummels Vol. 2.* They recorded a third, but before its release the financially struggling label shuttered its doors and sold the band's contract to Warner Brothers Records in 1966 along with the Mojo Men, the Vejtables, and the Tikis, who would subsequently find success as Harpers Bizarre.

Since the Warner deal did not include master tapes, the Los Angeles–based label immediately sent the band into the studio, where they recorded *Beau Brummels '66,* a fairly uninspired album of covers of other musicians' hit songs. Label executives came to their senses in 1967, and working with Warner Brothers producer Lenny Waronker, the band recorded *Triangle,* an album of original material. The Brummels' last LP for Warner Brothers, *Bradley's Barn,* was an acoustic country rock album. It was recorded at Nashville's legendary studio of the same name, and Norbert Putnam, who went on to become a highly successful producer of folk and country rock, was one of the session musicians. Both albums were highly regarded by those who knew music but received little supportive airplay. "*Triangle* came out just before the Beatles' *Sgt. Pepper* was released, and once that hit the air, nobody heard anything else," says Sal Valentino.

In 1968, not long after making *Bradley's Barn,* the group split up. They reassembled briefly in 1975 to record a reunion album, *Beau Brummels,* but the original chemistry that ignited the Brummels in 1964 had become inert.

As they went their separate ways to pursue new careers, Ron Elliott, Sal Valentino, John Petersen, Ron Meagher, and Declan Mulligan left behind a timeless body of work rich in lyrical substance, technical virtuosity, and artistic depth.

HIT SINGLES BY THE BEAU BRUMMELS

DEBUT	PEAK	TITLE	LABEL
1/65	15	LAUGH, LAUGH / STILL IN LOVE WITH YOU BABY	AUTUMN
4/65	8	JUST A LITTLE	AUTUMN
7/65	38	YOU TELL ME WHY	AUTUMN
10/65	52	DON'T TALK TO STRANGERS	AUTUMN
12/65	97	GOOD TIME MUSIC	AUTUMN
6/66	95	ONE TOO MANY MORNINGS	WARNER BROTHERS

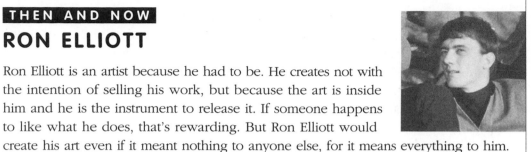

RON ELLIOTT

Ron Elliott is an artist because he had to be. He creates not with the intention of selling his work, but because the art is inside him and he is the instrument to release it. If someone happens to like what he does, that's rewarding. But Ron Elliott would create his art even if it meant nothing to anyone else, for it means everything to him.

Elliott, onetime composer, guitarist, and musical architect, is now a graphic artist working in acrylics, photography, and computer imaging. Elliott has considered himself an artist since a vision came to him at age 10. "That's when the music just started coming out of me. I had to write it, and I learned how to play guitar just so I could get my melodies out. Right then I knew I was an artist and would remain an artist for the rest of my life, no matter what. And that's what I've done.

"I've gone from music to a few years of painting to graphic arts. I haven't thrived but I haven't starved either. I'm one of the wealthiest people I know because I've done only what I was supposed to do, and I'm really happy. I don't regret being unable to write music anymore. When the music was in me, that's what I did. Strangely enough, when I was 10 years old, I saw a vision of what my life was going to be like. I knew I'd have a taste of success at a young age. And I knew that in the long run, in the end, if I pursued this self-premonition, I'd be recognized maybe even after my death."

Seated in one of his favorite restaurants on Clement Street, Ron Elliott speaks softly and deliberately, seemingly composing each thought before the words leave his lips. He is wearing a tan canvas photographer's vest and trademark wide-brimmed fedora, a likeness of which graces his business card. At his side is a thick travel case

which holds the two things that most dominate his life today: his portfolio of magnificent florals and landscape art, and the equipment and medications he needs to monitor and control his diabetes. He enjoys a life of quiet introspection amid the bustle of San Francisco, the city he's called home since childhood, savoring the anonymity that he was denied during his years as a reluctant pop star.

The only child of Charles and Lola Elliott, Ron was born in October 1944 and spent the first five years of his life on his family's ranch 70 miles north of San Francisco, in the rural Sonoma County town of Healdsburg. But two years of devastating drought

PHOTO BY EXPRESSLY PORTRAITS.

in the land irrigated by the Russian River destroyed Charles and Lola financially, and they moved to San Francisco in search of employment to pay off their debts. Charles learned steam engineering in the merchant marine, found employment with the PG&E (Pacific Gas and Electric) utility company, and ultimately erased all his debts.

Charles, who played drums, and Lola, who played accordion, contributed in large degree to Ron's interest in music. For their own enjoyment, they'd play popular songs of the day with a saxophonist or clarinetist. The Elliotts enjoyed country music, and Ron's earliest musical memories are of songs performed by Lefty Frizzell, a country music Hall of Famer whose tunes stayed on the country chart for weeks on end in the early fifties.

Ron's premonition about his life of artistry preceded by two years the diagnosis of his diabetic condition. During a protracted bout with the flu at age 12, he began losing weight. "I went from 120 pounds to 90 pounds within two weeks," he remembers. Realizing that Ron had been in bed for two weeks without taking a bath, Charles went into Ron's room. "When he took my pajama top off, he gasped at how much weight I had lost, even though I had been scarfing up food. The morning I went to the hospital, I ate six eggs, six pieces of bacon, and six pieces of toast. My parents were thinking, 'He's going to be a monster.' And there I was, shrinking away. The fact that I had the premonition before I got diabetes was the only thing that kept me focused."

Ron had become an instrument for the creative forces he felt within himself. "Diabetes attacks the nervous system, attacks sensitivity, and although I did not know it then, musical time was running out and creativity would eventually fade. At the start, however, the music was just pouring out. I had to write," says Ron, who shunned pop music in favor of the theatrical stylings of Jerome Kern, Irving Berlin, Rodgers and Hammerstein, Rogers and Hart, and Cole Porter. "I probably would have had more success had I gone to New York and gone into theater, because I was more of a composer than a songwriter."

Elliott is characteristically blunt in his description of the music he wrote for the Beau Brummels. "It was simple, unsophisticated music, lots of steps backward from the music I had been composing. 'Laugh, Laugh' has a very complex chord structure, but instead of using the major seventh chords and the passing chords that I prefer, I wrote the song in flat major and minor keys using a simplified tonal structure. But you have to remember, I was coming from a theatrical rather than from a rock and roll perspective. That was all new to me and I never really did figure it all out."

For Elliott, the role of pop music raconteur was an arduous task. "I felt under pressure from beginning to end to produce and keep it together. I worked three hours before we got together for a rehearsal or recording session, I was working the whole time we were together, and I worked three hours afterward organizing, writing chord charts, and figuring out lyrics." Elliott, who says lyrics were his curse, often collaborated with Bob Durand, a high school buddy of his who had a way with words.

Performance was an even greater source of agony for Elliott, a self-professed introvert who still becomes uncomfortable in the presence of more than two people. He required several hours of mental preparation before each stage performance, after which he was emotionally drained for the remainder of the day. "I was never good at performing because I had no relationship with the crowd. I was always testing myself, wondering, 'Am I OK? What's the next song?' When things went wrong, I always had a prepared solution, so I was inner-directed the whole time. I approached music like a playwright. I didn't have to learn the lines. I knew the lines. I knew the harmonies. I had no real communication abilities, but not because I resented the audience," Elliott explains. "It was a matter of self-preservation, the result of the combination of my personality and my health condition. And that's what I had to do to survive those ordeals."

The rigors of the road proved too great for Ron. He was unable to continue touring, which compromised his health and strength, as he tried without success to maintain his strict medication and dietary regimen. "In those days people with diabetes had no glucometers to test blood sugar. It was all guesswork. That was the biggest obstacle that I ever had to face."

Even so, the dissolution of the band in 1968 proved nearly as challenging. "When Tom Donahue sold the band to Warner Brothers, he sold our tapes to someone else, and he sold the publishing elsewhere. So he figuratively cut off our heads," Elliott asserts. "When Warner Brothers discovered what they didn't have, that marked the demise of the Beau Brummels. We became a tax write-off for them."

At that point Elliott called upon a skill that he had regarded only as incidental: guitar playing. He became a studio musician in Los Angeles, where he was in high demand through the '70s and well into the '80s. He rehearsed with Barbra Streisand; worked recording sessions for Dolly Parton, Little Feat, the Everly Brothers, Van Dyke Parks, and Van Morrison; and performed on seven Randy Newman albums. He produced a melodious album by Marc McClure on Warner Brothers and an album by a group called Joyous Noise for Capitol Records. Elliott also recorded a solo album of his own called *Candlestick Maker* for Warner Brothers. "It wasn't 'get your girlfriend in bed' music. It was a suite, a picture of a person in crisis." Despite Elliott's high aspirations for the album, it received little promotion and consequently was accorded little notice.

Disillusioned, he returned to the Bay Area, where he resumed playing weekend gigs with Dec Mulligan. Something was different, but he couldn't quite put his finger on it. He knew what it was by the time he turned 50. The music had faded away. "It just wasn't there anymore," says Ron, whose guitar has remained on its stand since 1994. "I walk past it 10 times a day, and I don't even look at it. It never even occurs to me." Elliott hardly even listens to music anymore. "I listen to sports and have very little desire to hear music. When I do listen to music, it's short bits of opera, American theater, or movies from the '30s produced by MGM. I love that stuff. I wish that we could again make entertainment programs that give people hope and laughter instead of despair."

When the music died Ron's art was born. He began working in acrylics in 1994, painting interpretations of floral and landscape photographs, such as those he takes in nearby Golden Gate Park. More recently, he's begun scanning his paintings and manipulating them with image-editing software on his Macintosh computer. The resultant impressionistic artworks are hauntingly beautiful, composed in delicately hued pointillistic patterns.

Elliott learned to paint the same way he learned to compose music and play guitar: by teaching himself. A voracious reader, Ron learns what he needs to know from books. "The main lesson you learn in school is how to learn," he observes. He studied the techniques of other artists and adapted them to the moods he wanted to convey. "Those paintings are my songs," he says. They're also his progeny. Elliott, who was twice-married and twice-divorced, has no children.

Even after completing well over 100 paintings and illustrations, Elliott has not exhibited his artwork. "I'm an extreme introvert, and consequently I don't talk to many people. I need to make some contacts," he admits. "But in the art world, I know no one."

Unlike the other band members, Elliott continues to derive some income from the Beau Brummels as composer of their songs. "The Brummels didn't make squat. But I wrote the material and that's what makes money. I'll make a penny here and a penny there and by the end of the year, I have a few pennies."

Elliott believes his life would have pursued a dramatically different course if not for his diabetes. "But having it isn't that bad. As long as you watch your stuff—watch the clock, watch your diet, watch the dosages, and live a relatively boring life, you're fine." The greatest limitation it imposes, he says, is time. "I have to watch my insulin doses and my blood sugar. That's much easier now than it used to be, when it was all guesswork. Still, when you're young and your blood sugar drops, you can sense it. Now, at my age, I don't have a clue. I don't know if it's low or high. That's because of the damage that diabetes does to the nervous system. That's why I have to rely on a glucometer to measure my blood sugar level."

Though some might be tempted to call him brutally honest, Elliott is driven by pragmatism induced to large degree by management of his diabetes. "I've sold a few paintings but not because I was trying to sell them. I just try to create artwork that is very harmonious. Like a good scheduled diabetic lives his life. That's the kind of artwork I want to do."

After spending the first half of his life manipulated by the sounds in his head, Ron Elliott is now enjoying the silence. Now, at last, he is fulfilling what he believes to be his destiny. "I continually explore the art I was born to create."

THEN AND NOW
SAL VALENTINO

The first time Sal Valentino appeared in Sacramento, in early 1965, he and the Beau Brummels were welcomed by thousands of screaming, adoring fans. When he returned to the Northern California city in 1994, he came quietly and unnoticed. After years of living in Southern California, the San Francisco native rented a small apartment in Sacramento, 11 blocks from the auditorium in which the Brummels had played their first concert. The apartment, at 27th and J, was owned by a friend of his who also owned Harlow's Bar & Grill, on the ground floor of the building.

One evening Sal wandered downstairs to "air out" and enjoy the music of the live band playing there. Sal, who says he doesn't "hang well" in bars, was sitting alone when a buddy of the bar's owner walked over to him to introduce a friend. "Catherine, this is Sal Valentino," he told her. Catherine pretended she knew who Sal was. The Beau Brummels meant little to her because she was from Detroit, one of the few markets in the country in which "Laugh, Laugh" had not been a hit. Sal hummed a few bars of the song. Catherine said, "Oh, yeah." Sal smiled, but Catherine saw the look in his eyes—a look that said, She doesn't know who I am. They began talking. He learned that Catherine Kopinski was a schoolteacher, that she and her friend had just come from a wedding they had attended, and that she didn't visit bars often. Neither did Sal. She said that since her arrival from Michigan she hadn't yet seen much of California. When Sal told her he was from San Francisco, she told him she'd like to see Golden Gate Park sometime.

"You're on," he replied. They went that weekend. In March 1995, they married.

Getting Sal Valentino to take you to San Francisco would be like touring Boston with Larry Bird. Or comparable to strolling the streets of Liverpool with Ringo Starr. Like Beau Brummels composer-guitarist Ron Elliott, Valentino grew up in the colorful Italian-flavored North Beach sector of San Francisco, where he was born Salvatore Spampinato

on September 8, 1942. Although he enjoyed singing from the time he was a young child, he never thought of it as a career. Like his father before him—who had, over the years, been a Golden Gloves amateur boxer, worked professionally as a boxing trainer and ringside "cutman" treating injuries, and acted as *Racing Form* agent for Northern California tracks—Sal tried his hand at a variety of jobs.

As Sal entered his teenage years, his parents paid for lessons from a voice teacher. Sal learned

PHOTO BY AMANDA MARCH.

to sing standards—"Don't Blame Me," "It Had To Be You." Sal received a lot of support from his mother, who worked for most of her life at a San Francisco credit union, as well as from his father, whose own youthful musical ambitions had been discouraged. "My father played saxophone when he was young, but he didn't play long. My grandfather, who was a fisherman, used to complain. He'd say, 'I go out, I hear the foghorns out there. Then I come home, I hear the foghorns here, too.' So I guess my father got discouraged. He didn't tell me about that until I was almost 20."

Like his father, Sal took up baseball. A lefty, Sal played first base until high school, when he made the school's football team as a receiver. His play earned him a spot on the All-City team and scholarship offers from the University of Utah, Oregon State, and the College of the Pacific, but Sal decided he didn't want to play football. He wanted to sing. Working solo and pairing with other musicians, Sal started working gigs in the neighborhood—weddings, dances, and clubs with names like Bimbo's, LaRocca's Corner, and El Cid. He first called himself Sal Valentino in 1961 at age 19, when he cut a record called "I Wanna Twist" for a couple of local guys. (Sal's father was the one who suggested the name Valentino, in honor of heavyweight boxer Pat Valentino.) Released on the Falco label, the record earned Valentino several appearances on *Dick Stuart's Dance Party*, which aired locally on CBS television affiliate KPIX.

His success with the Beau Brummels, then, was no surprise to those who had followed his rising star in the San Francisco Bay Area. But the sale of the Beau Brummels' contract to Los Angeles–based Warner Brothers in 1966 took Sal as well as his Bay Area fans by surprise.

After the Brummels broke up, Warners brought Valentino into the studio to record some tracks produced by Waronker and Van Dyke Parks. He then turned to background singing on an album for Screamin' Jay Hawkins. Sal also worked on Ron Elliott's *Candlestick Maker* album and he discovered Rickie Lee Jones for Warner Brothers. "I took her to Lenny, and he loved her demo tape," says Sal. "I wanted to get an A&R job out of it, but I didn't."

Meanwhile, Tom Donahue had returned to radio after the sale of Autumn Records, of which he was co-owner. He devised a format that was the antithesis of frenetic, jingle-punctuated, singles-dominated top 40 radio. His free-form approach transformed little-known FM station KMPX into the nation's first "underground radio" outlet, emphasizing long album cuts and a low-key delivery. Duplicated in Southern California at Pasadena's KPPC, as well as stations in New York, Chicago, Detroit, Boston, and other markets, the format metamorphosed into "progressive rock," the precursor of the "album rock" format.

By 1971, Donahue had turned his attention to another project and Warners had cut Sal loose. "Tom Donahue came to rescue me. In fact, with only one exception, Tom got me all the record deals I've ever had," says Sal. Donahue had become involved with production of a rock music film called *Medicine Ball Caravan*, the acts in which included a power trio called Stoneground. Promotion plans called for a five-week national concert tour to launch the motion picture. Donahue added Sal and three female backup singers to strengthen Stoneground's stage presentation. "We did three concerts—in Taos, New Mexico, Boulder, Colorado, and Winnebago, Nebraska—along the way to a final performance at the Lincoln Memorial in Washington, D.C. By the time we got to D.C., Warner Brothers signed us, and that's how we became a recording act."

Donahue produced Stoneground's first album, with Sal assisting on some tracks. Released on GRT Records, the album included several compositions by Ron Elliott, who became increasingly involved in writing for the band. In 1971 Stoneground headlined at Sacramento Memorial Auditorium, the locale of numerous Beau Brummels triumphs. Sal sang, played guitar, and produced cuts not only on Stoneground's self-titled debut album in 1971, but also on the follow-up *Family Album* the following year, and on *Stoneground Three* in 1973. Upon completion of the *Stoneground Three* album Valentino left the band, resurfacing two years later in Southern California with Elliott, Mulligan, Meagher, and Petersen in a Beau Brummels reunion. The band recorded an album titled simply *Beau Brummels,* but it lacked the spark of their previous efforts. Within a year, the band members had parted for the last time. In San Francisco, Tom Donahue died at the age of 46.

The reunion was a sad counterpoint to the glory days of 1965. Valentino thinks the band was misunderstood—in 1975 as well as in 1965. "'Laugh, Laugh' is listed as one of the 500 most influential songs in the Rock and Roll Hall of Fame, but I never thought we were a rock and roll band. You know, 'Laugh, Laugh' is not like a Chuck Berry or Fats Domino or Little Richard tune. Its chord structures are based in the musicals that Elliott was writing. In '75 he wrote some real nice songs for us. We just didn't have a market anymore."

The Brummels reunion soured Sal. "I found out too much about the music business then. It broke my desire to make any more records for anybody," he says. "And then my father was diagnosed with cancer." Sal returned to Northern California to be closer to his family. And to find work. As a teenager, he'd worked as a laborer. He could always do that again. "I've had other jobs outside of music. I didn't know what I was going to do, but I knew I didn't want to wind up singing in bars."

He worked a succession of jobs, unloading freight, driving forklifts, stocking warehouse shelves. Ultimately, he heeded the call of his father, who had regained his health and was employed by the company that published the *Daily Racing Form.* Although Sal wasn't really interested in horse racing, he didn't have anything else to do at the time. "So," says Sal, "my father put me to work as a parimutuel clerk at racetracks."

For the next decade, Sal's stage was a teller window, where he took bets and cashed winning tickets. Sal was working at a betting window in the Southern California coastal town of Ventura in 1993 when he bent down to pick up a $20 bill. A paralyzing pain seized his back, and he was unable to move. Sal was forced to go out on disability with a herniated disc in his lower spine. Sal once again was the victim of circumstances beyond his control. For the first time in 15 years, he thought about resurrecting his singing career. He considered singing jingles for commercials. "I was getting tired of the voices I was hearing on commercials, with the exception of Bob Seger [lead singer for the Silver Bullet Band]," he says. Still living in Los Angeles, he began practicing, using his tape recorder at home, but was unsuccessful in landing any assignments.

While the advertising agencies didn't call him, a member of a band in Reno did in early 1994. The caller had named his band the Beau Brummels, and he hoped to include at least one member of the original Brummels. Sal agreed, but didn't move to Reno, instead relocating 120 miles away in Sacramento because of friends and fond memories there. Valentino performed with the Reno Brummels for about a year, until concert producer Donnie Brooks called. Brooks, a singer who hit the top 10 with "Mission Bell" and "Doll House" in 1960, packages oldies shows on which he also performs. Sal did shows for Donnie in 1995 and 1996, resurrecting "Laugh, Laugh" and "Just A Little" for appreciative fans and starring for three months in "Juke Box Giants," a Brooks-produced review at the Flamingo Hotel in Laughlin, Nevada's newest gaming and entertainment town.

Gradually, Sal became interested in performing new material. He readily credits Ron Elliott as a pivotal musical influence in his life. "I'm fortunate I had Ron writing songs for me. That made a big difference. I didn't fully realize that until after I worked with others." With that realization, he's begun gaining new confidence in himself, and he's now considering recording a solo album and singing songs that he has composed. "I've never done a solo. I never thought I was good enough, to tell you the truth. But now I believe I should," says Sal with conviction.

Catherine and Sal now live in their own home in a Sacramento suburb. "This is the first time I've ever had a house, and I like it. My family is happy that I'm married and have a nice wife. So things are good." Sal's father died in 1985, but his mother remains in the San Francisco Bay Area, as do Sal's two younger sisters.

Sal has no children of his own from his first brief marriage, but he inherited two grown children when he married Catherine. Although he didn't have to take on the role of father for the boys, who were 19 and 23 when he married Catherine, the two young men affectionately began calling him "Papa Sal."

The children in Catherine's elementary school classroom call Sal something else. "When I go to the school to pick her up at the end of the day, I hear all these little voices saying, 'Hello, Mr. Valentino.' Nobody ever called me 'Mr. Valentino' before."

Sal says that regardless of the outcome of his renewed recording ambitions, he'll always remain proud that he was able to carve a place in musical history. "I could have done a lot worse if I weren't lucky. And that includes you," he says, casting an adoring smile toward Catherine. "I'm lucky."

THEN AND NOW

DEC MULLIGAN

When turntable tone arms lowered onto the debut Beau Brummels record in 1965, the first sound that emerged from the vinyl was Declan Mulligan's melancholy harmonica. Wailing like a lonesome train whistle across the prairie, Dec's playing set the somber tone for "Laugh, Laugh," the song that sent the San Francisco quintet to the top of the charts.

Pop music stardom was an unanticipated bonus in the life of Dec Mulligan, who had come to San Francisco three years before to learn the insurance trade in expectation of an eventual return to his native Ireland. But San Francisco has been his home ever since. Now semiretired, Dec never did pursue a long-term career in the insurance business. He does, however, continue to perform music.

Contradicting record label biographies and liner notes that said he entered the world in 1940, Dec freely admits he was born April 8, 1938. As a teenager in the town of Clonmel, County Tipperary, Ireland, in the 1950s, Dec was exposed to a lot of music. Although television wasn't available in the hilly, wooded Fethard region where he lived and BBC radio was out of range, he was able to receive Radio Luxembourg, which on Sunday nights relayed the U.S. Armed Forces Network's broadcast of the top 20 tunes. "It was a thrill to hear American accents. That's where I heard a lot of the early rock and roll, songs by the Everly Brothers, Fats Domino, and Elvis Presley," says Mulligan.

PHOTO BY TANYA G. MULLIGAN.

"My uncle, Dick Gough, lived in the United States and he would come to visit every now and then. One visit coincided with the release of Elvis' first movie, *Love Me Tender,* and my uncle brought two Elvis LPs—*That's Alright Mama* and *Mystery Train.* He brought me a guitar, but nobody in the town played guitar, and I didn't even know how to tune it. I saw somewhere that you tune it EBGDAE, but our piano at home was out of tune and didn't sound right, so I went into the convent where the nuns teach music and I tuned it there." Painstakingly, Dec taught himself to play guitar.

Because Dec's father, William, made a comfortable living as a divisional manager for a large insurance company, he was able to send Dec to boarding schools for the last three years of his high school education. "Although my father didn't attend college, he was a very refined man and articulated like someone with a college degree. My mother, whose name was Mary, was well educated."

As a student, Dec began to play with local skiffle bands and learned to play many of the American songs that were popular at the time. "Every hit that was a hit in America was copied by a British artist," recalls Dec. "For example, Tommy Steele copied Guy Mitchell's 'Singing The Blues.' Frankie Vaughn looked a bit like a young Tony Franciosa and he sang Jim Lowe's 'Green Door.' Cliff Richard was an English version of Elvis Presley." When Dec enrolled at University College, Dublin, to study business administration, he began playing in "show bands," which typically had acoustic bass, drums, guitar, piano, trumpet, trombone, and saxophone players.

"I was on guitar, and I was feeble because I was playing rhythm and also trying to play some of the leads. Ireland had a lot of natural talent but musical education was very much according to the nuns! Wind instruments and piano dominated the musical scene, not the guitars. You learned to play an E flat, an F, C sharp, B flat, and if you went into a band and someone asked, 'What key do you play this in?' and you say, 'I do it in A,' you could feel the vibes in the horn section—like get out of town right now. They didn't want to play in E or A or G—which are good-sounding keys for guitar. So most of the time I ended up in conflict with these guys. I'd sing a song in F or I'd play a song in B-flat and kill myself trying to play these bar chords on the guitar—with bad action, also, I recall. My fingers would be throbbing by the end of the night."

At that time, Mulligan didn't regard music as a potential career. His ambition was simply to travel to the United States. After completing college in 1960, Dec made it across the Atlantic and stopped in Toronto, Canada, where he stayed for two years after landing an underwriter's job with the Fireman's Fund Insurance Co. His father, who was several years from retirement, planned to open an insurance office of his own in Clonmel, and Dec intended to branch out from his father's specialty, life insurance, and learn the general insurance business. In the summer of 1962 Dec transferred to the San Francisco office of Fireman's Fund, fulfilling his dream to journey to the United States. The following year, at an Irish dance at Richmond Hall, an auditorium on Clement Street in San Francisco, he met three other young men who would change the course of his life: Ron Elliott, Sal Valentino, and John Petersen.

Dec was faced with a decision: choose between music and his insurance job. "Thinking about living a life as a musician was scary, even though I loved music. Coming from a strict Catholic background, as I did in Ireland, the guilt trip began working on me." But the lure of music was too strong and the pull of the stage lights was mesmerizing. And, after all, the Beau Brummels did work steadily during their extended stay as the house band in the Morocco Room in San Mateo. Dec vividly remembers the Wednesday night at the Morocco Room when Tom Donahue and Sly Stone caught the band's act.

"Rich Romanello's girlfriend Judy, who did some modeling under the name 'Judette the Nudette,' had told us that she wanted to help us. On this particular night, she walked in, accompanied by a big imposing figure and a black man. Heads turned. The big man was Tom Donahue of Autumn Records and with him was Sly Stone, his producer. Tom Donahue was a very handsome man, bearded, probably about 6 foot 2, weighed about 275, and when he spoke he had a commanding presence. He asked us to come to Coast Recorders on Bush Street that Friday. And that was the start of it. Tom liked the sound of Sal's voice and Sal looked good. Then he and Bob Mitchell began to talk about us on the radio. When Ron picked me up to drive to the Morocco Room, he said, 'Muggins'—that's what he called me—he said, 'Look at all of the people!' They were lined up around the block to see us, because of the power of radio. That's how the Beau Brummels were created, by Tom Donahue and Bob Mitchell."

During his time with the Brummels, Dec met another person who would later become very important in his life, Tanya G. Goodhill. Only 16 at the time, she was the editor of her high school newspaper and she wrote stories about celebrities. After interviewing Sean Connery at the Fairmont hotel, she went to the Morocco Room to do a story on the Beau Brummels. "I dated her for a little while but then I went away to Los Angeles, she went away to school, and we thought that was the end of it," says Dec.

But life on the road didn't sit well with him. Tensions that arose contributed to abbreviation of his tenure with the band. "I was unhappy on the road. But my departure was partly my fault. I thought things would come easier than they did. I thought if I had talent, I didn't have to work at it." Dec later realized that wasn't the right way to think, but his change of mind came too late. "When we came back off the road in the summer of '65, Donahue called me and said, 'Hey, the boys don't want to play with you anymore.' In every band some personalities don't fit," Mulligan says. "I've since learned that no matter how good you think you are, there's always someone out there better."

It didn't take Dec long to form his own band, called Mulligan Stew, which for three years was the house band at the Carousel Ballroom, a dance hall above an automobile dealership at Market and Van Ness streets—which was later to become

Bill Graham's Fillmore West. Looking for something new, Dec began assembling another group called the Black Velvet Band, just as the Beau Brummels were in the process of dissolving. Ron Meager reunited with Dec in the Black Velvet Band, along with lead guitarist Fuzzy Dean and drummer Don Abbott. "The Black Velvet Band was one of the hottest club bands in San Francisco in that era," declares Mulligan. He and Meagher remained with the Black Velvet Band until the ill-fated Beau Brummels reunion in 1975.

The reunion of the Brummels seemed like a good idea at the time because each of the original members had enriched his musical experiences during their time apart. But the band's resurrection germinated the seeds of dormant animosity, which resurfaced during the earliest rehearsals. Dec envisioned a larger role for himself in singing and songwriting. His suggestion that a couple of original songs from the Black Velvet repertoire be included was rebuffed and Mulligan became agitated. "Muggins, calm down, calm down," urged Ron Meagher. "Let's just go along with it. Don't worry about it. Let's just do the other songs. You blew it before when you left the band and everything went haywire. We might make some money this time." Four months after the band members signed their new contract, Ron Meagher was dismissed. The others managed to remain together for another year before parting for the last time.

"It became boring for me to play with the Beau Brummels in 1975 and revert to the old songs," says Dec. "By comparison, the Black Velvet Band had matured so much as a band. We were playing anything and everything." Unfortunately, they played too few self-penned compositions. "We probably could have signed with a label if we had more original material. The door opens only once and if you're not ready to walk in, it slams in your face. Then I got to be a smart ass on top of that. This was a period when bands were receiving large advances to sign. When a guy from Capitol told us, 'I really like you guys. You should be signed up,' I asked him, 'Where's the brown case?' He looked at me with a puzzled expression on his face and asked, 'What case?' I said, 'The case with all of the money in it that all the other bands are getting. Where is it? I don't see it.' As he turned and walked away, the Capitol rep hissed, 'Who's that smart-ass Irish guy?' I've kicked myself many times after that for not doing a little brown-nosing."

Although not as volatile as he once was, Dec is still driven by restless energy. In the years since the second breakup of the Brummels, he has worked in the San Francisco Department of Public Works and held a managerial position with the golf course at the Presidio. Through a short-lived relationship with a woman, Dec became the father of a son, Sean, who was born in 1980. Sean lived with Dec between the ages of 3 and 14 and subsequently spent the remainder of his teenage years with his mother in Oroville, a Sacramento Valley town about 150 miles northeast of San Francisco.

But Dec was not destined to live alone. In 1989, he got a phone call from Tanya Goodhill, who had recently been divorced and was calling to say hello. Today, Dec and Tanya are married and living in a comfortable home clinging to a San Francisco hillside.

Tanya's career in nursing inspired Dec in 1997 to join the staff of a residential care facility for physically and developmentally disabled people. In his position, as he transports residents to medical appointments and relays critical information about their care, he has discovered the power of music for bringing joy to and eliciting responses from people who are largely noncommunicative.

Energetic and trim, Dec still runs on nervous energy. Music remains an important part of his life. "I play a little. I write a little," he says with a shrug. Awaiting the arrival of a fellow musician before a wedding gig late one afternoon, he paces, craning his neck to see the street down below. Clearly a man who wears out shoe leather faster than he does seat cushions, Dec remains in a state of flux. "I'm kind of retired right now," he says. "My dad died in 1973 and my mom died in 1988, and they left me some money that keeps me going. I have to be frugal to exist."

Dec turns his thoughts abruptly to the Brummels. "Autumn Records neglected the Beau Brummels. [Beatles manager] Brian Epstein focused all of his attention on the Beatles. Why didn't Autumn do that with the Beau Brummels?" Dec gazes out the window. "We were like five guys pushing a Cadillac up a hill who were within 10 yards of the top but got tired and rolled back. And if they'd gotten us to the top of the hill, we could have been cruising down the other side for a long time."

But Dec doesn't dwell on the past. Far from it. He has plans: "To stay healthy," he says. And to continue performing. "I'd love to record some of my songs. Because I think I sing better now than I did 30 years ago."

The doorbell rings. Dec bolts down the hall, grabs his guitar case, and gives Tanya a tight hug as he heads out the door and down the stairs to sing once more.

THEN AND NOW

JOHN PETERSEN

Most people go through life wondering when their day of reckoning will come and what it will bring. John Petersen already knows. It was January 11, 1985. Unemployed after ownership squabbles crippled the Mother Lode restaurant in which he had worked as a chef, Petersen and his wife, Roberta, had driven 150 miles to San Francisco, where his mother had taken ill. They intended to care for her and cook some food to put up in her freezer. As his mother began to improve, John heard that his former Beau Brummels mates Sal Valentino and Dec Mulligan were performing at a bar across town.

"I'm sitting at an intersection in my blue Ford pickup, on my way to go hear them play, and my light turns green," Petersen recounts. "I go and some guy running the red light hits me going about 70 miles per hour. The crash broke my neck in five places." John was in the hospital when he regained consciousness, heavily braced and dazed. He spent the following three months in San Francisco in a "halo" brace that immobilized his neck and head. "I stayed at my Mom's with my wife in the room that I grew up in." Fortunately, the residual effects of the injury were limited to partial paralysis of his right thumb and forefinger.

Just as John had recovered sufficiently to permit him to travel, Roberta received a call from her former employer Warner Brothers Records, where she had been on the A&R staff. The label wanted her back, this time as a vice president. She accepted. John, who had during the previous two decades played with a half-dozen bands,

Roberta and John Petersen celebrating their 25th anniversary in 1994.

managed two ice cream parlors, sold men's clothing, operated a bed-and-breakfast inn, and rolled burritos, took stock of where he'd been and where he wanted to go. Still suffering from headaches related to the accident, he wasn't yet strong enough to work, but he was up to reading. And so he began studying for his real estate license. After passing his real estate test in April 1986, he began selling homes in Southern California. During the ensuing years, John avoided dwelling on the past, but every now and then he would pour himself a drink, put a Beau Brummels recording on the stereo, and listen with pride.

Born January 8, 1945, and raised in the Outer Mission District of San Francisco, John Louis Petersen began his childhood musical instruction with trumpet and accordion lessons. But he was more interested in banging on the kitchen pots and pans. That was a particularly prophetic fusion of two interests that would dominate much of his life: music and cooking. To stop his abuse of kitchen utensils, his parents, Louis and Marie, bought him a drum set when he was about 12. Says John, "My dad, who was a cabinet maker, played spoons and he played harmonica just for fun." His older sister, one of his four siblings, remains an accomplished piano player. But John pursued music more zealously than anyone else in the house.

Petersen played in the band in junior high and at Balboa High School in San Francisco. He also became involved with a musical group called the Sparklers, so named because the band members wore sparkle shirts and white bucks. The Sparklers played luncheon meetings for Lions Clubs, the Veterans of Foreign Wars, and other fraternal and civic organizations. They recorded two sides, "Sparklers Theme" and "Freight Train Boogie," at Sound Recorders, later renamed Coast Recorders, the eventual site of the Beau Brummels recording sessions for Autumn. At age 12, John sometimes made as much as $50 or $60 per week playing with the Sparklers. "I realized that if I just kept playing drums and making music I wouldn't have to shop at JC Penney anymore. Even then, I thought I would either play music the rest of my life or be in the restaurant business."

John continued playing with the Sparklers as well as with other San Francisco musicians, and by the fall of 1963, he was earning $21.40 union scale each Friday night while playing with Sal Valentino and Ron Elliott at the Irish dances in San Francisco, where they met Dec Mulligan.

John still feels pangs of distress about the friction that developed between him and Dec Mulligan in the months before the fiery Mulligan and the Beau Brummels parted. "Declan and I came very close to fistfights. But you know what? It was probably a big mistake for that band to break up at that point," Petersen declares. "Although we thought Declan was behaving like a jerk, it was a mistake for us to say, 'Leave,' instead of trying to work it out. We were all just too immature."

The disintegration of the band was foreshadowed even before Autumn sold the Brummels' contract to Warner Brothers in 1966. "Elliott was married and Meagher was married, and they and their wives were all living together in Laurel Canyon. Sal, Meagher, and I had actually started another offshoot of the band because Elliott wasn't healthy and they had drafted Don Irving to play lead guitar," explains Petersen. "Irving was really cool. He played all of Elliott's licks perfectly. By then we had three albums and we were still a good draw but the vibes in the band weren't healthy. It was really strained. I would go out to Laurel Canyon and people weren't talking to each other. By the time we got sold to Warner Brothers, we weren't the same band anymore."

In late 1966 Petersen got a call from Carl Scott, who had been the Brummels' manager. The Tikis, who had been on the Autumn roster and were dealt to Warner Brothers along with the Brummels, needed a drummer. At Carl's request, John met with Ted Templeman and Dick Scoppatoni of the Tikis. John agreed to join the Tikis, who soon became known as Harpers Bizarre. "And that's how I met my wife," says John.

Roberta Templeman is Ted's sister. She joined Warner Brothers in 1967 as a "listener," screening audition tapes and demo tracks by aspiring recording artists. Demonstrating a natural sense for detecting musical talent and hit-making potential, she rose quickly through the ranks and held A&R executive positions with increasing responsibility at Warners for 25 years, before joining Geffen Records in 1993.

The Tikis, as Harpers Bizarre, had recorded "59th Street Bridge Song (Feelin' Groovy)" before the arrival of Petersen. But Petersen was a part of the band when the song hit the charts in March 1967 and played at the session that produced Harpers Bizarre's follow-up hit, "Come To The Sunshine," three months later. "I found a second life," said Petersen, who toured with Harpers Bizarre for three years. "I had a lot of fun with Harpers, but I would have to say the Brummels were much closer to my heart."

John and Roberta married in Santa Cruz, California, in 1969, a year before Harpers Bizarre disbanded. Petersen subsequently took a job at a local Taco Bell fast-food outlet. "I did cooking jobs, I did whatever it took. I'm not ashamed of that. You've got to take care of yourself and your family. I had three cars and I couldn't put gas in them all." Petersen called Ron Elliott one day and asked if he'd like to form another band. "Cool," Elliott replied. They recruited Butch Engle to sing lead, Pappy Smith on bass, and named the band Crap. After playing some gigs in San Francisco, they relocated to Southern California, moving into a big house in Malibu together. "We were just this funky little band doing covers and acting goofy on stage," says Petersen. Unable to tolerate the communal environment in the Malibu house, Roberta moved in with Ted and his wife, Kathy, who lived in Pasadena. When Crap dissolved a couple of weeks later, John moved in with Roberta, Ted, and Kathy. A few days passed before Roberta told John, "You probably should go get a job."

After landing a job as a cook at a Pasadena coffee shop, John moved into management at the Pasadena and Beverly Hills locations of Wil Wright's, an upscale ice cream parlor chain. After some time Petersen responded to a "help wanted" ad placed by Bruno's for Men, a locally owned clothing store. Hired as a salesman at age 26, Petersen advanced to become a buyer and eventually general sales manager of Bruno's, which expanded from its single location to four stores during the time he was there.

Roberta and John were both doing very well in 1975, when Ron Elliott called to say he wanted to resurrect the Brummels. "That sounds cool to me," John replied.

He and Roberta rented out their house, Roberta moved back in with her parents in Santa Cruz, and John returned to San Francisco to rehearse with Elliott, Valentino, Mulligan, and Meagher. "We got a contract with Warner's, recorded the *Beau Brummels* album, went on the road, and it was a disaster." Ron Meagher quickly departed, John's drumming was criticized, and simmering tensions between Dec and John reached the boiling point. After appearing with Fleetwood Mac in Phoenix and Tucson, the band arrived in Portland, Oregon, the next tour stop. In John's room, he and Dec began a fierce argument. "I just about took off his head. I don't know if I could beat him up or if he could beat me up. It didn't matter. I was mad," says Petersen. "So I took a walk, bought a raincoat, and tried to figure out what I wanted to do with my life." At 5 the following morning, John boarded a plane. He and Roberta returned to their home in Southern California, where John rejoined Bruno's.

Now, over two decades later, Petersen admits that he'll probably always regret leaving the Brummels. "It was what I always wanted to do, ever since I was 10 years old. This is the first time I've ever vocalized that. But I guess my ego was too big. I couldn't take the criticism. I'm not Ginger Baker, I'm not Russ Kunkel, I'm not like some of the great drummers out there, but I was always good for the band. We were always about simple licks and simple lyrics. At the recording sessions for the 1975 album nobody ever got loose and it was all too technical. And on stage in 1975 we didn't play anything that we used to, other than 'Laugh, Laugh' and 'Just A Little.' The rest was new stuff. We should have been playing 'Still In Love With You Baby' and other fun old stuff. That's what people came to hear." After Petersen's departure the Brummels played only a few more gigs with a different drummer before disbanding for good.

At Bruno's, John was promoted to buyer, then manager. In 1981 John and Roberta became restless, sold their home in urban Pasadena, and moved 30 miles away to Thousand Oaks, beyond the western suburbs of Los Angeles. John quit his job and occupied his time by stripping furniture. Six months later they moved 400 miles north to Placerville, a Gold Rush town with a narrow, twisting main street lined by 19th-century buildings. John and Roberta bought and remodeled an old Victorian home at Coloma Road and Highway 49 and converted it to a bed-and-breakfast inn. Working with a local handyman, they fashioned bathrooms out of closets, stripped generations of paint from fine old wood, repaired leaks, and replaced poor plumbing and outdated electrical fixtures. When completed, the Petersen Inn accommodated eight guests.

In 1983 John and Roberta sold the inn and bought a house in Twain Harte, another historic California town along State Highway 108, a mountain pass route that is routinely closed in winter by Sierra snowfalls. John took a job as a night clerk in a liquor store for $4.25 per hour until the real estate agent who sold the Petersens their home decided to open a restaurant with a business partner. Since neither knew anything about the restaurant business, they persuaded John to quit the liquor store, and he became the chef and manager of Moby Dick's seafood restaurant, where he remained for the next two years. "I had some great recipes. I was doing San Francisco–style dishes like swordfish with avocado butter and great scampi dishes." But business declined and John was laid off after squabbles erupted between the two owners. It was then that Roberta and John drove to San Francisco to help John's mother during her illness.

During John's recuperation from his devastating automobile accident that occurred during that visit, Roberta sold the house in Twain Harte. Roberta accepted the executive position that Warner Brothers Records had offered her, and as soon as John was able to travel they moved to Pasadena, where John studied for his real estate license. He sold homes in the Pasadena area for 12 years, until leaving real estate in August 1998 to pursue a longtime dream: owning and operating his own record label. With two partners he formed Lawless Records, based in Pasadena, quickly signing alternative rock singer Caron and her band as the label's first act.

Petersen is modest about his background in the spotlight. When his real estate clients asked what he did before he entered real estate sales, he answered, "I was in the entertainment business and I was in retail." That's often as much as he reveals to new acquaintances. If pressed, he'll mention the Brummels. "I never tell people that I meet for the first time. When they find out later, they're thrilled but, still, that has little bearing on what I do today," says Petersen.

John's mother now lives in San Juan Capistrano, which is about 60 miles southeast of Pasadena, but John's father died in 1975 following a short illness. John learned something important about his father shortly thereafter.

"Some of the fathers of the '50s didn't express themselves. They didn't hug you and tell you they love you, like fathers do now," observes John. He was never certain how much his father loved him until after he died. "When we were going through my Dad's stuff, I went out into the car and I happened to pull down the visor on the driver's side. Clipped to the visor," John says slowly, "was a picture of the Beau Brummels. He was not unwilling, he was simply unable to say, 'I'm proud of you.' I never knew he was proud until that moment."

John still plays drums for personal enjoyment, but is developing new interests. Like fellow Beau Brummels member Ron Meagher, he's become interested in photography and has enrolled in a class. I've been thinking about my passions," he declared. "I'm comfortable, I drive a nice car, I wear nice suits, I have a great history behind me, but I'm looking to find another passion." Even before launching Lawless Records, Petersen mused, "One thing I'd like to do is open a night club. I'd like to do some acting. And I'd like to have a restaurant with maybe 15 or 18 tables and cook for people." John Petersen is not a person who wants his life defined by what he did when he was 22 years of age. "I think my future is probably a lot more important than my history."

THEN AND NOW

RON MEAGHER

Ron Elliott, Sal Valentino, John Petersen, and Dec Mulligan, members of the newly formed Beau Brummels, had begun practicing in the downstairs room of Ron Elliott's family home while awaiting the arrival of a bass player, Ron Meagher, who had been invited to audition for the band. The four boys had never met the bass player, who was an acquaintance of a girl Elliott knew. It was the fall of 1963 in San Francisco, but these teenagers were most definitely not part of the local sub-culture that had nurtured poets Lawrence Ferlinghetti and Allen Ginsberg, novelist Jack Kerouac, and other prominent members of the Beat Generation who made the city's North Beach district their headquarters in the 1950s. All four boys favored the Ivy League look, and the only leather they wore was a belt.

The staircase leading to the downstairs room revealed their visitor's feet first, shoed in black Beatle boots. Then black pants. A black guitar case. A black leather jacket. Black sunglasses. And finally a face framed by long, dark hair. That was their introduction to Ron Meagher, and it brought silence to the room.

Meagher plugged in his amplifier. One of the boys asked if he had heard of the Beatles, who were little known in America at that time. He had. They asked if he knew how to play "I Want To Hold Your Hand." He did. With Mulligan singing lead, the band began playing the song.

Barely 15 seconds into it, Mulligan laid down his guitar and, with an astonished expression, motioned with outstretched palms to stop playing. "Whoa, whoa, whoa! That's it, that's it! He's doing it!" Mulligan was indicating to the others that Meagher was playing the intricate bass line the way that Paul McCartney did. Replicating McCartney's playing required a difficult hand stretch, and other bass players that the group had

Self-portrait of Ron Meagher with his wife, Cheri, and their son, Aaron, taken in the late 1980s. The older boy, Canaan, is Ron's son from a previous marriage.

interviewed failed because they took a lazy approach. That night, Meagher became a Beau Brummel. No big deal to him, because he was already playing with 12 other bands.

Ron's early musical interest was a product of the public school system in Oakland, California, an industrial and commercial center across the bay from San Francisco. Ron, born October 2, 1945, displayed natural musical aptitude that an elementary school teacher spotted early on. Ron learned to play every stringed instrument he could wrap his hands around, but was disappointed to learn that the school would provide training only on orchestral instruments. Unable to learn to play the guitar in school, he decided to try the upright bass. "I remember carrying that upright bass home every afternoon so I could rehearse. It was unusual to see a 13-year-old kid walking around with a bass fiddle on his hip," Ron laughs.

But the ability to play that upright meant that he was in great demand. By the time he entered high school, he had played with jazz combos, folk groups, Latin ensembles, and dance orchestras. He started carving his own path into rock music after hearing a trio called the Offbeats performing music of the Ventures during one high school lunch period. Meagher approached the group, which consisted of drummer Richard MacDonald, lead guitarist Graig Cahill, and rhythm guitarist Jimmy Ela, and asked if they would like to have a bass player. They agreed. Given that opportunity, Ron declined his parents' offer of a '57 Chevy he had once coveted as a gift for his 16th birthday and instead chose an electric Fender Jazz bass guitar and an amplifier.

Every evening after completing his homework, Ron assiduously practiced with his new instrument. After his parents went to sleep, he'd plug headphones into his amplifier, muting the speakers, and perform bass lines into the early hours of the morning. Ron polished his skills, and during his junior and senior years of high school rotated among 12 musical groups, including the Offbeats, which by then were known as the Blue Echoes. At a time when few Americans had heard of the Beatles or Cliff Richard and the Shadows, Ron and the other Blue Echoes were buying British albums in a local record store that had a small selection of imports. "I Saw Her Standing There," the leadoff cut on the *Please Please Me* album, had an unusual bass line by Paul McCartney. Ron Meagher was intrigued. He studied McCartney's playing style until he was able to replicate it himself.

In his junior year at Oakland High School, Ron understudied the lead role in *Oklahoma*. During the staging of that play, he struck up a friendship with another cast member, senior Kay Dane. It was Kay, who had met Ron Elliott at San Francisco State College and was later to marry him, who suggested that Elliott and his buddies invite Ron Meagher to that basement audition.

At 18, Ron Meagher was the youngest member of the band, a year younger than Ron Elliott and John Petersen. Meagher celebrated his 19th birthday on

October 2, 1964, on stage at the Cow Palace, where the Brummels were appearing with a slate of 10 acts that included Sonny and Cher, Sam Cooke, the Temptations, and Glen Campbell. "Laugh, Laugh" had just been released, and Meagher was as yet the only member of the Brummels with long hair.

Meagher remembers being introduced by Tom Donahue, who was Master of Ceremonies. "That was our first performance before a large audience. I remember we were wearing yellow bolero jackets with no collar," Meagher laughs. He was the last band member in Donahue's introduction. "When Tom called my name, I bowed, my long hair came down, and the place went nuts. The girls were screaming like crazy. All the other band members looked over at me and thought, 'Oh. Isn't this interesting?' That was the end of the Ivy League look of the Beau Brummels and shortly after that, one at a time, they started growing their hair longer." After the introductions were complete and the screams had subsided, Donahue carted a huge layered birthday cake topped with a candle across the stage and presented it to Meagher. Later, offstage, Glen Campbell approached Meagher and the cake, affectionately said "Isn't this great?" and promptly smashed his hand into the cake. "We ate the cake anyway," says Meagher.

Ron remained with the band through its relocation to Los Angeles and through the sale of the band's contract to Warner Brothers in 1966. He left only after being called up for military service. "I remember being right in the middle of a recording session for *Bradley's Barn,* and I had to leave with about only three-quarters of the tracks laid down. I had to serve Uncle Sam." After his military discharge in 1970, Meagher returned to San Francisco. At the time Dec Mulligan was performing in an Irish bar in San Francisco with the Black Velvet Band. "Declan recognized me sitting in the audience. He was kind enough to ask me to come up and join his band, and I just happened to have a guitar sitting in the back of my car." The band became regulars at Paoli's Old Library, a San Francisco restaurant and night club stocked with old library books.

Meagher and Mulligan continued to perform with the Black Velvet Band until the 1975 reunion of the Beau Brummels. With Dec playing bass for the Brummels, Meagher moved into the lead guitar slot, but he was uncomfortable with the change. When the Brummels went on tour performing their new tunes, Meagher stayed behind, replaced by Danny Levitt. Meagher reactivated the Black Velvet Band in the East Bay, and recruited drummer Will Riddick and bassist Tony Del Fabero, later adding a female singer-keyboardist named Britani Barteleme. "She not only had a wonderful voice, she also had one of the first keyboard synthesizers in the area," says Ron. The trio began a gig in the Emeryville location of Tia Maria, a Northern California restaurant–cocktail lounge chain. Adjoining Berkeley and Oakland, Emeryville is a commercial center and transit hub for East Bay commuters. The band continued playing there for more than four years. "During that time, I met a beautiful blue-eyed blond named Cheri, and we became engaged," Ron smiles. (Ron and Cheri Staggs were married in 1979 in the lush fern grotto on the Hawaiian island of Kauai.) Unfortunately, the Tia Maria chain was sold by the owner to bankroll other investments in San Francisco. "If the chain had remained open, we'd probably still be there."

With the closure of Tia Maria, the Black Velvet Band increased its availability for dates at social events, including business parties and weddings. During one wedding gig at the prestigious Olympic Club in San Francisco, Ron's mind began wandering as he pondered his future. His gaze fell upon the bride and groom dancing as the wedding photographer snapped pictures of them. Leaping around the reception hall to capture memorable images, the energetic photographer riveted Ron's attention. Ron introduced himself to the photographer, Tony Machado, and told him he'd like to learn how to become a wedding photographer. "No kidding," Tony replied. "I always wanted to learn how to play the guitar." The two agreed to exchange lessons. Tony invited Ron to accompany him on several assignments. As Ron lugged the photographer's bag of equipment around, his determination to learn the trade solidified.

Ron began his quest for a new career by securing a sales job in Berkeley at Brooks Cameras, a chain of retail photographic equipment stores. As he learned more about the stock, he was promoted to assistant manager. Meanwhile, Tony introduced Ron to Jim London, another photographer who had just bought some new lighting equipment and was considering selling his old gear. Ron purchased the equipment then and there. (Years later, when London retired, Ron bought his house and studio as well.)

"I'm just starting wedding photography," Ron announced to Jim. "Would you like someone to come out and carry your equipment for you?" Ron had no idea that Jim London was among the most prominent wedding and portrait photographers in Northern California at the time. Ron observed that Jim didn't run around the way Tony did, but always seemed relaxed as he stood in front of the church waiting for the wedding party. Jim simply exercised control over the shoot and knew what was going to happen next. That impressed Ron. After his informal apprenticeship, Ron got his first paid wedding job, and he applied all he had learned. When the 200 proofs were returned from the color lab, Ron showed them to Jim before the bride and groom saw them. Impressed, Jim said, "You and I have to talk." Eventually Jim and his wife nicknamed Ron "the sponge" because of how much information he absorbed and applied so quickly. "It was just what I did with music—I heard it and duplicated it," explains Ron. "I simply observed photographic styles and applied them."

In 1978 Ron launched his new career, working weekends as a wedding photographer for the next seven years while working weekdays in sales management at Brooks Cameras. It wasn't long before Ron's talent as a professional photographer was recognized, and he won several local, regional, and national awards for his work in portait and wedding photography. Although photography was both artistically satisfying and lucrative, Ron felt drawn in yet another direction that would provide more long-term stability. And so after he finished counting receipts and shut down the Brooks offices at night, he would walk up the hill to the University of California, Berkeley, where he began taking extension courses in computer science.

Ron's interest in the computer industry went back to when the Black Velvet Band was playing at Tia Maria. There he struck up a friendship with a company financial executive, Marvin Katich, who balanced Tia Maria's books using IBM mainframe computers and software. After leaving Tia Maria, Katich went to work selling peripherals for California Computer Products, a Silicon Valley firm that devised pen plotter technology used for engineering drawings. Katich persuaded the branch manager of his office to interview Meagher, who was hired as a salesman in 1981.

Ron Meagher had made the transition to the corporate world. He did extremely well at Cal Comp, where he remained for nearly three years, until one of Katich's prophecies—that the brass ring would go to the first company to develop a color plotter—came true.

A Xerox subsidiary called Versatech was first to introduce a color electrostatic plotter, which printed images composed of tiny dots at high speed. In only one minute, an electrostatic plotter could generate a drawing that a pen device required a half hour to complete. As Ron considered approaching Versatech, the company's sales manager recruited him in 1984 after observing his effectiveness selling in their territory. Versatech's high-end equipment was not an easy sale, considering the cost: plotters and their controllers carried price tags of as much as $150,000. Nevertheless, Ron excelled at Versatech, earning a succession of promotions from senior sales engineer to regional manager of local OEM (original equipment manufacturing) accounts. Ultimately he became Western Regional OEM manager for Xerox, covering 11 western states. During an 11-year period, during which time the company became known as XES—Xerox Engineering Systems—Meagher opened several new markets in the reprographics and graphic arts industries.

"I'm proud of those accomplishments. Before my arrival at Versatech, architects would take their files on diskette to a service bureau, where a pen plotter would create the drawing, copies of which they would produce on a blueprint machine. So I was instrumental in introducing black-and-white electrostatic plotters to that industry."

Meagher, whose territory covered only the industrial areas of the East Bay cities, had customers who needed only black-and-white output. Color plotters were primarily marketed to the high-tech semiconductor firms of Silicon Valley across the bay, out of Ron's territory. "I could sell only black-and-white plotters, but I still made my quota," says Meagher, whose sales colleagues dubbed him "Monochrome Meagher." After one of Ron's customers told him, "I will never buy a color machine," Ron took that as a personal challenge. Meagher's breakthrough into a new color market came by means of a prospect in Berkeley named Harry Bowers, who was interested in the potential of color plotters in producing wallpaper or other large photographic images.

Versatech and Xerox Engineering Systems had concentrated on the semiconductor, petroleum, architectural, engineering, and construction industries, but disregarded the emerging desktop publishing segment. But after a new company called Bowers Imaging Technologies emerged from Harry's experimentation in electronic digital imaging technology, XES was persuaded to enter the graphic arts environment. Ron was credited for enabling the Xerox entry into the new graphic arts industry segment, in which plotters were viewed as tools to create photographic imagery rather than just engineering drawings. "Suddenly we were selling new color plotters to people we never imagined would be interested," Ron says proudly. XES plotters were being used to create advertising displays, billboards, and other applications requiring large color images. He racked up lots of sales awards, and "Monochrome Meagher" was given a new nickname: the "Color Guy." Xerox eventually created a new business unit called Xerox Color GraphX Systems, dedicated to this single vertical market. Meagher thinks it's kind of amazing that "a former rock musician could make a difference in one of America's premier corporations."

But Ron's success in creating the close affiliation with the graphic arts industry ultimately contributed to relocation of the entire division to Rochester, New York, where Xerox is headquartered. Ron's parents were elderly and Cheri did not want to uproot their family, so he left Xerox in the summer of 1995 and took a sales position with another computer firm in the San Francisco Bay Area.

Settled comfortably in the home he and Cheri purchased from photographer Jim London in 1984, Meagher has converted his former downstairs photo studio into a music studio—not for himself, but for the couple's son Aaron, who was born the year they moved into the house. Like Ron Elliott, Aaron was drawn to computer art. He's interested in the application of computer technology for music as well. "So I built him a studio to satisfy his growth in music," said Ron.

A display case in the Meagher home contains a singular collection of symbolic Beau Brummels mementos. Mint-condition copies of the two original Autumn albums. Playbills and tickets from Beau Brummels concerts. Newspaper clippings. Wonderful old photographs. Less than two miles away, cars park on an asphalt lot that had once been the site of the Morocco Room. Nothing remains today of the building in which five young guys in yellow bolero jackets made music that the world still recalls with fondness more than three decades later.

Wooly Bully

CHAPTER 8

Sam the Sham and the Pharaohs

Sam the Sham and the Pharaohs in 1965. Left to right: guitarist Ray Stinnett, saxophonist Paul "Butch" Gibson, drummer Jerry Patterson, bassist David Martin, and organist-singer Domingo "Sam" Samudio. FROM PHOTOFEST ARCHIVES, NEW YORK.

FROM THE TIME CAPSULE

APRIL 1965: Sam the Sham and the Pharaohs' "Wooly Bully" begins its record-setting chart run.

- APRIL 6: *Intelsat 1,* "Early Bird," the world's first commercial communications satellite, is launched.
- APRIL 9: The Beatles' "Ticket To Ride" is released in the U.K. Mickey Mantle hits major league baseball's first indoor home run, in the Houston Astrodome.
- APRIL 28: Lyndon Johnson sends 20,000 U.S. Marines to the Dominican Republic to back an army faction that overthrew the Dominican Republic's president in 1963.

DECEMBER 1966: The fourth hit single of the year for Sam the Sam and the Pharaohs, "How Do You Catch A Girl," climbs to No. 27.

- DECEMBER 23: The Who perform on the final broadcast of the British Broadcasting System's *Ready, Steady, Go!* television series, which ends a wildly popular three-year run.
- DECEMBER 30–31: Country Joe and the Fish, Moby Grape, and Lee Michaels usher in the new year with performances at the Avalon Ballroom in San Francisco.

JUNE 1967: "Black Sheep," the Pharaohs' last single to chart, reaches No. 68 on the Hot 100.

- JUNE 1: EMI releases the Beatles' landmark *Sgt. Pepper's Lonely Hearts Club Band,* a milestone in the history of studio recording techniques, in the U.K.
- JUNE 5: Israeli military forces capture the Sinai Peninsula, the Gaza Strip, the Golan Heights, and the east bank of the Suez Canal during a six-day war with Egypt, Jordan, and Syria.
- JUNE 17: The People's Republic of China detonates its first hydrogen bomb.

In early 1965, as President Lyndon Johnson's advisers were recommending a huge increase in U.S. involvement in Vietnam and racial unrest in cities was seething to a low boil, pop music lovers were showing a definite preference for light fare. Roger Miller tickled his fans' fancy with "Do-Wacka-Do," Freddie and the Dreamers flapped along with "I'm Telling You Now," and Herman's Hermits honed their huggable image with their serenade to puppy love lost, "Mrs. Brown, You've Got A Lovely Daughter."

Through that squeaky-clean panorama a flamboyantly attired group from America's South burst onto the charts with a raucously improbable blend of Tex-Mex salsa and Memphis rhythm and blues. While parents settled in for a quiet evening watching Lawrence Welk set the bouncy rhythm of his televised "champagne music-makers" with his trademark "uh-one and a two-and-uh," their kids cruised the boulevard with radios blaring a far different beat, one launched by Sam the Sham with his inimitable Tex-Mex countoff: "Uno, dos, one-two, tres, cuatro." So began the boisterous "Wooly Bully," which remained on the charts longer than any other record in 1965, and so began the improbable hit recording career of Sam the Sham and the Pharaohs.

Dressed in robes and feathered turbans inspired by the attire of King Ramses in the motion picture *The Ten Commandments,* Sam and the Pharaohs arrived at gigs in an old Packard hearse. Sam had polished his act over a two-year period, beginning in clubs around Dallas, at isolated roadhouses in steamy southwest Louisiana, and finally in the thumping nightspots of the legendary home of the blues, Memphis.

Bearded Texan Domingo "Sam" Samudio, singing lead vocals and playing rhythm on organ, fronted the four Pharaohs: bassist David Martin, guitarist Ray Stinnett, saxophonist Paul "Butch" Gibson, and drummer Jerry Patterson. In their hometown of Dallas, Samudio and Martin had been high school classmates, performing together in a local band with drummer Vincent Lopez before going their separate ways.

As an aspiring singer in the early '60s, Sam worked any kind of gig that would pay a few bucks and put him in the spotlight. When the house band at a Dallas bar called the Blue Room needed an organist who could sing, he auditioned and was hired even though he'd never played the organ. Sam traded a bass guitar and a flute for a Wurlitzer 4040 organ to practice at home, and three days later his phone rang.

David Martin was on the line from Louisiana. He and Vincent Lopez had joined Andy and the Night Riders, a band led by guitarist Andy Anderson. They were playing at a club in Louisiana when their organist quit, and they heard that Sam had picked up the organ. Sam agreed to join them, but after he arrived in Louisiana, his rudimentary keyboard skills earned him a new nickname.

"Andy and the Night Riders started introducing me as Sam the Sham because they knew I couldn't play the organ well," says Samudio. "Shamming also refers to cutting up, and I did a lot of that." It was the spring of 1963. As Leroy Cooper orbited the earth 22 times in the last Mercury space mission, Andy and the Night Riders were kicking in the afterburners down in Newllano, Louisiana. "Every night was like Saturday night on Highway 171 in Vernon Parish. We were a hot band," Sam proudly recalls.

The lights were bright and the music was loud, but home was a motel room that Samudio shared with David Martin. There, the two forged their dreams. Lying on his bed one muggy sleepless night, Martin said, "You know, while we're sitting here in this rathole, there's bands out there not half as good as we are making thousands of dollars a night."

"So I asked him what he thought it would take to get there," remembers Sam. "David answered, 'one gold record.' I told him, 'Let's go get one.' David got closer to my face and he said, 'I'm not joking.'"

"Neither am I," Sam affirmed. They shook on it.

By the summer the band members felt ready. "We packed everything up in a U-Haul and headed for Memphis, eating onions and sardines," said Sam.

When they pulled into Memphis, they checked into the Crystal Motel and took a look around town. The place was pulsating. Jerry Lee Lewis was pounding piano at the Hi Hat on Highway 61, the Mar-Keys were struttin' in a club across the way, Willie Mitchell was bumping out blues just up the road, and Ace Cannon and Bill Black's Combo were gigging in town. Undaunted by the competition, Andy and the Night Riders started making the rounds. Within four days they landed a gig at a place called the Diplomat Club. They hit the stage in full stride.

"Oh, we were hot," confirms Sam. "We were playing six hours a night and we never came out in the daytime. But about sundown that hearse would roll out of the driveway. We were on our way to rock. On stage, Andy would hit a couple of notes on lead guitar and we were on. He was way ahead of his time."

Time was running out for Andy and the Night Riders, however. After a couple of months in Memphis, Andy's homesickness for Louisiana became overpowering. He announced his intention to quit the band and return home. Vincent Lopez was losing confidence as well. Figuring that meant the breakup of the band, Sam was tempted to follow Andy. But David Martin, whose musical talents Sam deeply respected, persuaded him to stay and form a new unit. Sam was worried about how the band would survive the loss of its lead guitarist and drummer. "We'll find others," David assured him.

Guitarist Ray Stinnett and drummer Jerry Patterson had been close friends for two years before Sam and David had even arrived in Memphis. Ray recalls he was standing at a Memphis bus stop in 1961 when he first met Jerry, who ran stock cars at the time. "Jerry had a big ole pink Oldsmobile that he called the pink elephant," says Ray. The initial conversation focused on engine rebuilding before the two discovered their mutual interest in blues music. "We instantly became buddies. I helped him build his car back up, and the two of us started playing music together at roadhouses, honky-tonks, clubs, bars, anywhere we could play."

After a while they started doing gigs with Sonny Wilson, an early Sun recording artist, and Memphis singer-pianist Eddie Caroll. That led to some backup work on demo sessions at Fernwood Recording Studio on North Main. Ray and Jerry began moving easily through Memphis music circles. They hung out at Satellite Record Shop on East McLemore just as it was metamorphosing into Satellite Studios—the precursor to STAX Records. Satellite Record Shop was run by Estelle Axton, the mother of Charles "Packy" Axton, who played baritone sax with the Mar-Keys.

Ray, who with Jerry also began doing some session work at Sonic Studios, remembers a particular recording date one morning late in the summer of '63. "While I was waiting for Sonic to open, I looked across the street and noticed this tall dark-haired guy with a big beard. He looked kind of like Fidel Castro," says Ray. "He was with a guy who looked like Cochise or something. I said to myself, 'These are some weird-looking dudes.' I walked across the street to them and said, 'You've gotta be musicians,' and they said, 'We're from Dallas.' So we sat down on the stone wall and started talking." The guy with the beard was Sam Samudio. With him was David Martin.

"They said they had a band called the Night Riders and that the other two guys were off having breakfast," recalls Ray. "They told me they had been in Memphis a few weeks and they had a gig playing at Eddie Bond's place, the Diplomat Club." Then Andy and Vince, the two other Night Riders, showed up. "They said they thought they were wasting their time in Memphis and wanted to go back to Texas or Louisiana. Sam and David said they wanted to stay but they needed a guitar player and drummer." Ray asked them what kind of music they play. "Blues, rock, soul, gut-bucket kind of blues," Sam responded.

"That sounds like something I'm familiar with," said Ray with a sly smile. "This might be your lucky day."

As they talked, the studio opened its doors for a scheduled demo session with Dick and Dee Dee. Ray invited the Night Riders in. "On that session, Sam contributed a little organ and I played a little rhythm guitar, and when the demos were done, the Night Riders hooked up and played a couple of tunes. But the whole time Andy was mumbling and complaining that they were wasting their time in Memphis," recalls Ray.

Sam spoke next. Pointing to Ray, he said, "Hey, look, let this red-headed guy sit in and see what he can do." As Ray began to play, Andy packed his guitar and left. Sam said, "We're staying. We found a guitar player already. You want a job, Booger Red?" he asked Ray.

"He started calling me that. He had a talent for coming up with names for people," says Ray, who was hired on the spot. "I told them about this drummer friend of mine. Sam said, 'If he can play as well as you can, bring him on in to the Diplomat Club.' Jerry joined us, and that was the beginning of the Pharaohs."

The quartet had good chemistry and quickly evolved into a tight unit. Their repertoire consisted principally of funky rhythm and blues tunes like "Long Tall Sally" and "Every Woman I Know (Crazy 'Bout An Auto)." The Diplomat was a big club, and Sam the Sham and the Pharaohs quickly drew crowds. "We were the only predominantly white band in Memphis that played hardcore blues. The club was packed every night," says Ray. In addition to their own shows, the band also backed two nightly performances by singer Jumpin' Gene Simmons, who owned an independent label called Tupelo Records. On Tupelo, with their own money, Sam the Sham and the Pharaohs recorded their first single, the 1958 Chuck Willis hit "Betty And Dupree," backed with "Manchild," a tune penned by Sam. Disappointed by their inability to penetrate the soul music market with that release, the band members decided they needed the added dimension that a saxophone player could provide.

As a premed student at Southwestern-Memphis in 1962, saxophonist Butch Gibson began moonlighting with a band named Joe Davis and the All-Stars that was fronted by a trio of black vocalists. The band, which played dates at colleges throughout the South, had a brush with stardom in 1963 when they recorded as the Avantis. They cut a tune called "Keep On Dancing" that became a top 10 hit two years later for the Gentrys. In January 1964, when Butch was halfway through his second year of college, Joe Davis called him aside. "Hey, man," Joe told Butch, "there's a group in town that you need to hear. They play your kind of music, but they don't have a sax player. They call themselves Sam the Sham and the Pharaohs."

Butch headed to the Little Black Book, the club where Sam the Sham and the Pharaohs were playing at the time. He introduced himself and they invited him to audition on stage with them. The Pharaohs liked what they heard. And that evening as Butch became a Pharaoh, he decided to quit college.

"That was a real smart thing to do," says Butch sarcastically, "but I wouldn't change that now because it afforded me a lot of opportunities and exposure to the world that I wouldn't have had otherwise." Butch had begun a two-year adventure that would take him to the heights of bliss and the depths of depression.

After the arrival of Butch, the band members recorded their second single, Johnny Fuller's "Haunted House," and tried their best to promote the record, which was released on the independent Dingo label. "We went on George Klein's TV show, *Dance Party,* and I sat on Butch's shoulders and we were made up like some kind of 10-foot-tall spooky 'haint' from the haunted house," recalls Ray.

"Sam and the other guys acted out the story line of the song and then Butch and I chased them all over the studio in this ridiculous getup. We worked really hard at promoting 'Haunted House.' We went out on the road knocking on radio station doors, asking them to play the record," said Ray. "We went to see Wolfman Jack, who was running a late-night R&B show in Nashville, and he started giving us airplay."

After the band had shopped the record from Memphis to Birmingham and everywhere in between, Gene Simmons said that a larger label, Hi Records, was interested in releasing "Haunted House," but wanted Sam and the Pharaohs to re-record it with a somewhat different arrangement. The deal didn't feel right to Sam. Simmons appealed to Sam to reconsider, but Sam was resolute in sticking with Dingo. "So Gene went over to Hi Records and recorded 'Haunted House' himself," says Stinnett. The Simmons version eclipsed the Pharaohs' disc and charted nationally in August 1964.

As chart success eluded them, Sam the Sham and the Pharaohs continued enjoying a strong following in the nightspots of Memphis. After the Diplomat Club was closed for curfew violation, the band quickly found other gigs, first at Quentin's Club and then at a place called Smoochie's Show Bar. Owner Smoochie Smith was the original piano player with the Mar-Keys and a member of the famed Sun Rhythm Section. As a solo act, Smoochie had a local hit called "Hot Nuts," with eye-winking lyrics. Sam the Sham and the Pharaohs decided to go back into the studio also, and recorded a novelty song called "The Signifying Monkey," released on XL Records. Stinnett remembers that to promote the record Sam bought a small spider monkey, which sat on his shoulder and occasionally bit him on stage. Although the song failed to live up to their expectations, the next recording session for XL was more productive.

"Do you have anything else to record?" producer Stan Kesler asked. "Yeah, we got something," replied Sam.

What he had was little more than a rhythm pattern without any words. "I told the band, 'Kick it off, and we'll make up some words.'" There, in the same recording studio in which Elvis Presley, Roy Orbison, Jerry Lee Lewis, Johnny Cash, and Carl Perkins had laid down tracks for Sun Records, Sam the Sham and the Pharaohs improvised, jotted down some lyrics, and recorded another novelty tune: "Wooly Bully."

Pivotal to the tune's eventual success was its riveting downbeat, the staccato "Uno, dos, one-two tres cuatro" spark plug that ignited the band. The famous countdown was no big deal to Sam, who thought it was "just a Tex-Mex count-off." Sam used it as a timing device to pace the musicians, but hadn't intended it to be part of the recording. Kesler liked it, however, and argued in favor of retaining it on the pressing. Sam finally agreed. "Put a label on it, that's a hit," Sam said. It was, but not right away.

During the smoldering days of "Wooly Bully," before it became a wildfire hit, the band continued playing at Smoochie's. Wishing to increase business at the club, the band members decided they needed a gimmick. "At the time we wore brocade jackets and we looked kind of like the Blues Brothers. We bought our clothes at Lansky Bros. and we were mod, dapper dudes," says Ray.

"Then we got the idea that the Pharaohs should dress up like pharaohs, so we went to a drapery shop and bought some pieces of fabric and decorative cording. We made some head coverings out of them and dyed some bed sheets, and made them into robes. We didn't wear the pharaoh outfits all of the time, just for special occasions." Ray admits they were a pain. "We couldn't hear very well, they were hot, and we tripped over the sheets. But we used them to attract attention. We started riding around town in Sam's hearse dressed like the pharaohs. We got ourselves boots with real high heels and we looked like we'd just ridden in on camels. We'd run into clubs and yell, 'Smoochie's Show Bar' and leave, and Smoochie's started filling up."

Even while playing at Smoochie's, the band made short runs on the road, promoting their record and doing one-nighters in other southern cities. Duke Rumore, a Birmingham disc jockey who liked the band's music, packaged rock shows at the local National Guard Armory and at a beach stage in Panama City, Florida. "He would rent out those places and we would pack them," says Ray. Opening for Sam the Sham and the Pharaohs one night was a band called the Sundowners, whose guitarist was a very young Tom Petty. With help from Duke, "Wooly Bully" hit No. 1 in Birmingham. That's when MGM Records took notice. "A couple of MGM reps came out to Smoochie's Show Bar, took one look at us in our pharaoh outfits, and said, 'That's it, deal's closed. You guys are on MGM Records.' It was just that fast," says Stinnett.

"Wooly Bully" was released nationally in March 1965, at the height of the British invasion, on MGM Records—the label of Herman's Hermits. It shot to No. 2 on the *Billboard* Hot 100, went on to sell 3.5 million copies, and was named record of the year for 1965 by *Billboard* magazine. The solemn pact that Samudio and Martin had made in that dim motel room in Louisiana had been fulfilled; they had their gold record.

In short order, the band that had existed by living in flophouse motels and eating balogna and onion sandwiches was on tour in Europe and introduced to a national television audience by Ed Sullivan. Making the leap to the drive-in screen, the fully garbed Sam and the Pharaohs appeared with Herman's Hermits in the MGM motion picture *When The Boys Meet The Girls,* starring Connie Francis, Harve Presnell, and Sue Ann Langdon, with cameo appearances by Louis Armstrong and Liberace.

Dick Clark booked the band even before "Wooly Bully" had made it to the top of the charts. "He's a visionary," Ray says with admiration. "He knows a good thing when he sees one coming. We were booked on the Dick Clark Caravan of Stars tour for a small amount of money. We lived on a bus for about 30 days and slept in the luggage racks, on the floor, whatever."

Butch also recalls with fondness his days touring with the Caravan of Stars. "We toured on the West Coast with Ike and Tina Turner, James Brown, the Beach Boys, the Righteous Brothers, and others," Butch says wistfully. "Dick Clark is without a doubt the greatest guy in the music business in the whole world and always will be. If Dick Clark tells you that tomorrow is Easter, you have to color your eggs tonight. Whatever he says is real. We went up the West Coast into Portland and then down to Reno. I'll never forget the night that we played in Oakland, with James Brown the marquee leader on the show. We had a blues song called 'I Found A Love' that was done originally by the Isley Brothers. We held it for the last song of our set, and I mean we really *played* it. James Brown came out of his dressing room with his silk robe on, and stood in the wings with his hands on his hips and watched us sing that song. He wanted to know who was singing because the crowd was going crazy. He didn't smile, applaud, nothing. When we were done he just turned around and walked off. And that was kind of like his approval."

Capitalizing on the success of "Wooly Bully," MGM rushed the group into the studio to record a couple of cookie-cutter follow-up hits, "Ju Ju Hand" and "Ring Dang Doo." For 10 months the band toured relentlessly throughout the United States and Europe, pausing only to record three albums. The pace took its toll by the spring of 1966.

"Our management unmercifully worked us on the road," says Ray. "We were all young, married, and had young children except for Sam, even though we lied and told all of the fan magazines that we were single. As soon as we'd get home and see our wives, the phone would ring, and we'd be told, 'You gotta come to the studio' or some such thing."

Despite the grueling schedule, touring seemed to have its rewards—at first. Initially, the band members managed their own funds, counting their earnings after each show and keeping their mounting cash reserves in shoe boxes. Then they assigned financial management duties to a team of New York accountants. The band members were given expense accounts, and small allowances were sent to their homes. That arrangement seemed satisfactory until the day Butch called the accountants' office and asked for $1,000 to buy a motorcycle. "The accountant laughed and told Butch, 'You don't have $1,000,' and we all freaked out because we'd figured we should have had about $100,000 in the account by then," says Ray. "So we went to meet with them and they showed us stacks of statements showing where all of our money had been spent. We had 70 people working for us who we didn't know, in offices we'd never seen, and bills we were unaware of. It was horrible."

Sam remembers the day the band broke up. They were staying at a Ramada Inn on the road. "It was a Wednesday. They asked when we would be going home. And I told them, 'This *is* home.' They were weary. They wanted to go out and try it on their own. I said, 'OK,' but I turned to David and asked, 'Where are you going Dave?' He said, 'I think I'll go with them.' And that's how we parted. The following day I flew to New York."

Legal action with the record company and talent agents over the use of the band's name ensued. For a settlement of $1,000 apiece, Patterson, Martin, Stinnett, and Gibson agreed to relinquish use of the name Pharaohs.

In New York, Sam assembled a new group of Pharaohs from a band called Tony G and the Gypsies. The recruits included musician Frank Carabetta, singer Tony Gerace, drummer Billy Bennett, and guitarist Andrew Kouha. Searching for a new hit formula for the reconstituted group, MGM concocted a nursery rhyme scheme. Surprisingly, the initial effort of that new direction, "Li'l Red Riding Hood," clicked and gave Sam and company their second top 10, million-selling single. But personnel turmoil continued. Billy Bennett exited and was replaced by Louis Vilardo. Ronnie (Spiderman) Jacobsen became bassist. The band was given a new dimension with the addition of the Shamettes, a female vocal backup trio consisting of Fran Curcio, Loraine Genero, and Jane Anderson.

By the time "Black Sheep" was released in June 1967, the novelty of Sam the Sham and the Pharaohs had worn off. The group's next single, "Banned In Boston," appeared to be banned everywhere else as well; it didn't even crack the top 100. But that was probably more a measure of the times than of the music made by Sam the Sham and the Pharaohs. In their prime, Sam and the group had surmounted heavy odds and taken their barroom beat to the top of the charts.

But by the summer of 1967 the lights had changed. That was the summer of love, of Monterey Pop, of Haight-Ashbury, when the Beatles' landmark *Sgt. Pepper's Lonely Hearts Club Band* helped to usher in the era of psychedelia. America left Tex-Mex and Memphis behind as it tripped off to San Francisco.

HIT SINGLES BY SAM THE SHAM AND THE PHARAOHS

DEBUT	PEAK	TITLE	LABEL
4/65	2	WOOLY BULLY (Certified Gold)	XL, MGM
7/65	26	JU JU HAND	MGM
10/65	33	RING DANG DOO	MGM
2/66	82	RED HOT	MGM
6/66	2	LI'L RED RIDING HOOD (Certified Gold)	MGM
10/66	22	THE HAIR ON MY CHINNY CHIN CHIN	MGM
12/66	27	HOW DO YOU CATCH A GIRL	MGM
3/67	54	OH THAT'S GOOD, NO THAT'S BAD	MGM
6/67	68	BLACK SHEEP	MGM

SAM SAMUDIO

Fort Polk, Louisiana. 1963. A car rolls to a stop at the entrance gate of the U.S. Army base. A young soldier steps out of the guard shack, approaches the vehicle, and addresses the driver.

Solider: "Sir, please state your business."

Driver: "My passengers and I are expected at the Officers' Club."

Soldier: "I'll need to see identification."

Voice from the back seat: "¿Que dijo?" ["What did he say?"]

Soldier: "Hold it right there."

The soldier peers into the vehicle and does a double-take. There, seated in the rear, are three other men, one of them a dark-haired, bearded man wearing military fatigues and a garrison cap and clenching a large cigar in his teeth. To the young guard, the man looks very much like Cuban Premier Fidel Castro.

PHOTO BY MICKEY O'KEEFE/MAJESTIC ENTERTAINMENT CO.

Soldier (placing his hand on his holstered .45 service weapon): "Sir, you'll need to report to the Provost Marshall's office."

The driver was Andy Anderson and the man in the fatigues was Domingo "Sam" Samudio, and he and the other musicians went on to play their set in the Officers' Club without incident. The band was called Andy and the Night Riders, the precursor to Sam the Sham and the Pharaohs. Although the Fidel Castro impersonation was typical of the stunts the band members occasionally pulled for their own mischievous enjoyment, it reflected the proclivity for costumes that would help propel Sam to international stardom in a robe and turban.

Sam had put in some military time of his own, a four-year stint in the U.S. Navy. After his discharge in December 1959, the lanky 6-foot-1 Samudio became a construction laborer—as his father, Jim Samudio, was—in order to save enough money for the entrance fee to the University of Texas, Arlington. While studying English and music there, he worked beer joints, singing and playing harmonica for $6 a night. Sam grew restless in college, however, as he pondered his ambitions. He wanted to be a movie star. He wanted to be a bull fighter. He wanted to be a singer. More than anything else, he wanted to be a singer.

Born February 28, 1937, Sam made his performing debut as a first-grader singing "I'm Always Chasing Rainbows" in a contest broadcast on a radio station in his hometown of Dallas. As a high school student at Crozier Tech, Sam took voice lessons and began performing lunch-hour concerts in a band with two fellow students: bassist David Martin and singer Trini Lopez. After quitting college, Sam united with Martin, drummer Vincent Lopez, and two other friends in forming a band that pounded out Tex-Mex music and blues. They called themselves the Pharaohs. Mirroring the interest in ancient Egypt stirred by the motion pictures *The Ten Commandments* and *Cleopatra,* an image of King Ramses adorned the Pharaohs' bass drum. The Pharaohs played funky clubs that paid each musician as little as $5 per night. After the group disbanded, Sam did what he could to survive, including selling french fries and hot dogs on the midway at the Texas State Fair and cutting truckloads of fir trees in the forests of New Mexico for the Christmas season.

Not everyone in Sam's family was pleased that he had begun to pursue an entertainment career. His sister, Esterina Samudio, who received a master's degree in education and special education and still teaches in Laredo, encouraged Sam to continue with his studies. Sam's older half-brother, Onesimo Hernandez, who was a physician, offered to pay Sam's way through law school if he'd promise to relinquish entertaining. But the siren call of the stage was too strong, and it drew him to Louisiana and then to Memphis, where Sam the Sham and the Pharaohs began their rise to fame.

Although distressed by the breakup of Sam the Sham and the Pharaohs in the spring of '66, he took pride in the success achieved after he re-formed the band.

"People were saying I'd never do it again. They said I was a one-trick pony," says Sam. "That was before we recorded 'Li'l Red Riding Hood.' It sold over a million and a half." That was in the summer of '66. Sam and the reconfigured Pharaohs went on to drive two more novelty tunes into the top 30, but the group's popularity sagged after the release of their January 1967 single, "How Do You Catch A Girl?"

Sensing the inevitable demise of the group, Sam recorded and released a solo album titled *Ten Of Pentacles* in 1967. The title, which refers to a Tarot card that symbolizes material wealth and success, was indicative of Sam's interest in the mystical arts, including Tarot card reading and astrology.

Four years passed before his next recording endeavor. Long after the expiration of the MGM contract, Sam was in a club in London hanging out with bluesmen Freddy King and Charlie Hooker. A man walked up to him and tersely introduced himself. "Sam. Sam the Sham," he said. "Ahmet. Ahmet Ertegun. Atlantic. Do you have a contract with anybody?"

"No, I'm not signed," Sam replied.

"Would you like to do an album for us?" Ertegun asked.

"Yeah."

"When you get back to New York, call me," Ertegun said as he walked off.

Freddie King turned to Sam and said, "Man, that was Ahmet Ertegun from Atlantic Records."

Sam returned to New York, took up Ertegun's offer, and went to a Florida studio to record with a cadre of top-notch musicians. The Dixie Flyers formed the rhythm section and the Sweet Inspirations sang backup. The result was a heavily blues-flavored album of which Sam was proud but which received little airplay or public attention. Still, his work on the album, called *Sam Hard And Heavy,* didn't go totally unrecognized, as Samudio won a Grammy Award for best liner notes. Written as a personal acknowledgment of those who had helped and inspired him, the liner notes also revealed Sam's pain and exposed those who inadvertently strengthened his character by mistreating him. His list of those to thank began with "The people who mistreated me as a child, 'cause they made me strong." He thanked "the people who refused me service, for they made me save my money." He thanked "the people who rejected me because of the color of my skin and the texture of my hair, for they made me realize that I was different." He thanked "the towns I was run out of, for they ran me to better places." He thanked the women who loved him, and acknowledged that loving the wind would have been easier. He thanked his children "for having chosen me as their father in this life; for they alone gave me the will and strength to continue when all other sources of energy were depleted." Finally: "And most of all, God for letting me be a musician, for in doing so he's given me a taste of Paradise."

Sam packed and went west to fulfill the acting ambitions he'd harbored since his college days. But when he was unable to navigate his way into the inner circles in Hollywood, Sam took up a pen and began writing music and recorded some tracks with a number of top session musicians in L.A. He was surviving financially, he said, on a guaranteed 10-year salary from MGM. Just about the time he began to experience some artistic freedom, the Internal Revenue Service came to call. Sam and the Pharaohs had long questioned royalty payments they said they never received and expenditures by their agents they say they never authorized. "I was doing OK until the IRS came after me for money I had never seen," says Sam. He let himself slip into a boozy, hallucinogenic mire. He'd previously been hospitalized for collapse of the lower lobe of his left lung, which he almost lost. "It was caused by smoking, cocaine, and the dusty dumps I'd played in for so many years." He reached bottom, figuratively and literally, when he found himself on the floor of his Hollywood Hills apartment, staring up at the sky. Sam heard a voice—the voice, he said, of God.

"Lord, give me a break, because I know this is going to take me out," Sam pleaded, referring to drug abuse. "If you would just remove the desire, I'll go wherever you want me to go and do whatever you want me to do. I just want to ask you to take care of my kids." Sam, saying he "felt a peace," experienced a transformation. "That night I felt the power of God come into the room. He spoke to my heart and said, 'I gave you a talent and look what it's come to. I'm going to put it back together for you and the way I'll put it back together no man will be able to take it apart.' And I said, 'God, I love to stay high.' And the Lord spoke to my heart and said, 'I'll keep ya high. But it won't be on anything cheap. The high that I'll keep you on is so expensive, it cost my son his life.' And I said, 'You know Lord, I love to run that highway.' And the Lord said, 'You can run that highway, but you'll run it for me.' And when I made that deal with the Lord I walked away from rock and roll."

Sam concluded that he really was a sham. Uncertain about what to do with his life, he lingered in L.A. until 1976. "Then I returned to Memphis and went through some more changes," says Sam, ticking off a succession of events. "Got married. To the wrong woman. By that time it was the third marriage."

When that marriage went awry, Sam headed back to Texas—not to Dallas, but down the Louisiana border through Sabine Pass to the shipyards on the Gulf Coast. There he signed on as a deckhand, doing labor on the ships that shuttled workers and supplies to the offshore oil rigs in the Gulf of Mexico. Sam shaved his trademark beard and quietly, anonymously toiled, working his way up through the ranks and reading his Bible in his room. No more hearses, no more turbans, no more "Wooly Bully." Just Sam, the sea, and his God. Sam rose to the rank of engineer, then mate, then captain, piloting vessels. He commanded a 100-ton crew vessel and though he battled 23-foot swells in stormy seas, his spirit was becalmed.

Sam did surface briefly from anonymity when Ry Cooder called in 1982. Cooder, an admirer of Samudio's music, wanted him to record a couple of tracks for the Universal Pictures film *The Border,* starring Jack Nicholson, Harvey Keitel, and Valerie Perrine. One of Sam's former wives, Brenda Patterson, also a singer, helped Cooder track Sam down in the Gulf. The script appealed to Sam and he wrote two songs, "Palomita" and "No Quiero," in Spanish. The project brought

Sam, Freddy Fender, and Flaco Jimenez into collaboration. Once his work on the project was completed, Sam slipped back to the Gulf oil fields.

Then while out at sea one day in 1985, another conversation with the Lord persuaded him to do more with his life. As easily as he came to the shipyards, he left, and headed once again for Memphis. This time, Sam was on a mission from God. That mission was to spread The Word.

He did so wherever people would listen. Driving a pickup truck with a small trailer in tow, he'd stop on a street corner, set up shop, and begin preaching and singing gospel songs. And that's what he does today, speaking and singing wherever anyone will listen, in nursing facilities, homeless shelters, jailhouses, and maximum-security prisons. He exists on commercial-use royalties from "Wooly Bully" and other songs he's written. Today his accompaniment is provided not by Pharaohs, but by a group called Gideon's Few, whose members include reformed drug abusers.

Sam hasn't completely forsaken his musical roots. In 1995, he went back into the studio and recorded an album of gospel songs backed by the Ambassadors for Christ. Released in cassette format on his own Samara label—a name that means "protected by God"—the album contained nine songs, including "Prayer Line," "Maranata," and a power medley ("What A Friend We Have"/"There Is Power In The Blood"/"I'll Fly Away").

Sam says his family wasn't religious, although one of the few memories he retains of his mother, who died when he was only 3½, is a prayer she liked to recite. "I'm not into religion," Sam says. "It was religious people who nailed Jesus to the cross. I don't really preach. I teach." Sam speaks proudly of the Bible study courses he conducts at several prisons in the Memphis region. He's even journeyed to Latin America as an interpreter with a missionary organization called Health Care Ministries. Sam paid his own way. "That was just part of my end of the bargain with the Lord," Sam explains.

Sam married his present wife, Ann Dearborn, in 1986. Of Ann, he says, "I was resolved to live the rest of my life alone when the Lord blessed me with a fantastic person." His two sons, now in their 30s, are successful in their careers. One is a jazz and symphony musician, and the other is a bright computer programmer who enjoys playing music. Sam also has a daughter who was born in 1980, just about the time he went off to sea.

For a long time Sam tried to suppress memories of the old days. While he still performed, he'd sing only gospel, refusing requests for "Wooly Bully." A few years ago, however, he began to come to terms with the past. Today Sam does consent to do a few of the old tunes, along with a gospel number or two. And he holds pleasant memories. His fondest thoughts, he says, are of bassist David Martin, who died in Dallas of a heart attack in August 1987. "I loved him.

Sometimes you can have a bond with a friend that other people don't understand. Even wives. It was rough in Louisiana, and we went through a lot together down there."

Speaking of his previous wives, Sam says, "Today I have great relationships with the mothers of my children. And I really appreciate that." Looking back, Sam candidly says, "I imagine any of those situations would have worked if I'd have worked at it." He tempers his tart self-criticism with an apologetic philosophical nugget: "You can't blame a dog for being a dog."

So comes to mind the paradoxical question: Who is the real Sam the Sham, and what kind of person is he? "You should ask my enemies," replies Sam in his salt-dried drawl. But quoting Scripture, he found an answer. "Paul the Apostle said, 'In this flesh dwelleth no good thing.' What kind of person am I? I'm not anything but by the grace of God. I guess I'm critical and, at times, I can get full of myself. You know, you must always guard against becoming a legend in your own mind. And, if we're going to serve God, let's really serve God," he urges. "That doesn't mean you have to walk around with a long, drawn face trying to be sanctimonious. Look at me," he offers, grinning that mischievous Sam the Sham grin. "I still keep company with publicans and sinners."

DAVID MARTIN (1937–1987)

Although the colorfully costumed Sam the Sham and the Pharaohs were most often identified with lively novelty tunes, their roots were in the blues. And while Sam Samudio personified the group's on-stage image, the musical soul of the Pharaohs was embodied in David Martin.

If anyone was truly accountable for the formation of Sam the Sham and the Pharaohs, it was David. It was he who had recruited Sam to join Andy and the Night Riders in Louisiana. It was he who had solemnly declared with Sam the intent to capture a gold record. It was he who had encouraged Sam to persevere as Andy and the Night Riders were preparing to abandon their plans for stardom in Memphis. And it was he who provided musical direction in shaping the repertoire of Sam the Sham and the Pharaohs.

David Allen Martin was born on March 20, 1937, into a family with a rich heritage of Dutch, German, and Native American blood. Both Martin and Sam

The late David Martin in 1986. PHOTO BY JEAN MARTIN.

Samudio, who met in high school, grew up in West Dallas, the poor, working-class area that produced notorious '30s gangsters Bonnie and Clyde. Looking for something more than West Dallas could give him, Martin quit school and enlisted in the Army. Assigned to duty in Germany, he promptly joined a country music band called the Redeye Four. He also completed the requirements for his high school diploma. On his discharge in 1959, he returned to Dallas, where he worked in construction for a time before joining a rhythm and blues band called Tommy Brown and the Tom-Toms.

David first showed musical inclinations as a preschooler, when he became separated from his parents at the Texas State Fair. After a frantic search, they found him at the bandstand, where he was mesmerized by the musicians. David's father, Calvin, a superintendent for an electrical contracting firm, and his mother, Edna, both encouraged David's musical development. According to Jean Martin, who was married to David from February 1964 until his death in August 1987, "His daddy gave him a guitar when he was 11 years old and let him have lessons with a teacher in downtown Dallas. He'd take the bus there every Saturday from the Cement City neighborhood where they lived." The first song he learned to play was "Red River Valley," which was popular in the late '40s.

Martin, 6-foot-3 as an adult and tall and regal in appearance, was so small at birth compared to his four older brothers that his mother started calling him "Tiny." The name stuck. To his brothers and his friends at school, he was always "Tiny." Jean met David on Christmas Eve, when a few friends took her out for a night on the town to celebrate her 19th birthday. They went to the Colonial Club, a nightspot in Arlington, midway between Dallas and Ft. Worth. There, David was playing bass with Tommy Brown and the Tom-Toms. One of Jean's friends was dating a member of the band, and at the break the musicians came over to the table where Jean was sitting. David asked Jean to dance. That began a four-year courtship, during which David told Jean he would marry only when he was sure of his future. Jean herself was cautious.

"He was tall, well-mannered, and good-looking," Jean recalled upon first meeting David. "But I was very leery of dating him because he played in a band and I thought at that time that a man wanted only one thing, and I wasn't about to let him have it. And that's what I told him on our second date. That shocked him, but he was also pleased." Apparently so, because David went home and awakened his mother. "He told her that he'd just met a girl—a good girl. And then he took me to meet her. She told me I was the first girl he'd brought home in five years."

At about the same time in 1960 that Martin quit his construction job to devote full attention to music, Tommy and the Tom-Toms signed on as the house band at Guthrie's—the hottest club in Dallas. It was at Guthrie's that David met Andy Anderson and his band. David accepted Andy's invitation to join the Night Riders, who had club dates lined up in Louisiana. Before long, David began making a name for himself. Barely in his 20s, he backed and toured with blues greats Jimmy Reed, Elmore James, and Lightnin' Hopkins as well as R&B pioneers Chuck Berry and the Drifters. Jean said his talent was self-evident. "He had a natural ear and perfect pitch, and he could play about anything he set his mind to playing," she observes.

David and Jean continued dating on his frequent returns to Dallas, where she worked in the billing department of Lone Star Steel. In Louisiana in the spring of 1963, David was joined by his former schoolmate Sam Samudio. As the band's sound solidified, the bond strengthened between Sam and David, and both envisioned a recording career. On the encouragement of David and Sam, Andy and the Night Riders migrated to the music Mecca of Memphis that summer in quest of a gold record. Did David really believe at that time that a gold record was within their grasp? "Oh, yes," says Jean. "He believed that with all his heart, and of course he did get that gold record, and he was happy."

When the Night Riders retreated to Louisiana after only a few months in Memphis, Martin and Samudio formed Sam the Sham and the Pharaohs. "David," says Jerry Patterson, "was the soul of the band. He was the one who picked all the songs that we played. David knew way more than we did about the blues."

Ray Stinnett characterizes Martin as a man of creativity, quiet intelligence, and unpretentious goodness. Ray was close to David—off stage and on. "He's the guy who I shared a microphone with on more gigs than I can count," says Stinnett. "We used to make lots of jokes about all those onions that Dave ate corroding the mike. I never minded because we loved to sing harmony together. He made the most handsome Pharaoh when we were in our costumes," Ray adds. "He had enough charisma to inspire the whole band."

As popular as the band was becoming and as close as he felt to his fellow performers, David couldn't ignore the empty spot in his heart.

At 3 o'clock one morning in January 1964, the phone rang at Jean's house in South Oak Cliff. Jean answered. Dave was on the line. "He'd had a little bit to drink," Jean recalls. "Will you marry me?" he blurted out. She asked him to repeat that. Mustering up a bit more confidence, he repeated, "Will you marry me?" Jean sat silent for a moment before replying, "Yes. Tomorrow will be fine."

The next morning at about 11, Jean phoned David.

"Do you remember calling me last night?" she asked him.

"Yes," he replied.

"And do you remember what you said?"

"Yes," said David.

They were married in a small church wedding on February 17, 1964, the first date David could get off work. They moved into the rented house that all the band members had previously roomed in together, while the other band members rented apartments elsewhere in deference to the newly married couple. And as the Pharaohs began touring, their wives frequently kept each other company, stayed overnight at each others' homes, and looked after each other. So it was when "Wooly Bully" hit. The night the boys headed off on their initial tour, Jean suffered a miscarriage. Saxophonist Butch Gibson's wife, Gwynne, took care of Jean during the difficult weeks that followed.

Even at the height of the group's popularity, David and Jean tried to live normal lives. He treated touring as if it were a day at the office. "To him, that was going to work. That was his job," says Jean.

Their daughter, Denise, was born in 1966, just as the band was breaking up. Leaving Sam behind, David, Butch, Jerry, and Ray remained together for a time and played in a few nightspots around Memphis and other cities in the South. But they were unable to land a steady gig. Money became tight for David and Jean because her accounting job at the home office of Holiday Inn couldn't quite stretch far enough to pay all the bills.

David decided to use his GI Bill benefits and enrolled in an electronics training course through the DeVry Institute. He played gigs by night, and baby-sat Denise during the daytime, studying while Jean worked. "We were kind of passing ships in the night for a while," Jean smiles wistfully as she recalls those times. "David finished his electronics course early and got excellent grades, because he had a high IQ," she says. David landed a job with a big retailer in Memphis that sold home entertainment products and operated an in-store repair service. "He worked for them for about seven months before deciding it wasn't for him because the owners were dishonest. After David would repair a TV that somebody had exchanged because it was defective, the store would turn around and sell it as new again. He didn't care for that. He was a very honest person. He didn't like cheating people."

David and Jean opened their own television repair shop in Memphis called Martin Electronics and built up the business until it had a steady clientele. But in 1975 Jean's allergies worsened and she developed asthma. They returned to Dallas. "He moved back for my sake," says Jean. There in Dallas, they started a new Martin Electronics store, offering TV and VCR repair. They closed shop nine years later, when their inventory of unclaimed repaired televisions became unmanageable. David remained in television repair, working as a technician for others.

Sale of the business permitted him to spend more time at home with Jean and Denise, which he relished. He had purchased a drum set for Denise when she was 8 years old, and he taught her how to play. Denise has fond memories of those days. "The first song he taught me was 'California Dreamin' by the Mamas and the Papas, and then 'Sloop John B' and 'Tequila.' We liked to clown around and play that. It started out just me and him and then all the kids in the neighborhood wanted to play, too," recalls Denise. "And we'd sing and he'd try to teach me harmony."

Denise says her dad continued playing his guitar long after he'd gone into TV repair. "That was his relaxation, his comfort zone." Those informal jam sessions rekindled David's interest in music, and he began to consider managing the career of drummer Jeff Hilliard, with whom he had developed a close, paternal relationship. It was not to be.

David was home relaxing one August day in 1987 when he mentioned feeling ill. "He didn't like to go to the doctor, and when he got a feeling of heartburn he didn't think much of it. But when it didn't go away after a few hours and then he said his arm ached, I thought I'd better phone the doctor." David went to the bedroom. As she phoned the doctor's office, Jean heard a thud. David had collapsed. He was rushed to the hospital, where doctors reported he'd suffered a massive heart attack. They were unable to save him.

Denise, who was 21 when her father died, confesses to having no particular interest in school as a young girl. "My interest was just getting home and being with my dad," she said. "He always gave. He always called me 'Baby,' and he would give me his last dollar for my lunch at school. He was usually home by the time I got home and we'd ride the lawnmower together and play guitar or swim. We had an above-ground pool in the backyard and we'd play water volleyball all the time. You know, he was a mentor, he was a friend. He had an open-door policy with you to find out what was on your mind. And he was that way with all my friends, too."

Now married and a mom herself, Denise bought her son, Dalton, a snare drum for his second birthday. One of Denise's best friends, a young man who studied drumming and talked music with Denise's dad, gave the name David to his first-born son. "What I miss most in my dad I get to see and enjoy in my son, Dalton," Denise confides.

Jean Martin says three things mattered most to David: privacy, love for his family, and humankind. "He was a religious person, even though he didn't go to church," said Jean. "He knew his Bible inside out, and he lived life as a Christian daily."

Although David Martin did get his gold record, he never did achieve substantial riches. But that didn't matter much to him. "We both came from struggling families so we thought we were well off," explains Jean. "David always said when he was growing up that he thought the rich kids lived in the projects. We didn't know we were poor. We had love."

THEN AND NOW
RAY STINNETT

The rocky canyons carved in the parched foothills beyond Ray Stinnett's Southern California neighborhood rise to the flanks of Mount Baldy. From the mountain peaks overlooking the mustard-colored haze blanketing the Pomona Valley the ozone glare obscures all but the faintest outline of the Pacific coastline at Santa Monica Bay, 50 miles away. Though the view may be veiled, Ray's memories of the days he and his wife, penniless, slept on those beaches remain clear.

The journey from that era on the beach to Ray's present foothills home was a test of faith and patience, one stop on a philosophical odyssey that took him from obscurity in his native Memphis to international celebrity, from blues to country music, from redneck bars to life at a "hippie" commune. Along the way he crossed paths with some of the legends of the music world, sold health foods, helped build hotels and houses, and fashioned a musical instrument from a door. And Ray is still redefining himself today, still looking for answers.

Ray learned the answer to one of his most puzzling musical questions early in his career. Although he was an apostle of blues music, he was unable to replicate the particular lonesome, melancholy whine that legendary African American blues artists coaxed from their guitars. He found out how one night from one of the masters, when he and drummer Jerry Patterson heard that B.B. King was playing at Club Paradise on Beale Street. They went there and got a front-row table. Ray sat mesmerized through B.B.'s set, intent on watching his intricate fingering.

Ray and Sandra Stinnett. PHOTO BY JEFF MARCH.

"After the set, B.B. stepped off the stage and we went over and talked to him. It was pretty obvious we were musicians because we were the only white guys there," says Ray. "I asked him, 'How do you get that sound with those strings?' And B.B. told me the secret. He said, 'I go down to the drugstore and buy myself a packet of Black Diamond strings and I buy an extra second string and I put that where the third string is supposed to go. All of the white guys use those wound third strings and you just can't pull those strings to get the blues sound, even if you know how to play the blues.' And that's what B.B. told me. The second string is unwound. It's just straight steel and it's thinner. So nowadays," says Stinnett, "everyone uses an unwound third string. It's more pliable, you can pull it, and that's how the blues sound is developed on the guitar. B.B. is the guy who started that sound. I think I was one of the first white guys to use that technique. I started stringing my guitar that way and from that day forward, I was able to play the blues much better than I had before."

Ray attributes his early interest in music to his uncle Mitchell "Mickey" Stinnett, who had played guitar and bass with bluegrass music pioneer Bill Monroe. "When my dad first came home from the war, my uncle broke his guitar out from under the bed, and I was hooked."

Born James Ray Stinnett in Memphis on February 18, 1944, the red-haired guitarist has gone by his middle name ever since he can remember. Ray had developed a strong interest in boogie-woogie music by the age of 7, three years before the debut of the earliest rock and roll songs. Inspired by a 12-year-old neighbor who played boogie-woogie on the piano, Ray persuaded his parents to buy a piano and enroll him in lessons. Ray's mother was a beautician and his father was a civil service employee who worked for a time in the U.S. space program. Although Ray took lessons for several years, his teacher disliked boogie-woogie and taught classical style only. "I'd occasionally get rapped across the knuckles with her ruler for playing boogie-woogie. She finally gave up in disgust and advised my parents to sell my piano. She thought I was off on the wrong foot. And my parents listened to her."

Ray continued his musical pursuits at school, where he began playing horns and joined the school band. But "Daddy-O" Dewey Phillips's "Red, Hot And Blue" radio program on WHBQ caught his ear, and after the station began playing Elvis Presley's recordings, Ray decided he had to have a guitar. "So in 1956 my folks took me down to Nathan Novick's on Beale Street, the same place Elvis bought his guitar, and they bought me a guitar for $29," recalls Ray. "That same night, as fate would have it, Elvis was cruising Beale Street in his pink Cadillac, and pulled right up beside us at the stoplight. I said, 'Hey, Elvis,' and he answered, 'Hey, cat.' That provided all the inspiration I needed."

Ray took a few lessons from premier instructor and solid-body guitar maker Lynn Vernon, then began practicing with upright bass player Jimbo Hale, nephew of rock music performer Bill Black. Within a year Ray had hooked up with many other young musicians and eventually formed a band called Johnny and the Electros, which began playing sock hops and other local engagements. "We were highly competitive at Kingsbury High School, where kids who later formed the

Gentrys had a rival band. I started getting paid to play when I was 13 years old." Johnny and the Electros remained together for about four years. "I decided it was time to move on as I became more interested in jazz and black music."

Ray immersed himself in his music, to the exclusion of everything else. Or so he thought. "In January 1963, after telling a close friend I felt so dedicated to my musical pursuits that I was sure I would never get married, I met my true love, Sandra Crofford," said Ray. They were married a few weeks later. "She loved me and my music, and still does today."

A few months after Ray and Sandra were married, Sonny Wilson returned briefly from California, where he'd been working, and he invited Ray and Jerry to join him at a gig in San Bernardino, California—about 20 miles from Ray's home today. They played a few country music places in the area, but that didn't appeal much to Jerry and Ray and before long they returned to Memphis, where in the summer of 1963 they first encountered Samudio and Martin. Ray says that although he sort of knew that "Wooly Bully" was a huge hit in major capitals as well as remote outposts, he didn't fully realize the magnitude of its success until years later, when he met a man who had done combat duty in Vietnam in 1965. "The guy hung out at a joint in Saigon where the only American tune on the jukebox was 'Wooly Bully' and they literally wore out the record. He said his company used 'Wooly Bully' to march cadence."

After Ray and the three Pharaohs parted with Sam in the spring of 1966, they began calling themselves the Violations and recorded "The Hanging," a song that Butch Gibson and Ray wrote protesting their treatment. Released on Dot Records, the song failed to capture attention and Butch decided to leave the recording business. David Martin, Jerry Patterson, and Ray Stinnett took a new name, the First Century, and landed a gig in Naples, Florida. They recorded some songs, including "Dancing Girl" and "Looking Down," written by Ray. "On 'Dancing Girl,' I played harpsichord and recorder flute, which I had bought just the day before. On 'Looking Down,' I also played an instrument that I had made out of what used to be my dining room door. The door was played like a slide guitar."

The trio hooked up with Sonny Wilson, who invited them to come to California. Once again, Ray found himself playing in San Bernardino. It was the summer of 1967. The Beatles had released *Sgt. Pepper's Lonely Hearts Club Band,* 50,000 people converged on the Monterey Pop Festival for performances by the Grateful Dead, Jefferson Airplane, Buffalo Springfield, Quicksilver Messenger Service, and a dozen other acts, and Scott McKenzie's "San Francisco (Be Sure To Wear Flowers In Your Hair)" was an open invitation to America to come to Haight-Ashbury. Ray responded. In San Francisco, he heard about a place called Morningstar Ranch, a commune in the redwoods of Sonoma County on property owned by Lou Gottlieb, a former member of the Limeliters. Ray called Sandra at home and passionately described what he had found. She promptly sold off most of their furnishings and appliances, shuttered their house, and she and their 4-year-old son, Bobby, joined Ray at Morningstar, where they spent the "summer of love" living in a tent amid the redwoods.

"Before Morningstar, I was heavy into liquor, cigarettes, and the night life. While there, I learned how to have fun again, enjoy nature, and listen to other people play music. It was a sort of spiritual rebirth," explains Ray. Morningstar began to attract more widespread attention. The BBC told the story of the commune in a documentary film. "Lou deeded the property to God, and God wouldn't pay the taxes, so that led to the eventual demise of Morningstar," deadpans Ray.

He and his family returned to Memphis, where Ray reunited with Jerry, who had been playing with other bands. With Jerry, bassist Mike Plunk, organist Bruce Smith, and guest performers, Ray formed the group Sun Tree to perform his original material. In the summer of 1969 he recorded a double album for Buddha Records, produced by R&B stalwart Booker T. Jones. The album was never released, nor was a subsequent Stinnett-Jones collaboration for Los Angeles–based A&M Records two years later—not because of problems with agents or distribution, but for quite another reason. "I had my second child by that time and A&M wanted to make a superstar out of me, throw me into the bubblegum music market. That sounded like a nightmare to me. I had already gone that route with 'Wooly Bully.' I didn't want to be a superstar. I just wanted my songs released. That's what I told them at A&M and they weren't too impressed. They said, 'We're going to release you from your contract instead.'" At that point, Ray made a momentous decision—to quit music.

Returning to Memphis once more, he pursued an interest in landscape design inspired by his experience at Morningstar and by a little gardening he'd done while staying at Sam Samudio's apartment in the Hollywood Hills. Ray took a low-paying job with a Memphis landscaping outfit and found out, he says, what hard work was all about. Ray also began taking Yoga classes. He and his Yoga instructor became friends and went into the landscape gardening business together, working out of an old truck that Ray bought. He and Sandra then tried their hand at operating a health food store, Alfalfa's Good Earth Shop, for three years.

In 1982 they moved to Florida, where Ray first did some construction work and then sold vacation time-shares. The time-share company transferred him to Breckenridge, Colorado, a ski resort, but when the time-share market weakened, Ray took a job with a construction firm building a Hilton Hotel at Breckenridge. For a while the Stinnetts settled down, enrolled the kids in school, and enjoyed life. When the construction job ended, though, the money ran out. "In 1986 we moved to Southern California the hard way: broke," says Ray. "We lived in our RV at the beach at Playa del Rey and went surfing a lot."

Then Ray started getting residential construction work in nearby Manhattan Beach and in other communities around L.A. Still living in the RV, they moved to Castaic, while Ray worked as a carpenter at a new housing development for two years. Next they moved to Malibu, where Ray was hired by Sandpiper Construction, which had a heavy roster of celebrity clients. Stinnett's projects included a Malibu ranch house, which he and Sandra restored. The Stinnetts were able to move from their RV into the house, which overlooked the Pacific, around the bend from Dick Clark's home.

One morning Ray couldn't resist the urge to visit Clark. "I knocked on the door, Dick opened it and he asked, 'Are you the carpenter?' I said, 'I am a carpenter but probably not the one you're expecting.' When I told him that I'd worked for him years ago and handed him my card, that blew him away. Dick's a great guy. He showed me around his newly constructed home."

The Stinnetts have four children: Marea, born in 1971, Aaron, born in 1972, Christy, born in 1974, and Laurie, born in 1978. At Santa Monica High School, Aaron played in the drum line of the school's highly regarded marching band, while Marea played orchestral percussion, including xylophone. Marea became the century-old school's first female drum major and conducted from the podium.

Like other proud dads, Ray enjoyed watching his children perform with the band at Santa Monica High football games. As Ray sat in the bleachers at the football home opener one September evening in 1988, he had an unexpected and emotional reunion with an old friend. There to watch his own son Justin play football was Carl Wilson of the Beach Boys, with whom Ray and the Pharaohs had appeared in concert at the Seattle Coliseum in 1965. They hadn't seen each other since. The two men who had played to thousands of adoring, screaming fans sat side-by-side in the stands.

In 1991 the Stinnetts moved to Upland, where they established their own business, Ray Stinnett Custom Carpentry. But Ray is more interested in the music activities of his other family business, Stinnett Enterprises. Ray and Sandra have begun exploring music publishing, production, and distribution opportunities available through computer networking on the Internet by means of their "www.axemanmusic.com" Web site.

Ray believes he hasn't yet experienced his greatest moment, saying, "I believe it's possible for people to achieve their heart's desire. My proudest accomplishment will be when I manage to achieve and fulfill everything I started out to do in my life. My family is still a work in progress, and even though it's had a lot of ups and downs, somehow we're all still playing in the same game," says Ray, who believes in the virtues of patience and hard work. "I intend to continue working hard on my music, which I have never really given up on. I've never hung up my rock and roll shoes. I try to break mine out every now and then and polish them up."

JERRY PATTERSON

Until a momentary catastrophic event deprived drummer Jerry Patterson of the pursuit that had defined more than half his life, he thought he knew who he was. But through tragedy, Jerry learned a lesson in courage that opened an unexpected avenue of achievement.

As a teenager in 1950s Memphis, Jerry wasn't sure what to do with himself. Working the Cotton Exchange or the barges that floated down the Mississippi held no appeal for him, but Shelby County kids didn't have many choices back then. Upon graduation from high school, Jerry took a job in a bread bakery. Even while some of his buddies took an interest in auto mechanics, truck driving, or assembly-line work, Jerry was drawn to Beale Street, immortalized by composer-performer W.C. Handy in his 1912 tribute called "Memphis Blues."

As played by the legendary Johnny Ace, T-Bone Walker, Memphis Slim, Lowell Fulson, Bobby Bland, B.B. King, and other blues artists, the subtle pitch inflections, or "blue notes," that define the blues were infectious. They hooked young Jerry Patterson. Particularly captivated by the beat of many of the blues numbers he heard, Jerry bought a set of drums at the age of 19. He bought B.B. King's "Sweet 16," put it on his phonograph, and began playing along. "That was the first record I ever practiced with, and that's how I learned to play," says Patterson.

Jerry was born November 30, 1941, one week before the bombing of Pearl Harbor made it impossible for the United States to stay out of World War II. His father worked in a variety of trades in the postwar years. "He had cafes, stores, he worked on the river some," says Jerry. His folks encouraged his musical ambitions. "They were proud of my music career, especially Momma."

Jerry pursued his newfound interest with passion, and began practicing with a couple of local guitarists. "I always had my drums in my car and was ready to play at any time," he recalls. Before long he landed his first paying gig with a rockabilly band at a dance club in Jonesboro, Arkansas. "The place was a concrete block square building along a country road out in the cotton fields. It paid $12 per night, and I had to drive 120 miles from Memphis three nights a week.

PHOTO BY CHARLES GAGE.

The bass player in that band, Marcus Van Story, later became part of the Sun Rhythm Section." Jerry had been playing there intermittently for more than a year at the time he met fellow musicians Ray Stinnett and Sonny Wilson.

Although Patterson wasn't getting rich from the music he and Stinnett and Wilson were making, he was working steadily, enough so to settle down, he thought. In 1963 he met and married his first wife, Alma Josephine Brammer, shortly before he and Ray became part of Sam the Sham and the Pharaohs.

"We were young and crazy," remembers Patterson. "I was drinking a lot, doing pills. I was into alcohol and drugs more than anybody else in the band. I liked to have a party every night and sometimes went too far." All the while the British invasion was spreading across the country, Sam the Sham and the Pharaohs continued pumping out the blues at nightclubs through the spring and summer of '64. That Halloween, the boys decided to have a little extra fun. That's the first time they wore the sheets that eventually led to their costumed stage persona. "During that whole period of time we had standing room only at our gigs, and we just got light-headed about it. Ray and I had never been around any kind of success. We were like stars. We'd drive there to do our show and we'd find a line of people outside waiting to see us. Even a little success can spoil some people," Jerry admits. "So we got a big head and started getting goofy about it. I'd dye my hair bright orange or blond, and I caught a lot of grief from the rednecks there. But when you're a star, it doesn't matter. We were playing six hours a night and making $80 a week.

"I guess I knew we were going places when we met at a restaurant one night with a couple of MGM record company guys and a lawyer," says Patterson. "They had mapped out a concert tour, and they had bought us a late-model Ford station wagon to ride in. It looked so exciting. We headed out in the station wagon and the hearse because we had a lot of equipment, including Sam's organ. It was heavy. The first date on the tour was in Holyoke, Massachusetts, and we had to drive there straight from Memphis. The rest of the tour was just as ridiculous, driving long distances like that. Still, we thought it was all right then because we were having so much fun. Later, we started flying to gigs."

Jerry regrets that the high-flying days of Sam the Sham and the Pharaohs lasted such a short time and left them with so little. "'Wooly Bully' sold a few million copies. By the time that happened, it was all sour. We figured we'd have a lot of money, about $30,000 apiece, when the first royalty checks came in just before Christmas in 1965. We went to a meeting but instead of money we got a huge statement sheet showing where all our money went for hotels, touring and managers and stuff, and we walked away with nothing. The stack of statements was about an inch and a half thick. There were expense items in there like Playboy clubs and limousines, and we had never seen a Playboy club. I had a wife and a 2-year-old daughter, Randy Lynn, at home who I'd hardly ever seen. All the fun went out of it because my wife had no car, no money month after month, and for a year I kept telling her that it would get better." Even after he and the other musicians quit and headed home, Jerry somehow thought a solution would materialize because they had planned to retain the name Pharaohs and resume performing on their own. "When we got back, they said we owed them some money. That broke our spirit right there."

Jerry's memories of the "summer of love" experience that followed are a little different from Ray's. "We couldn't stand playing that redneck music we tried for a while and we loved the hippie ideals. So Ray and I drove to San Francisco and we lived in a car on the street for weeks. Our wives were in Memphis with no money. After a while Ray brought his wife out [to Morningstar]. We stayed high a lot, but then I had all I could take of it. My mother sent me some money so I could fly back home. That's when Ray and I finally parted."

Back home in Memphis, Jerry returned to session work, which he did through the 1970s. In 1973 Jerry played with Tony Joe White on the last Creedence Clearwater Revival tour. "It was my last real party. Every night for three months, we had a time. I did a little of everything until age 40." That's when he noticed some lumps on the right side of his neck. A physician told him he suspected the growth was cancerous and ordered a biopsy. During that procedure, the physician nicked a nerve in Jerry's neck. "The whole right side of my body immediately drooped," says Jerry, who is right-handed. "I couldn't raise my right arm for about a year. The biopsy showed that it wasn't cancer, after all; it was cat scratch fever." That's a benign short-term condition characterized by fever and inflammation of the lymph nodes.

Jerry, who knew only to play the drums, was confronted with a stunning reality: his playing career was over. "It was tough, but I think God wanted to get me out of music. I knew it was time to leave music but I couldn't do it on my own." Jerry was undecided what to do until an old friend called him. "Jimmy Day was a musician who I recorded with in the early 1960s. He once had a group called Jimmy Day and the Knights, but he had gone into paint contracting back in the 1970s." Jimmy asked Jerry if he wanted a job. "I don't know anything about painting," Jerry protested. "Well, I'll teach you," came Jimmy's reply. Jerry agreed, and spent the next year and a half working for Jimmy. "After he taught me how to paint, he decided to quit painting. He had a long list of customers and he gave me his list. I started calling people and got jobs."

Jerry and Alma were divorced in the mid-1970s, and in 1982 Jerry married Joanne Cook. Joanne helped him through his painful recovery, but their marriage didn't survive. By this time Randy Lynn was married, and his other daughter, Lara Spring, born in 1972, was living with him. He built his paint contracting business, which is named Master's Touch. He began to hire painting crews to handle the growing volume of work. "But they got to be way too much of a hassle," says Jerry, observing an eerie parallel. "Getting a good paint crew together is like trying to get a band together. Many painters are temperamental and drink too much and do drugs. You can't depend on them." Jerry has scaled down his operation a bit, and now hires only one or two painters at a time as needed. He does home repair work and plastering as well as painting. "Whatever comes up," he says.

Jerry credits his resiliency to a seminal event that occurred in 1978, three years before his life-changing bout with cat scratch fever. "The Bible says no man can come to the Father except through Jesus and you can't come to Jesus unless the Father draws you," says Jerry. "In 1978, I was living with a woman named Virginia Jarvis, and cutting up and getting drunk every night, but she was patient and she was Christian. One day I came in drunk and Virginia started reading the Bible to me and led me into prayer. The next day I got up and I didn't want any drink or smoke or anything anymore. It's been like that since."

In 1994 Jerry married Lorie House, whom he had met in church. He and Lorie say they are now at peace with God. His oldest daughter, Randy Lynn, now has three children of her own.

Jerry doesn't make a big deal of his past. "I never tell people that I was in that band, but somehow people find out even now," he says. Even though that was a long time ago, Jerry's music career remains his greatest source of pride. "I think I'm most proud of the fact that I made a living in music for so many years. It's a hard life and most people couldn't do it. Sam and the band went through a lot together, and I'm happy I can call him my good friend today." Jerry said he still regards drumming as his greatest talent. "I can play at church now, but I can't play over 30 minutes at a time because there's a lot of pain."

Through all the years, Jerry has remained true to his musical roots. "The black music of the 1950s had a profound influence on me. I was really caught up in it all the way. I wasn't a Christian then, but it didn't matter. The rhythms that the black singers adapted from gospel music and the emotion that they sang with, I still love." Jerry's greatest regret is his abuse of drinking and drugs. "That's what killed my music career," he says candidly. "I would get a really fine job where I could have made steady money and I'd get too drunk some night and couldn't play. Or I'd get in someone's face. You know alcohol is like that. It's the devil. It cost me my first family and a lot of money. But pain is a relative term.

"I've been Christian long enough to realize a lot of fundamental truths; one is that God's in control," Patterson declares. "I believe the Bible, and the Bible says that all things work together for good to those that love the Lord. The bad things that happened to me don't seem so bad because they're working toward my good in the long run. God's not concerned about my comfort here. He's concerned about my spiritual well-being and my eternal life. So not many things cause me pain. I get angry like everybody else. But the pain like I used to feel, I don't feel that anymore." Citing Philippians, Jerry adds, "For to me, to live is Christ, and to die is gain."

PAUL "BUTCH" GIBSON

Butch Gibson's saxophone rests in a closet in his Memphis home. The horn that helped coax James Brown to his feet stands in silence. Dusty and tarnished, the instrument has worn pads that for years have rendered it unplayable. As Butch prepares to begin a new stanza in his life, the horn remains a bittersweet reminder of the sadness and happiness of years gone by.

Butch remembers well the first time he heard "Wooly Bully" on the radio. He was listening to WHBQ in Memphis when disc jockey George Klein gave it a spin. Butch should have been excited, but he had other things on his mind. "I've got $2 in my pocket, and if we don't get paid at the club tonight, I won't be able to buy enough gas to get home," he thought. A month later, Butch and the other Pharaohs were performing on stage in Atlanta with the Beach Boys.

The skyscrapers and crowds of Atlanta were leagues away from the small west Tennessee town of Adamsville, where Paul "Butch" Gibson grew up. There, in the country about 100 miles east of Memphis, his folks operated the town's hardware store and a real estate business. Butch took a liking to blues and R&B when he began listening to John R. and Big Hugh Baby around 1956 on WLAC, a Nashville radio station that drifted in through the blackness of the nighttime sky. "I listened to them playing Slim Harpo, Lightnin' Hopkins, and those guys, and I thought, man, that's really good music," recalls Butch, who was born October 2, 1944, in Corinth, Mississippi.

After taking his first music class in junior high, he began playing sax in his high school band. Following his sophomore year, Butch

Butch Gibson with his late wife, Gwynne.

PHOTO BY MARY FRANCES ABERNATHY GIBSON.

left Adamsville to attend a military institution, the Webb School in Bell Buckle, Tennessee. It didn't take Butch long to break out his sax and break into a music combo composed of fellow students. After graduation from military school in June 1962 he entered college at Southwestern-Memphis. Following the lead of other medical professionals in his family, Butch enrolled in Southwestern's premed program, but he moonlighted in music.

His work with Joe Davis and the All-Stars led to his encounter with Sam the Sham and the Pharaohs, which he joined in January 1964. During his two years with the Pharaohs, Butch met and married his wife, Norma Gwynne Mowdy of Union, Mississippi, and Amy, the first of the couple's four children, was born. That event presaged a dramatic change in priorities for Butch. "When Gwynne gave birth to Amy, I realized I really didn't want to be a musician forever," says Butch. His career change came sooner than Butch had anticipated. "The group broke up over money. It's always about money, the same thing that breaks up homes." So when Sam the Sham and the Pharaohs disbanded in early 1966, Butch was perhaps more prepared than other group members to move on. And while he knew he needed to change directions, he made a lot of wrong turns up dead-end streets before he found his way.

His first post-performing foray was into his uncle's used-car business, but it didn't take long for him to realize he didn't like selling automobiles. From there he spent three years pounding on doors as a collection agent for a Memphis finance company. "That was pretty scary," he admits. Then he got an inside job, working as a loan officer for a bank and subsequently went back outdoors again when he and one of his relatives formed a business installing and operating truck wash equipment at truck stops.

When the truck wash business partnership dissolved, Butch hired on as the manager of a truck stop he had been servicing in West Memphis, Arkansas. Within three years, the company, which operated truck stops throughout the South, appointed Gibson vice president of sales and marketing. In that position he developed a wholesale fuel program called Mid America Petroleum Suppliers. "I bought and sold enough gasoline and diesel fuel in the Memphis area every day to raise or lower the price of gasoline on the street by a penny. We sold a lot of petroleum." Butch's high-volume dealings drew news coverage in a national petroleum trade publication, *U.S. Oil Week* in Washington, D.C.

He remained happily in that post for eight years until the early '80s, when his friend and company founder Frank Wagner died and Butch found himself in business with Frank's wife and son. Butch sold his share of the business to them, then with his profits launched his own oil wholesaling business, which he named Phoenix Petroleum. He bought petroleum from refineries and sold it to independent service station operators and regional chains including Total Petroleum Vickers in Memphis. Oil wholesaling is a tricky high-stakes business requiring impeccable timing. And deep pockets. A wholesaler must have sufficient finances on hand to take delivery as product becomes available at good prices, and try to have the right quantity on hand to match the needs of the service station owners. "Ideally, you want the checks to pass one another in the mail," explains Gibson. "It takes about a million dollars in credit to do it. You don't sleep real well in that business. You just stay in the fast lane, and you either get used to it or get out." Gibson quotes a Chinese proverb: He who rides the tiger has fear to dismount. For Gibson, the fear was well-founded. "The business was doing real well until the summer of 1986, when the price of crude oil dropped from $30 to $10 per barrel. I lost about $600,000 in eight weeks."

Butch decided to try his hand at real estate. Plunging in headfirst, he earned a broker's license to sell commercial real estate and sold properties totaling $1 million within his first three months in the business. "That was easy because I was dealing in commercial properties costing $300,000 to $500,000 or more. I sold $3 million in my first year of real estate business, but I earned only $30,000 due to commission splits. I thought, what's wrong with this picture?"

While in real estate he began taking an interest in the computers he was using. He saw new opportunity, and joined a division of the Ralston Purina Company after taking some courses in computer programming and systems management at Christian Brothers University in Memphis. "I went to work for Ralston as a computer nerd. Another example of being in the right place at the right time."

Gibson became the financial information systems administrator of the company's Protein Technologies International subsidiary in Memphis, which was acquired by DuPont in November 1998.

After joining the company, Butch decided to complete his college education. He enrolled at Christian Brothers University, where he earned his bachelor's degree, then his master's degree in business administration in 1999. In September 1999, still with Protein Technologies, he began teaching a night course in management information systems at Crichton College in Memphis.

Butch is also interested in teaching philosophy and theology. The interest in theology is attributable in part to a close call with death he had in 1992. When complications arose during gall bladder surgery, physicians told Butch's family they didn't expect him to survive the night. "I had an out-of-body experience during which I stood at the junction of two tunnels," says Butch. "One goes there, and the other comes back here. While I was in the tunnel I saw my old friend Frank Wagner, who had already gone on." Miraculously, Butch survived. Sadly, his wife Gwynne did not. In 1996, after 32 years of marriage, she died of cancer.

Today, Butch is proud of all four of his children. Amy, the oldest, is now a creative director with Sony Music Publishing in Nashville. Second daughter Lauri, the mother of Butch's grandson, still lives in Memphis and is a customer service agent at Northwest Airlines. Julie, Butch's youngest daughter, is a high school band director in Nashville. Butch's son, Paul, is a lieutenant in the Air National Guard stationed in San Juan, Puerto Rico, where he pilots C141 transport aircraft. Butch is clearly proud of each of them.

Butch says, "I'm very humble because I know that I have been blessed. I've been through a whole lot, but I can see God's hand in it all. I've always felt protected. Even when the bottom completely dropped out from under me, I felt like somebody caught me."

Gibson feels bolstered by what he calls the four Cs in his life: character, charisma, credibility, and Christ. "Character is something you get from your own life's experiences—the ups and downs that put the scars on you but give you soul. Charisma is something that you're born with to a degree, but which you enhance as you develop people skills. Credibility is something you earn by going to the well and coming back with water. You can gain credibility from successes, or from awards like college degrees. Then, of course, Christ is available to everybody. You just have to open your heart and say that you want Christ to take over your life and handle it." In that regard, Butch still has much in common with Sam and the other original Pharaohs. "Sam and I talk on the phone periodically. He was in touch with the family when I was so sick, and he was in touch with me when Gwynne died. He does a whole lot of good in his ministry for the homeless and for prisoners."

Butch performed professionally in the early 1980s, when he sang lead for a Memphis gospel quartet called the Confederates. "We opened up with the Blackwood Brothers for a couple of years in Mississippi, Arkansas, and West Tennessee." Musical performance is in his past now, however. "I'm a lot different from the person I was in the '60s when we did the records. And I'm different from the way I was in 1995 before my wife died. I'm settled and comfortable, yet I'm still anxious about what I'm going to see next. I kind of amaze myself sometimes. I'm not afraid to take a risk and to change venues to take advantage of new opportunities. Every move I've made has been with myself and my family in mind. You have to measure the risks."

Although he's generally content with the choices he made, Butch occasionally wonders about one opportunity he let pass him by. "Al Jardine of the Beach Boys was a good friend. We traveled with them. A lot of people have worked for the Beach Boys at various times. When Sam the Sham and the Pharaohs broke up, the Beach Boys came through town. Al called me and said, 'I heard you guys are breaking up.' When I told him we had, he asked, 'Would you like to come to work for us and do some studio work?' I turned him down. There were times later that I'd have changed that decision if I could have."

But Gibson doesn't agonize over the past. He continues to focus on the future. "You know, persistence is the key. Just don't give up. It's hard to have an absolute career as a life goal. I think it needs to keep changing, because sometimes the worst thing that can happen to you is for all of your dreams to come true. Because then you ask, 'What now?' A lot of my dreams came true when I was in music, but I really look forward to teaching college. I came from a small town and had a real strong Christian background. When I went to college, there were a lot of atheist and agnostic professors there who tried to challenge my faith, and that hurt me a lot." Although scholars have an obligation to raise questions and introduce their students to new and sometimes controversial ideas, Butch believes a predominant number of academics willfully blur the line between raising questions and forcing their own agendas. "Those professors are out there in increasingly greater numbers. I want to be able to tip the scales in the other direction a little bit."

Even as Butch prepares to move on, his time with Sam the Sham and the Pharaohs remains an indelible part of him. "Sam had a great stage presence," he reaffirms. Still etched in Butch's memory is the whimsical rap that Sam recited to his audience at the close of each nightclub gig:

"That old clock on the wall done caught up with us all, and we're going to roll outta here like a hole in a doughnut.

"Remember, you've got to be yourself or else you'll wind up by yourself.

"And like the old gypsy woman told me, life is short and talk is cheap, don't make promises you can't keep.

"And you know I love you baby, cause if I don't love you baby, grits ain't groceries, eggs ain't poultry, and the Mona Lisa was a man."

"We were cool, man," said Butch. "We had it all."

CHAPTER 9

Summer in the City

The Lovin' Spoonful

The Lovin' Spoonful in 1967. Left to right in foreground: drummer Joe Butler, guitarist Jerry Yester, composer-musician John Sebastian (wearing glasses), and bass player Steve Boone. Guitarist Zal Yanovsky, then departing the band, peers out from behind the barn door. PHOTO BY HENRY DILTZ.

FROM THE TIME CAPSULE

AUGUST 1965: The first of the Lovin' Spoonful's 13 hit singles, "Do You Believe In Magic," makes it into the top 10.

- AUGUST 11–16: Rioting in the Watts section of Los Angeles results in 34 deaths, 1,000 injuries, 4,000 arrests, and more than $200 million in arson damage.
- AUGUST 13: In San Francisco, Jefferson Airplane make their first stage appearance.
- AUGUST 14: At CBS Studio 50 in New York City, the Beatles tape the final dress rehearsal for their upcoming appearance on the *Ed Sullivan* show.

JULY 1966: "Summer In The City" heats up the airwaves, hitting No. 1 and staying there for three weeks.

- JULY 1: The federal government enacts Medicare, underwriting the cost of medical care for older Americans.
- JULY 4: President Lyndon Johnson signs the Freedom of Information Act.
- JULY 18: Bobby Fuller, whose hits with the Bobby Fuller Four included "I Fought The Law," is found dead in a parked car in Los Angeles. Carl Sagan turns 1 billion seconds old.

JANUARY 1968: The Lovin' Spoonful's "Money" doesn't make as much money as their last few singles, getting only to No. 48 on the charts.

- JANUARY 12: AT&T adopts "911" as a nationwide emergency telephone number.
- JANUARY 22: *Rowan & Martin's Laugh-In,* a show hosted by Dan Rowan and Dick Martin with sketch players Goldie Hawn, Arte Johnson, Lily Tomlin, Henry Gibson, Judy Carne, JoAnne Worley, and Ruth Buzzi, debuts on NBC-TV.
- JANUARY 23: The government of North Korea seizes the U.S. Navy ship *Pueblo* in the Sea of Japan and holds 82 crew members captive as spies.

In pop music, the class of 1965 was resplendent in fresh talent, comprising a striking honor roll of new artists who graduated to the national singles charts for the first time. Performers making their debut on the *Billboard* Hot 100 that year included flamboyantly attired Sonny & Cher, British motion picture star Petula Clark, rough-hewn Bob Dylan, Los Angeles–based Dylan disciples the Byrds and the Turtles, the San Francisco quintet the Beau Brummels, Great Britain's Yardbirds, and an electrified jug band quartet from New York's Greenwich Village called the Lovin' Spoonful.

The Spoonful emanated from the same roots that produced the Mamas and the Papas and Richie Havens, among others. During a prolific three-year run, the Spoonful put 13 memorable singles on the pop charts, the first seven of which all cracked the national top 10. Most were ballads and ditties fashioned with the band's lilting "good-time" folk-flavored blend of instruments. But the group is perhaps best remembered for "Summer In The City," a hard-driving full-on dose of rock and roll that jackhammered its way to the top of the charts in July 1966.

The band's bilateral repertoire reflected the divergent backgrounds of its founding members: folk music aficionados John Sebastian and Zalman Yanovsky, who had been entrenched in the Bohemian scene of Greenwich Village, and rockers Joe Butler and Steve Boone from Long Island, New York.

Native New Yorker John Sebastian had honed his musical skills by hanging around the coffeehouses of the eclectic Village, where in his late teens he sat in with John Hammond, Fred Neil, and Mississippi John Hurt, formed a backup duo with Felix Pappalardi, did extensive session work playing harmonica for Elektra Records, and performed with the Even Dozen Jug Band. John also worked with a baritone singer named Valentine Pringle, a protégé of Harry Belafonte. At one gig in late 1963 at a club called the Shadows in Washington, D.C., Sebastian and Pringle opened for a group called the Big Three, the members of which included Cass Elliot.

"Cass was instantly likable and funny, and conversationally astute. I loved her from the minute I met her," says John. The two became friends and kept in touch as the Big Three grew to include members of a dissolved Canadian group called the Halifax Three, which included Denny Doherty and Zal Yanovsky. The merger of the two groups produced the Mugwumps, which John briefly joined as well.

Sebastian clearly remembers when he met Yanovsky in February 1964. "It was the evening of the Beatles' first appearance on the *Ed Sullivan Show,* which we all watched at Cass's house." A friendship soon developed as Zal and John discovered common musical interests. When the Mugwumps disbanded, Cass and Denny became members of the New Journeymen, which evolved into the Mamas and the Papas. Meanwhile, Zal and John began looking around the Village for a bass player and a drummer.

Since the early '60s, singer-drummer Joe Butler and guitarist Steve Boone had been playing together in a band on Long Island called the Kingsmen. When Steve first joined the Kingsmen as a college freshman in 1962, he was playing rhythm guitar, but was asked to switch to bass when the Air Force transferred the band's bass player to Louisiana. "OK," Steve told the others. "That's two less strings to play."

Joe grew up in a working-class family in largely affluent Great Neck, New York. He led his first band at age 13 and continued to perform music even while he was in the Air Force, in which he had enlisted after graduating from high school in 1959, at age 17. While stationed at West Hampton, Long Island, he enrolled in college courses through Long Island University, but found himself drawn to Greenwich Village. For over a decade, the Village had been America's version of Paris's Left Bank, and in the early 1960s, the last wave of the Beat Generation mingled with the first wave of the Folk Generation in cafes like the Gaslight, where Allen Ginsberg and Gregory Corso had read their poetry and Noel Stookey (later Paul of Peter, Paul and Mary) got his start. Steve, too, slipped into the Village on weekends, taking advantage of the Long Island Railroad's student discount fare. "The Village," says Steve, "was always exciting. That's where all of the action was."

After Joe's discharge from the Air Force in 1963, he continued working toward his college business degree while the Kingsmen changed their base to Greenwich Village, and changed their name to the Sellouts. Joe soon underwent a change as well. "I was introduced to my ex-wife's cousin, Peter Yarrow, one of the first musical celebrities I had met. It struck me that he was just a guy. If he could be a star, I realized that so could I." That revelation provided all the incentive Joe needed to quit school in early 1964, just before completing his degree requirements.

When the Sellouts were playing six 40-minute sets a night at the Playhouse Cafe in the Little Italy section of New York, Joe attracted the attention of Mercury Records, for which he cut a few demo tracks beginning in late 1964. Producer Erik Jacobsen introduced Joe to John Sebastian and Zal Yanovsky, who were seeking a bass player and a drummer. Joe suggested bassist Steve Boone.

Steve had taken a three-month break from college that fall, motorcycling through Europe with a friend. He had just returned from that trip in December when he met Sebastian and Yanovsky, and quickly agreed to join them in forming the band that would become the Lovin' Spoonful. Joe Butler hesitated, reluctant to leave the Sellouts.

Still unnamed, the band rehearsed throughout January at a hotel in Bridgehampton that had been closed for the winter. Steve and John broke camp only to do some session work with Bob Dylan in New York City. The band's eventual name was inspired by a Mississippi John Hurt song, "Coffee Blues," in which the legendary scotch-and-coffee-drinking blues singer professed his love for his "baby" by the lovin' spoonful. As the new band took the name Lovin' Spoonful and began playing at the Night Owl Cafe on West Third Street the following month, the members of the audience included Joe Butler.

"Zally totally hypnotized me and captivated me," says Joe. "He had a tremendous sense of crazy humor. He was loose, relaxed, and was having the time of his life. John was a little serious, a little professorial in his presentation. They were doing mostly old jug band things, but a few John Sebastian originals were in the set, and they were good."

Erik Jacobsen finally convinced Joe that joining Sebastian, Yanovsky, and Boone would be a good move. It was late January 1965 when Joe agreed. The quartet began playing at various clubs in the Village—the Night Owl, the Village Music Hall, the Circus—where they worked for peanuts. The four members of the Spoonful, along with Cass Elliot and Denny Doherty, all roomed that icy winter at the rickety Albert Hotel, where they rehearsed in the basement. "We lived on tuna fish and ice cream. Whenever we needed to pay the bill, we'd send Denny down to romance the girl who was keeping the books, and he got us a free ride many times," says Joe.

Bob Cavallo, manager of the Shadows nightclub in which Sebastian had previously played, caught the Spoonful's act and inked a deal with them—not for a booking, but as their manager. With front money put up by Erik Jacobsen, the band bought studio time and recorded some original material, including several sides that would go on to become hit records. The major labels were uninterested, but when Kama Sutra Records offered the band a recording contract as well as a publishing deal, the members signed. Though it was small, Kama Sutra had a distribution arrangement with powerful MGM Records.

Issued as Kama Sutra No. 201, "Do You Believe In Magic" was a prophetic debut single for the group. Magically, the record took off in the summer of '65, and the band appeared on a wondrous succession of television programs. On *Hullabaloo*. On the premier broadcast of the *Sonny And Cher Show*. On stage with Sammy Davis Jr. and the Supremes. "We went from playing to 200 seats in the Night Owl to playing in front of 60,000 at the Pasadena Rose Bowl," says Butler.

Although John Sebastian and Steve Boone wrote most of the Spoonful's material, all the band members played a songwriting role. They were versatile instrumentalists as well. John played guitar, piano, Autoharp, harmonica, and other instruments. Steve played organ, piano, and bass guitar. Zal played guitar and bass. All four sang and contributed song arrangement ideas.

The guys clearly had fun in the studio, evidenced by their playful use of an old manual typewriter to set a syncopated beat in "Money," and their rollicking performance of Sebastian's "Lovin' You," a good-time tune if ever there was one. The band played credible country music as well, delivering a mischievous poke in the ribs with "Nashville Cats" and "Darlin' Companion." The soundtrack that the Spoonful recorded for Francis Ford Coppola's 1967 motion picture *You're A Big Boy Now* included one of the band's lovelier recordings, a wistful harmonica instrumental called "Lonely (Amy's Theme)." That was their second motion picture effort. The year before, the Spoonful had created the score for a wacky Woody Allen spoof of the spy-film genre, *What's Up, Tiger Lily?*

On the road, audiences adored the Spoonful. Glorious moments included a stellar performance at the Hollywood Bowl in 1967 with Simon and Garfunkel, and an appearance at Fordham University in New York in which the audience coaxed the Spoonful out for nine encores. "Performing was a big party. It was rare to do a concert without continual yelling and screaming. It was wonderful. When they went ape shit, I was in heaven. It was the best response I ever got out of anybody," Joe laughs.

The band found itself amid controversy in 1967, following disclosure of the arrest of Yanovsky and Boone in San Francisco the year before for possession of one ounce of marijuana they had obtained at a party. Under threat of Yanovsky's immediate deportation to Canada, he and Boone reluctantly acknowledged their source of the illegal weed. The story was kept quiet for nearly a year, until the *Berkeley Barb, Los Angeles Free Press,* and *Rolling Stone* learned about the incident.

"It was such a heart-wrenching ordeal that stigmatized me and Zally," says Boone, who with Yanovsky and the other band members paid for an attorney to defend the individual who was charged with selling the pot. Although their cooperation with police was vilified in the "underground press," mainstream kids outside the counterculture enclaves were largely unaware or unconcerned about the incident. Still, the harsh public reaction was a distraction for the band members, precipitating Yanovsky's departure from the Spoonful within a couple of months and leading to the eventual collapse of the band.

Because he was a close friend of Erik Jacobsen's, guitarist Jerry Yester was aware in May 1967 of Zal's impending departure from the Spoonful. But Jerry says he was surprised when John Sebastian phoned and asked him to join the band. Jerry replaced Zal as lead guitarist in June.

Yester, a member of the highly regarded Modern Folk Quartet, had produced albums for the Association and Tim Buckley and performed on recording sessions for the Monkees. He had also long been friends with the members of the Lovin' Spoonful. He had, in fact, done vocal arrangements for the band and played piano on the recording session for "Do You Believe In Magic."

The Spoonful took part in a pioneering technical experiment in 1967, when the group became the first rock band to record an album on an Ampex 16-track tape machine. The well-received album, *Everything Playing,* yielded three hit American pop singles—"Darlin' Be Home Soon," "Six O'Clock," and "She Is Still A Mystery"—as well as two singles that charted in the United Kingdom, "Boredom," and "Money." Following release of that album—their fourth—the Spoonful made a triumphant appearance on the *Ed Sullivan Show,* where they performed "She Is Still A Mystery" to a wildly appreciative audience.

Although many pop artists of the era, including the Monkees, Dion, Elvis Presley, and Glen Campbell, felt compelled to use their music as a forum for political and antiwar statements, the Spoonful purposely avoided doing so.

"What set us apart was that we did decide against supporting any political cause," Steve explains. "We felt that if we could be nonpolitical and provide some uplifting moments during some very tense times, that would be a fine mission in itself. But," he adds, "by the time 1967 rolled around and a lot of our buddies were coming back in bags or with ugly stories to tell, we could see the handwriting on the wall for the end of good-time music."

After John Sebastian left the band in June 1968 to embark on a solo career, Joe, Steve, and Jerry maintained the Spoonful as a trio. Under Joe's guidance, the band produced two final charted singles, the country-tinged "Never Goin' Back" in the fall of 1968, and "Me About You," which barely broke into the Hot 100 in February 1969. Although the trio disbanded at the end of 1968, they were able to look back with pride on an association that left behind a catalog of memorable music for millions of lovin' fans.

HIT SINGLES BY THE LOVIN' SPOONFUL

DEBUT	PEAK	TITLE	LABEL
8/65	9	DO YOU BELIEVE IN MAGIC	KAMA SUTRA
11/65	10	YOU DIDN'T HAVE TO BE SO NICE	KAMA SUTRA
2/66	2	DAYDREAM	KAMA SUTRA
5/66	2	DID YOU EVER HAVE TO MAKE UP YOUR MIND?	KAMA SUTRA
7/66	1	SUMMER IN THE CITY (Certified Gold)	KAMA SUTRA
10/66	10	RAIN ON THE ROOF	KAMA SUTRA
12/66	8	NASHVILLE CATS/FULL MEASURE	KAMA SUTRA
2/67	15	DARLING BE HOME SOON	KAMA SUTRA
4/67	18	SIX O'CLOCK	KAMA SUTRA
10/67	27	SHE IS STILL A MYSTERY	KAMA SUTRA
1/68	48	MONEY	KAMA SUTRA
7/68	73	NEVER GOING BACK	KAMA SUTRA
2/69	91	ME ABOUT YOU	KAMA SUTRA

THEN AND NOW

JOHN SEBASTIAN

Throughout his durable career, John B. Sebastian has performed with some of the most prominent folk and blues artists of the 20th century. Bob Dylan. Judy Collins. Fred Neil. Tim Hardin. Maria Muldaur. John Hammond. The Serendipity Singers. Peter, Paul and Mary. Mississippi John Hurt. Lightnin' Hopkins.

But he derives his greatest sense of professional pride and some of his fondest memories on stage from his association with a blues mandolin player named James "Yank" Rachell, whose recording career spanned an astonishing 68 years. Already a celebrated artist in Memphis 15 years before Sebastian was born, Yank Rachell was in his eighties when he recorded some tracks and performed on stage a few

PHOTO BY CATHERINE SEBASTIAN.

times with the jug band in which Sebastian now blows diatonic harmonica and plays guitar.

Sebastian will never forget the day he was stepping off the stage following a performance with Rachell, who had diabetes and who had undergone dialysis the day before. Turning to Sebastian, Rachell crowed, "Man, if I had a guitar player who could play as strong as you, I might be able to do this for another 40 years." Even though Rachell had grown frail and suffered from painful arthritis, the stage energized him and he continued performing until his death at the age of 87 in April 1997. With an air of reverence, Sebastian says, "To play with Yank and to hear him say the things he told me were every bit as valuable as all the screams for the Spoonful on the *Ed Sullivan Show*."

While some contemporary pop music stars have professed that they drew their inspiration from rock and roll performers of the 1950s and '60s, John Sebastian cherishes the music upon which the rock and roll genre itself is based: blues, country music, traditional folk, ragtime, and jug band music. It was no accident that jug band music was mentioned by name in the very first Lovin' Spoonful hit, "Do You Believe In Magic." Jug band music was a formative interest for John Sebastian as a young man, and the desire to preserve that element of Americana remains a driving force in his life today.

With an interest in music stemming from his childhood, Sebastian had learned to play harmonica, guitar, electric bass, and Autoharp before the age of 20. While a member in 1964 of the Even Dozen Jug Band, the members of which made about $25 apiece per gig, Sebastian began getting an increasing amount of work as a session musician, making $51 per three-hour recording session. Sebastian's harmonica was heard on most of the early output of Elektra Records, on recordings by Tom Paxton, Judy Collins, Fred Neil, Tim Hardin, and other folk artists emerging from the Greenwich Village music scene.

Unlike most of his contemporaries, Sebastian didn't migrate to the Village. His family lived there from the time he was born, on March 17, 1944. John Benson Sebastian (known to his family and friends as J.B.) and his only brother, Mark—who co-wrote "Summer In The City"—grew up in a musically rich environment. Their father, John Sebastian Pugliese, was a classical harmonica virtuoso from Philadelphia who later truncated the family name to Sebastian. As a soloist, he played with the New York Philharmonic and the Philadelphia Orchestra, the Tokyo Philharmonic, and orchestras in Rome and Milan. "My father was the greatest classical harmonica virtuoso who ever lived," proudly declares John. Jane Bishir, John's mother, was a scriptwriter in the heyday of radio.

John began playing harmonica as a 4-year-old. "A diatonic harmonica like the ones I learned to play can produce two or three notes between the regular notes based on chords," Sebastian explains. "If you inhale, you get a seventh chord and that technique came from an African American tradition. That's the key to playing the blues."

Although he had an idle interest in veterinary medicine and acting during his high school years at Friends Seminary in New York City, he was far more intrigued by what was happening in the neighborhood of his parents' Greenwich Village home on Bank Street. "I was 16 in 1960, a perfect time for my attraction to folk music." Washington Square Park, where folk musicians like Burl Ives and Woodie Guthrie performed at folk music singalongs (hootenannies), was just down the street. His acquaintances there included another 16-year-old kid, at that time a portrait artist from Brooklyn who worked with chalk and enjoyed singing doo-wop. The portrait artist was Richie Havens, who in 1969 would appear along with Sebastian on stage at Woodstock.

During the two years of his early adolescence when he had lived with his family in Italy, J.B. picked up a bit of the language. So when he was told to go to college, he enrolled at New York University in the fall of 1962 with a major in Italian. "I was a total goofball," he laughs. He spent more time working in a Greenwich Village guitar shop trying to earn a guitar than he did at his studies. He didn't need much of a nudge the day he received a phone call from fingerpicker Stephen Grossman.

"We started a jug band and you're in it and rehearsal is today," Grossman blurt-ed. The model for the new assemblage, called the Even Dozen Jug Band, was the Jim Kweskin Jug Band. The jug band music genre, popular in the South when Yank Rachell was a young man, draws its rich sound from skilled players who can evoke just about any note in any key from ceramic maple syrup jugs. Before the members scattered, the Even Dozen Jug Band quickly achieved notoriety, playing Town Hall and Carnegie Hall.

The Even Dozen, which had as many as 14 members, also brought J.B. into contact with Paul A. Rothchild, who would later produce the Doors and most of the artists in the Elektra catalog. It was Rothchild who booked Sebastian for much of that session work. And it was Rothchild who would produce the solo *John B. Sebastian* album for Warner Brothers after Sebastian's departure from the Lovin' Spoonful in 1968.

Sebastian defines the Spoonful's place in the evolution of pop music. "The Lovin' Spoonful was truly the first American band in post-Beatle America that was not seeking to imitate the English sound," he declares. "We were seeking to combine as many American influences as we could. Now, granted, the Beatles had taken as many American influences as they could to incorporate into their sound. But part of what made them who they were was the fact that they were Englishmen. Rather than try to imitate Englishness, we decided to follow them only in the sense that we were going to be a self-contained band, without using session musicians and by doing our own writing."

Sebastian left the band in June 1968 because it seemed to him that it had run its course. "As somebody who was there in the beginning, I had a sense of the arc of the success of the group," he says. "By then, not only had I learned a lot about the studio, but I had accumulated friends who were studio musicians. Once three years had gone by, people I knew had advanced as members of groups or producers. I also wanted to move forward musically and try to carve out a solo career. I never conceived that the Spoonful would go on. I began to build another body of material and I began to record."

Sebastian's departure from the Spoonful coincided with dramatic change in other aspects of his life. Newly divorced after a marriage that had lasted only 18 months, Sebastian sold his suburban house on Long Island. He accepted the invitation of a friend, Modern Folk Quartet member Cyrus Faryar, who owned some outbuildings that were part of an old hunting lodge behind the Warner Brothers television production lot in the hills of Burbank, California. John took up residence on the property in a Volkswagen bus tent. "It was sufficient because I was mainly on the road at that time," says Sebastian. "I had accumulated a lot of debt, because I had not realized how much I was going to be taxed." Sebastian's financial austerity was exacerbated by a prolonged legal tussle between MGM, parent of the Kama Sutra label for which the Spoonful had recorded, and Warner Brothers, with whom Sebastian had contracted as a solo artist. Release of his first solo effort was delayed a year and a half as a result.

Faryar's property during that time became somewhat of an artistic haven populated by other musicians and actors. During his months in Burbank, Sebastian developed a strong friendship with Catherine Cozzi, a photographer. In 1971 John decided he wanted to take a leisurely drive across the country in a truck and he wanted Catherine to accompany him. She agreed, and during the cross-country drive their friendship grew into a relationship. That trip, on which they were accompanied by another couple, Art and Carolina Carpinelli, fueled the idea for a future Sebastian solo album called *Four Of Us.*

During the following years, John was content to record as a soloist and play small club dates. He and Catherine married in 1972 and settled in the Los Angeles suburb of Tarzana in a home they bought from Iron Butterfly guitarist Erik Braunn. John had just signed with manager David Bendett of Brooklyn in 1975 when a TV producer phoned Bendett. "I'm trying to find a John Sebastian–type guy to write a song for me for a new television show," the producer said. "How about John Sebastian?" replied Bendett.

Sebastian was interested. After reviewing a 10-page show synopsis and a couple of potential scripts, Sebastian wrote "Welcome Back," the theme for the hit television series *Welcome Back, Kotter.* The project came at a time when Sebastian had decided to extricate himself from his contract with Warner Brothers Records.

"With Alice Cooper posters on the walls at Warner Brothers, it had become obvious to me that it could be hard to be a John Sebastian–type guy with that label, because I was not going to suddenly show up with studs and leather," Sebastian explains. Some Warner Brothers execs seemed to be coming around to the same conclusion until the label began receiving phone calls from record stores throughout the country inquiring about the *Kotter* television theme. The label rushed Sebastian into a studio, and he assembled an album incorporating other material he had already written. The single and the album were released in 1975 on the affiliate Reprise label. "It was an odd period. I couldn't get the attention of the record company, yet 'Welcome Back' became the second biggest-selling single of the year," Sebastian says wryly.

"Welcome Back" became a welcome back for Sebastian: "It permitted me another long breath in my solo career. It resulted in some tours that were a lot of fun." He spent a summer opening stage appearances for Steve Martin, who had just unveiled his "wild and crazy guy" persona. Sebastian also worked with Robin Williams, George Carlin, and Billy Crystal. "I was a very logical opener for a comedian because I didn't need a band, so it made for a very compact traveling unit."

Sebastian quietly continued recording and performing solo through the 1980s, as well as with a group called the Little Big Band, which included drummer James Wormworth and guitarist Jimmy Vivino, who later would join Conan O'Brien's television show. But 1991 brought another professional change into Sebastian's life. A Sony Music executive phoned and said, "You know, Sebastian, I'll bet you could put together about the best jug band in the world." Sebastian replied, "You know, you're absolutely right." Sebastian recruited his friend Fritz Richmond, once the washtub and jug player in the Jim Kweskin Jug Band, along with guitarist Paul Rishell and harmonica player Annie Raines. They formed the core of a musical group called John Sebastian and the J Band, which began playing summer concerts, rock and roll bars, folk and blues festivals, fairs, and just about any other kind of musical venue.

While touring, Sebastian met Yank Rachell and began the association from which he derives so much pride. "Yank was pleasantly surprised that we were playing in a style he had played 50 years before. He loved the fact that I would stay on this old six-string banjo and that the jug player could play in any key. He knew how unusual that was."

For part of their first jug band album, Sebastian and his group members traveled to a studio in Indianapolis, where Yank lived in his last years. There, Yank recorded two tracks for the first album release by John Sebastian and the J Band, *I Want My Roots*.

"Yank was 87 years old at the time, and after that we traveled with him to Brownsville, Tennessee, his old home and did a concert there at a location where he was never allowed to play as a young man." In early 1997 Sebastian's ensemble played a benefit concert in Indianapolis that raised funds to help pay medical costs for the ailing Rachell, who was suffering from kidney failure in the months before his death. Tracks recorded at that concert were included in the J Band's CD *Chasin' Gus' Ghost,* which was released in early 1999. The album's title honors pioneering jug band musician and composer Gus Cannon, who died in 1979 at the age of 94.

Although Sebastian does a lot of session work these days, the J Band remains his principal musical interest. His dream is to provide greater visibility for jug band music, perhaps by providing background music for a motion picture or other theatrical project.

John, who appeared on stage at the Woodstock Music Festival in 1969 crooning his tender song "Younger Generation" about the joys and trials of parenthood, now leads a comfortable life with his family near Woodstock, New York. Catherine Sebastian is a recognized anthropological and portrait photographer whose work has graced scores of album covers, including all of John's solo releases, as well as releases by Muddy Waters and a folk group called Mud Acres with which John often performs. In 1999 she and an anthropologist completed a seven-year photographic project in the British Virgin Islands. John and Catherine have two children of their own: Benson, born in 1972, and Charlie, who was born in 1986. John expects Benson to find a career in the music business. "And my younger son is incredibly talented as a snowboarder and a bicyclist and a lot of sports that scare the hell out of me," confesses John, sounding remarkably like the parent he had anticipated when he wrote "Younger Generation" three decades before. Justifiably proud of his kids, John is quick to identify the greatest challenge he's faced in his life, musical or otherwise: "Parenting. I think that's a real challenge," says John. "Music is easy."

THEN AND NOW

JOE BUTLER

For more than half of his life, Joe Butler had been a musician, earning income behind his drums and behind a microphone. Then suddenly, when he was 27 years of age, it came to a halt. The breakup of the Lovin' Spoonful in 1968 was devastating to Butler. "It happened very abruptly," he says. "I didn't have any kind of grace time. We received far less money than we had been expecting. I was on the street instantly, and needed to earn money right away." However, he was in anything but the right frame of mind to find other work. "The hardest thing I've ever had to do is keep my spirits up when I was down and out and had given up on myself," he acknowledges. "In the music business, a lot of bodies have washed up on the shore, not because of drugs but because of having their hearts broken."

But Joe, always emotive on stage, took stock of his resources and decided to try his hand at acting. Immersing himself in method acting studies, he achieved remarkable success, doing Shakespeare and Chekov with the prestigious Circle Theater Company, and landing leading roles in Broadway productions of *Hair, Mahogany,* and *Soon.* Drawn by the cinema, Joe sold his apartment on Bank Street in Greenwich Village to John Lennon and Yoko Ono, and moved to Los Angeles. There, he was cast in a half-dozen motion pictures, including *Born To Win* with George Segal. Even so, he became disillusioned with Hollywood. "I didn't know the system well enough. I didn't know how to make that crossover from stage to films."

He decided to enter a more welcoming labor market: residential construction. Two years after he was pounding his drums before

PHOTO BY AMANDA MARCH.

thousands of fans, Joe was pounding nails into sheetrock. One of his first jobs was construction of a home for comic Dan Rowan. Following Joe's marriage in September 1967 to Leslie Vega and the birth of his daughter, Yancy, in July 1970, construction work supported his young family. Moving with them back to New York, Joe graduated to more polished finish carpentry and eventually became a foreman, supervising large construction projects. Although he survived the career change, his marriage didn't. By 1978 the relationship was on the rocks and the couple divorced.

Living once again in Greenwich Village, Joe answered his phone and heard a voice from the past. It was Kim Ablondi. "She had been a neighborhood kid when I lived on Bank Street in the Village in the early '70s," Joe explains. He had heard that she had moved to San Francisco several years before. She was working as a congressional aide in Washington, she told him. They decided to renew acquaintances. "When I saw her I fell like a ton of bricks," he says. They were married in 1982, and they've lived in the Village since.

Through the first decade of their marriage, Joe was content to work, anonymously, in construction. After all, he'd been working since he was a kid, unlike many of his more privileged childhood friends. Born September 16, 1941, in Glen Cove on Long Island's largely rural north fork, Joe had a newspaper route during his grammar school years, and at age 12 got a job washing dishes at a soda fountain. "I was under age, and my apron was so long, I had to fold it at the waist so I didn't trip on it. I remember being so proud of having that apron. I didn't want to take it off. It was like I was a grown-up because I was earning money. I wanted to contribute to the family."

Joe, whose father was a police officer, credits the formation of his childhood interest in music to his mother, who once sang in a talent contest in which she lost to a skinny adolescent named Frank Sinatra. Joe tried his hand at trombone in grade school, but quickly dismissed that instrument when he realized he wanted to sing. He tried guitar but had an unsatisfying experience because of the poor quality of the instrument he was using. Then he paid a kid a couple of bucks for a pair of drumsticks and some brushes, and began pounding out rhythms on newspapers and chair seats. His folks set him up with an old drum set in the basement, where he practiced for hours, singing and playing along with records by Danny and the Juniors and other early rock music performers.

At age 13, Joe started playing in a combo with a guitarist and an accordion player. The group played mostly country music in a local delicatessen, and Joe reveled as Elvis Presley took his rockabilly tunes into the mainstream of pop music. "I shied away from the Irish music," says Joe. "My family was Irish and it was embarrassing when the old-timers played their fiddles. Now I love the stuff. Somehow it raises the hackles. If I hear a bagpipe, I'm looking for my sword and a hill to charge down." But Joe grew up in a community in which 93 percent of his high school graduating class was Jewish. He was one of few *goyim*—gentiles, non-Jews. Only later did he learn that his heritage included some German-Jewish ancestors.

Joe took courses at Long Island University toward a business degree through much of his four-year stint in the military, but his heart wasn't in it. He felt pressured to get a business degree. "It was the curse of the working class, the fear of the Depression that forced parents in that era to press for something to fall back on," Joe says. Although Joe had enough credits to graduate, he hadn't quite completed the requirements for a business major when he decided to pursue music and moved to the Village in early 1964. "We were in the war, I had grown to dislike the military, President Kennedy had died, and there was a lot of bitterness in the nation." Joe said he viewed the focus of the Greenwich Village music scene on peace and love as a "noble attempt to try to find another solution."

Joe is proud of his years with the Spoonful, and proud that he survived the dissolution of the band as well. Difficult as that was, it was not nearly as emotionally draining as the breakup of his first marriage. "We went for therapy, which was healing and helping. A lot of people laugh at therapy until they need it. With the help of therapy, we scrapped the marriage and kept the friendship. We never used our daughter as a weapon, or resorted to other cruel things that some people endure." But the process still brought Joe to his lowest ebb. "I had a feeling of real worthlessness."

His work in construction was the mechanism by which he began pulling himself out of his depression. "Getting some money in my pocket, so I wasn't always out of money and always frightened, helped a lot." But most instrumental was a remark in a speech at his daughter's high school graduation in Brooklyn. When a speaker said, "Remember, it's not the road you take, it's how you take the road that you find yourself on," that struck a chord with Joe. "That thought really gave me solace and comfort. It reestablished me. I had joined the human race as a working person and realized that's okay."

Although he came to terms with anonymity, his past shadowed him. Like a scene from the motion picture *Eddie And The Cruisers,* in which the ephemeral success of a fictitious early '60s band haunts the dispersed members years later, each time Joe heard a Spoonful song, it brought a painful reminder of the money he said the band members were still owed. That unrest ultimately led to the reformation of the Lovin' Spoonful in 1991. "One of the reasons we got back together was to fight back and claim our money. We had been given a large advance and then cut off and still to this day, we don't have one piece of paper accounting for that money. We fought for and received a settlement. We were granted future royalties, which we collect now," says Joe.

In October 1991, Joe, Steve, and Jerry rented a house near Pittsfield, Massachusetts. After a month of rehearsals, they played a date on Thanksgiving in Kitchen, Ontario, then a New Year's Eve party in Athens, Ohio. The band members lined up a schedule of dates for the following summer, and have been doing summer tours since then. In the new incarnation of the Spoonful, Butler has stepped out from behind the drums as lead singer, performing the classic Spoonful hits, as well as new material.

"One of the reasons we put the band together was to serve as a vehicle for this new music that Jerry, Steve, and I have been writing," Joe explains. "Jerry is a virtuoso and could certainly be making records by himself, but I think the most interesting recordings are made by groups of people. I'm a believer that if you have one person, that's just one, but if you have two the square is four, if you have three it's nine, and so forth. So the group concept becomes very powerful. John [Sebastian] had been the only representative in the Spoonful with any visibility, and rightfully so. After all, John is one of the great American songwriters of this century. But none of us had that kind of visibility on our own. Steve and I had some skills and we got a new level of confidence when Jerry joined in with us. And now with the addition of Jerry's daughter, Lena, who also writes, we all have something to contribute. We're getting good reaction to the new stuff. Our audiences are excited about it." And he believes that's with good reason. "I'm performing better than I ever have in my life."

In doing so, he's drawing upon some of his earliest experiences. In 1998, at the Hotel Seville in Harrison, Arkansas, the Spoonful recorded an "unplugged" (acoustic) set in which Joe drummed on a vinyl chair cover and on a phone book, reminiscent of the kitchen surfaces he played as an adolescent before he acquired his first drum set. "I had just those two sounds, a tambourine and some maracas, and that was one of the most charming recordings," says Joe. That session was recorded and released in early November 1999 on a CD called *Lovin' Spoonful Live At The Hotel Seville* on the Varèse Sorabande label.

Following Joe's footsteps onto the dramatic stage, his daughter Yancy has starred in two television series, *Mann And Machine* and *South Beach,* as well as the motion pictures *Hard Target* and *Drop Zone.* His wife, Kim, whom Joe refers to as "an obsessed marathon runner," is on the staff of the graduate illustration department in New York's School of Visual Arts.

Among all 128 tracks that the Spoonful recorded, Joe says he's fondest of the band's hits. "I always loved the hits. There's a reason why they're hits. They say something to a lot of people, and they're basic and open, and a lot of people can envision them like a book. When you read the *Green Leaf,* it's your green leaf. So I love 'Summer In The City,' 'Magic,' and 'You Didn't Have To Be So Nice.' And I like 'Full Measure' because I got to sing lead on it, and it's a great song. Now it's so much fun doing them. I look forward to the shows because the songs are so good. I don't ever get tired of them."

THEN AND NOW
STEVE BOONE

Sometimes Steve Boone isn't easy to recognize. Particularly when he's wearing his giant green Mr. Frog costume. Most 6-foot-tall green frogs are indistinguishable from one another, but Steve's Mr. Frog is easy to identify because he's often found standing near a mermaid—his wife, Susan B. Peterson. Together, they operate Mermaid Productions, a Florida company which is really several businesses in one. One arm of the company (the Mr. Frog and Ms. Mermaid branch) produces theatrical shows for children. Mermaid Productions also provides costumed swimming mermaids for special events and television specials such as the *Mermaids For Manatees* children's ecology show broadcast in 1997 on Swedish public television. As freelance writers specializing in Florida nautical history, Steve and Susan have written numerous articles published in *New River Times* and *Waterfront News,* regional periodicals.

Since 1988, twenty years after the breakup of the Spoonful, Steve has been living in Ft. Lauderdale, where he met Susan. During the course of those two decades, Steve lived a life of adventure in the Caribbean, acquired a valuable business at a time when he had little cash and few assets to his name, and watched to his horror three years later as his investment sank—literally—to the floor of Baltimore's inner harbor.

Steve's association with the sea began early in his life. He was born September 23, 1943, on the U.S. Marine Corps base at Camp Lejeune on the North Carolina coast,

just down the road from Cherry Point Naval Air Station where his father was stationed. It was wartime, and Steve remained there with his mother when his father, Emmett Boone Jr., was shipped out for duty in the Pacific. Steve's mother, Mary, was the daughter of a coal miner from the Scranton area of Pennsylvania, and his father's family had operated a hotel in Philadelphia. Steve's mom and dad met while working in a hotel in the Pocono Mountains.

When Steve's father returned from the war, the family moved several times,

PHOTO BY AMANDA MARCH.

first operating a resort hotel in Southern Pines, North Carolina, and later managing a resort hotel in Westhampton on Long Island. Steve began taking piano lessons at age 10, but his career as a pianist ended before it really got going after Steve's younger brother, Charles, accidentally tipped over a pot of boiling water, burning himself badly. When the family's physician recommended a moist climate to promote healing, the Boone family moved in 1954 to St. Augustine, Florida, where Steve's grandfather Emmett had retired.

"In the 1950s St. Augustine was still a very charming small southern town and a fun place for a teenage boy who liked the outdoors and the water," recalls Steve. His mother worked as an administrator at a hospital, then later became an office manager for a newspaper before entering real estate sales. As a high school kid, Steve learned the skills of cabinetry and furniture making in the woodworking shop his father opened. During those years, Steve's older brother Emmett III—nicknamed Skip and six years his senior—formed a rock and roll band. But Steve remained focused on another goal: becoming a U.S. Navy aviator. Those plans were crushed, however, after his family moved back to eastern Long Island. There, on the last day of his junior year at Westhampton Beach High School in June 1960, Steve was involved in a serious automobile accident that fractured his collarbone, hip, and both legs and paralyzed his right foot. He spent most of the summer in rehabilitation in the hospital and nearly a year on crutches, and began to think of what other career path he might pursue. That Christmas, his parents gave him the acoustic guitar he requested. His self-taught folk strumming eventually led him to join with Skip's band, the Kingsmen, first on rhythm, then on bass—a talent that persuaded him to abandon his preengineering studies in college and participate in forming the Lovin' Spoonful in January 1965.

An orthopedic brace that was fashioned for Steve carried him through the Spoonful years gracefully. Steve's injury, which disqualified him for military service, left him unable to raise his foot as he walked. His corrective brace pulled his foot back up in place and prevented it from dragging. Gradually, he learned to compensate for the foot injury and eventually shed his brace. "It's still a little awkward," says Steve, who never recovered full use of his foot.

Still, his injury never prevented him from pursuing an adventurous career. After the Spoonful dried up in 1968, he heard about a band in Virginia called the OxPetals that had been doing some interesting experimentation with music. Steve agreed to produce their sessions, and was instrumental in landing a recording contract for them with Mercury Records.

That was in the fall of 1969, when Steve married his first wife, Patty Curtis, sold his six-room apartment on West 79th Street in Manhattan, and bought a house alongside a trout hatchery in Eastport, Long Island. Only eight months later, Steve sold nearly everything he owned, packed everything else he wanted to keep in a shipping crate, and sent it off to St. Thomas in the Virgin Islands, where he and Patty moved. There Steve bought a 54-foot sailboat on which they lived frugally, and for nearly four years he concentrated on writing songs and thinking about what he might do next musically.

Steve returned to the United States in the summer of 1973 and stopped off in Baltimore to visit members of a band that he had met in St. Thomas shortly before his divorce from Patty. At the time, the band was recording in a 24-track studio that was part of International Telecom Inc., a state-of-the-art complex encompassing three studios, an engineering department, and record-cutting equipment in an industrial park owned by the McCormick Spice Co. The manager of the facility, who was a fan of the Lovin' Spoonful, asked Steve if he was interested in leasing the facility because the owner wanted to get out of active management. "I don't have any pockets, much less deep pockets," Steve told him. "I'll see what I can come up with."

Steve phoned some friends, including Bob Cavallo, the former manager of the Spoonful. Cavallo asked Boone if he had ever heard of a band called Little Feat. Steve said he hadn't because the only music he heard during the previous four years in the Virgin Islands was Latin Caribbean music and *Soul Train* once a week. Cavallo was by then managing Little Feat and had been trying to get the group to record a new album. The problem was that Lowell George, the group's leader, would record only if working with George Massenburg—the recording engineer who had designed the Baltimore studio complex. Massenburg, engineer for albums by Linda Ronstadt, Ramsey Lewis, and Earth, Wind and Fire, had done a session for Lowell George in Washington a year earlier.

"I learned that the engineer had done almost the same thing I had done—he got the hell out of the business and he moved to Paris to be with his girlfriend," says Boone. Before leaving, Massenburg had invited Lowell George to the Baltimore studio, and Lowell loved it. When Steve called Massenburg, he was able to persuade him to return to the states to perform session work for Little Feat. On the strength of the contract he arranged with Massenburg, Boone and a business partner leased the studio complex, where Little Feat recorded the classic 1974 album *Feats Don't Fail Me Now*.

Boone and his partner changed the name of the recording complex to Blue Seas Studio, began writing and producing commercial jingles, and developed a strong clientele in the Washington-Baltimore area. Blue Seas continued renting studio time to rock bands as well, and at the beginning of 1975 the McCormick Company, believing that the recording studio was incompatible with other businesses in the industrial park, issued an eviction notice to the studio owner. When the studio owner, who was in arrears in rent payments, refused to cooperate, Baltimore authorities sanctioned a public auction of the studio's assets.

Caught in the middle of the legal dispute between the studio owner and McCormick, Boone thought he'd show up the day of the auction and spend perhaps

$100 to buy a microphone. Instead, he walked away with a whole studio through a combination of nimble thinking and luck.

The auction was set up to offer the equipment two ways: a comprehensive offering of all the gear in the recording complex, followed by a second, piece-by-piece auction. The company would accept the bid total of whichever process netted the highest earnings. By the day of the auction, Boone and his partner had interested a prospective investor from New York. But the investor's arrival in Baltimore that February morning was delayed by a snowstorm en route. The auction opened with bids for the whole complex. After a long silence, Steve Boone was the first to speak. "I offer $15,000," he said. Another bidder blurted, "$18,000." Steve countered, "$18,500," and the auction room fell silent. After a few moments the auctioneer announced, "The bids are closed and now we're going to go piece by piece." But before those proceedings began, a vice president from Maryland National Bank leaned over and whispered something to the auctioneer. The auctioneer drew in a breath, then announced, "Ladies and gentlemen, the auction is over. Steve Boone is the buyer of the entire studio complex for $18,500."

At that point, Steve still didn't have any money and needed a 25 percent deposit by 3 o'clock that afternoon to hold his bid for 24 hours. "So I set up this furious sale on the floor of the auction," says Steve, who began doing what the auctioneer hadn't done—selling equipment piece by piece. "I sold an eight-track reel recorder, two echo chambers, and a couple of microphones for $19,100." Steve paid the auction house and had $600 to spare. After it was all over, the New York investor came bursting into the studio and gasped, "Am I too late?" Steve replied, "You're too late for the auction, Tom, but if you want to be my partner, we already own the place."

Steve and his two partners had to move all of their newly acquired gear quickly. And they knew just the place: a 130-foot-long barge owned by John Armour, heir to the Armour Meat Packing Company. Armour had converted it into a beautiful, Danish modern houseboat for his new bride and anchored it in Baltimore's inner harbor. When she stepped onto it and became seasick, she said, "I'm not living on this thing." Steve and his partners leased it and christened the new facility Blue Seas Studio. They were back in business—for three more years anyway. "Blue Seas," named after a freighter that Steve had seen stranded on the rocks at St. Thomas, may have been an unfortunate choice.

Blue Seas Studio attracted numerous pop and country music recording artists, including Emmylou Harris, Bonnie Raitt, Robert Palmer, and Ricky Scaggs. But on Christmas day in 1977, the barge sank in the harbor. "We salvaged most of our electronic gear, but the tapes all tipped over and fell into the salt water," says Steve. "We lost all of our master tapes, safeties, and backups, including stuff by Lowell George and Earth, Wind and Fire. We weren't insured." The partners sold the surviving electronic equipment and managed to pay off almost all of their debts.

Steve stayed in Baltimore but he'd had enough of the recording studio business. "I joined the Scott Cunningham Blues Band. It was a pickup band, never the same cast of characters. Baltimore was so rich in talent that I played with some of the best musicians I'd ever played with. It was fun, but we didn't make a lot of money," Steve admits. To make a few bucks, he began renovating abandoned houses in downtown Baltimore. Renting out the houses he renovated, Steve began to earn a respectable income. In 1982 he married a second time, to Jonell Ryan. The couple administered the rental properties until 1989, when they divorced and Steve moved to Florida, where he had lived as a teenager.

After looking around, Steve settled in Ft. Lauderdale, where he began sailing again. There he met Susan Peterson, with whom he formed Mermaid Productions Inc. in 1990, a year before they married. The house they bought contains a musical instrument digital interface (MIDI) computerized studio in which Steve records the musical compositions he writes. Steve and Susan are actively involved in numerous public service organizations, including the Ft. Lauderdale Historical Society, the Sierra Club, and the Legal Environmental Assistance Foundation. Steve, an avid boating advocate who conducts tours of local waterways, is a founding member of an organization dedicated to recreational boating access in the Broward Blueway river system, and he has volunteered extensively in connection with swimming meets at the International Swimming Hall of Fame Aquatics Complex.

Now living comfortably, Steve has a new goal. "I have an ambition to see the Lovin' Spoonful record a successful album of new music," acknowledges Steve. He is thinking not just of himself. He's written a number of songs in collaboration with Jerry Yester's daughter Lena, who performs on the road with the new Lovin' Spoonful. The band members would like to see Lena achieve some recognition for her work. "I think we've produced some real good songs," says Steve, acknowledging they're not typical Spoonful songs. "They're more in a sarcastic and humorous vein than you would expect."

Currently, three members of the band are thinking of developing their own project separate from the Spoonful—recording an album of new music under a different name: Forq. If they go through with the project, the album will be titled *In The Road*. The three-piece band will be made up of the rhythm section of the Lovin' Spoonful tour band—drummer Mike Arturi, Steve on bass, and Lena on guitar and keyboards. "Of course, we'll invite other musicians in for the recording," he smiles.

Beyond that, Steve has a more personal plan in mind. "When it comes time for those last golden 20 years to wind down, I, too, would like to write a book," he says, "and pursue some less strenuous artistic endeavors. Rock and roll music can wear you out if you let it."

THEN AND NOW

JERRY YESTER

Jerry Yester, perhaps best known as a producer and arranger, is the musician who replaced Zal Yanovsky in the Lovin' Spoonful. But that one-year stint represented just one facet in the busy life of a guy who wore so many hats that he'd need a separate closet to store them all.

When he began touring and recording with the Spoonful on the Kama Sutra label in June 1967, Jerry was already signed as a solo artist to Dunhill Records. Racking up a track record as a songwriter, producer, and musical arranger, Jerry even developed a partnership with Zal Yanovsky. And he gives some of the credit for a long, varied, and distinguished music career to his parents, not just because they had musical talents of their own but because they gave him a plastic ukulele for Christmas when he was 14.

PHOTO BY AMANDA MARCH.

Although Jerry was born in Birmingham, Alabama, on January 9, 1943, his parents moved only six months later to Burbank, California, in the Los Angeles metropolitan area. Jerry's father, Larry, was a professional musician who played piano, organ, and accordion. Attracted to the movie studios of Burbank and Hollywood, Larry played the part of a musician in about a dozen motion pictures, including *Fort Apache* and *April Showers*. A year after receiving the ukulele Jerry graduated to the guitar and was playing in a local garage band by the summer of 1958. Playing music for enjoyment, Jerry was interested in becoming a commercial artist. But music was in his family. And in his destiny.

When his parents decided to move to the high desert town of Joshua Tree in late 1960, Jerry decided to remain with his brother Jim in Burbank, where they moved into a house. Jerry's mother, Martha, who had worked as an accountant, became a singer in the bar that she and Jerry's father bought in Joshua Tree. While attending Notre Dame High School in Sherman Oaks, a few miles from Burbank, Jerry had enrolled in glee club. His classmates in glee club included Danny Hutton, who had a brief solo career before rising to fame as a member of Three Dog Night.

After graduation from high school Jerry enrolled at Glendale College to pursue a major in music and art, but quickly grew bored with theory classes that discussed what he had already learned in practice. Captivated by folk music, in particular by the songs of the Kingston Trio, Jerry bought a banjo and learned to play it. Performing as the Yester Brothers duo, Jim and Jerry played the coffeehouses of Hollywood. Jerry dropped out of college after a semester, enrolled the next year again, and left college for good after one more disappointing semester. When Jim joined the U.S. Army in 1961, Jerry formed a trio with John Forsha and Karol Dugan called the Inn Group, which became part of the original New Christy Minstrels. The Minstrels were really a collective of several individual groups, and Jerry appeared on the Minstrels' first album that yielded a hit single: "This Land Is Your Land."

In January 1963, Jerry joined the Modern Folk Quartet upon the invitation of the group's manager, Herb Cohen. The MFQ was originally formed in Hawaii by bassist Chip Douglas, who later was a producer for the Turtles, the Monkees, and Linda Ronstadt; by rock photographer, banjo player, and clarinetist Henry Diltz; by Cyrus Faryar, who had been a member of the Whiskeyhill Singers, a group led by former Kingston Trio member Dave Guard; and by Stanley White, who Jerry replaced. During the next four years, Jerry played hundreds of college concerts with the Modern Folk Quartet. Jerry, who habitually bought music books and studied orchestration, arranging, and composition on the tour bus, shared vocal arrangement responsibilities with Chip Douglas. Upon the addition of drummer Eddie Hoh in 1965 at the onset of the British music invasion, the band went electric with Jerry on lead guitar, changed its name to the Modern Folk Quintet, and the following year scored a moderate-sized regional hit single called "Nighttime Girl."

From 1963 to 1965 the MFQ was based in New York, where Jerry and the other MFQ members met and befriended the Lovin' Spoonful members during their formative months. "In the spring of 1965 the MFQ worked a gig at the Bitter End in the Village, and John Sebastian was our drummer. At the time, the Spoonful were together and working down at the Village Music Hall on Third Street, and John would run over to the Bitter End between the Spoonful's sets and get on stage and play a few numbers with us. We'd do our folk sets until he showed up and then we'd do folk-rock songs. We worked a week that way," Jerry recalls fondly.

Yester says the Beatles' initial appearance on the *Ed Sullivan Show* in February 1964 exerted a profound effect on the Greenwich Village folk music scene. "That was the arrow through the heart of folk music," Yester intones. "Before then, folk music was the most popular music in the country. But after that Sullivan program, folk musicians started growing long hair and buying electric guitars."

In all the years since 1963, the MFQ has been an off-again, on-again entity, periodically going into hibernation for a few years, then regenerating for a few more. When the MFQ members went their separate ways for the first time, in 1966, Jerry produced an album for the Association, in which his brother Jim was a member. He also produced Tim Buckley's debut album, *Goodbye And Hello,* and had been signed as a solo artist with Dunhill Records at the time the Spoonful invited him to join. Jerry cherishes the year he spent with the Spoonful, from June 1967 until the group's breakup in June 1968, when he and his wife, Judy Henske, moved to Los Angeles.

By that time, Judy had given birth to their daughter, Kate. Jerry welcomed the opportunity to stay closer to home, and began to concentrate more on writing. He and Judy—who had worked with Dave Guard's Whiskeyhill Singers and recorded under her own name for Elektra—set to work on an album for Straight! Records, which was owned by Herb Cohen and Frank Zappa. The album, which featured a potpourri of folk, jazz, and classical music that Judy and Jerry performed together, was called *Farewell Aldebaren,* named after a red star in the galaxy of Taurus.

Zal Yanovsky was coproducer of *Farewell Aldebaren,* but that wasn't the first Yester-Yanovsky collaboration.

About six months after Zal left the Spoonful, he had asked Jerry to collaborate in producing his solo album, *Alive And Well In Argentina,* which Buddah released in April 1968. Their coproduction of Zal's album led to an alliance between the two called Hair Shirt Productions, based in Los Angeles. Under that banner, they produced recordings for Pat Boone, Tim Buckley, and a group called the Fifth Avenue Band, managed by Bob Cavallo, who later guided the careers of Prince, Savage Garden, Alanis Morissette, and other popular artists of the 1980s and 1990s. On his own, Jerry produced the last recording the Turtles made in that era, then with Judy formed a band called Rosebud. Just after completing an album for Warner Brothers in 1971, Jerry and Judy broke up.

After knocking around for six months, Jerry was asked to produce the debut Elektra album for a new duo called Aztec Two Step in New York. There in 1972, he unexpectedly saw someone he knew—a woman named Marlene Waters, who had been but a girl when he met her eight years before. At about the same time he renewed his acquaintance with Marlene, Jerry formed a songwriting partnership with another old friend, Larry Beckett, who had been Tim Buckley's composing collaborator. Yester and Beckett continue to work together today.

Back in Los Angeles in 1973, Yester produced Tom Waits's moody debut Asylum album, *Closing Time,* did the orchestration and arrangements for Rob Reiner's recording of *Peter And The Wolf,* and then joined the Association, with which he remained for about a year and a half. In 1975, a particularly memorable year for Jerry, he and Marlene were married. That same year, the MFQ was reactivated, and Yester answered the call, performing with them for about three and a half years. He kept busy on the side as well, doing string arrangements for Tom Waits and Merrilee Rush and vocal arrangements for Manhattan Transfer, America, and other performers. And during that same year, Marlene gave birth to a daughter, Lena. Five years later, Hannah was born. Jerry recorded a solo album in the early '80s and moved into session engineering at Annex Studios in Hollywood.

By 1984, Jerry and Marlene decided they needed a change in scenery, and moved to Hilo, Hawaii. Jerry's brother Jim followed shortly, and the two brothers formed a band called Rainbow Connection with another local musician, Rainbow Page, stepson of Charles Mingus. The band used MIDI technology to synthesize instrumental sounds. They began playing local hangouts—the Banyan Broiler, a popular disco called CJ's, and additional clubs, as well as for weddings and other occasions. "It was just the three of us, but we sounded like a nine-piece band if we wanted to. We had a computer on stage doing bass and drums and strings. We played guitars, flute, and conga, and we became the most popular dance band in Hilo for about five years," says Jerry. After recording *Moonlight Serenade,* an album of '40s standards, in 1984 for John Stewart's Homecoming label, the MFQ reconvened four year later and signed with a Japanese label, for which the band made five albums during the next four years.

By 1990 the isolation of island living had set in, so Jerry and Marlene moved to Portland, Oregon. "Beckett lived there—still does—and I always loved Portland." But Jerry and Marlene didn't stay there long. Not long after the MFQ finished *Wolfgang,* an album of Mozart music in 1991, Steve Boone called Jerry to see if he'd be interested in resurrecting the Lovin' Spoonful. Jerry agreed after thinking about his previous experience in the Spoonful. "My relationship with John Sebastian wasn't as strong as the partnership he had with Zally. It just couldn't have been. One reason we decided to get back together was that feeling of unfinished business." Even though John and Zal declined to join them, Joe, Steve, and Jerry greatly enjoyed their reunion in 1991—so much so that they've stuck together since.

Jerry and Marlene have been based in Arkansas since 1994. That's when Bob Richards, a friend from Hawaii, landed in Memphis, bought a motor home, and decided to drive until he found the "perfect place." That place was Marble Falls, Arkansas, in the Ozark Mountains. Unable to afford a home in Portland, Jerry and

Marlene somewhat reluctantly accepted Bob's invitation to visit Arkansas. "We fell in love with the place," says Jerry. In 1994 they bought a parcel of land in a small town called Harrison. The neighbors include bears, cougars, skunks, opossums, squirrels, and groundhogs.

Jerry remains connected with both the Lovin' Spoonful and the MFQ, which became a quintet once again in 1988 with the addition of Jim Yester. All of the other members remain with the MFQ as well. "The MFQ never stops. So once you're in, you're in. It's like the Mafia."

Their Arkansas home has permitted Jerry to fulfill his childhood dream of having his own recording studio, which he calls Willow Sound. In two 15- by 15-foot rooms containing a piano, a pump organ, drums, and shelves filled with tapes and equipment, Jerry produces sessions for local artists and runs a service for songwriters who need to record demo versions of their songs. Jerry and daughter Lena also use the studio to work on their own music.

Although Jerry's mother died in 1998, her passing helped sweeten one of Jerry's fondest memories of his folks. A few years before the death of his father in 1977, Jerry and the MFQ played a gig at the Ice House in Pasadena, sharing the bill with a 15-piece jazz band. Engaged to write arrangements for the band's appearance, Jerry invited his father to collaborate with him. "My dad had an 18-piece band when he was 18 years old. Music was all he knew. He taught accordion and did gigs at night. That arrangement he did with me was actually the best arrangement for that jazz band."

"So, there's still a lot I want to do," he says. "When Beckett and I first started writing together, we wanted to compose a cantata, and we still do. I'm working on two albums of my own and I'm real interested in recording with the Spoonful. Joe and I have written some really good songs together and Steve and Lena are writing some fine compositions. I'm also getting more into producing and arranging again. It's funny, since the MIDI revolution in the 1980s, string arrangers or orchestrators have been hard-pressed to find work. But now people are discovering that it's one thing to simulate an orchestra on a computerized keyboard and it's another thing to do actual orchestration. Now these young artists are calling up and saying, 'I want the real thing.' So arrangers and orchestrators like me are getting work again."

For Jerry Yester, it's a daydream come true.

Lady Willpower

Gary Puckett and the Union Gap

CHAPTER 10

FROM THE TIME CAPSULE

NOVEMBER 1967: Columbia Records releases the first of the million-seller hit singles by Gary Puckett and the Union Gap, "Woman, Woman."

- NOVEMBER 7: Cleveland, Ohio, elects Carl B. Stokes mayor—the first black mayor of a major U.S. city.
- NOVEMBER 17: *Surveyor 6* becomes the first manmade object to lift off the moon. (Actually, it was more of a "hop," as the spacecraft moved up 4 miles, then laterally 2.5 miles to a new spot on the lunar landscape.)
- NOVEMBER 27: The Beatles release *Magical Mystery Tour.*
- NOVEMBER 30: Julie Nixon and David Eisenhower announce their engagement.

MARCH 1969: "Don't Give In To Him," the fifth of six top 20 Union Gap singles, debuts on the charts.

- MARCH 1: Doors lead singer Jim Morrison is arrested and charged with indecent exposure and public drunkenness during a Doors concert in Miami.
- MARCH 2: The Concorde SST supersonic airliner makes its inaugural flight.
- MARCH 11: The Jackson Five sign a recording contract with Motown Records.
- MARCH 20: John Lennon and Yoko Ono marry at the Rock of Gibraltar, and two days later begin a seven-day "bed-in" for peace from their bed in the Amsterdam Hilton.
- MARCH 28: Dwight D. Eisenhower, president from 1953 to 1961, dies in Washington, D.C., at the age of 78.

AUGUST 1969: Columbia releases "This Girl Is A Woman Now," the last Union Gap single to make the top 10.

- AUGUST 9: Actress Sharon Tate and four other people are brutally murdered in Los Angeles; cult leader Charles Manson and members of his "family" were later convicted of the crime.
- AUGUST 15–17: The legendary Woodstock Music and Art Fair held on a farm near Bethel, N.Y, draws an estimated 400,000 people to performances by Jimi Hendrix, the Who, Janis Joplin, John Sebastian, Country Joe & the Fish, Ten Years After, Sly and the Family Stone, and others.
- AUGUST 24: Arlo Guthrie's film *Alice's Restaurant* opens.

OPPOSITE: Gary Puckett and the Union Gap in Civil War uniforms, early 1968. Left to right: singer, guitarist, and keyboard player Gary Puckett (standing, in general's uniform); keyboard and bass player Kerry Chater (seated in foreground, corporal's uniform); keyboard, woodwind, guitar, and bass player Dwight Bement (sergeant's uniform); drummer Paul Wheatbread (standing, in private's uniform); and keyboard and woodwind player Gary Withem (seated, private's uniform).
FROM PHOTOFEST ARCHIVES, NEW YORK.

Amid the tourbillion of young revolutionaries against the establishment, a growing interest in politics and the Vietnam War, and a rapidly emerging subgenre of heavy metal bands such as Cream, Iron Butterfly, and Led Zeppelin, the serenades of Gary Puckett and the Union Gap consistently adhered to a tried and true pop ballad formula conveying the pathos of young love. The band unleashed a consistent string of ballads of which five remained in the top 10 for more than 11 weeks. In 1968, San Diego–based Gary Puckett and the Union Gap enjoyed four consecutive million-selling singles—"Woman, Woman," "Young Girl," "Lady Willpower," and "Over You"—and sold more records that year than any other recording act.

Formed in January 1967, Gary Puckett and the Union Gap began with longtime friends Gary Puckett and Dwight Bement, members of a San Diego cover band called the Outcasts. They were soon joined by Kerry Chater, Gary Withem, and drummer Peter Carrillo of another local band called Jerry and the Jeritones, members of which went on to become Iron Butterfly. The band's first road performance took them to the Pacific Northwest, an area in which Gary spent much of his childhood. Calling themselves Gary and the Remarkables, the members of Puckett's band dressed in powder-blue double-breasted jackets and striped pants and performed for a month each in Seattle, Washington, Portland, Oregon, and Vallejo, California, before returning to San Diego's popular Quad Room in the Clairemont Bowl, where they landed their first recording contract with Columbia Records.

While the band was on its first road trip, Puckett, who had an interest in Civil War history, decided that Gary and the Remarkables needed a new name and image. Seeking a stronger identity for the band, he conceived the idea of wearing Union soldier uniforms. "Gary Withem insists I got the idea while watching *F Troop* during leisure moments on the road," says Puckett. "Probably so." And having grown up in Union Gap, Washington, Puckett thought that name would be appropriate. "I remember telling the guys at this hotel in Seattle that we were going to dress in Union soldier outfits and we were going to call the band the Union Gap," recalls Puckett. "They laughed about it for days, but I wanted to be different than the tie-dyed, paisley-patterned '60s flower child mode."

After the band members returned to Southern California from their Pacific Northwest tour, they began searching for Union soldier uniforms. "Western Costume in L.A. said they could make the uniforms for us for $400 apiece," says Puckett. Instead, Gary decided to rent a Union soldier outfit and took it to a tailor in Tijuana, who was willing to make five coats and hats for about $400. "We were going to debut our outfits and new name at the Quad Room in San Diego's Clairemont Bowl. So everyone met at my house and we went down there en masse. As we walked in the door, people in all 52 lanes stopped bowling, one lane at a time, and stared at us." Quad Room patrons initially were unsure how to respond, but as word about the costumed quintet began to draw appreciative crowds to their performances, the band members relaxed and began feeling more comfortable in character, growing sideburns and mustaches to evoke a Civil War appearance.

Shortly after Gary Puckett and the Union Gap made their debut at the Quad Room, Paul Wheatbread replaced Peter Carrillo on drums. At about the same time, Gary and the band's manager, Dick Badger, presented a portfolio of the band, including song lyrics, photos, and a demo tape, to Columbia Records producer Jerry Fuller, who had written "Travelin' Man" for Ricky Nelson. "Jerry Fuller heard us and could see potential, especially in Gary's voice," says Kerry Chater. "So he came down to the Quad Room and we signed right there without any legal counseling. Lucky for us Columbia Records was a reputable organization."

The Union Gap was a multitalented group of musicians. Kerry Chater played bass and keyboards; Gary Withem played keyboards, clarinet, and sax; Dwight Bement played keyboards, clarinet, sax, guitar, and bass; Gary Puckett switched back and forth between bass, guitar, and keyboards; and everyone sang, including drummer Paul Wheatbread. "It was a very talented band," says Puckett. "During concerts, we enjoyed impressing the audience by switching instruments. We also sang a barbershop quartet number, which was a real crowd pleaser."

On August 17, 1967, the band recorded Puckett's "Believe Me" and "Woman, Woman" by Jim Glaser and Jim Payne, as well as a song called "Don't Make Promises," written by Tim Hardin. A month later the band's first record—"Woman, Woman" backed with "Don't Make Promises—was released. The record's first regional success was in Columbus, Ohio. "Bob Harrington, a local disc jockey on WCOL, was a Civil War buff, and he thought the record jacket picture was so authentic that it might be a good record. He auditioned it, liked it, and added it to the playlist. It went to No. 1," says Puckett.

"Woman, Woman" received its first major market exposure in Cleveland, which catapulted it onto the national charts. Chater recalls, "It was right in the middle of the psychedelic era and, although we looked like we fit into that mode, we didn't play that kind of music." The record sleeve portrayed the band in Union soldier uniforms in a battlefield scene, which was actually photographed at a demolished Los Angeles area school auditorium. "Steve Popovich, the promotion man for Columbia Records in Cleveland, went to the top radio station there to get some airplay," explains Chater. "The program director looked at the cover and said, 'Oh, that's just another psychedelic group,' and he didn't want to play it. But Steve Popovich said, 'No, no, no. Just listen.' So the programmer put it on and it sounded so different from what he had expected that he fell in love with it and played it and played it."

The band returned to the studio to record a song written by Jerry Fuller that he thought would be a good follow-up song to "Woman, Woman." That second single, "Young Girl," quickly climbed the charts, but was held out of the No. 1 position by Bobby Goldsboro's "Honey," which dominated the pop and country charts in the early spring of 1968. "Jerry always said the hardest thing for anyone with one hit record to do is to have two," recalls Puckett. "And we were fortunate to follow a song as great as 'Woman, Woman,' which had great production qualities, with another solid hit." Three months later the band's next single, "Lady Willpower," peaked at No. 2, and in another three months "Over You" made its debut, climbing to No. 7.

For the next three years, Gary Puckett and the Union Gap rode a wave of popularity, performing with acts such as the Association, the Grass Roots, the Beach Boys, Paul Revere and the Raiders, the Byrds, the Turtles, and the Mamas and the Papas. The band spent most of its years performing in the United States and Canada; however, a trip to Mexico City is etched in the mind of Dwight Bement. The band was scheduled to fly from New Orleans to Mexico City to perform a concert at the Plaza de Toros arena with the Byrds, but flight trouble delayed their arrival for four hours. Their appearance was canceled due to a riot that broke out in the stadium when concertgoers thought the band had simply not shown up. For the next two weeks the band performed at a nightclub in Mexico City, and the obliging owners hired a young driver to take them sightseeing.

"It's 4 o'clock in the morning and this club owner wants to take us to Maximilian's castle," recalls Bement. "So we start up this hill for about a quarter of a mile and a couple of guys step out from behind trees with pistols drawn. The club owner sticks his head out the window and yells something in Spanish and then hits the driver in the back of the head and yells *andele*. The driver responds and hits the gas, and further along we see another couple of guys with rifles. And when we get to the gate there are two more guys with submachine guns." Puckett remembers the group getting out of the limo, submachine guns at their backs, and walking through the gate toward the front door of the castle where they were met by the commanding officer with his guards telling them that was as far as they go. "That's when we turned around and headed back down the hill," says Bement. "You're not supposed to be going to national historic sites at 4 in the morning!"

In 1969 the band was invited by then-governor Lurlene Wallace to perform for Alabama's Shower of Stars fund-raiser—a risky proposition for a band performing in Union soldier uniforms. "We told them we didn't want to chance it," says Withem. "We could see ourselves getting up on stage in our Union soldier outfits and becoming target practice for the boys down there." After concert organizers promised to provide extra security, the band uneasily agreed to the performance, which turned out to be a huge success. Bement adds, "I got hold of a bars and stars [Confederate] flag and after we played a couple of songs, I let it unfurl over the front of my organ, and the roof went off the place. They loved it. We were made honorary lieutenant colonel aides-de-camp in the Alabama State Militia. We went over really big in the South."

Paul Wheatbread recalls a concert for about 40,000 people that took place in New York City's Central Park. "We were really popular at the time. I remember we were driven there by limousine, and the fans were breaking the mirrors off the limousine for souvenirs. It was cold so we were dressed in scarves and turtleneck sweaters. They tore the scarf off my neck for a souvenir. The only way we could get out of the park, as I remember it, was by helicopter."

The band made numerous guest appearances on a variety of popular television programs, including the *Jerry Lewis, Jonathan Winters,* and *Red Skelton* shows. But when they were invited to perform on the *Ed Sullivan Show,* Gary Withem was convinced the band had finally made it to the top. "I remember the Rolling Stones performed right before us and they had to change their song lyrics to 'let's spend some time together.' It was too risqué in those days to refer to going too far, so in 'Young Girl' we had to sing, 'How can this love of ours go on.'" Since the Stones had to change their lyrics it was okay with us."

Gary Puckett and the Union Gap appealed to a wide spectrum of fans including teenagers and their parents and college-age kids. The band recorded "Dreams Of The Everyday Housewife," a song that charted for Glen Campbell in 1968. "Glen Campbell was a good friend of Jerry Fuller's," says Withem. "In fact, Glen was the guy who showed us 'Woman, Woman.' He had brought it back from Nashville, and that's how we recorded it."

Gary fondly recalls the time in 1970 when he worked a Las Vegas engagement at the same hotel in which Elvis was performing. "Elvis came to see my show one night. That was an exciting moment. The maitre d' brought a note backstage that said, 'Tell the boy he sure can sing.' I loved his records, especially the early ones—'Don't Be Cruel,' 'Heartbreak Hotel,' and 'I Want You, I Need You, I Love You,'" says Puckett. "Later on, in her book, Priscilla said I was one of the artists that Elvis enjoyed listening to, and he had my records in his collection."

By 1970 Kerry Chater and Gary Withem had left the Union Gap to pursue careers as team songwriters for Irving/Almo, the publishing company for A&M Records. A new seven-piece Gary Puckett and the Union Gap emerged, which included Paul Wheatbread and Dwight Bement as well as new members Dick Gabriel on tenor saxophone, Tom Manasian on trombone, Barry McCoy on B3 organ, and Mike Crawford on trumpet. The band re-formed once again in late 1970 to include Puckett, Bement, Wheatbread, and new members Rob DeKarr on guitar and Brian Griffin on piano, and continued performing until May 31, 1971, when Puckett decided he was ready to take a break from music for a while.

"When we broke up it was a new generation basically—a new decade at least," says Puckett. "Times were changing rapidly and much of the '60s, including the music, was mostly a memory."

But as the years rolled on, a nostalgic generation would long for the music of their youth. Now, decades later, the memories associated with songs such as those recorded by Gary Puckett and the Union Gap and other hit groups of their time seem sweeter than ever.

HIT SINGLES BY GARY PUCKETT AND THE UNION GAP

DEBUT	PEAK	TITLE	LABEL
11/67	4	WOMAN, WOMAN (Certified Gold)	COLUMBIA
3/68	2	YOUNG GIRL (Certified Gold)	COLUMBIA
6/68	2	LADY WILLPOWER (Certified Gold)	COLUMBIA
9/68	7	OVER YOU (Certified Gold)	COLUMBIA
3/69	15	DON'T GIVE IN TO HIM	COLUMBIA
8/69	9	THIS GIRL IS A WOMAN NOW	COLUMBIA
3/70	41	LET'S GIVE ADAM AND EVE ANOTHER CHANCE	COLUMBIA

GARY PUCKETT

A truly gifted singer and musician, Gary Puckett has found meaning in music for as long as he can remember. His grandfather played banjo, sang, and danced, and both parents played instruments and were active in barbershop-style singing groups. "When I was a child, we always had a piano," recalls Gary. "My parents would rent a tape recorder a couple of months before Christmas and we would record songs and messages, which they would have transferred onto little records. My folks would send those records to my grandparents for Christmas. My mom told me one time, 'You know, I just always thought that all little boys could sing like you could sing. But that's not the case.' I inherited the qualities of their voices. They're both wonderful singers and musicians."

Gary began piano lessons when he was 6 years old, and played classical music for about four years. "I now wish that I had continued studying seriously," says Gary. "I still play piano but I don't have the ability that I once had because I became enamored with the guitar at some point, when rock and roll came along."

The oldest of five children, Gary was born October 17, 1942, to Leona and Arlon Puckett in Hibbing, Minnesota. Shortly thereafter, Gary's father enlisted in the Army and was stationed in Germany during World War II. Within a couple of weeks of his birth, Gary and his mother went to live with his grandparents in Pelican Rapids, Minnesota. "My father was reported missing in action but returned safely after being held in a German prison camp for five months toward the end of the war." When his father returned in 1946, the family moved to Watertown, South Dakota, where Gary's sister Kathy was born.

Gary says his whole family is musical. "Music was just a part of our everyday lives.

PHOTO BY TIM STAHL.

Kathy, four years younger, and David, seven years younger, both studied and play the piano. Brian, who is nine years younger than I, studied clarinet but in high school took up the drums. He's quite a good drummer today. My youngest sister Kris jokes that she has none of the 'family talents,' but she does have a beautiful family as do the others."

Gary spent a good part of his childhood in the Yakima Valley in Washington State, as well as two years, during the fourth and fifth grades, in Tacoma. His father was in the merchandising business for the Allied Corporation, working his way up the ranks to manager of major department stores. When Gary was about 16, the family moved to Twin Falls, Idaho, where he graduated from Twin Falls High School.

"I really didn't know what I wanted to do when I grew up. My parents were hoping that I would go to school and maybe go into medicine or something at least with a college education. I was one of those kids who just didn't have a clue about what I really wanted to do with my life. Rock and roll just had a feeling about it, as opposed to what classical did for me. I love classical music today and wish that I had not been such a lazy kid and continued my studies. I envy people who can play the classics."

Gary's first band was called the Redcoats, which he formed in the Yakima Valley when he was 15. The group consisted of piano, guitar, and drums, and Gary was the lead singer. "The guitar player was Barry Curtis. He's been in the Kingsmen of 'Louie Louie' fame for many years now. Now and then we get a chance to work with them, so Barry and I get together and reminisce about the good old times, like the time he tried to steal my girlfriend," laughs Puckett. "We played rock and roll! Songs by Elvis, Jerry Lee Lewis, Everly Brothers, the Platters, the Coasters, and others." Later on, in Twin Falls, Idaho, Gary joined a folk group called the Continentals. "We had three singers. I didn't even sing; I was just a guitar player."

After graduating from high school in 1960, Gary attended San Diego City College for two years. He had an interest in pursuing some aspect of psychology, but found himself becoming more and more involved in the San Diego music scene. "I was playing in a band called the Ravens while I was going to school, and eventually I just gave up on school and went to work from 9 a.m. to 5 p.m. as a delivery boy for Foreign Auto Supply. We sold basic engine parts for foreign cars. At the same time, I was working 9 p.m. to 2 a.m. in different clubs in town." Foreign Auto Supply personnel consisted of the two owners, a secretary, and two delivery boys. By the time Gary left two years later, he had been given managerial duties over the parts department, machine shop, and the company's 11 employees.

Meanwhile, by 1965 Gary's band, the Outcasts, had become one of the hottest bands in San Diego, performing regularly at a nightclub called the Quad Room.

"We were just a trio but somehow we had a finger on the pulse, and were rocking hard every night," declares Puckett. The Outcasts tried unsuccessfully to launch a recording career, releasing two singles, "Would You Care" and "Run Away" on Prince Records and "I Can't Get Through To You" and "I Found Out About You" on Karate. Even though the two small labels lacked sufficient promotional punch to propel the band to stardom, their stage appearances drew good crowds.

"There was a waiting line to get in the club from about 9:30 p.m. until about midnight every night of the week." The band included guitar, bass, drums, and all three handled lead singing roles. And Gary recalls the three had distinct personalities, "like oil and water. Bobby Brown was a great bass player. He and I were good buddies. Tommy Kendall was an excellent drummer, but Bobby and Tommy were pretty much the oil and the water. The band was kind of volatile. We would find ourselves breaking up every week or two. But as soon as we thought it was over, we'd all realize that we had a great band and an excellent job, so we'd apologize and show up for work again."

After Tommy left the Outcasts in 1966, Bobby and Gary brought in three other members, including Dwight Bement. The five-piece band consisted of Bobby Brown on bass, Willy Kellogg on drums, Puckett on guitar and organ, Bement on tenor sax and organ, and Bob Salisbury on baritone sax. "It was a real good band, but it was another pretty unstable mix of individuals, and I finally just got tired of it all," says Puckett. "We played in Northern California for a short period of time, but it didn't take me more than about six weeks to decide that if I'm going to stay in music, I want to have a band that—one—is my own, and—two—everyone has the same desire for success in the music business. So Dwight Bement stayed with me. He was a great player and we got along well. We went looking for other players." Puckett and Bement found Kerry Chater, Gary Withem, and Peter Carrillo, later replaced by Paul Wheatbread.

Gary Puckett and the Union Gap enjoyed a fruitful but exhausting three and a half years together. But late 1970 was the beginning of the band's demise. "It was kind of like being married to four people instead of just one," says Puckett. "We all had different goals and were heading in different directions. Chater and Withem wanted to spend more time with their loved ones, and they had been hired at A&M Records Publishing to write songs; they're both excellent writers."

With the dissolution of the Union Gap in the summer of 1971, Puckett decided to take a break from music. "I had decided at that point I was going to go on hiatus. I thought I would take some time off, maybe a year, reflect on past events, decide what I wanted to do next, and go back to work. Columbia Records had said to me, 'Gary, just re-sign the contract. We know what to do. We'll make you rich and famous.' In retrospect, that's what I should have done. The record company and I were somewhat at odds then, so I thought I'd wait a little longer to re-sign. A year later, nobody cared about the '60s. My so-called sabbatical had turned into a mandatory exile from the music business. The world had moved on with glitter rock and disco."

The '70s were difficult for Gary, who not only endured the demise of his band and the loss of his popularity, but also the breakup of a 10-year relationship and divorce from his first wife. The divorce settlement left him with few material possessions.

Before that, during the late '60s, Puckett had begun searching for a spiritual foundation and reading books espousing Eastern philosophies. While studying acting in 1974, Gary was introduced to transcendental meditation (T.M.). "One of the students had a book called *Tranquillity Without Pills*. I asked her if I could borrow it and found that I was somewhat impressed with what Maharishi Mahesh Yogi had to say about transcendental meditation," says Puckett. Before long, Puckett found himself being initiated into T.M., meditating morning and night and studying books about spiritual learning and health-promoting foods.

"I found meditation to have an effect of some sort in my life at times. It gave me feelings of equanimity, but ultimately it left me feeling empty. I meditated from 1974 to 1985 and the last couple of years of meditation, I was in an emotional pit," confesses Puckett. "In the middle of meditation one day, I found myself in tears, just at the lowest that I'd ever been in my life, and I started to pray to God to fix my life. And I did that morning and night for two years. Finally, the Lord Jesus said to me, 'Stand up. Walk away from Maharishi Mahesh Yogi, and I'll show you the way.' Gradually things started happening. Christian people and situations entered my life."

Gary met Grant Goodeve, an actor from the '70s TV series *Eight Is Enough*, during a benefit he was doing for the Make-A-Wish Foundation. "Grant helped me a lot. He was very patient, and encouraged me to understand Christianity and know the Lord," said Puckett. "I also worked on the film *My Boyfriend's Back* with Sandy Duncan, Jill Eichenberry, and Judith Light, and with John Sandaford, who was also an inspiration to me. So I moved out of L.A., bought a condominium in San Diego, and started attending Horizon Christian Fellowship, a Bible-based church."

Following his return to San Diego in 1978, Gary began working in local venues. Still struggling with his spirituality Puckett continued working quietly and writing songs in his beachfront condo. His mother, Leona, is a born-again Christian and a believer in God and the power of prayer, but Gary had distanced himself from Christianity for many years. "I was too caught up in the '60s generation 'if it feels good, do it' kind of thing, but I found myself losing all of the things that the Lord had given to me," says Gary. "I know that I'm extremely fortunate to have been blessed with the success of the Union Gap in the late '60s, but it's even more a blessing now. That's because I know it was not by my own devices, although I worked hard for it, but it was by the grace and love of the Lord Jesus. I want people to know that we are given eternal life but only through Jesus Christ, no other way but through Him. The Lord wants me to use the celebrity he gave me in the '60s to tell others about him now. He tells us that if we stand up for him now, here on earth, by believing he is the son of God, he will stand up for us on judgment day and he'll give us the right to walk through the gates of heaven."

Sharing that message is now a driving force in Gary's life. Today, his concerts appeal to a wide audience from young to old who enjoy the music of the '60s. His band includes bass player Michael Fiore, who likes to say, "It's the Michael Fiore band featuring Gary Puckett." David Page, who was once the band leader for the Grass Roots, is the drummer, and Howard Laravea is the musical director and keyboardist. "It's a great band and we enjoy working together," says Gary.

Gary and his brother David have written many songs together and collaborated on an album released in 1998 by Rivière International Records called *Europa*. David co-wrote 4 of the 13 songs for the CD on which Gary sang to the accompaniment of top German studio musicians. "*Europa* is a good album and well produced," says Gary. "It's just different. It's very keyboard-oriented and it doesn't sound like you'd expect it to sound. The arrangement is typically German."

Europa reflects the versatility of Puckett's voice and reveals his interest in adventurous projects that apply his talents in new ways. "I'd love to do a great pop project again, but I'm much more interested in the Christian songs the Lord has given my brother and me," says Puckett. "A Christmas album is also at the top of my list."

That would be a particularly fitting project for Gary Puckett, whose first recordings were the Christmas carols he sang as a child for his grandparents.

THEN AND NOW
DWIGHT BEMENT

As the house lights dimmed and the curtains parted, the school principal announced the names of the two young performers and gestured to the side of the stage. No one appeared. After an uneasy pause, a young trumpet player by the name of Neil Waters shuffled hesitatingly partway across the stage. All eyes, including Neil's, gazed stage right as the curtain ruffled. Finally the bell of Dwight Bement's clarinet poked out past the edge of the curtain. Gripped by fear, the young musicians began to blow the opening notes of the "Marine Hymn." That fifth-grade assembly marked the performing debut of Dwight Bement, who later would overcome his stage fright enough to perform before thousands of fans throughout the country.

Now a partner in a commercial remodeling company in Colorado Springs and a long-time member of Flash Cadillac and the Continental Kids, Dwight Bement has succesfully intertwined his identity as both a craftsman and a musician.

The Bements have deep roots in the construction industry. "My grandfather was a carpenter who crafted his own furniture, and my father, Dwight Richard, who worked at Ryan Aeronautical in San Diego for 30 years, would pick up con-

Dwight Bement (in checked jacket, second from left) with other members of Flash Cadillac: Warren Knight, Sam McFadin, and Dave Henry. COURTESY FLASH CADILLAC.

struction work whenever his union shop went out on strike. He would take me along and let me help in any way that I could."

Born December 28, 1940, in San Diego, Dwight first became interested in music in the fifth grade when he learned to play the clarinet, an instrument his father had played in high school. Dwight wanted to play the trombone but at the age of 9 he wasn't able to reach all the stops on that instrument. In the eighth grade his mother, Virginia, bought a piano and Dwight and his father began taking piano lessons. "Not too long after that, I was telling my mom all the things she was doing wrong," laughs Dwight. "After I learned the piano, I found it very easy to pick up just about any other instrument."

Dwight grew up in National City, which is just south of San Diego near the Mexico border, and attended Sweetwater High School. By the eleventh grade he was playing saxophone in a band that included some of his Spanish-speaking classmates, who taught him the style of Latin-influenced music that Bement calls "Chicano Rock."

"When deciding on a name for the band, we combined Medallions, a popular group at the time, and Hi-Fi, a recent technological wonder that preceded stereo, and came up with the Fydallions. My mom sewed that name on a square of burgundy silk and we stretched it over the bass drum head. We all went down to Penneys, bought matching burgundy corduroy jackets, and we were in business."

The Fydallions performed instrumental music for car club dances and various other events. "I knew clarinet wasn't going to get it at these dances, so I chose to use the saxophone, and the first song I learned was 'Night Train,' which I continue to play to this day," says Dwight.

Following graduation in 1958, Dwight went to San Diego State, planning to major in music. He joined the Nomads, a popular band that performed at big dances and socials throughout the San Diego area. The Nomads are still quite active today.

In 1960, Dwight and some musician friends moved to Sacramento where they formed a band, once again taking the name Fydallions. "Hey! It's a good name," says Dwight. "We played night clubs and bowling alleys and stayed up all night doing stupid things." The money wasn't very good so Dwight supplemented it by working in construction. He recalls, "We would play in bars until 2 a.m., then go to an after-hours joint and play there for a couple more hours and then go to the construction site, climb up on the roof, and wait for it to get light enough to see a nail head. We would hammer away until three in the afternoon doing subfloor, framing, and roof sheeting. Afterwards, we would either go drink beer or go get some sleep, depending on which was more urgently needed. Then the whole process would start over again. I don't know how I survived it all," says Dwight. That version of the Fydallions eventually became the Spiral Starecase, which recorded the 1969 hit "More Today Than Yesterday."

On his way back to San Diego in 1960, Bement was waylaid in Ontario, California, by his longtime friend, Ronnie Williams. Ronnie talked him into joining a band called the Blackouts. This band included Ronnie's neighbor, Frank Zappa. Bement performed with the Blackouts for a couple of years until another friend, Tommy Kendall, coaxed him into returning to San Diego to play for the next three years in a band called the Gentrys, which had no relationship to the Memphis-based band of the same name that recorded "Keep On Dancing" in 1965.

"We decided on the name by opening a dictionary, covering our eyes, and placing a finger on the page," recalls Dwight. "The word was 'gentry' which means people of good birth. Perfect." Kendall left the Gentrys to form the Outcasts, which Bement joined in 1964.

"The Outcasts was an excellent group, a *really* good band, and in 1966 we tried to take the band on the road," recalls Bement. "We went to San Francisco to play but a couple of the guys got into an argument over something and the band broke up before we had a chance to play." About a month later, Puckett and Bement formed a group specifically for recording, which was to become Gary Puckett and the Union Gap.

Although Bement was justifiably proud of the success that he and the other Union Gap members achieved, he admits, "I never particularly cared for the music of the Union Gap. It wasn't my style, and I didn't play saxophone in the band; I played organ. I never liked keyboards until four or five years ago when my level of proficiency improved to the point that I could stand to listen to myself."

Following the breakup of the Union Gap in 1971, Bement returned to San Diego and played with a local band for a few months before moving back to L.A., where he became involved with Flash Cadillac and the Continental Kids. Peter Rachtman, who managed the Union Gap, also managed Flash. Rachtman recruited Bement when the band was looking for a sax player.

"Flash Cadillac was the first band to appear on *American Bandstand* without a record," said Bement. Flash, which specializes in old-time rock and roll, recorded the only original music used on the soundtrack of Francis Ford Coppola's *American Graffiti*. The band also appeared in the movie and received a platinum album (then signifying 1 million units sold) in 1973. Bement didn't join until after shooting on *American Graffiti* was over, but was part of the group when Coppola asked Flash to do some location shooting and soundtrack work for his 1978 movie *Apocalypse Now*. Flash also appeared on an episode of *Happy Days* as Johnnie Fish and the Fins.

"The whole band lived in this huge, three-story house on Wilton Place near Wilshire Boulevard. Every Friday night that we were in town we threw a party, *Animal House* style," says Dwight. "Everyone attended. Famous musicians, infamous musicians, the Fonz, and other celebrities. Some of the Los Angeles Dodgers would occasionally drop in."

Bement, who has been with Flash Cadillac since 1973, continues to perform with the group two or three weekends a month, at venues all over the country. The other members are the original bass player, Warren Knight; guitarist and lead vocalist Sam McFadin; and drummer Dave Henry. Flash Cadillac has been together since 1969.

In 1975, Flash moved to a 117-acre ranch in the Colorado Rockies. They built a studio, which is used for Flash recording sessions and is also leased to other bands.

About half of Flash Cadillac's engagements are performed with symphony orchestras. The band's joyous vocal renditions of the '50s and '60s have been accompanied by orchestras in Salt Lake City, Long Beach, Reno, Atlanta, Cincinnati, Charlotte, Portland, and many other cities. The band uses a talented group of arrangers, including Bement, and a librarian who sends the music to the different symphonies prior to rehearsals. "The symphony players are better than we are; no one will ever deny that. We have a lot of respect for them," says Dwight. "We don't think of them as just backup music. The orchestra members help form an 80-piece rock and roll band."

Flash Cadillac performs for many of the conventions hosted at Colorado Springs' Broadmoor, a five-star hotel set at the base of Pikes Peak on the front range of the Rockies, 50 miles south of Denver. With the U.S. Air Force academy located 10 miles to the north, Colorado Springs has attracted quite a bit of high-tech industry, which has stimulated the regional economy.

"It's nice being the house band for the Broadmoor. People call them up and ask, 'What kind of entertainment do you have in the area? We are bringing in an insurance company from Ohio for the week and we need a good dance band for the weekend.' We also do a lot of corporate jobs like that all over the country."

Dwight still supplements his music with construction as he did in Sacramento in the early '60s. He and his two business partners specialize in commercial building and remodeling. Bement has recently been licensed as a general contractor, but, he is quick to add, "music is *numero uno.*"

Dwight speaks fondly of his partner, Kathy Ryan, who is a real estate broker in Colorado Springs. "I met Kathy in 1968 when I was with the Union Gap and she worked for WCFL Radio in Chicago," says Bement. "We were just kind of ships passing in the night until 1983, when we hooked up permanently. We've been together ever since."

Kathy and Dwight spend time hiking, skiing, and snowboarding. Dwight also plays a lot of golf with his business partner, Dan Zemler.

Dwight hopes to achieve additional fame in some area of music. He says, "I still feel that I can write a hit song, be an actor, or write a book. I believe when you are an artist, you can be famous at anything, at any age."

KERRY CHATER

Composer, arranger, keyboardist, and bass player Kerry Chater has spent most of his life making other people shine. His name is little known by the public, but he is well known and respected by Lee Greenwood, Alabama, George Strait, Reba McEntire, and other country artists for whom he's written numerous hits. He has composed about 20 songs that have done well on both the pop and country charts. Three of them, "You Look So Good In Love," "I.O.U.," and "If I Had You" hit No. 1 in the country music market. In 1984, Chater received a Grammy nomination for Lee Greenwood's recording of "I.O.U.," which received BMI's 2 Million Broadcast Performances Award. Chater has received 16 BMI awards, and his songs appear on more than 8 platinum and 20 gold albums.

Kerry's father, who loved to play piano, bought an upright piano when Kerry was born, but it wasn't until Kerry was 10 years old that he became interested. "I met a school friend, a kid named Doug Ingle, and we used to get together and teach each other boogie-woogie piano licks," recalls Chater. In his early teens Kerry took lessons from a jazz pianist in San Diego, and by the time he was a sophomore in high school, he knew that he wanted to be a songwriter.

Kerry was born on August 7, 1945, in Vancouver, Canada; a year later the family moved to Toronto. In 1951, Kerry's father, Melville Chater, who was an executive director for the YMCA, moved the family to Southern California. "We had music going on all the time at my house, everything from classical music— Rachmaninoff—to big band music and jazz," recalls Kerry. "My father had some albums called *Backroom Piano,* which was kind of early blues piano-only albums."

Kerry attended Helix High School in La Mesa, California, where he was in the choir and wrote songs for the girls in the choir. After high school graduation in 1964, he attended Grossmont College in El Cajon, near San Diego, for about a year, but found that performing in bands didn't leave much time for studying.

"I started working in bands when I was about 15, and I was the leader of a lot of them. I could get us bookings at a lot of military clubs. The only problem I had was I'd put these really good bands together, but they'd all want to play for their high school peers, and would get mad at me for booking them into service clubs. I kept telling them, 'Hey, you get one gig a month at a high school, and you get four gigs a week at these other places.' We were making lots of money."

Kerry Chater with Doberman puppy, Titan. PHOTO BY LYNN GILLESPIE CHATER.

Doug Ingle, a childhood friend and keyboardist, played with Chater in many of the same bands. "We both wanted to play piano, but I always felt he was better than I was," says Chater. "I picked up the bass so that we could be in the same band together."

Chater's first band, called the Shadows, lasted for about six months. He then started a band called the Progressives, which included Gary Withem, Doug Ingle, and Danny Weis. The Progressives later became Jerry and the Jeritones, named after Chater's girl-friend, Jerry Martinson, who sang in the group. The Jeritones played at the Moose Club, the Elks Lodge, and at military base clubs around San Diego, and in 1965 the Jeritones auditioned for an opening as house band for a new teen club called the Palace. The band changed its name to the Palace Pages, but the new group was short-lived.

Kerry and Jerry were married in 1966, the same year the Palace Pages broke up. Ingle and Weis went on to form Iron Butterfly, and Gary Withem and Chater became members of the Union Gap.

"When I met Gary Puckett I was working in a San Diego club with a union group called the Nomads. Puckett's group had been working across town, but they had broken up and Gary was going around to the clubs to see who was playing and what they were playing. I was playing some instruments stacked on each other, which is real popular now, but it was unheard of at the time. I had a Fender Rhodes piano bass, which produced two and a half octaves of bass sounds, and a Fender Rhodes electric piano on top of an organ. So we saved one guy and we made a little more money. Gary and I just sat in a coffee shop and discussed the band he was putting together, and I told him about Gary Withem. So originally, the Union Gap was me playing this stack of keyboards, Puckett playing guitar, plus two saxophonists, and a drummer. And then I got tired of playing so much, and I really wanted to be playing bass because you can run around and do more stuff on stage. Since Dwight played keyboard, I went to bass."

Chater did most of the arranging for live performances of Gary Puckett and the Union Gap, and wrote the song "His Other Woman," which appeared on the B-side of "This Girl Is A Woman Now." Chater says, "Although Jerry Fuller is a great songwriter, and he was writing our hits, that was a problem for me because I couldn't get enough of my material going in there. I had to compete with our producer. So after about three years I left the group to pursue songwriting." In early 1970, Kerry felt that he had made enough money to support himself for a few months during his pursuit of a career in songwriting. The band's manager, Marty Erlichman, helped Chater and Withem get jobs as staff songwriters for April-Blackwood, which was the publishing company for Columbia Records. The two wrote as a team for about a year before joining A&M Music's Irving/Almo Publishing.

"I had publishers showing my songs, and I worked my way up. I had always wanted to write country music. That was a part of it, the biggest part of it. So finally, after I got some successes in country music, I felt I had enough impetus to move to Nashville." Chater adapted easily to the "music city" culture of Nashville, where he soon established a reputation as a prolific songwriter.

Chater works with other songwriters, including his wife, Lynn, who began writing with him in 1991. (Chater's first marriage ended in 1976; and he married Lynn Gillespie in 1988.) The two share song credits on recordings by numerous country artists including Mindy McCready, Paul Brandt, Lorrie Morgan, Jessica Andrews, and Anne Murray. He often collaborates with other writers, a common practice in Nashville. "Quite often I'll write with two other people because in Nashville songwriters are almost like a rock group. You can have three or four of them writing together. They might work independently of each other as well, but it's not unheard of here to have three writers on a song."

Kerry moved to Nashville in 1987 after spending several years commuting back and forth from Los Angeles. He says he prefers the work ethic in Nashville over that of L.A. "Songwriting here in Nashville is very 9-to-5. Even if the hours don't synch up, the attitude does. And that was one of the inspirations that got me to this town. I could have written country music in Los Angeles, and I had several successes out of Los Angeles that would normally be thought of as Nashville records. In L.A. it's not unusual for writers to get together at noon, take a lunch break at 3, and work until 9 p.m., and that isn't the way I like to work."

Most of Chater's inspiration for songs comes from what he sees in people. "I guess you could categorize most songwriters in one of two categories: either they're writing about something they experienced, or they're writing about something that they're fantasizing. For example, I don't know Joni Mitchell, but I get the impression that her songs are derived from experiences that she has had. Other writers are inspired by a fabricated event such as observing people walking down the street who were obviously married and having an argument. You can build a fantasy around that situation. I write from that second scenario most of the time, because when you're continually churning out songs, you don't have time to have all of the experiences. It's like writing fiction novels. You have to invent the scenarios, and you try to pick scenarios that generally could happen to anyone."

Just as the musician continually longs for that perfect opportunity to impress the right person at the right moment, the songwriter hopes that his or her song will be heard by an artist who will then record it. Since most of Chater's songs are written on speculation, he welcomes any opportunity to present his songs to anyone of influence—whether it's the producer, the artist, the manager, or a spouse, a boyfriend, or a girlfriend. "It's like selling anything—insurance or shoes or cars. The publisher goes to the marketplace and says, 'Here's a song that I represent.' And if the artist likes it and eventually records it, then the publisher and the writers share the royalties."

Chater rarely writes on assignment; however, after "I.O.U." was nominated for a Grammy, Greenwood's producer contacted Kerry looking for more songs to record on a subsequent album. Kerry admits that some of his favorite songs are the ones that have become hits, such as George Strait's recording of "You Look So Good In Love"; Reba McEntire's first No. 1 song, "You're The First Time I've Thought About Leaving"; and "I Know a Heartache When I See One," which was a hit for Jennifer Warnes in 1978, was recorded 20 years later by Jo Dee Messina, and has placed on all of the charts except R&B. In 1999, "You Go First," a song written by Kerry and Lynn Chater with Cyril Rawson, recorded by Jessica Andrews, was featured in the film *Forces Of Nature* and on an episode of the TV series *Providence*.

"The fact that they've become hits is a confirmation that I'm doing the right thing," says Chater. "And I think they're honestly good songs that deserve the recognition they're getting. In the case of 'I Know A Heartache,' I happen to like the rhythm. Even if I hadn't written it, I would have liked the song."

Kerry and Lynn live and work south of Nashville in a community called Brentwood. "When we bought the property, there was only one tree on it, and we had to move it because that's where we wanted to build the house. Now we have about 75 trees that my wife planted, and it's just beautiful."

Kerry's hobby is tactical pistol shooting, which he practices at a target range. "As in any sport, there's lots of gear, and it's real expensive. We wear hearing protection gear that looks like headphones in a stereo system. You can hear actually better than your normal hearing would be until there's any loud noise, and then it shuts down automatically, so that your ears are protected," says Chater.

Kerry's ambition today is to continue writing music. "I know that there's no real retirement from songwriting. You can do it as long as you live. But I think the longer you go at it, the harder it gets," says Kerry. "People start to want a new generation, new voices, and new ideas, and my hope is to keep going and get those new ideas to stay in the business."

Kerry, who describes himself as "quiet" and "a thinker," says performing in the Union Gap was always a vehicle for getting involved in songwriting. "It helped me in a lot of ways, because the success didn't go to my head. I realized it could be over at any moment." He relates his feelings to something he heard Clint Eastwood say during an interview. Eastwood said that he knew from the time he was 6 years old that he wanted to be an actor. But, Eastwood went on, a 6-year-old doesn't mind getting up and doing something silly in front of everyone. And if you can remember to be that 6-year-old, then you can have a lot of fun in life. "I think that's kinda where I'm coming from, too," says Chater. "I'm trying to stay this teenager with the joy in the music and writing it."

Nowadays when Chater sees himself and the Union Gap on reruns of old *Ed Sullivan* shows he says, "It feels like another life that somebody else lived. I was so sure, even with the Union Gap and its success, that I would leave the group as soon as I could, because I always wanted to be a songwriter."

THEN AND NOW

PAUL WHEATBREAD

Paul Wheatbread loves to entertain people, and whether it's from the stage or through his consulting agency, which specializes in travel, entertainment, meeting planning, group trips, and fun, everyone's guaranteed a good time. In 1995 Paul took over the Judy Francis Agency, a hospitality consulting firm that his wife, Judy Francisco, started in 1990. As the company grew, Judy, who is the senior sales and marketing manager for the La Jolla and San Diego Hard Rock Cafes, could no longer manage the business, so Paul took over. The agency's clients include corporations, professional associations, meeting and convention planners, lawyers, and various business organizations. Many of the firm's clients grew up listening to the music of Gary Puckett and the Union Gap.

"I consult with people who need entertainment, people who want to arrange fishing trips or group travel to destinations such as Las Vegas, San Francisco, or anywhere. I arrange for all of the accommodations, entertainment, and anything they might need," explains Wheatbread, who now manages all of the details that

Judy and Paul Wheatbread on their 1970 BSA A-65 Thunderbolt in 1999.

road managers once handled for Gary Puckett and the Union Gap. "We plan a group trip, for example, to Las Vegas, and then we send out fliers announcing the trip, dates, and times to our regular clients, hospitality business associates, family, and friends. We get group room rates, and discounts for flights and shows. I've also taken groups to the Fabulous Forum in Inglewood for Lakers games," says Paul, who works out of his home office. "I'm kinda like the old road manager, making sure that everything is happening the right way it's supposed to happen. That little travel bug is still in me after being on the road for so many years."

Born in San Diego on February 8, 1946, Wheatbread began playing the drums when he was 5, after his parents, Leonard and Ermine, bought him a drum set for Christmas. His first interest in music was stirred by the big band sounds of Gene Krupa and Benny Goodman. Originally from Buffalo, New York, Paul's parents had moved to Southern California to work in the aircraft factories in the late '30s. During World War II his mother helped build bombers while his father put in military service. Ermine became an elementary school teacher and gave piano lessons, teaching Paul and his older brother, Mark, and younger sister, Karen, how to play. After the war, Leonard returned to the aircraft factories as a civil service worker and didn't retire until 1983. "My brother followed my Dad into the civil service, working on aircraft, and my sister works for preschools—kinda followed my Mom's footsteps. I was the oddball."

During his junior year at Clairmont High School in San Diego, Paul worked in a laundromat after school for three to four hours, then played music at night. He met Gary Puckett when members of Gary's band, the Ravens, were looking for a drummer to play at the local military clubs in San Diego.

"At 15½ I wasn't quite old enough to join the musicians' union, but they made an exception for me after talking to my Dad and Gary. And we'd have to go down and work in these military clubs that at the time were union."

Following his high school graduation in 1963, Paul studied music at Mesa Junior College for a couple of semesters, but his love of performing lured him to the club scene full time. About six months later, the Ravens decided they would like to play at the local night clubs rather than at military clubs. Since Paul wasn't yet 21, it was illegal for him to play in clubs, so he had to leave the band.

A few weeks later Paul joined a local group called the Hard Times, which consisted of Wheatbread on drums and vocals, lead guitarist Bill Richardson, lead vocalist and 12-string guitar player Rudy Romero, bassist Bob Morris, and harmonica player Lee Keifer. The band started rehearsing in Wheatbread's garage and after two months decided to go to Hollywood. The Hard Times began performing at the Sea Witch on Sunset Boulevard in Los Angeles. Dick Clark, who was looking for new talent for his teen television show *Where The Action Is,* came into the club, liked the band's sound, and signed them up on the spot. The show aired five days a week on ABC-TV from 1965 to 1967. Regularly featured performers on the program besides the Hard Times included Paul Revere and the Raiders, Steve Alaimo, Keith Allison, Tina Mason, The Robbs, Tommy Roe, and the Action Kids Dancers.

"We recorded for a subsidiary of Liberty Records called World-Pacific. We put out a song called 'Fortuneteller' about a month before the Stones put it out in 1966, but we didn't quite have the hit with it that they did," says Wheatbread. "They were just trying to draw new talent, and thought the Hard Times would do the trick for that show. We had a great time, played with a lot of great rock and roll performers. Dick Clark had all the top acts on all the time—James Brown, Otis Redding."

Where The Action Is was filmed on location throughout the country, and the performers traveled by bus. Wheatbread recalled a particularly memorable Dick Clark tour through the South in which he performed with the Hard Times but also had the opportunity to sit in with some other acts. "Neil Diamond was the headliner and his drummer got sick, so I backed him on stage for quite a few days of that tour. Neil was and is a real nice guy. He'd sit there in the back of the limo with his acoustic guitar and write songs, and a couple of months later I'd hear them on the radio."

Paul lived with other members of the Hard Times in a house in Laurel Canyon in the Hollywood Hills. "The Turtles lived down around the corner, the Byrds lived down at the end of the street, and the Mamas and the Papas lived up at the other end of the street. So I got to know them all pretty well. When I went back on the road again with Gary, I kept running into them, sharing bills."

After *Where The Action Is* went off the air in March 1967, Paul returned to San Diego. Gary Puckett, who was looking to replace the drummer in the new band he had assembled, heard of Wheatbread's return and asked him to join the band. "I had just turned 21 so I was finally able to play in night clubs," says Wheatbread. "They had just changed the band's name from Gary and the Remarkables to Gary Puckett and the Union Gap, and they were getting the Civil War uniforms. About that same time Jerry Fuller came to see us, liked us, and signed us up."

The next five years were remarkable for Wheatbread, who tasted the success he had admired in others. Following the breakup of the Union Gap, Paul stopped playing music for about six months before joining a local group called Burt Torres and the Charades in which his brother-in-law Ronny Legrette was playing. "Then I got a call from Flash Cadillac and the Continental Kids' manager, asking if I wanted to play drums for them," says Wheatbread. Paul agreed, reuniting with Dwight Bement, who had begun performing with Flash Cadillac about six months earlier.

Recalling Flash's work in *Apocalypse Now,* Wheatbread says, "Our role in the movie was portraying a USO band entertaining the troops in Vietnam. We played the song "Susie Q" on this floating pontoon stage on a river in the Philippines, where much of the movie was filmed. We were set up on risers on the sides of the stage so a helicopter with these Playboy bunnies on it could land between us. At the same time it was raining and windy, and we were looking up at this helicopter hoping it was going to land straight. They had to fly us over to the Philippines again because the first time all the roads and the set got wiped out by a typhoon."

Flash Cadillac and the Continental Kids recorded three *Billboard* Hot 100 hits in the 1970s, including "Dancin' (On A Saturday Night)," issued by Epic Records in 1974; "Good Time, Rock And Roll," released by Private Stock in 1975; and "Did You Boogie (With Your Baby)," which included spoken interludes by Wolfman Jack, produced by Private Stock in 1976. "Did You Boogie" reached No. 29, and charted for 14 weeks.

"We traveled pretty much worldwide but mainly in the states, playing the local college circuits and fairgrounds," says Paul. "We played at the Diamond Head crater in Hawaii, down in the bowl itself, a natural amphitheater, with the Turtles." In 1976 Paul and Judy sold their house in San Diego and moved to Colorado with Flash Cadillac.

"The band had a 117-acre ranch, and we built a recording studio on it. I was the only one who had a family at the time, so rather than live at the ranch, we bought a house nearby. I could get to the ranch in about 10 minutes. I was with the group for two years, but the touring was kinda coming to an end, we were getting homesick, and I wanted to raise my two boys [Paul II, born in 1970, and Andrew, born in 1978] and get off the road. So I decided to stay home and take care of them."

With his family, Paul returned to San Diego, where he began performing locally with several bands, including Red Eye, another called Steer Crazy, and one called Haywire. "I decided to start playing country and western music because at that point in rock clubs it was disco or nuthin'," says Paul. "I started playing with a group that opened for a lot of top country performers—Johnny Lee, Eddie Raven, Steve Wariner, and Gary Morris."

Paul, who still owns the original drum set he played with the Hard Times on *Where The Action Is,* and the original Union Gap set, as well as a newer Gretsch set, occasionally sits in with some of the local bands. "If I'm playing a concert situation, I'll take the Gretsch set. But if I'm playing a local function I'll take the old Union Gap set and use about half of it."

The Fabulous Pelicans, a San Diego band that plays classic rock, is one of the bands in which Paul enjoys performing. He appeared with the Pelicans in Olympic Village at the 1996 Olympics in Atlanta, Georgia, on the same bill with Eddie Rabbitt and Chubby Checker. The band has also performed at corporate functions in the Cayman Islands, Hawaii, and Disney World in Orlando, Florida. The band consists of featured vocalist Caroline Martin; front man, guitarist, singer-songwriter

Bob Garrett; slide guitar player and songwriter Greg Douglas (formerly of the Steve Miller Band); bass guitarist and vocalist Joe Hastings; keyboardist and vocalist Ethan Brown; singer-guitarist Mel Vernon; and Wheatbread on drums and vocals. "A couple of the band members have day jobs. Ethan Brown, for example, works as a seismologist," says Wheatbread, who enjoys performing for a "live and appreciative audience." He also sits in with a rockabilly band featuring a young up-and-coming singer and songwriter named Jake Crawford.

While many of the best songs of the '60s and their performers are still beloved by those who lived through that era, the marriages of many of those recording artists are not nearly as durable. Among the rare exceptions is the union of Judy and Paul Wheatbread, which began more than three decades ago. For their 25th wedding anniversary in 1994, Paul and Judy were remarried in the same church in which they had been married 25 years earlier in a ceremony performed by the same priest and with the same wedding party in attendance. They placed their original wedding rings on their right hands and bought new ones for their left hands.

"One of the main ingredients in a good marriage is to be able to talk to one another," says Wheatbread. "You also have to be open to each other's views on different things. I've always let Judy go after her own career and she's always let me go my own way since the beginning. We have always supported each others' careers, so our marriage has always worked out."

Paul is most proud of his natural ability to adapt his singing and playing to all styles of music. "I've always been fortunate to be in the right place at the right time, and have my natural talents to guide me through my career. I never even knew I could sing lead vocals that well until I started performing in Flash Cadillac. I kinda surprised everybody."

Wheatbread enjoys collecting antique motorcycles and he and Judy belong to the San Diego Antique Motorcycle Club. They own four motorcycles—two British BSA bikes, for which they have won awards at shows, a 1961 Super Rocket, and a 1970 Thunderbolt.

Paul says he's satisfied with the direction his life has taken him. "I like staying in contact with local musicians and playing with them, but I kinda miss the stage and the touring. If that opportunity ever arises again, I'll give some serious thought about doing that before I get *too* old. But so far, no problems. Still healthy. Still playing."

Paul manages to keep the performing aspect of his life distinct from his other role as a group tour organizer. But every now and then, when a patron of a group tour who is escorted to a Las Vegas stage show wonders aloud about the lives of glamour that performers lead, Paul's face stretches, almost imperceptibly, into a knowing smile.

GARY WITHEM

A positive role model can make a big difference in the choices children make on their path to adulthood. If they have the inspiration to work hard toward a goal and to achieve small successes along the way, they'll likely excel. Gary Withem hopes that he has wielded a positive influence on the lives of the high school students that he has taught since 1975, and on the lives of his five children, because that is one of his main goals in life.

A high school music and dramatic arts teacher, Withem says he enjoys being around people who are trying to make the world better. "What I admired most about my high school music director is that he inspired me to go to college to pursue music," says Withem. "I think you can make a difference with kids if you can show them that there are other things to do besides drugs and partying all night long. I don't think the kids have gotten worse. I think the temptations have gotten worse. The kids are great. They just need structure, they need role models. And there are not a whole lot of role models around anymore. The athletes don't think it's worth their while. Basically it's not their job. A lot of musicians don't feel it's their problem, either. Politicians, you're not going to find many role models there. I like to show kids that there is a way to have good, clean fun and to be proud of what they're doing in their work and to make their families proud of them. That's why I enjoy teaching so much."

Throughout elementary, junior high, and high school Gary Withem was involved in music. He was a member of a marching band, concert band, orchestra, and choir. He enjoyed Stravinsky just about as much as he loved rock and roll. Withem began playing the clarinet in the fourth grade, and in high school

PHOTO COURTESY OF GARY WITHEM.

added the flute and alto saxophone to his repertoire, becoming a member of the school's stage band, which performed big band music.

"I was lucky enough to play all the old arrangements—*In The Mood* and all those Glenn Miller tunes, and the big band styles. We had a great band director, and the pep band was also a jazz band. So when we played at basketball games, the stage band would play the traditional fight songs, and at halftime we would put on a concert of Benny Goodman tunes and all the big band sounds."

Withem, who was born in San Diego, California, on August 22, 1944, moved with his parents back and forth between San Diego and Terre Haute, Indiana, until 1955 when his father settled into a job in San Diego working with computers for a company called Convair, which later became General Dynamics. Gary began taking private woodwind lessons at a local music store in the fourth grade, and later took piano lessons.

"By the time I was in the Union Gap I had a pretty good background in writing and arranging. Kerry and Dwight also studied music and were pretty good at writing music and reading rhythms, and Gary Puckett, of course, could also read music and was a good musician. And so it made rehearsals and studio work a lot easier."

Gary recalls growing up with a variety of musical talents in his family. His grandfather was the fiddler for square dances in the Midwest. Gary's father played harmonica and guitar, his mother played violin, and his only sister, Gay La, who is five years younger than Gary, played string instruments in high school. So on weekends and holidays, the family would perform and sing together.

Throughout high school and into college, Gary performed in bands for extra spending money. One of the early bands included Kerry Chater. "All of the members of the band could read music and we could read 'fake books,'" recalls Withem. A fake book provides the melody and the symbols for the accompanying chords for popular songs. The accompaniment is then improvised or faked by the performer. "When someone would ask for 'Blue Moon' or 'In The Mood' we could just whip out the 'fake book' and play tunes that the older people really liked. So we played just about every weekend and made more money playing two or three nights a week than most of our friends could make flipping hamburgers all week."

After graduating from San Diego's Mount Miguel High School in 1963, Gary enrolled at San Diego State College to pursue music, playing with Jerry and the Jeritones, which in 1965 became the Palace Pages. Gary remembers one night in 1966 hearing a group from San Francisco called the Friendly Stranger. "We had been sheltered from the very basic acid rock groups that were getting off the ground. But these guys were wearing paisley outfits, and appleseed necklaces. They had hair down to their waists and they were driving a van that was decorated in seashells and pine cones and stuff. Danny [Weis] and Doug [Ingle] really loved their sound and all of our rehearsals started getting more and more into that area and we could see that the Palace Pages were doomed."

Danny and Doug ultimately went to Los Angeles and formed Iron Butterfly. And, with only nine units left to graduate from college, Gary put his degree on hold and went on the road with Kerry Chater, Gary Puckett, and Dwight Bement, and helped evolve the sound of Gary Puckett and the Union Gap, with which he enjoyed three years of success.

In 1970 Chater and Withem joined April-Blackwood Music as team writers and later the duo went to A&M Music. "We shared the office with Paul Williams, who wrote 'We've Only Just Begun' and John Bettis, who wrote a lot of the Carpenters' songs with Richard Carpenter."

During the nearly three years together Withem wrote a couple of hundred tunes with Chater and other writers in the catalog. They wrote jingles for national commercials and soundtracks for movies and television shows, and some of their songs were recorded by Tom Jones and Bobby Vee. "It was a project writing situation. We were paid a salary and we'd just turn out the product that they wanted. We didn't really get a big movie theme, but we came close a couple of times."

In 1973, Withem decided he wanted to complete his college degree and pursue a career in teaching, so he left A&M Music to return to school, enrolling at the University of Southern California and San Diego State University. During the early seventies he dated Penny Packer, who was working for Marty Erlichman, former Union Gap manager and manager for Barbra Streisand. After Withem graduated from San Diego State University and received his teaching credentials in 1974, he and Penny got married and moved to San Diego, where Gary began teaching music in the San Diego Area school district. In 1985 he completed his master's degree in education, and since then has continued teaching band, vocal music, and theater production in San Diego. The Withems also own a florist business in San Diego, which Penny manages.

Gary and Penny have five children, born between the mid-1970s and mid-1980s, and their youngest son, Michael, enjoys playing the guitar. "Whenever everybody's in the house at the same time, we knock out some harmonies. It's fun," says Withem. "Penny is musical, too. She played strings in high school, and she has a beautiful singing voice. So we have a good girls' choir in our family."

The Sweetwater School District, in which Gary teaches, has very successful, well-rounded, and highly supported arts programs, which is extremely rare in public schools. "We have more musicians, more actors, and more artists than any other school district in the state. We have choirs, bands, and art and photography teachers at every school in our district. And that's unusual because arts programs are usually the ones that are cut back when the budget crunch comes. So I'm real proud of what we're able to do, and I think we are making a difference with some of these kids."

Some of the kids from Gary's school have gone on to acting careers, from Broadway to commercials, and several of his students play in major symphonies. "I've had some pretty successful kids that are making money not only in the rock and roll business, but have become road managers, and are working as techs and light people and traveling with groups."

Gary, who is also a church musician and directs the choir at his church, still hopes to get back into writing music. "I think as the years have gone by I have developed a pretty good idea of what it takes to make a hit musical. That's one of my goals professionally."

But Gary's main focus today lies with his family. "When I had to decide whether I was going to stay in the music business, I visualized that lifestyle as one that isn't really conducive to keeping a marriage together. That lifestyle was not something that I thought was going to make me happy. So I really enjoy my reclining chair on the weekends, and going out fishing with my kids and that kind of thing. A lot of rock people love the get-up-and-go type thing—new people every night and new arenas, but it was not what I wanted to do."

No wonder Withem enjoys being around people who are trying to make the world better. That's exactly the kind of person he is.

CHAPTER 11

I Feel Like I'm Fixin' to Die

Country Joe and the Fish

Country Joe and the Fish in 1967. Clockwise, from left: drummer Gary "Chicken" Hirsh, guitarist Barry "the Fish" Melton (top), guitarist-bassist Bruce Barthol, guitarist Joe McDonald (wearing necklace), and guitarist-organist-pianist David Cohen (lower left).

FROM THE TIME CAPSULE

APRIL 1967: Vanguard releases the first Country Joe and the Fish album, *Electric Music For The Mind And Body.*

- APRIL 7: Veteran "top 40" disc jockey Tom Donahue unveils the first album-oriented "progressive rock" format on San Francisco FM station KMPX.
- APRIL 9: Svetlana Alliluyeva Stalin, daughter of Soviet dictator Josef Stalin, defects to the United States.
- APRIL 29: "Respect," written by Otis Redding and sung by Aretha Franklin, climbs to the top of the pop charts.

AUGUST 1968: Country Joe and the Fish's third album, *Together,* comes out. It is dedicated to Bobby Hutton, a member of the Black Panther Party who was killed in a police raid on Black Panther headquarters in Oakland, California.

- AUGUST 8: Richard M. Nixon wins the Republican nomination for president at his party's convention in Miami and chooses Spiro Agnew (later forced to resign because of charges that he took bribes in the mid-sixties when he was a county official in Maryland) as his running mate.
- AUGUST 11: The Beatles' new Apple label releases its first four singles: "Thingummybob" by the Black Dyke Mills brass band, "Sour Milk Sea" by Jackie Lomax, "Those Were The Days" by Mary Hopkin," and "Hey Jude" by the Beatles.
- AUGUST 28: Police and National Guard troops clash violently with antiwar demonstrators outside the Democratic convention in Chicago, where Vice President Hubert Humphrey and running mate Edmund Muskie are chosen as the party's candidates for the presidential election.

JULY 1969: The Fish release *Here We Are Again,* their fourth album.

- JULY 3: Former Rolling Stones guitarist Brian Jones drowns in the swimming pool at his home in England.
- JULY 14: The film *Easy Rider,* starring Peter Fonda, Dennis Hopper, and Jack Nicholson, premieres.
- JULY 18: Mary Jo Kopechne drowns when a car driven by Senator Edward M. "Ted" Kennedy crashes off a bridge at Chappaquiddick, Massachusetts.
- JULY 20: *Apollo 11* astronauts Neil Armstrong and Edwin Aldrin Jr. become the first humans to walk on the moon.

More a collective than a traditional band, Country Joe and the Fish coalesced as a medium of protest in late 1965 and used the San Francisco ballroom scene as a podium from which it launched a litany of antiwar political satire so potent that the band members were named on the Nixon administration's "enemies list." The formation of Country Joe and the Fish occurred a year after the initial upwelling of student protest at the University of California, Berkeley, that kindled the fires of the Free Speech Movement.

The seeds of unrest had surfaced in the dwindling days of the summer of 1964, barely 10 months after the assassination of John F. Kennedy. The man who inherited the presidency, Lyndon Baines Johnson, was on a roll in the 1964 presidential campaign in which he would trounce Republican challenger Barry Goldwater. The Warren Commission had just issued a controversial report concluding that Lee Harvey Oswald had acted alone in Kennedy's assassination. The release of the Warren report followed a seething summer in which three civil rights workers in Mississippi were killed by members of the Ku Klux Klan but their bodies were not discovered until six weeks after the murder. While Congress approved the major provision of LBJ's War on Poverty bill, it also passed the Tonkin Gulf Resolution giving the president authority to take "all necessary steps, including the use of the armed forces," to support South Vietnam.

In the fall of 1964, America's most divisive foreign policy action of the century had not yet become a target of mass protest. For politically and socially conscious college students, the most compelling cause was civil rights, and many of them were returning to school that year after a summer of participation in antisegregation rallies and voter registration drives in the South. One of those students, a quiet philosophy major at the University of California in Berkeley named Mario Savio, was to play a pivotal role in the transformation of general student support for civil rights issues into national resistance to U.S. intervention in Vietnam.

On October 1, 1964, the Berkeley campus police placed graduate student Jack Weinberg under arrest for passing out leaflets on behalf of the Congress of Racial Equality, in violation of a recently beefed-up policy prohibiting political activity on campus. When police led Weinberg to a squad car, dozens, then hundreds, of angry students surrounded the vehicle. Savio, jumping on top of the squad car that held Weinberg, called for total freedom of political expression. His impassioned oratory mesmerized the crowd, which continued to surround the police vehicle for 32 hours. The initial refusal of the university administration to relax the political speech ban incited ongoing student meetings, teach-ins, and demonstrations. The upwelling of student protest there, which became known as the Free Speech Movement (FSM), expanded in scope and channeled growing mistrust of educational, governmental, and military institutions—"the establishment." On December 2, thousands of students participated in a sit-in at Berkeley's Sproul Hall, where Joan Baez led the protesters in song. The next day Savio and 782 others were arrested by a police phalanx organized by Alameda County deputy district attorney Edwin Meese, later attorney general under Ronald Reagan. It was in this explosive theater of protest that Country Joe and the Fish began their rise to fame.

The protesters began targeting the military establishment after the United States initiated Operation Rolling Thunder—continual bombing raids against North Vietnam—in March of 1965. At the Oakland Induction Center near Berkeley, folksingers invigorated demonstrators as enlistees and draftees reported for military duty. The musical performers included Joe McDonald, a Navy veteran who had migrated from Southern California to Berkeley in 1964 to attend school but found participation in social causes more compelling. With a partner named Ed Denson, who later would manage Country Joe and the Fish, McDonald had begun issuing a local social commentary publication called *Rag Baby Magazine.*

At the same time, McDonald began composing musical satire. On an extended-play (EP) four-cut vinyl pressing that was billed as "the first talking issue of *Rag Baby Magazine,*" McDonald and a few acquaintances—guitarist Barry Melton, vocalist Mike Beardslee, Carl Schrager on washboard and bells, and Bob Steele on bass—recorded two songs: "Superbird," which skewered the president, and the first version of the satirical, stridently antiwar "I-Feel-Like-I'm-Fixin'-To-Die Rag." Copies of the EP recording, on which McDonald and Melton called themselves Country Joe and the Fish, were sold at the first teach-ins against the war in Vietnam that were held in Berkeley in the fall of 1965. A folk music program on Berkeley's nonprofit KPFA-FM broadcast the songs from the EP. The popularity of the recording led to a booking by the Students for a Democratic Society (SDS), which by then was organizing antiwar protests on college campuses throughout the nation. Traveling by Greyhound bus, the duo of Country Joe and the Fish played at college campuses throughout the Pacific Northwest.

Upon their return to Berkeley, Melton and McDonald began playing regularly at a Telegraph Avenue coffeehouse called the Jabberwock. There they were joined by several local jug band musicians, including Barry's two roommates, singer and guitarist-bassist Paul Armstrong and guitarist-bassist Bruce Barthol, and bluegrass guitarist David Cohen, with whom Melton had played briefly in a rock band. With the addition of drummer John Francis Gunning, the six-piece band started its metamorphosis.

Because the Jabberwock was in a narrow old building, the small stage was built along the left wall. A piano sat on the floor to the left of the stage. At the rear of the building was the kitchen. "It was a funky old place, with a legal audience capacity of maybe 60 to 70. We used to pack 100 people in there, night after night. Our pay was $3 apiece, along with all the food we could raid from the refrigerator," laughs Cohen.

"We became the hottest band in Berkeley," recalls Melton. "But we were no longer a jug band. We became a rock band because we could reach more people that way. We played there five nights a week and it was packed, two shows each night. It was a great time. We weren't making any money but the Jabberwock had food and we lived right next door. Joe had left his wife and moved in with me, Bruce, and Paul. We had this great landlady who lived downstairs. She was deaf, so we got to make as much noise as we wanted to, and she thought we were the most wonderful young men in the world."

In deference to the band's repertoire and motivations, manager Ed Denson advised them to keep their offbeat name—Country Joe and the Fish. The band members agreed. "When Joe and I began the band, we figured they all think we're commies for doing this stuff, so why not call it Country Joe and the Fish? Country Joe was a nickname for Joseph Stalin, and Fish is a reference to a saying of Chairman Mao's: 'The revolutionary moves through the peasantry as the fish does through water.' The reference was so obscure. It was a dumb name. Still is," asserts Melton. "We were certainly not the first people to insert political expression in music, but we were probably among the first performers to be political and popular at the same time."

The release of the second Country Joe and the Fish EP on the Rag Baby label in June 1966 attracted local radio airplay and mention in *Billboard* magazine. By autumn the quintet graduated to appearances presented by rock music impresario Bill Graham at San Francisco's Fillmore Auditorium, sharing the bill on October 23 with the Yardbirds and on December 22 with Otis Redding, before headlining for the first time on New Year's Eve at the Avalon Ballroom. The composition of the group solidified following the departure of Armstrong—who as a conscientious objector to military induction began a two-year alternative service obligation driving a truck for Goodwill Industries—and the replacement of Gunning with drummer Gary "Chicken" Hirsh. At the close of 1966, Joe McDonald, Barry Melton, Bruce Barthol, David Cohen, and Chicken Hirsh signed with the distinguished folk- and blues-oriented Vanguard label, for which Joan Baez, the Weavers, Doc Watson, Ian and Sylvia, and Buffy Sainte-Marie also recorded.

As American involvement in the Vietnam conflict increased, Country Joe and the Fish assumed the mission of mobilizing opposition to the war through the powerful medium of music. The first of the band's six Vanguard albums, *Electric Music For The Mind And Body,* released in April 1967, produced the group's initial single. Titled "Not So Sweet Martha Lorraine," the single received light top 40 airplay but the song became a favorite on newly emerging underground radio stations, including the Bay Area's KMPX.

Barry Melton attributes the success of the band not so much to Vanguard Records or their association with the Family Dog and Bill Graham's Fillmore Auditorium concerts as to a single musical event: the Monterey Pop Festival of June 1967. As the first large rock festival, it set the stage for the American debut of the Who on a staggering bill that included the Jimi Hendrix Experience, Big Brother and the Holding Company with Janis Joplin, Otis Redding, Ravi Shankar, Hugh Masekela, the Grateful Dead, Jefferson Airplane, the Byrds, the Association, the Electric Flag, the Paul Butterfield Blues Band, Canned Heat, Laura Nyro, Booker T. and the MGs, the Mamas and the Papas, Buffalo Springfield, the Blues Project, and Quicksilver Messenger Service.

Playing colleges, ballrooms, and rock festivals across the country, Country Joe and the Fish recorded a second album, *I Feel Like I'm Fixin' To Die,* released in November 1967. The tracks on that album included the group's second single, "Janis," an ode to Janis Joplin, with whom McDonald had a brief but incendiary relationship. Country Joe and the Fish had become the spokespeople for a generation of young Americans expressing abhorrence of the horrors of war and resistance to American military policy.

In 1968, the band became involved in the planning for a massive protest demonstration in Chicago. That spring, Abbie Hoffman and Jerry Rubin had called for the formation of the Youth International Party, members of which would be called Yippies. With fellow activists, they planned a "Festival of Life" to coincide with the Democratic National Convention that August at the Chicago Hilton. Rubin and Hoffman said they wanted to attract thousands of antiwar protesters to Chicago's Grant Park with a celebration of peace, live bands, and demonstrations against racial discrimination and the Vietnam War.

Yippie organizers Rubin and Hoffman met with Joe and Bruce to seek the participation of Country Joe and the Fish. The band, which already had a gig scheduled in Chicago a few days before the convention, was initially supportive of the festival. But as spring turned to summer, the potential for violence became increasingly apparent.

"Joe decided the festival was going to be too out of control, too dangerous, feared that our equipment would get busted up, that we might be encouraging people to get hurt. He even wanted to take out an ad in the paper announcing withdrawal of our support. I believed exactly the opposite," recalls Bruce Barthol. "I felt that if anyone could afford to get hurt and have their equipment busted, it was us. I felt we had an obligation to take part, but I was the only member of the band with that position."

Following a few weeks off in June and July, the group members traveled to Chicago for their performance at a dance hall called the Electric Theatre. They arrived as convention delegates began streaming into town. "As we got off the plane at O'Hare Airport there were signs all over saying, 'Mayor Daley welcomes you' and girls in straw hats called Daly-ettes were greeting people." Their smiles did little to erase the tension gripping the city. Reacting angrily to rumors that the Yippies planned to lace the city's water system with LSD and initiate other disruptive actions,

Mayor Richard Daley dispatched an army of 12,000 police, accompanied by 7,500 Army troops, and 6,000 Illinois National Guardsmen, to confront demonstrators.

"After our performance at the Electric Theatre we returned to our hotel on North Lakeshore Drive," Bruce recounts. "Chicken and I already had our room keys so we got into the elevator and pressed the button for our floor. As the doors closed I saw Barry, Joe, and David waiting for their keys, and I also noticed a guy with a crewcut hairstyle running from across the street toward the hotel door. The next morning I found out that he had run into the hotel lobby yelling, 'I'm back from Vietnam, hippies,' and punched the totally surprised Joe, Barry, and David before running out the other door."

The Democratic Convention facility was encircled with electrified barbed wire as Aretha Franklin sang the National Anthem inside. Committed to the Vietnam policies of President Johnson, Vice President Hubert Humphrey withheld support of a peace platform, triggering its defeat at the convention. In Grant Park, amid a noisy crowd of nearly 10,000 antiwar demonstrators, a young man shinnied up a flagpole to tear down the American flag. Police closed in, teargassing and clubbing demonstrators. As police rampaged in response to the taunting demonstrators, those injured in the melee included convention delegates and news reporters. The crowd chanted "the whole world is watching" as television crews broadcast images of police and national guardsmen wielding clubs and Mace against demonstrators and bystanders alike, underscoring the contention of the Yippies that the United States was increasingly becoming a police state.

Bruce Barthol's conviction that the group should have taken a larger role in the demonstrations in Chicago precipitated his departure from the group that fall, when he moved to England.

"The first person to leave was Bruce, who was probably the conscience we should have listened to," says Barry. "He was the first person who said, 'This isn't for me. This isn't what we set out to do. We're just pop musicians.' There was a push from the business side of things not to shake the boat too much. I think Bruce had a distinct aversion to fame and money, but I also think he sensed that the mission was being lost."

Bruce was initially replaced by Mark Ryan, later a member of Quicksilver Messenger Service, then by Jack Casady, formerly the bassist for Jefferson Airplane. Following the expiration of their recording contract with Vanguard at the close of 1968, Country Joe and the Fish were undecided about how—or whether—to proceed. David Cohen remembers a conversation he had with Bill Graham at that time. "This band's not breaking up without a farewell concert," Graham said. The result was a memorable performance in January 1969 at Bill Graham's Fillmore West in San Francisco.

"Jack was playing bass with us, and a bunch of our other friends showed up and sat in with us, including Jerry Garcia, Jorma Kaukonen, Steve Miller, and Mickey Hart," Cohen recalls. The staging of the concert demonstrated how far

Graham and the band members had come since they first met three years before. "The first time we ever met Bill Graham we were on stage doing a sound check. This demon came tearing across the stage yelling at us to get off the stage because he had a show to begin," Cohen recalls. At the January 1969 concert, Cohen heard Graham utter in hushed tones, "What a band!" The bittersweet concert was captured on tape, and Vanguard warehoused the audio recording for three decades until its ultimate release in 1997 on a compact disc titled *Live! Fillmore West 1969*.

McDonald's performance of "I-Feel-Like-I'm-Fixin'-To-Die Rag," prefaced by a ribald version of the infamous "Fish Cheer," at the Woodstock Music and Art Fair in Bethel, New York, in August 1969 was immortalized in the 1970 documentary/concert film *Woodstock*. Bill Belmont, the group's former manager, now an executive with Fantasy Records in Berkeley, observed that "Five years after its debut at a demonstration in Oakland, it became an anthem."

Country Joe and the Fish remained together after signing a new Vanguard recording contract, but by the time they got to Woodstock, Joe and Barry had replaced all the other members of the band with a succession of musicians. "Joe and I stayed on and got a whole new crew of musicians," says Barry. "There's never been a Country Joe and the Fish without Joe and me. But sometime after the Woodstock festival we figured we had gone as far as we could go with each other. We shook hands, we split up the name—he took Country Joe, I took the Fish—and off we went."

On March 29, 1973, four years after President Richard Nixon began military reductions in Vietnam, the last American troops were withdrawn. During the previous 12 years, 47,369 Americans had died in combat and 153,303 had been wounded. Country Joe and the Fish, the group that had set out to end the war in Vietnam, ultimately contributed to the achievement of that goal by raising awareness of the war and encouraging a generation of young people to speak out against Washington policy.

ALBUMS BY COUNTRY JOE AND THE FISH
RELEASED DURING THE SIXTIES

YEAR	TITLE	SINGLE FROM ALBUM	LABEL
4/67	ELECTRIC MUSIC FOR THE MIND AND BODY	NOT SO SWEET MARTHA LORRAINE	VANGUARD
11/67	I FEEL LIKE I'M FIXIN' TO DIE	JANIS	VANGUARD
8/68	TOGETHER	BRIGHT SUBURBAN MR. AND MRS. CLEAN MACHINE	VANGUARD
7/69	HERE WE ARE AGAIN	DOCTOR OF ELECTRICITY	VANGUARD
12/69	GREATEST HITS	HAPPINESS IS A PORPOISE MOUTH	VANGUARD

BARRY "THE FISH" MELTON

Three decades after the formation of Country Joe and the Fish, guitarist Barry "the Fish" Melton concludes that the political potency of the band was the product of a fleeting moment in the cultural evolution of the nation, a phenomenon that emerged in shifting sands now eradicated by changing technologies.

"We were correct in our assumption that rock and roll was the medium through which to reach young people," says Melton. "It had been just pop music before the '60s and it returned to being pop music after the '60s, but for a brief moment in time it was one of the exclusive channels of young people's expression in this country with the growth of underground radio, and it seemed to be controlled by young people rather than by adults. Such dominance by one medium is improbable today because there are so many channels on television, so many radio stations, newspapers, and now the Internet. But for a moment in the '60s, music, the counterculture, and the antiwar movement became very closely identified with one another."

PHOTO BY AMANDA MARCH.

Country Joe and the Fish fused the prevailing interests in Melton's life: music, political activism, and the legal system. Since May 1999 Melton has been chief assistant public defender of Yolo County, California, an administrative and policy-making position in which he oversees 19 lawyers as well as handles his own caseload. His duties include criminal defense litigation, working with offenders who are facing lengthy prison terms or even a death sentence. Each year his office handles 3,000 to 4,000 felony cases—the majority of which are drug-related—along with an equal number of misdemeanor cases. He says his current occupation is consistent within the continuum of his lifelong pursuit of social justice. Melton, whose days on the job are spent meeting with clients in county jail, preparing legal pleadings, and searching documents and other evidence for subtle factors that can reduce a lengthy prison sentence or a death sentence, says he is in the business of saving lives. That is his principal obligation to his clients. He was recruited for his present position while he was a California deputy state public defender, a position in which he was assigned to postconviction appeals in capital litigation, working with offenders who were under sentence of death.

For people who wonder how a lifelong peace campaigner can reconcile defending offenders convicted of violent, gruesome crimes, Melton has a ready response: "My job within the framework of government is to question authority and to defend people against authority being arbitrarily and capriciously meted out. I like being a public defender, because I'm working in the only branch of government that is funded to fight the government. It's a branch of government whose job is to stop police, courts, and prosecutors from dealing with people unjustly. It makes sense for me. My legal career has mostly been involved with defending the poor, and it serves my view of what social justice is, as did my musical career to some extent. I'm not saying that's entirely why I do what I do. It's to make a living, like anyone else. But I need the element that I'm accomplishing some greater societal purpose in my work. Being a criminal defense lawyer, working for indigent clients, in many ways is consistent with this kind of progressive political outlook I've had all my life."

Left-wing activism was inbred in Barry's family, and his parents, Jim and Terry Melton, encouraged him to pursue a career in music. Barry, however, was drawn to the legal profession. Born in New York on June 14, 1947, he lived as a young child down the block from folksinger Woody Guthrie and his family.

"I went to Marge Guthrie's dance school as a young kid, and I grew up in the American left wing that had arisen in New York City and resulted in Senator Joseph McCarthy's pursuit of people who had been labor organizers in the 1930s." Jim Melton, a merchant seaman, was a founder of the National Maritime Union. "In our house, I grew up listening to records by the Weavers, Pete Seeger, Woody Guthrie, and others."

With that early influence, Barry began his musical education at age 5. "I learned to read and write music from the time I could read and write English," says Melton. He took classical guitar instruction under Charles D'Aleo, who had been a violinist with the New York Philharmonic. Barry, his older brother, Mike, and their parents remained on Avenue Z near Brighton Beach in Brooklyn until 1955, when they moved to North Hollywood, California, where Barry's younger sister, Abby, was born. There Barry resumed studying guitar with Milton Norman, a jazz guitarist with the Kay Kyser Band.

At Ulysses S. Grant High School in North Hollywood, Barry played trombone and baritone horn in the school band and orchestra. He was also president of the school's folk music club, which allowed him to pursue an increasing interest in folk music, and it was there Barry first met fellow student Bruce Barthol. Barry, Bruce, and other friends jammed and performed together at parties and hootenannies. At fraternity parties, Barry often played in a group called the Three Prominent Bastards, dabbling in the irreverent as well as the socially relevant.

Melton began commingling his interest in music with civil rights causes. "I was a CORE [Congress of Racial Equality] volunteer doing Freedom Rider support, and I managed to get myself arrested during a sit-in at Van De Kamp's Restaurant, one of a chain which refused to integrate their lunch counters in the South."

Barry also demonstrated upon the arrival of Madame Ngo Dinh Nhu and her husband in Los Angeles. Madame Nhu was the sister-in-law of South Vietnamese President Ngo Dinh Diem, who was murdered in a 1963 coup supported by the United States. Known derisively as the "Dragon Lady," Madame Nhu acted in an official capacity on behalf of Diem. She referred to self-immolation by Buddhists in Saigon and Hue protesting South Vietnamese government policies as "barbecues." Barry Melton was among the crowd that protested loudly outside the Los Angeles hotel where she was staying.

By 1963, Barry had started performing in folk music clubs in Hollywood, including the legendary Ash Grove on Melrose Avenue. In the summer of 1964, he hitchhiked to the San Francisco Bay Area, where he first met Joe McDonald during a performance by folksinger Malvina Reynolds, who wrote the song "Little Boxes" that was popularized that year by Pete Seeger.

But Melton stayed in the Bay Area only a short time before traveling on to New York to perform at the Greenwich Village "basket houses," cafes in which young folk performers would play a set, then pass a basket among the audience for donations. All the while, though, Barry sought to apply both his stage presence and his interest in social causes in a career that required both—criminal law. "Music was my parents' thing, and law was mine," says Barry, who decided at age 15 that he wanted to become a lawyer after reading a book on the life of Clarence Darrow. "I wanted to defend people, advance social justice, and all of those lofty covenants."

During his senior high school year, Barry also took an interest in the writings of semanticist S. I. Hayakawa, who taught at San Francisco State College and later would become its controversial hard-line president during the height of student unrest. After graduation from Grant High in January 1965, he enrolled at San Francisco State but was unable to take classes from Hayakawa, who taught only in the upper division. After 10 weeks, Melton dropped out of college. "I was lured away by the music," he says.

Ineligible for induction into military service because of leg injuries he had suffered in a motorcycle accident while in high school, Melton headed across San Francisco Bay to Berkeley. There he began hanging out and playing in clubs, including the Jabberwock, where he reunited with his high school pal Bruce Barthol and again ran across Joe McDonald. Melton joined McDonald in the Instant Action Jug Band, an ad hoc group of musicians who performed at political demonstrations. Their union ultimately led to formation of Country Joe and the Fish, which, by the fall of 1966, had become a ballroom headliner.

The band, which had ignited spontaneously in the heat of protest, burned brightly for three years. When it began, the Vietnam War was barely on the radar of the national consciousness. By the time the quintet disbanded three years later, its antiwar message was seared into the American political landscape. Objection to the war in Vietnam was widespread, crossing social, philosophical, and generational lines.

The initial breakup of Country Joe and the Fish after Woodstock coincided with the breakup of Barry's first marriage. Melton dropped out of the music scene and took a six-month rest, after which he signed as a solo artist with Columbia Records and recorded an album produced by Mike Bloomfield. In 1971, Grateful Dead drummer Mickey Hart introduced Barry to Barbara Langer, whom he subsequently married. In 1973 Melton and McDonald paired again and toured together for the next several years. But as Barbara was expecting their first child in 1977, Barry began to ponder the wisdom of life on the road. "I wanted to prevent this relationship from going down the tubes, and I wanted to be around as my child grew up." That's when he decided to resurrect his interest in the law.

Melton enrolled in a correspondence law preparation program that had been advertised on a matchbook cover. "Matchbook U," Melton jokes. Actually, the program was offered through LaSalle Extension University in Chicago. While on the road, Barry performed by night and studied law independently during the days. After studying five years under the LaSalle program and another correspondence course, he passed the California Bar exam in 1982 and opened a small law office in San Francisco's low-overhead Mission District. His clientele was "whatever walked in the door," he says.

Melton welcomed both civil and criminal cases. His first client was the owner of a health food store who was encountering difficulty with city government regulations requiring businesses with more than 10 employees to provide separate restroom facilities for men and women. "I helped keep the city at bay for like a year while the store moved to a new location with two bathrooms. The store didn't pay me money, but they gave me groceries. I was playing music at night so I had a way of making money, because I sure wasn't making anything practicing law."

By night, Barry was playing with a band he had formed, the Dinosaurs, the members of which included Grateful Dead lyricist Bob Hunter, Jefferson Airplane drummer Spencer Dryden, Big Brother and the Holding Company bass player Peter Albin, and Quicksilver Messenger Service guitarist John Cipollina. Melton and Cipollina also periodically played as a duo, under the name Fish and Chip.

After an internship at the San Francisco Public Defender's Office, Melton was able to get on the court appointment panels and handle juvenile and criminal cases by referral. A year after Melton went into partnership with two other lawyers in 1984, he was earning more money as a lawyer than as a musician. Even then, he continued playing until John Cipollina died of a lifelong respiratory ailment in May 1989. "John and I had worked a lot together for seven to eight years before he died, and we had been in three different bands together at the same time. I've got to admit, his death took the wind out of my sails."

Concentrating on his practice, Melton focused on criminal law, in which he became a board-certified specialist. In 1992, he ran for judicial office. "I got only 80,000 votes, and I was mad at San Francisco," Melton laughs. "I was! I had bet my wife that if I lost we could move, because she had always wanted to move." Barry began looking for the right opportunity. In late 1993 he spotted a job opening for deputy public defender in rural Mendocino County, north of San Francisco. He wanted that job. He got it. And he quickly developed a reputation for ingenuity, intensity, and diligence.

"I've had some really great cases," says Melton. "I've never experienced a greater feeling of satisfaction from anything I've done than I have in winning a jury trial for someone who I truly believe in. There's no greater feeling even from performing before an audience. It's funny, but being a trial lawyer is a performance art in many respects. When you really believe in a client with the odds against you and yet you vindicate your client in front of a jury, there's no better feeling," says Melton, whose expertise in criminal law gained widespread recognition.

After serving as a guest lecturer in professional workshops presented by the California Public Defenders Association and the California Attorneys for Criminal Justice, Melton was offered a position as deputy state public defender for the state of California in Sacramento, which he accepted in July 1998 and held until accepting his present position in Yolo County. Melton considers criminal law the most interesting and most theatrical specialty in law. "I've spent many hours of the week on my feet in court. Probably the vast majority of lawyers out there are in their office most of the time," says Melton, who has chosen to specialize in cases involving violent crimes because he relishes the challenge of unraveling real-life whodunits.

Just as the music of Country Joe and the Fish had a strong philosophical under-carriage, Melton espouses deep-seated views about crime and punishment. "A lot of what criminal lawyers do is more akin to what people think of as social work than it is lawyering skills. I believe that our society has become overly punitive, particularly with regard to nonviolent crimes, particularly drug offenses. From a humane perspective, punishment is not the right approach for crimes that concern lifestyle choices. I'm a pragmatist. I know that's the way it is. But if someone has a problem, I'd rather work hard to see that they get help rather than to see that they simply get punished, especially when there is no victim," Melton says.

Barry and his wife Barbara have two sons: Kingsley, born in 1977, and Kyle, born in 1986. Kingsley, educated at the University of California, Davis, is interested in a career in journalism. Barbara, a licensed marriage and family therapist with expertise in substance abuse, is in private practice. As an independent contractor, she provides counseling services and supervises interns at Diogenes Youth Services, an agency that has a public service contract with Sacramento County.

Barry Melton's passion for the law is not at the expense of music, which continues to offer him a creative outlet and relief from stress. He still records and performs on occasion. "I really find that as an adult, my life runs best if I'm doing both law and music," says Melton, whose latter-day musical exploits included performing before an audience of 50,000 at the 1997 "Summer of Love Reunion" in San Francisco's Golden Gate Park.

"I think I'm a better musician than I've ever been. I don't play as fast as I used to play, but I've developed a certain simplicity that in a way is more expressive than things that I used to do. It felt good to get out in front of a crowd of 50,000 people. But I also like arguing a case in front of 12 people, or presenting a brief to a panel of judges. I think it's unfortunate if you have to drop things to pick new things up. I can see a time in the future when I'll do something else in my life that is neither law nor music," Melton muses. "But I hope that I would still have the skills to take a case that interests me from time to time and play a gig if it seems like fun."

THEN AND NOW

DAVID BENNETT COHEN

The lotus flower blooms in a muddy swamp. The muddier the swamp, the more beautiful the flower. "That tells us that whatever mud exists in our lives, whatever kinds of negatives we have made, we still have the potential of the pure lotus flower in our lives," says guitarist and pianist David Bennett Cohen, whose life is given power and purpose by this gentle Buddhist philosophy.

A disciple of folksinger Pete Seeger, grandson of anarchists, self-described revolutionary, boogie-woogie enthusiast, organist with Country Joe and the Fish, published music technique instructor, and now a grandfather and a pianist with a blues band, Cohen beseeches those he meets to call him David rather than Dave, saying, "Don't leave out the 'id,' please," with a laugh. While Cohen once used music to ridicule the military and discredit government leaders as a means to end the war in Vietnam, his objective today is spiritual: "I hope my music will show people the power of my practice."

PHOTO BY ACISCLO A. LOPEZ.

Cohen is a member of the Soka Gakkai, an international Buddhist lay organization whose name is derived from a phrase meaning "value creation society" in Japanese. "We try to create value in everything we do. We believe that if each individual takes responsibility for his or her own life and own happiness, then world peace will occur as a natural by-product," Cohen declares. "It's a slow process that transcends politics, but this is the only way it's going to work."

David Bennett Cohen grew up in Brooklyn, New York, where he was born August 4, 1942. He and his brother, Michael, lived with their parents, Max and Molly Cohen, on Maple Street in a neighborhood known as Pigtown, between Crown Heights and East Flatbush. "There were a few Jewish families, two black families, and everyone else was Italian," recalls David, whose father was a dentist and whose mother became a teacher.

David, who was raised without a religious background, started taking classical piano lessons when he was a 7-year-old kid attending Public School 91. "My mother wanted me to play the piano. She thought maybe it would help round me out. I studied piano for about seven years and I hated it." David's eventual abandonment of piano lessons was undoubtedly influenced by a discovery he made at about age 9.

"We went to visit some friends of my parents and there was a guitar there. I couldn't stay away from it. The next thing I knew, that guitar ended up at my house. I started playing it even though I didn't know what I was doing. The summer I turned 14, I went to a camp in upstate New York called Lincoln Farm Work Camp, which was run by radicals and Communists. My parents weren't radical, but my grandparents were active anarchists, and this camp matched their political and social philosophy." There David saw Pete Seeger, with whom he was totally entranced. "I took guitar lessons from the instructor there, but I learned more from playing with people in the camp. I spent a month or two there, and it was one of the greatest experiences of my life."

As the summer of 1956 drew to a close, David returned from that camp with a driving obsession for music. His days at Brooklyn Tech High School were little more than a distraction from his pursuit of music. "I would come home from school and go to my room and play guitar for six hours. I would do homework for about 15 minutes and go to sleep. Somewhere in there I would run to the kitchen and wolf down something to eat. I had a straight C average in high school," acknowledges David, who lived for the weekends—specifically, Sundays. That's when he'd go to Washington Square Park, the eclectic little Greenwich Village park later immortalized in a 1963 bluegrass instrumental by the Village Stompers. Every Sunday afternoon, folk musicians would gather and play their stringed instruments in the square as artists displayed their canvases and sculptures.

"I tried not to miss a Sunday. I would take my guitar, my banjo, and sometimes my mandolin. I used to take the subway with my friend Perry Lederman and as soon as we got on the train, out would come our guitars and we'd play all the way to the park. There would be clumps of musicians strumming different types of music all around, and I would gather with my friends and play. Those years from 1956 up until about 1962 were really formative for me. When it rained on Sunday, we were real miserable."

David managed to develop an indoor interest to fill those rainy days. While in high school, years after quitting piano lessons, he happened to tune in to a televised performance by boogie-woogie piano virtuoso Meade Lux Lewis. His interest in piano rekindled, David bought a record album by Lewis and two other leading boogie pianists, Albert Ammons and Pete Johnson. "They used to tour together back in the '30s and '40s, and that record they made was unbelievably wonderful. It was recorded with just their three pianos, and it just cooks." The album inspired Cohen to resume playing piano. He learned to play piano as he learned to play guitar and banjo—by immersing himself in music, studying the techniques of others, eventually crafting his own style.

After graduating from high school in 1960, David enrolled in George Washington University in Washington, D.C., but his grades suffered as he longed for the New York music scene. A year later, he moved back in with his folks and enrolled in classes at Brooklyn College, eventually managing to move out on his own by teaching private guitar lessons. "My parents helped support me, because I was barely supporting myself," says Cohen. He frequented a Greenwich Village hangout called the Folklore Center, a Macdougal Street institution where books, records, and musical instruments were sold and folk music performances were staged.

One day in 1962, David brought a friend, Sherry Tenzer, to one of the folk music concerts hosted by the Folklore Center, run by Israel Young. As he paid for his tickets at the door, David announced, "Izzy, this is my wife," to the startled owner. "It was a joke, but the rumors started that David Cohen got married. So we went and got married. We didn't do it just to give a truth to the lie. We really cared for each other. The first year was total rapture and after that it was hell," says Cohen, who gave up music during his marriage. "I was 19 years old—definitely too young. We never had any kids, but all through the marriage some voice was calling to me that I was stuck and I needed to get out of it. I felt I had a mission and that I was being stifled." The marriage lasted a little more than three years, until 1965. "That's when I split," says David, who dropped out of college, hitchhiked, and rode by bus to Berkeley, California, where Burt Soloman, a friend from the Washington Square days, had moved to attend UC Berkeley.

Although David intended to visit only briefly, he was electrified when he arrived in Berkeley in May 1965. "The Free Speech Movement was still percolating. You could feel the music in the air. I would go hang out in the music stores, like the Campus Music Shop run by a fellow named Campbell Coe, and John Lundberg's guitar store." That summer, word reached him that Sherry had found someone else. "I was ecstatic," says David, who returned to New York, where he and Sherry divorced. Cohen once again immersed himself in the New York folk scene. "I didn't like electric music, I didn't like jazz, I didn't like rock and roll. I liked blues and folk music. I was pretty arrogant."

David's admittedly narrow view broadened considerably that fall when he and a friend, Joan Silverberg, went to see a Beatles double feature at a theater in the Village. "We sat in the back and she brought wine and chicken and joints.

Other people brought food and we were passing it around, and we had so much fun. We sat through *A Hard Day's Night, Help!* and *A Hard Day's Night* again. We would have stayed longer, but the theater closed. At that point I decided I wanted to play rock and roll."

Cohen returned to California, bought an electric guitar, started hanging out at music stores and clubs, and was soon playing with a couple of bands. The members of one of those bands, called Blackburn and Snow, included drummer Gary "Chicken" Hirsh.

One day after a Blackburn and Snow rehearsal, Jeff Blackburn asked Cohen if he'd like to go see the Grateful Dead, who were playing at UC Berkeley. "When we got there I was blown away. I had never heard anyone play guitar like that. After the set, I introduced myself to Jerry Garcia, and we became friends."

Shortly afterward, Cohen left Blackburn and Snow to concentrate on playing with another band in which Barry Melton was a member. Melton had already been playing with Joe McDonald, who was looking for an organ player. "I had banged on the piano at the Jabberwock every now and then. I'd do some boogie-woogie stuff and played tunes like 'St. Louis Blues,' but I wasn't serious. I wanted to play guitar. But Barry told Joe, 'Oh, David can play the organ.' I had never even seen an organ up close. But I joined the band anyway and played guitar because they didn't even have an organ. The first gig we played was on campus in early 1966. Then the band bought this Farfisa compact organ, and that's what I started playing. The only person that I had ever heard play organ like I wanted to play was Al Kooper. So I took all of my guitar licks and applied them on the organ. It worked fine. We were playing so much that I didn't have much time to listen to other people playing."

Cohen says that from the outset the band had two missions: to stop the war in Vietnam, and to legalize drugs. "Basically we were iconoclasts. We were not mainstream and we were proud of it. We were trying to revolutionize society." In that, Cohen believes the group succeeded. "Look at all the long hair on Wall Street. Part of our mission was to raise the consciousness of people. Joe's songs were very intelligent. They never were written for the lowest common denominator. I also think that through the music, the band had a sense of humor—a satirical sense of humor. There was a very beautiful side of Country Joe and the Fish," says Cohen, pointing to "Bass Strings," "Pat's Song," "Section 43," and "Janis" as representative examples.

"Janis," says Cohen, "was really something. Our band hung out together with Big Brother and the Holding Company. We were all friends, but one day Joe and Janis were an item. Janis and the band had lived together in Lagunitas in Marin County until Janis bought a house in Larkspur. She threw a party when she bought the house and we came, and I told her, 'Janis, this is great.' She took me by the hand and took me outside and she throws her hands up and says, 'One record. One [expletive] record.' She meant that the album *Cheap Thrills* enabled her to afford to buy the house.

"I remember Joe telling me that they were sitting in Joe's car in front of her house when she was living on Lyon Street at Oak near the Panhandle in San Francisco. They had the windows rolled up and they were having a screaming fight. People would come up and knock at the window and say, 'Hi. Where are you playing next?' I know that Janis said to Joe, 'Why don't you write me a song before we split up?' So he wrote 'Janis' with the notion that it would be recorded by Big Brother and the Holding Company." When Big Brother decided against recording it, Country Joe and the Fish took it into the studio, releasing it on their second album and ultimately as a single in 1967.

Cohen last performed with Country Joe and the Fish during the album recording sessions for *Here We Are Again* in the spring of 1969, leaving the group just before its appearance at Woodstock that summer. His departure stemmed from what he perceived as a loss of direction and integrity. "The band became perverted. We shifted from being serious to being clowns," he says, referring to the group's performances of "Rock and Soul Music" accompanied by a baseball game pantomime. "It wasn't satire, it wasn't even funny. It was just dumb." Cohen was newly married at the time to his second wife, Marjorie Sutler, with whom he had a daughter, Sara Cherokee Lyndall Sutler Cohen. The marriage lasted only three years.

After that, Cohen played with or opened for numerous bands and musicians, including the Blues Project, the Luther Tucker Blues Band, Huey Lewis, Bonnie Raitt, Jerry Garcia, the Mick Taylor Blues Band, Johnny Winter, Rufus Thomas, Kenny Rankin, Michael Bloomfield, Melvin Van Peebles, Leo Kottke, Meatloaf, Booker T., Elvin Bishop, Tim Hardin, Eric Anderson, the Roches, Norton Buffalo, and Happy and Artie Traum, as well as several bands he formed.

But Cohen also found a new interest. Happy Traum had started a business called Homespun Tapes, offering audio guitar instruction lessons. By 1975 Traum had decided to expand the Homespun instructional catalog beyond stringed instrument lessons. He asked David to record a piano instruction lesson. Since then, Cohen has completed three videotapes on blues piano, an audio set on blues and rock piano, and another set on ragtime piano, and he's written a book packaged with an instructional CD called *David Bennett Cohen Teaches Blues Piano*. He's also completed two guitar instruction albums for Kicking Mule Records, and he continues to compose music. In recent years, David has performed as a sub in the band of the hit musical *Rent*, on Broadway and on tour.

In the important decisions of his life, David always followed his instincts. Doing so took him to Greenwich Village, and then to Berkeley, which led to his involvement with Country Joe and the Fish. However, David initially resisted the path that would end by being the most important in his life. In 1985, a friend of his in San Francisco introduced him to Buddhism. Cohen, who had received no religious instruction in his youth and who subscribed to no religion as an adult, rebuffed his friend's initial invitation to attend a meeting. "But as soon as I started chanting and meeting people who had been practicing for a while, I felt the attraction. It's the best thing I've ever done."

Unlike many ritualistic Western religions, Buddhism imposes relatively little formal structure and places emphasis upon introspection. "We chant Nam Myoho Renge Kyo, the mystic law of the universe, in the morning and evening. We also read two chapters from the *Lotus Sutra,* which says that anybody can attain enlightenment to become absolutely happy. Judaism and Catholicism are both steeped in superstition. We don't worship a God that is more important than we are. We have the same potential within our own lives," Cohen believes. "Through chanting I've developed the wisdom to help me influence people in a positive way. That's my mission now. I'm still a revolutionary but I'm going through a human revolution now."

Buddhism has brought order and tranquillity to David's life. He married his third and present wife, Maureen Trant, on October 21, 1989. He speaks with pride of his daughter, Sara. Now divorced from her husband, Sara is raising her son Devin, who was born in 1994. "It was one of those situations in which marriage ruined a good affair," David notes wryly. A writer and editor of two lesbian magazines in the San Francisco Bay Area, Sara is studying to become a midwife.

David and Maureen now live in Forest Hills, New York, just seven miles from the neighborhood he grew up in. Although he has resurrected his musical passion for the blues, he speaks of his rock and roll years with fondness. "Monterey Pop was a fabulous gig," says Cohen. "And I'll never forget traveling up and down the West Coast after Monterey Pop with the Jimi Hendrix Experience. Sitting in dressing rooms with him playing guitar made for great moments. He was an exceptional musician."

Cohen offers a disarmingly honest appraisal of Country Joe and the Fish. "Judging from today's standards, the group wouldn't even have a chance to succeed. The musicianship wasn't all that great, and the material was very controversial," says Cohen. He attributes the success of the group to what he called "a combination of fortune"—the result, he says, of being at the right place at the right time. While critical of the band's execution, he praises the group's musical repertoire. "Every now and then I'll go back and listen to the first two albums, and I really believe that Joe wrote some masterpieces."

As a pianist with the Bobby Kyle Blues Band, David Bennett Cohen no longer plays cavernous ballrooms and open-air festivals. The four-piece group, led by Kyle—formerly a guitarist with Johnny Copeland—plays blues and hot jazz in clubs in New York, New Jersey, Pennsylvania, and Connecticut.

To David, music is a parable for life itself. "The violinist plays the violin, the trombonist plays the horn, the cellist plays the cello, the harpist plays the harp, but the conductor plays the orchestra. Even if you have a four-piece band there's a fifth piece—the band itself. When you're hearing yourself play within the band, it just overwhelms you. That's the best high I've ever experienced," says David. "One of the most important things that I teach is the concept of the ensemble. It's not enough to show somebody how to play something on the guitar or on the piano, but you need to demonstrate how that fits with other instruments, and how to create unity, which is so powerful. And that's the Buddhist philosophy as well— the concept of unity. We keep our individuality with a common goal."

THEN AND NOW
BRUCE BARTHOL

Awaiting his flight to London, Bruce Barthol sank disconsolately into a chair in the passenger waiting area at New York's Kennedy International Airport as a television set flickered results in the November 1968 election that would send Richard Nixon to the White House. Although Democratic candidate Hubert Humphrey nearly equaled Republican Nixon in the popular vote, Nixon handily captured the electoral vote as Barthol left America behind.

Only five years earlier, as a high school student in Southern California, Bruce imagined joining the Army, attending Officers' Candidate School with a specialty in a foreign language, and entering the foreign service. "That was my plan, but Vietnam made some career alterations," says Bruce, whose illusions were abruptly shattered during a conversation that left him incredulous and disillusioned. One day in 1962, a friend of Bruce's brother asked him, "Do you know what we're doing in Vietnam? We drop this stuff on people that's like flaming jelly and it adheres to human flesh." Bruce, then 14, indignantly rejected that notion. But the military lost all appeal for him when he learned the truth about American use of napalm, a compound of gasoline suspended in a gelatinous thickener which, when set ablaze, sticks to the skin of people upon whom it is fired. "That reality was very distressing because I had always considered my country in the right. Vietnam turned into a series of gut-wrenching horrific surprises."

PHOTO BY T. QUIRINO.

His initial disbelief subsumed by outrage, Barthol joined his high school friend Barry Melton in protesting a visit to Los Angeles by South Vietnam's Madame Ngo Dinh Nhu. From then until 1975, when Bruce participated in his last march protesting the Vietnam War, he committed himself to protesting actions by the military that he had once hoped to join.

Eighteen years before it became the flashpoint for the youth protest movement, Berkeley was the birthplace of Bruce Barthol on November 11, 1947. Bruce's grandparents were from the San Francisco Bay Area, and Bruce knows that Berkeley tilted toward eccentricity even in the fifties. As Bruce approached school age, his family moved to State College, Pennsylvania, when his father, Richard, accepted a teaching assignment in psychology at Penn State. A social worker by profession but an activist in spirit, Bruce's mother, Esther, demonstrated the power of personal conviction. "My mom was active politically and worked to repeal some of the 'blue laws' that had not only kept the county 'dry' but also prohibited movies on Sundays," recalls Bruce. He attended elementary school in Pennsylvania for three years, during his first three grades before his family moved to Los Angeles in 1956, when his father began teaching at UCLA.

In early 1959, Bruce and his family relocated to Spain. There, at age 11, Bruce attended Air Force Dependent School in Madrid, where his family lived in an off-base apartment. Bruce enjoyed the adventure. "There were new foods, some of which were really good and some were really weird," Bruce laughs. "On my first day of school I found myself in the Madrid Army Personnel Center, a huge complex that contained the enlisted men's family housing building and all of the schools, first grade through high school."

Bruce, whose family enjoyed absorbing local culture, says he ran into the narrow-minded attitudes common among military personnel overseas. "I pulled out my lunch my mom had made—a sandwich on a Spanish roll with Spanish ham. And these four boys in my class came over, stood around my desk, and said, 'You eat *spic* food?' Most of the kids in that school wanted nothing more than to get home."

Returning to Los Angeles, Bruce's family settled in the Sherman Oaks section of the San Fernando Valley. There Bruce enrolled in Millikan Junior High in the fall of 1960, against the backdrop of a presidential election year in which Senator John Kennedy from Massachusetts defeated Vice President Richard Nixon. Following his graduation from junior high, Bruce went on with other neighborhood kids to Ulysses S. Grant High School in North Hollywood, where he met and became friends with Barry Melton and cultivated an interest in music that had been inspired by his family. Bruce's father, Richard, played piano; his older brother, Clark, played upright bass; and his mother, Esther, enjoyed singing. As college students, both of Bruce's parents had performed in theater, a pursuit that Esther continued in New York after her graduation, studying with the Group Theater. Unable to eke out a living in theater during the Great Depression, Esther returned to California to pursue a career in social work.

So it was with the encouragement of his parents that Bruce took up music in school when he was 12. Inspired by Benny Goodman's playing, he chose clarinet and joined the school orchestra. To his disappointment, however, he soon discovered that playing in the orchestra was not as much fun as he had imagined it would be. "You played either first, second, or third clarinet on 'Song Of The Volga Boatmen.' That was fun to a degree, but it wasn't as much fun as playing 'When The Saints Go Marching In.' All I wanted to do was jam."

It wasn't surprising, then, that Bruce began to fool around with the guitar that his family had purchased while in Spain. He was about 14, and his interest in the guitar coincided with the rise of the folk music scene. Initially attracted to traditional folk music, Bruce was particularly captivated by a singer he heard for the first time on a folk music radio program. He went to the record section in the local White Front department store. "I asked if they had the *Freewheelin'* album by Bob Dylan, spelled D-I-L-L-O-N. What the heck did I know? I heard the name on the radio," he laughs.

As Bruce became proficient in his guitar playing, he picked up harmonica and Autoharp and began to play music with friends, including Barry Melton. "Barry and I were in the Young Democrats as well as in the folk music club at high school. We were the youngest members of a private beatnik coffeehouse in Hollywood called the Thirsty Ear, and we would see each other not only at the UCLA Folk Festival, but also on picket lines," says Barthol, who was also a member of the Los Angeles chapter of CORE. As a result of skipping ahead halfway through fifth grade and accelerating through high school by taking summer classes, Bruce graduated from Grant High in the summer of 1964 and enrolled at UC Berkeley that September at the age of 16.

The Free Speech Movement erupted on the Berkeley campus as he turned 17 two months later. Studying Spanish and history, Barthol quickly became involved in protesting the university's prohibition of political expression, which he called "a collusion of authorities engaging in idiotic and unconstitutional behavior." Bruce heard and was persuaded by protester Mario Savio's impassioned cries for resistance. "The university forced many people to become active members of the Free Speech Movement," says Bruce, who joined protesters on campus and at other locations including Jack London Square in neighboring Oakland, where demonstrators targeted discriminatory hiring practices at restaurants. "We would picket every Friday night, and we just hoped we wouldn't get pulled over by the Oakland cops on our way back to the Berkeley line. People were busted on concealed weapons charges if the cops found picket signs in their car trunks. It was pure harassment." After boycotting classes during a student strike, his grade-point average fell to 1.98 and he was placed on academic probation for a semester.

On his 18th birthday Bruce filed for conscientious objector status with the Selective Service. After completing that third semester, he decided to step away from his academic studies for perhaps a year. "I was tired of going to school. I was getting Cs and Bs and just wasn't feeling engaged. "I wanted to go to the Bahamas and listen to Joseph Spence [a legendary Bahamian fingerstyle guitarist].

I no longer wanted to be bound by the interminable tyranny of studying." Instead, after taking a job as a lineman with the telephone company in March 1966 to earn the money to travel, Bruce found himself bound by the tyranny of work. Assigned as an installer and repairman, Bruce climbed telephone poles to connect and disconnect lines. At that time, he lived with some friends: Barry Melton and percussionist Paul Armstrong, joined soon afterward by Joe McDonald. While working weekdays for the phone company, Barthol spent his evenings and weekends next door to his apartment building, in the Jabberwock. "My time with the phone company was the longest three months of my life," says Barthol, who began performing with the band. "When I quit the phone company in June, the Fish had already begun happening." The band went electric with Bruce on bass guitar.

As the band increased in notoriety and popularity, Barthol found playing in the increasingly larger rooms both exciting and challenging. "Country Joe and the Fish had an adventurous artistic impulse, and an intelligent consciousness of what songs might accomplish." Still, Barthol believes the band could have been more aggressive in pursuit of its goal. "Throughout our time together, that war remained a constant irritant. I wish we had been a little braver. We should have gone to Vietnam, but we were too scared to contemplate it. We actually could have played Saigon and we wouldn't have been killed. We would have had a real appreciative audience of GIs. I guess for me the sum of the good things about the band was in contradiction to the very success the band was enjoying. And those pressures of success and that changed world eventually spiraled the band apart." Evidently the other band members perceived Bruce's diminished sense of satisfaction, and decided it would be best for him to go his own way.

Three months after the band's appearance in Chicago in August 1968, Bruce boarded a plane for England with no plans other than leaving the United States. "I was so relieved to get away from the psychotic, tense, 'soon-you'll-be-dead' feeling I had at the time. What a year 1968 was! Hardly anybody who started out that year ended up where they thought they'd be."

Bruce moved to London, where he formed a rock band called Formerly Fat Harry, consisting of two other Americans—friends from Berkeley—and a Brit. The band played throughout England and toured in Europe before recording an album released on EMI in Europe and Capitol in the United States. The breakup of Formerly Fat Harry three years later wasn't particularly disturbing to Bruce. "I guess by then I was tired of being an expatriate and wanted to come back to the United States and reengage." Bruce moved back to Berkeley in 1972, quickly involved himself with the campaign of Democratic presidential candidate George McGovern, and joined a local satirical theater group called the East Bay Sharks. Passing the hat, the East Bay Sharks performed for the McGovern campaign and in support of ballot measures for rent control, legalization of marijuana, and other sociopolitical issues.

In 1974, Barthol formed a band called the Energy Crisis, which briefly served as Joe McDonald's backup band. But the lure of musical theater proved stronger than Bruce's diminished interest in rock and roll. In 1976, through his involvement with the East Bay Sharks, he began his enduring association with the Tony Award–winning San Francisco Mime Troupe, a musical theater collective specializing in political satire. Bruce was intrigued by the troupe's somewhat rambunctious history, and at the same time he saw an opportunity through which he could combine music and politics. "I remember the epiphany I experienced just before I was invited to join the mime troupe. At the time I was playing with a rock group called Delicia and the Darvons at the Long Branch in Berkeley, where the audience was mostly high on beer and Seconal. I wanted both sides of the brain engaged. The chance to work with material with some meat on it drew me to the troupe."

The troupe's audacious character also held strong appeal for him. "The park commission had busted the mime troupe in 1964 on an obscenity charge and the troupe beat it in court, opening up Golden Gate Park for free performances. Bill Graham was the business manager for the mime troupe, and it was his first famous benefit dance that led to the creation of the Fillmore Auditorium and the Avalon Ballroom dance halls," says Barthol. "The troupe's history snakes in and out of the whole San Francisco scene in the '60s and since."

Bruce, whose composing credits date to songs recorded on the first Country Joe and the Fish album, *Electric Music For The Mind And Body,* has been a composer-lyricist and musician for the San Francisco Mime Troupe for more than two decades. During that time he has amassed an impressive succession of critical and artistic successes, writing more than 100 compositions for more than two dozen shows performed in San Francisco and on tour. His credits include music for 1982's *Factwino Meets The Moral Majority* and 1988's *Ripped Van Winkle,* both of which won Original Score honors presented by the Bay Area Drama Critics Circle.

Although most people associate the term "mime" with pantomime, the San Francisco Mime Troupe has been anything but silent. "The term 'mime' actually means to mimic," observes Barthol. "That name has been a pain in the ass for 20 years. Every year or two there's been an effort to change the name, but it's always fizzled." Barthol is one of 10 collective members who together operate the mime troupe, which is based in San Francisco's Mission District. In the time he's been with the mime troupe, he's participated in five European tours and performed in Mexico, Cuba, Nicaragua, Israel, the Philippines, and Hong Kong.

Barthol has supplemented his modest income from the mime troupe not only by composing for other theatrical groups, but also through academic assignments, which he has pursued ever since his appearance as a lecturer at Frei Universitat in Berlin in 1982, where he discussed the cultural history of San Francisco. Bruce split his time between San Francisco and West Berlin from 1981 to 1983.

In subsequent years, he has lectured about American musical history, political theater, and the contributions of the San Francisco Mime Troupe in appearances at other institutions, including the University of Connecticut, Fordham University, New York University, and Golden Gate University in San Francisco. He served as artist-in-residence both at California State University, Long Beach, and at San Francisco State University where, in 1988, he drew upon his own experiences living in Franco's Spain for a student production of *Spain '36,* about the Spanish Civil War.

Barthol's involvement in academia influenced his decision to return to school 25 years after he had dropped out. In 1993, he was awarded a master of fine arts degree in musical theater from New York University's Tisch School of the Arts. The following year, he served as an instructor for the summer arts program at Humboldt State University in Arcata, California.

Bruce's musical theater compositions are not limited to the San Francisco Mime Troupe. In 1991, he collaborated on the score for the Oscar-nominated documentary film *Forever Activists.* Since 1990, musical compositions by Bruce have been performed in the Working Theater presentation of Mathew Maguire's *The Window Man* in New York City, in the Intersection Of The Arts production of Robin Karfo's *Cages* in San Francisco, and in a production of Joan Holden's *They Are So Sweet, Sir* in the Philippines. In 1998 he wrote the score for a bilingual version of 16th-century Spanish playwright Lope de Vega's *Fuente Ovejuna,* produced at Borderlands Theater in Tucson, Arizona. Bruce served as musical director and conductor for that production. He also continues to play bass with an old friend, folksinger Rosalie Sorrells, and occasionally with Midnight Rodeo, a band formed by Big Brother and the Holding Company drummer David Getz.

Although he's had enduring relationships in the past, Bruce was never as close to marriage as he is today. Childless, he's now engaged to Tina Quirino, a woman he met in 1995 in the Philippines. They now live in the cabin that Bruce's uncle built on two acres of redwood forest in Sonoma County about 50 miles north of San Francisco.

There, Bruce plans to continue writing, recording, and teaching. While he's mellowed in some respects, he's still driven by the same sense of outrage that propelled him into public view three decades ago. "I've always been motivated by a certain social political consciousness, mostly because some things are so annoying, you can't ignore them. In any era there are myths and assumptions that serve the forces of greed, hate, and reaction. As a former supporter of the cultural revolution in China, and I do have to confess that really didn't work out too well, you learn to look at things clearly." But lest anyone think he's become conciliatory, Bruce quickly adds, "However, the sanctimonious hypocritical drivel that spills out of Republicans in Congress is enough to make you want to write a song. I have more to do."

In-A-Gadda-Da-Vida

Iron Butterfly

FROM THE TIME CAPSULE

AUGUST 1966: Doug Ingle launches Iron Butterfly.

- AUGUST 10: NASA launches the first Lunar Orbiter. Four days later it begins orbiting the moon and thirteen days later takes a spectacular photo—the first moon shot of the Earth.
- AUGUST 29: The Beatles hold their last public concert, in Candlestick Park, San Francisco.

JULY 1968: Atco releases the first Iron Butterfly album, *In-A-Gadda-Da-Vida.*

- JULY 1: The United States, the United Kingdom, the U.S.S.R., and 58 other nations sign a nuclear nonproliferation treaty.
- JULY 5: Bill Graham relocates his San Franciso auditorium to the much bigger Carousel Ballroom, which he renames the Fillmore West.
- JULY 15: The Agnes Nixon–ABC soap opera *One Life To Live* (which is still very much alive 20 years later) premieres.
- JULY 17: The Beatles' animated film *Yellow Submarine* opens in the U.K.

FEBRUARY 1969: Iron Butterfly's "Soul Experience" becomes their second single to chart.

- FEBRUARY 2: The Palestine National Congress appoints Yasir Arafat leader of the Palestine Liberation Organization (PLO). President Nixon signs the Endangered Species Act into law.
- FEBRUARY 8: The *Saturday Evening Post* publishes its last issue, and Boeing's 747 flies commercially for the first time.

Opposite: Iron Butterfly in 1969. From left: guitarist Erik Braunn, drummer Ron Bushy, bassist Lee Dorman, and organist Doug Ingle. FROM PHOTOFEST ARCHIVES, NEW YORK.

The mid-'60s emergence of free-form rock and roll reflected the revolutionary attitudes of youth searching for their own musical style and means of expression. American bands such as Jefferson Airplane, the Grateful Dead, and the Doors performed lengthy instrumentals that relied upon improvisation. This new counterculture gave way to progressive, underground FM radio, such as that launched in April 1967 by former top 40 DJ "Big Daddy" Tom Donahue at San Francisco's KMPX. The success of Donahue's album-oriented format in California and at underground stations evolving throughout the United States, in turn, contributed to the advent of heavy metal bands such as Iron Butterfly. About the same time, a whole new counterculture was evolving that included freedom of expression through underground newspapers such as the *Los Angeles Free Press,* the *Village Voice,* in New York, and the *Berkeley Barb,* whose mission was philosophical and deviated from traditional papers' daily dose of violence, sports, and business. Long hair, love beads, sex, drugs, and radical politics became the symbols of psychedelia, and music became a principal means through which the emerging hippie culture communicated its dissatisfaction with the establishment.

Heavy, loud, and improvisational acid rock evolved from psychedelic rock. This short-lived music style gained widespread popularity with the distorted lyrics and long jams of Iron Butterfly's monumental LP *In-A-Gadda-Da-Vida,* featuring the 17-minute long title track that remained on the charts for 140 weeks, more than half of that time in the top 10. From the gossamer opening organ chords to its closing pronouncement, "In-A-Gadda-Da-Vida" is a work of surprising complexity that musically conveys the stark contrast of delicacy and power that the group's name symbolizes. The melodramatic Baroque organ and guitar signature that periodically weave in and out amid searing solos lend cadence to the song's free-form expressiveness. And not since the Surfaris' "Wipe Out" in 1963, and

before that Sandy Nelson's recording of "Let There Be Drums" in 1961, h̶
ming been given such prominence in a record. Iron Butterfly truly popu
drum solos, which became a staple of many late '60s and early '70s ban
the first year of its release, the album had sold 8 million copies, 16 times more
than the Recording Industry Association of America (RIAA) standard for the highest-ranking Gold Album Award. Iron Butterfly was subsequently awarded the first Platinum Album, and in 1993, received a Multi-Platinum Award from RIAA for *In-A-Gadda-Da-Vida*. The album has sold more than 25 million copies.

The name Iron Butterfly is a contradiction in terms deliberately chosen by keyboardist Doug Ingle to suggest the interweaving of a delicate, intricate fabric with a superstructure of raw amplified power. Ingle, who refers to himself as a ballad writer, confesses, "I've never written anything but ballads. My songs always turned into something quite different once the group got their hands on them. We call it the Butterfly filtering system. It always comes out distorted from its original format."

Launched in San Diego by Doug Ingle in August 1966, Iron Butterfly began its musical metamorphosis at Bido Lito's, a family-owned underground club located on Cosmo Alley, a couple of blocks west of Vine Street between Sunset and Hollywood boulevards. "Bido" was short for "Bill and Dorothy," and "Lito" was a contraction of the names of their kids, "Linda and Tom." Leading off for weekend headline acts such as the Seeds and Love, Iron Butterfly played three to four shows a night, six nights a week—the club was closed one night—and was earning $20 to $25 a week per man. Doug Ingle recalls, "We slept on the office floor above the club. Jerry Penrod, our bass player at the time—he was also on the first album, *Heavy*—was a *big* guy. They called him mountain. He was like a Mongolian warrior. If you didn't know him you'd think, 'Oh my God, let's cross the street now before we have to make eye contact.' But to actually know him, you couldn't have asked for a nicer guy. At any rate, I woke up one night in this Ma and Pa Kettle sleeping arrangement with my arm across his chest. And I opened my eyes and his eyes were just kind of glaring at me like, 'What's this?' I quietly went downstairs and took one of the reclining chaise longues and dragged it upstairs and took over the ladies' rest room. I had hot and cold running water, a private stall, and for the first time, I had my own room."

The police would frequently raid Bito Lito's after hours, looking for drugs. "Like SWAT teams they'd come flying across from the other businesses, on the rooftops," says Ingle. "They were looking for illegal stuff—marijuana—and that was the kind of club where they might find it. They were crazy times."

Over a period of about a year, the band found itself leaving the underground and gradually moving up Sunset Strip in West Hollywood to tourist clubs such as the Castle on Hollywood Boulevard, Pandora's Box, and finally the Galaxy, which was on the north side of Sunset Boulevard, two doors up from the trendy Whisky à Go Go.

As the band's following continued to grow, the weekend lines to get into the Galaxy were surpassing the lines for the Whisky à Go Go. "The Whisky would have a headliner, and our line would pass their line, go up the street, up Doheny, down the alley, back down to Sunset, and past itself. So this attracted attention," says Ingle. "By that point the Whisky à Go Go didn't look good, so they brought us on. That had never happened before." As house band for the Whisky, Iron Butterfly began opening for acts such as Buffalo Springfield, the Doors, the Turtles, Jefferson Airplane, Big Brother and the Holding Company, and Smokey Robinson and the Miracles.

The Butterfly's quotient of cover songs had begun yielding to increasing amounts of original material when Charlie Green and Brian Stone of Atlantic Records discovered them in early 1967. "Buffalo Springfield and Sonny and Cher had signed with them," says Ron Bushy, "and so did we." The group recorded its first album, *Heavy,* with Green and Stone, but the label held up its release for nearly a year as the band underwent substantial personnel and management changes. During the interim, Danny Weis left the group and joined Rhinoceros, an L.A.-based rock group. "The guy was a great guitar player," says Bushy. Erik Braunn agrees: "Danny Weis was an excellent guitar player and a brilliant musician. Jeff Beck and Eric Clapton used to come by and watch Danny play."

During the band's brief hiatus, Ron came home one night to find Ingle working on a new song. "Doug had a little too much red wine and he sang this song for me that came out 'in-a-gadda-da-vida,' but he was trying to sing 'in the Garden of Eden,'" says Bushy. "I liked it, so I wrote it down on a piece of paper phonetically. The next morning we looked at it and liked it, so we kept the name."

In August 1967, Ingle and Bushy auditioned and hired 16-year-old guitar player Erik Brann, who later restored his last name to the original Danish spelling: Braunn. Vocalist Darryl DeLoach and bassist Jerry Penrod left and soon after Douglas Lee Dorman joined the band. To avoid confusion with Doug Ingle, Dorman agreed to go by Lee.

With Atlantic Records holding up release of *Heavy,* the Butterfly was struggling to stay afloat in Hollywood. "We lived on the streets for a long time," says Bushy. "I got hooked up with Bonnie Ward, the ex-wife of Burt Ward of 'Batman.' She had a huge mansion in Brentwood, so half the guys would come over and stay there, too."

Following performances in 1967 at Notre Dame High School, a private Catholic school in Sherman Oaks, and a teen center in Van Nuys, the Butterfly performed their first big concert as the second of five bands opening for the Doors at the Shrine Auditorium in Los Angeles. From there, the Butterfly opened on short notice for Jefferson Airplane at Pauley Pavilion at UCLA because the Airplane's intended opening act didn't show up. The Butterfly turned in such a crowd-pleasing performance that the Airplane invited them on a two and a half month tour of the United States.

"We were doing colleges with the Airplane," recalls Braunn, "and Marty Balin comes into our dressing room while I was practicing, and he said, 'You know, Gracie Slick really has a crush on you.' And I said, 'Really?' because when *Surrealistic Pillow* came out I thought they were a great band, and I thought she was really neat. So I said, 'I don't know what to do about that.' He looked at me perplexed and asked, 'How old are you?' And I said, '17.' Knowing that Gracie was 28 at the time, Marty went back to their dressing room and I just heard this enormous amount of laughter, and I never saw Gracie again on tour. She always stayed away from me."

In July 1968, Iron Butterfly's *In-A-Gadda-Da-Vida* made its debut, featuring its celebrated 17-minute title track containing one of the longest and most explosive drum solos in the history of rock. "When we recorded 'In-A-Gadda-Da-Vida,' a guy named Brian Ross, who is deceased now, mixed the drums. He had conceived the idea of what they call phlange phasing to get that whooshy sound, only it was done manually by mixing the simultaneous playback of two identical recordings that are slightly out of synchronization. Now they have machines," explains Dorman. "The cost of that album to Atlantic was about $17,000." In contrast, the recording and production work for an album today typically costs about $200,000, nearly 12 times the amount it cost Atlantic to produce *Vida*.

The popularity of the band's recordings propelled them on the touring circuit. They headlined at ballrooms, auditoriums, stadiums, and at numerous rock festivals, including the two-day Newport Pop Festival in Costa Mesa, California. That event featured an extensive entourage including Sonny and Cher, Steppenwolf, Country Joe and the Fish, Jefferson Airplane, the Grateful Dead, Eric Burdon and the Animals, the Byrds, Tiny Tim, Quicksilver Messenger Service, and Big Brother and the Holding Company.

On August 15, 1969, the day the Woodstock Music and Art Fair opened, Iron Butterfly's equipment truck was stuck in traffic about 20 miles from the festival site. The group, which had been on tour for the entire summer, was waiting at their hotel in Manhattan, New York, for word from their manager on how to get to Woodstock, and once they arrived, what equipment they'd be using.

"We were told that the Who was going to let us use their amps and drums, and that Sly Stone would let us use his Hammond organ, so that was solved," recalls Dorman. "Our manager told us to go to the Port Authority Building at 10:15 a.m. to catch a helicopter, but it never showed up. So the entire weekend we went back and forth from our hotel to the heliport until our manager finally called back at 7 or 8 o'clock Sunday evening and said, 'Come home. It's over with.' It's just too bad that we weren't there because we, along with so many of the bands that were there, were part of an era, and I don't think anybody knew that was the end. That was, for some reason, the changing of the guard. We had no idea of its significance at the time."

Erik Braunn had an opportunity to play with Jimi Hendrix before Hendrix's death in September 1970. "The Butterfly was playing at the Spectrum in the summer of 1969, and I got a call from my manager saying, 'Jimi Hendrix just called me and he has sent a limo and wants to know if you'll come up to Manhattan to play guitar for him on a project he's producing.' For me it was a great honor to have Jimi Hendrix want me to play guitar," says Braunn. "I played with Hendrix, Mitch Mitchell, my longtime friend Harvey Brooks, who was the bass player on all of the great early Dylan stuff, and Keith Emerson, before the formation of Emerson Lake and Palmer. It turned out to be just a jam, and it was recorded, but never released."

Iron Butterfly went on to play many pop festivals throughout the country. Doug Ingle recalls a 1970 festival in which Iron Butterfly shared the bill with Janis Joplin following the breakup of Big Brother and the Holding Company. "We were flown in via military helicopter—big Hueys—which was an experience in and of itself. Janis was on stage just prior to our going on, and after the show, she ran up to me, threw her arms around me, crying, saying, 'Doug, what am I going to do? They don't like me.' Up to this point I didn't know if she knew me from Adam. I was flabbergasted. But the best I could come up with was, 'Janis, you know, they're slow to respond. They absolutely love you. I saw the twinkle in their eyes and you triggered their imagination. You gave them everything you've got. Bottom line is they're waiting to hear 'Piece Of My Heart' the way they heard it on the record. And until they have a little bit more time, they're not going to know how to respond to the new material until it's more familiar, until they've heard it a few more times on the radio.' And that was the last time I saw her. It was within two months after that she'd passed on." Janis was found dead on October 4, 1970.

The deaths of Joplin, Hendrix, Jim Morrison of the Doors, and Brian Jones of the Rolling Stones collectively brought to a staggering conclusion many of the musical excesses associated with the late '60s, and helped precipitate a return-to-the-land musical movement advanced by the gentle country-rock ballads of John Denver, Linda Ronstandt, Jackson Browne, James Taylor, Carly Simon, Cat Stevens, and Elton John.

The Butterfly quietly fluttered to a halt amid the shifting sands of musical tastes.

HIT SINGLES BY IRON BUTTERFLY

DEBUT	PEAK	TITLE	LABEL
8/68	30	IN-A-GADDA-DA-VIDA (Album Certified Multi-Platinum)	ATCO
2/69	75	SOUL EXPERIENCE	ATCO
7/69	96	IN THE TIME OF OUR LIVES	ATCO
10/70	66	EASY RIDER (LET THE WIND PAY THE WAY)	ATCO

DOUG INGLE

Although Lloyd Ingle never achieved his dream of becoming a professional musician, he derived vicarious joy from the successful musical career of his son, Doug, a career that took off quite unexpectedly. When Doug decided to move to Los Angeles with the intention of working as a theme music writer for the motion picture industry, the band he had taken with him in order to pay the bills unexpectedly became one of the hottest bands on Sunset Strip.

Doug's father was a music major at Drake University in Des Moines, Iowa. "My dad was a first-string classical pianist who could not provide for a family of four on a symphony salary, so he became a church pianist and leaned on his backup, which was accounting, and that's what he did throughout his professional life," says Ingle.

Doug Ingle was born in Omaha, Nebraska, on September 9, 1945. When he was 2 months old, Doug moved with his family into a one-bedroom cottage in Evergreen, Colorado, an isolated village in the mountains west of Denver. He and his sister, Pat, who is six years his senior, spent several years in a cabin with no indoor plumbing and a coal-burning stove for heat. Although Evergreen now has a population of about 7,500, when Doug was a child fewer than 400 people lived there.

"My dad was my inspiration. He introduced me to such a wide gamut of musical references from gospel to classical music, the boogie-woogie, and the standards such as 'Peg O' My Heart,'" says Doug. "We had an upright Boston Everett piano,

Doug Ingle in 1997, on Iron Butterfly's European Tour.

which was a wedding gift to my parents, and when I was about 5 years old, my father would slip me between the sound board and the wall of the cabin and he would rock out with the boogie-woogie." Doug still owns the piano.

Small though it was, Evergreen had a nondenominational community church, for which Doug's father was the piano player. "Every Sunday after church in the spring and summer we had parades through town that just constituted the kids pulling their favorite pet in their red wagons," recalls Ingle. "And then we'd go to the park for the spring and summer rodeo circuit. At that point, I was torn between being a cowboy in the rodeo and, of course, being an Indian. I ended up being a musician, probably a little of both."

While vacationing in San Diego in 1954, Doug's mother, Virginia, decided she'd had enough cold, snowy Colorado winters and decided she wanted to stay. She took a job with San Diego County, and over a period of two years the family joined her. "My sister, Pat, and I came out first on the Union Pacific train. My dad came later, taking a job as an accountant at a local music store."

Ingle began his music career performing in cover groups in high school. One of the early bands in which he performed was called the Progressives. The band included Ingle, guitarist Danny Weis, Kerry Chater, and Gary Withem. Chater, who played bass, and Withem, a sax player, later became members of Gary Puckett and the Union Gap.

"We played Mancini and 'Louie, Louie' and everything in between. We found a lot of work in the military enlisted men's clubs and petty officers' clubs. If you could play a variety of music, then you had a real good opportunity to work," says Ingle. The Progressives later became Jerry and the Jeritones and then the Palace Pages. Following the breakup of the Pages, Ingle and Weis moved to Los Angeles and a new band evolved with a new sound and new members. Doug called the band Iron Butterfly.

Although Doug had not formally met Ron Bushy, he knew of him. Ron was a member of a cover group called the Voxmen, named after the brand of amplifiers that the Beatles used. "We were archrivals," says Ingle. "The Jeritones and the Voxmen were not on speaking terms. We were top competitors in the same market. At the battle of the bands, we'd often glare at each other across from the wings of the stage. One year the Voxmen would come in first, and the next year we would come in first. It was a real rivalry."

Doug graduated from Hoover High School in San Diego in 1964 and attended UCLA Extension in San Diego for one semester, taking a course on musical counterpoint. "I don't know how, but I got an A-plus-plus, and I decided I wanted to write theme songs for motion pictures. I wasn't interested in the scoring. I actually wanted to write the theme music and then they could do with it as they pleased." Ingle decided to take the Iron Butterfly to L.A. so that he would have a source of income while pursuing a new career. "Then the darn thing took off. It wasn't supposed to do that."

A bit too naive and caught up in the limelight, Ingle paid little attention to the fruits of his labor. "I was just so happy to be doing what I enjoyed doing that I never really paid too much attention to the money. And quite frankly, it all came so fast and so unexpectedly, and the emphasis was never placed on monetary subsistence. I'm afraid that I became somewhat agnostic in the sense that, gosh, all my life I've been told, 'You really need to get some kind of a backup system because the likelihood of succeeding in music is slim to none.' I just thought, 'Gee, these people don't know what they're talking about. Making a living and a good one at that is a piece of cake.' But I was a child among men. The management back in L.A. was getting extremely wealthy, and my wife at the time was having quite a good time, I guess."

Tickled by the initial success of the Butterfly, Doug lost his focus on theatrical scoring and concentrated on the band, which began traveling to club dates out of the area. Doug recalls the time the Butterfly played at a nightclub in Dallas called the Phantasmagoria. "When we'd finish for the night, the cowboys would drive by in their pickup trucks throwing empty quart beer bottles at us for target practice." The band also experienced bomb threats. In Phoenix an entire auditorium had to be evacuated after an anonymous telephone caller reported planting a bomb in the building. A bomb was later found under the stage. Another unnerving incident occurred at the Kinetic Playground in Philadelphia. "This guy opened a club, and a competitor, which presumably had an interest in a rival club, sent a message saying, 'Don't open your doors or your club's going down the same night.' Sure enough, he opened the doors, and that night after hours our equipment was in a blaze with the rest of the club."

The enormous popularity the band enjoyed on stage and on the *Billboard* charts between 1968 and 1970 was a wondrous blur. But the group's decline after that was precipitous. In 1971 Ingle decided to call it quits after performing a month and a half farewell tour of U.S. colleges. By then Erik Braunn was gone and Mike Pinera, formerly of Blues Image and co-writer of the song "Ride, Captain, Ride," and Larry "Rhino" Reinhardt came on board. "Pinera, who was of Cuban descent, had a Latino R&B influence on his guitar playing, and Rhino, who we picked up out of Macon, Georgia, was a blues-oriented slide guitar player," says Ingle. Almost overnight, the Butterfly transformed from a keyboard-oriented rock group to a guitar-oriented rhythm and blues band. Ingle wasn't happy with the direction in which the group was heading. Halfway through a European tour in 1971 he gave notice that at the conclusion of that tour he would be willing to perform a farewell tour of the United States.

"At first I was elated to be off the road. I had a nice home in Calabasas, which is in the foothills between Malibu and the San Fernando Valley," recalls Ingle. "But then I started leaning more heavily on drugs. I started drinking more and smoking marijuana, and when that got boring I was smoking primo hash regularly, to the point that I actually lost track of two and a half years of my life. Then I got levied by the Internal Revenue Service." Ingle owed $185,000 in back taxes. He lost his house, but was able to hold on to $10,000, which he used to buy a mobile home.

In 1975 Doug and his wife, Alice Kidd, and their four children moved into a mobile home park for which Doug became manager, which entitled him to a free parking space and utilities. He began training as an apprentice house painter, becoming an independent subcontractor in 1977. By then he and his family had moved to a duplex in Sierra Madre, near Pasadena, and Doug was painting houses. When forced bussing came into effect in Los Angeles and their children weren't coming home until well after dark because they had been bussed to the far side of Los Angeles, Doug said to Alice, "Let's just get out of here and put the kids in a place where they can get a grasp on life, a good start."

They decided to move to Port Angeles, Washington, "the farthest northwest tip of the continental United States, up by Victoria, Canada," says Ingle. "It was as beautiful as you could get with somewhat mild winters." But the timing was bad. It was raining, and no one was hiring painters. "I ended up bartering my services in exchange for furniture because we didn't have any," recalls Doug. He then sought a job through the state of Washington's employment services, taking tests to determine an occupation for which he was best suited.

"The results indicated that I should be dealing directly with the public in the field of entertainment, more specifically, in the field of music," says Doug. "When I told my wife, she said, 'Does that mean that if you got a call from somebody in L.A. and they weren't willing to pay you but they would give you studio time, for instance, for a spec-type recording, you would go?' I said, 'You're damn right I would.' And the next thing I knew she was seeing another guy."

In 1979 Doug returned to Southern California on a Greyhound bus and took up residence in a warehouse in Northridge. Inside the warehouse, Ron Bushy and Taylor Kramer had built a studio—Bushwhack Studios—and Ron and his girlfriend Nancy Braverman had been living there. Ingle remembers that after Ron and Nancy moved out to live in Nancy's West Los Angeles home, "a rather undesirable lot of individuals began to frequent the place. It was often referred to by the neighboring businesses as the 'bottomless pit,' a flop house." Ingle cleaned up the place, living in it and allowing local bands to use it as a rehearsal facility. Since he didn't have any equipment of his own, Ingle gave bands cut rates on rehearsal time in return for the opportunity to use their equipment during their absence. Bushy paid the rent.

After leaving Northridge, Doug became a landscape foreman and ranch hand for the Smoketree Recording Studio in Chatsworth, California, which was built and owned by longtime friend Doug Parry. Gino Vanelli, Dolly Parton, and a few other acts had recorded at the ranch.

"I made $50 per week, had a free place to stay, and if there was any downtime with the clients, I had access to the studio for my own projects, which worked out fairly well. But after a year of doing that, I found that the downtime was precious little, if any, so I moved to Beaverton, Oregon, a suburb of Portland, and continued painting houses."

In September 1983, Doug returned to California to reestablish Iron Butterfly with Lee Dorman and Larry Reinhardt. "We toured all over the country but never made any money. We called them our Western Union tours. We had to go 120 miles out of our way to get a line of credit via Western Union just to continue, and we kept getting involved with scavengers of the industry, just cleaning up what's left as opposed to supporting something new." After two years, Ingle called it quits and moved to San Diego, where he took a job with Lifestyle Music Network, selling adult contemporary (easy listening) music via satellite to businesses to provide as background music.

Meanwhile, Erik Braunn, Lee Dorman, and Ron Bushy had resurrected the Butterfly and asked Doug to join them on a tour leading up to Atlantic Records' 40th anniversary concert, "It's Only Rock 'n' Roll," on May 14, 1988, at Madison Square Garden in New York City. About that same time, Doug met the woman who was to become his second wife, Cheri Taylor, who was a friend of Nancy Bushy's.

"During one of the dates we shared the marquee with Spirit at the John Ford Amphitheater in Hollywood. Nancy brought Cheri, and from that point forward, Ron played Cupid," says Doug. "I called Cheri from Philadelphia at the end of the New York anniversary concert, and she sounded so thrilled to hear from me that I asked her if she could pick me up at the airport. I've never heard anybody sound so happy to hear from me, and from that time on, it just got better and better."

Doug and Cheri were married in 1992, and between them they have nine children—Doug has six and Cheri has three—and as of 1998, five grandchildren. Doug speaks warmly about his children, most of whom live in the Pacific Northwest. One of his proudest achievements is his recent ability to be able to openly communicate with his children. "That suggests a level of mutual trust and respect," says Doug. There was a time when alcohol prohibited him from communicating clearly with them.

Doug was very close to his father, Lloyd, who died in December 1998, and remains close to his mother, Virginia. Both were extremely proud of his accomplishments. "When I would take my dad to a medical appointment, for example, I would say, 'Dad, do me a favor and don't mention the Butterfly,' because then the time spent with the doctor became more a discussion about me and the '60s, and my main concern was understanding exactly what his medical needs were."

In July 1994, Doug rejoined Lee Dorman and Ron Bushy in Iron Butterfly. The current group, which also includes lead guitarist and vocalist Eric Barnett, has been touring and performing live throughout the United States and Europe, doing classic hits as well as new material.

Although pleased with the direction in which his life is going and his involvement in the rekindled Iron Butterfly, Doug says he is still committed to "a genuine sense of inner peace." He hopes that through reading about his experiences, others will be encouraged to triumph over destructive vices such as those that nearly destroyed his life, and that he can in some way enlighten people's lives through his music.

RON BUSHY

Ron Bushy's childhood passion was to become an orchestra conductor. He loved classical music and opera. In the sixth grade he would sit in his bedroom conducting to Tchaikovsy's *1812 Overture* and *March Slave,* or he would sing along with Mario Lanza. Born in Washington, D.C., on December 23, 1941, Ron had decided at an early age that he wanted to play drums. His parents were opposed to it and urged him instead to take accordion lessons, which he hated.

After his parents divorced in 1951, Ron and his sister, Karon, who is three years younger, went to live with their grandparents in Clinton, Connecticut, for three years. His grandfather, a retired Connecticut state police officer and commissioner of the Clinton Police Department, taught him how to whittle. With his newfound skill, Ron went to the local hardware store, bought himself a dowel, and proceeded to whittle a couple of drumsticks. He picked up an old tire inner tube from the local gas station, cut the rubber in two sections, stretched it across a board, and fashioned himself a practice pad.

"I used to go out in the garage, where I taught myself how to play drums on my practice pad with the drumsticks I made. No one even knew what I was up to in the garage." In 1953 Ron's father, then a Navy lieutenant working for the Bureau of Personnel and the Pentagon, remarried and the family moved to Alexandria, Virginia. After demonstrating his recently acquired skills to his father, Ron joined the Alexandria Police Boys' Band as a drummer. He attended Thomas Jefferson Junior High and George Washington High schools in Alexandria until he was a sophomore. Then his family moved to San Diego, where his father served as a commander and executive officer of the U.S.S. *Henderson.* There, at Mission Bay High School, Ron joined the school band.

PHOTO COURTESY OF RON BUSHY.

"I didn't know how to read music, I just faked it. I remember Mr. Freeburn, the conductor of the band, used to get really upset with me, because I would always be playing parts that weren't written in the score. He even threw the baton at me a few times."

After graduating from high school in 1959, Ron attended San Diego City College, where he received his associate's degree in science. He then went on to San Diego State College, majoring in zoology and psychology. "I changed my major several times," he says. "I actually wanted to become a marine biologist and later attended Scripps Institute of Oceanography, but I never did get my four-year degree."

While in college, Ron worked the graveyard shift as a GFP (Government Furnished Parts) analyst at General Dynamics Astronautics for the Atlas Missile project for three years. While still attending San Diego State, he then joined Turquoise Animal Hospital in La Jolla, where he assisted the resident veterinarian, Dr. Custer, in surgery. That lasted for two years. "I drove a Vespa scooter and Austin Healy 3000 while living at Pacific Beach, Mission Beach, and La Jolla commuting to and from college."

Ron enjoyed playing bongos on the beach, where he met a guy named Frank, a steel pedal guitar player who had a band that needed a drummer and asked Ron if he'd like to join them. When Ron told him that he'd never played a drum set before, Frank replied, "We can go to Ace Music and rent one for 15 bucks a month." And they did. Ron recalls, "I took the drum set back to my apartment and learned how to play drums to 'Green Onions' by Booker T and the MGs. I caught on real fast."

After performing a few gigs at the Naval Training Center in San Diego, Ron formed another rock and roll band called the Bushmen in 1965. "We played a lot of Yardbirds, Turtles, Byrds, stuff like that. That band was together for about a year, and just kind of part-time." At the same time, Bushy was working as an automobile repossession investigator for Pacific Finance, a job he took to support his first wife, who was working on her master's degree in English at San Diego State College.

"One time I was repo-ing a car because this guy hadn't made payments for over a year. As I was hooking up his car to my tow bar the guy came out and pushed me, and I was arrested for assault and battery. It was his word against mine. The county sheriffs showed up and handcuffed me and the whole bit. The guy said, 'Tell him to give me my car back.' And they said, 'No, he's got it hooked up. It's his.' But they took me off to jail. I went to court, and I got summary probation. That, along with my deferment from college and being married, put me over the hump from going to Vietnam. So, in some respects, I was lucky. My roommate from college and my best friend, David Rose, became a paratrooper and was shipped off to Vietnam. On his first jump he was shot in midair and died."

Tired of dealing with all of the "flakes and deadbeats" associated with the repo business, Bushy quit Pacific Finance in 1965 and took a job at Ace Music, where he met members of a band called the Voxmen. After sitting in with the Voxmen for one night at Art's Roaring 20s in El Cajon, Ron was invited by the band members to join them, which he did. "I didn't make enough money with the Voxmen in San Diego to support myself and my wife, so at the same time I took a part-time job driving a Good Humor truck for almost a year. It was wild. I didn't make much money, and I ate up all of my profits."

When the Voxmen decided to go to Hollywood, they got a job playing at the Sea Witch, about two miles from the Whisky on the Sunset Strip. There Ron discovered that his San Diego acquaintances with Iron Butterfly were playing at a club just down the street. "We started hanging out together and then Bruce's mother got sick. He had to go back to San Diego and the Butterfly was without a drummer so I sat in and played with them for a week," recalls Bushy. "In essence what happened was we switched drummers. Bruce liked the Voxmen's music better, and I liked the Butterfly." Ron remained with the Butterfly for the next six years, throughout the era of their most triumphant successes.

During the Butterfly's European tour in 1971, Doug Ingle announced that he wanted to call it quits. The group, by then consisting of Larry Reinhardt, Mike Pinera, Doug Ingle, Lee Dorman, and Bushy, had agreed that they would fulfill one last obligation to perform a farewell tour: Music For The People, a bus tour of the United States with Black Oak Arkansas. "I never got to play that tour," laments Ron. "While I was getting off the plane at 4 a.m. in Nashville, I was carrying two Haliburton camera cases, and as I threw one over my left shoulder, it ripped my arm right out of the shoulder socket. They drove me to a hospital, which seemed 100 miles away." The band completed the tour with former Blues Image drummer Manny Bettamate. Ron rented a car and tagged along to seven or eight concerts. "I remember this one gig. I was out in the audience with my arm in a sling. I just couldn't take it anymore, so I ran up on stage, got on the drums, and played the solo. I paid dearly for that in pain."

In 1972, following the breakup of Iron Butterfly, Bushy built the Bushwhack recording and rehearsal studio and formed a group called Gold. "We recorded an album at Doug Parry's Smoketree Recording Studio in Chatsworth but it never went anywhere," says Bushy. Iron Butterfly was reincarnated in 1974. With Philip Taylor Kramer on bass and Howard Reitzes on keyboard, plus Braunn and Bushy, the group recorded an album called *Scorching Beauty.* In 1976, during recording of a subsequent album, *Sun And Steel,* Bill DeMartines replaced Reitzes on keyboard. The next few years Bushy played with Iron Butterfly and other bands, and in 1979, he went to work for Fisher Lumber, a hardware store on 14th Street and Colorado Avenue in Santa Monica, where he struck up a friendship with a Makita power tools sales representative.

"I started bugging him, saying, 'Hey, I'd like to drive around in a company car and travel, go see all the different buyers and sell them tools.'" His persistence eventually paid off. Bushy joined Makita in 1981, selling power tools and accessories for five years and becoming one of the company's top salesmen. He was named Salesman of the Year in 1984 and earned Salesman of the Month honors six times, and he trained all new sales personnel from 1983 to 1986. He was made a member of the company's Research and Development Committee for New Products and designed the company's ML700, a 7.2-volt Ni-Cad flashlight along with its own successful marketing program. Bushy convinced the company that if they'd package the flashlight as a kit with the cordless grinder, it would appeal to heating and air conditioning professionals and plumbers, who often have to work in dark spaces. The kit is still popular today.

Bushy then served a brief stint in 1986 as a sales representative for GTE Directories Corporation in Culver City, responsible for selling Yellow Pages advertising, before joining Bosch, a German power tool maker. "When I hired on at Bosch, they promised to give me the same sales territory I had with Makita [all of Los Angeles, Ventura, Santa Barbara, and San Luis Obispo counties], but they reneged on it and instead gave me a geographically sprawling region that included part of the east San Fernando Valley, all of Riverside County, and San Bernardino County all the way to Palm Springs. Sometimes I wouldn't get home until 10 or 11 p.m."

In 1988, Ron, Erik, Lee, and Doug got back together to perform for Atlantic Records' 40th anniversary concert at Madison Square Garden. "I quit Bosch, and we re-formed the original 'Vida' band. The band did a two-month tour leading up to Atlantic's 40th in New York, but it was just impossible. Atlantic even offered us a record deal, but the band just didn't see eye-to-eye musically," recalls Bushy.

Bushy rejoined Makita in August 1988, working for another three years until he suffered a back injury while loading a Makita generator into the back of his company mini van. The injury required a lot of physical therapy, and Bushy ended up on disability. While on disability, he attended Platt College in Pasadena, where he received diplomas in computer graphics and graphic design. A longtime artist and photographer, Bushy had designed Iron Butterfly's *Live* album cover, worked on the *Metamorphosis* album cover, and etched the gorilla with wings on the *Evolution* album cover.

After graduating from Platt in 1994, Bushy got the itch to get back into music. "Mike Pinera and I got back together and started playing and then he kinda bowed out, so Lee and I got together. We went through several guitar players and keyboard players until Doug returned in 1996."

Bushy uses his computer graphic skills to design Iron Butterfly T-shirts and merchandise to sell at concerts and through the group's Web site at www.ironbutterfly.com, for which he designs the graphics. "We're incorporated now, Iron Butterfly Music Inc. The art and merchandise company is called Mariposa Art and our booking agency is Papillon Ltd. Mariposa is Spanish for butterfly and Papillon is French for butterfly," explains Bushy. "This time, we're trying to do everything right."

Bush married Nancy Braverman in 1982 (it was his third marriage), during his first stint at Makita, and Ron has helped raise Nancy's two daughters, Brooke and Nicole, who were 5 and 7 at the time. "Meeting and marrying Nancy is the best thing that ever happened to me," says Bushy with a smile.

A self-proclaimed perfectionist, Bushy says, "If I can't do something right I won't do it. I usually figure out everything myself, without asking anyone for help. I'm also resourceful and adaptable. If I was stranded on an island I could probably survive, I'm sure. I can make do with anything. I have a real inventive mind, and I'm very curious about everything."

In February 1995, a good friend of Bushy's, scientist and fellow musician Philip Taylor Kramer, mysteriously vanished, leaving Ron an enigmatic message. "He called me and left a message saying, 'Bush, it's Taylor. I just want to let you know I love you more than life itself,' and then he hung up. He left behind his wife, Jennifer, and two children. He was a straight-arrow." Greatly disturbed, Bushy appeared on *Phil Donahue, Unsolved Mysteries,* and many other television shows in an attempt to gain leads into his friend's disappearance. It wasn't until May 29, 1999, that a hiker discovered Kramer's 1993 Ford Aerostar and skeletal remains in a Los Angeles ravine.

Bushy has continued writing songs and has composed the lyrics for many songs including "Unconscious Power," which is on the Butterfly's first album, *Heavy.* He also wrote the lyrics for "Soul Experience" and "In The Time Of Our Lives," from the *Ball* album. "I wrote 'Pearly Gates' on the *Scorching Beauty* album together with Jon Anderson from Yes while we were on tour in Europe in 1971. You can hear the Yes and Jon Anderson influence in it," notes Ron.

Bushy enjoys performing these days, and especially enjoys talking with the fans and signing autographs. He observes, "What's amazing is that we're playing for audiences of all ages, from 9 years old to 90. It's unbelievable. These young kids who weren't even born know our songs."

Nine years old. Just about the age Ron was when he whittled his first set of drumsticks.

THEN AND NOW
LEE DORMAN

In his mind, Lee Dorman can journey back to the misty mornings in the late '40s and early '50s when as a child growing up in Hermosa Beach, California, his father would take him to watch the fishing vessels chug in and out of the harbor near his home. And he would imagine what it must be like to be the captain of one of those vessels. That vision must have remained indelibly in his mind through the years for he became a captain musically as well as literally.

Not more than six months after the breakup of the Butterfly in 1971, bassist Dorman became involved in the formation of a group called Captain Beyond in Los Angeles. The group consisted of Dorman, guitarist Larry Reinhardt, former Deep Purple lead singer Rod Evans, and drummer Bobby Caldwell, who performed with Johnny Winter. "The four of us got together, made a demo album on a four-track machine, and took it to Phil Walden, who was just signing his Capricorn-Warner deal at the time and was about ready to unleash the Allman Brothers album *Eat A Peach* on the world. He agreed to sign the band."

PHOTO BY RON BUSHY.

Southern rock label Capricorn released the self-titled *Captain Beyond,* and the following year the group recorded a second album called *Sufficiently Breathless,* with Marty Rodriguez replacing Caldwell on drums. Captain Beyond toured Europe for a while, then broke up in 1974 for lack of work.

"We kept drawing a salary even though we weren't working," says Dorman. "The president of the record label, who was the manager of the band, was so tied up with other acts that he unfortunately just kind of put us on a shelf rather than turning us over to somebody who might have had us touring with Black Sabbath or a more related band. But to put a jazz-rock band opening for the Allman Brothers doesn't make sense. So ergo, the band just kind of wasted away." The band's demise was particularly frustrating to Dorman, whose commanding bass lines gave the power and presence to Captain Beyond, just as they had provided the substructure for the Butterfly.

Ironically, the genesis of that throbbing energy was a ukulele that his grandmother taught him to play when he was 5 years old. Lee, an only child, was born in St. Louis, Missouri, on September 15, 1942. That same year his family moved to Hermosa Beach, California, when his father took a job for Lockheed. The same grandmother who taught him to play the ukulele, a former vaudeville performer who lived in Berkeley, also gave him piano lessons. When Lee was 8 years old his parents signed him up for accordion lessons. He disliked the instrument, but it, along with the ukulele and piano, became part of his musical foundation.

"Most everything musically I've picked up I was able to learn because of my training on the ukulele. Later I switched to bass when a friend of mine, who was a bass player, asked if I wanted to learn. And I said 'sure.' So he showed me and I just picked it up. I taught myself how to play guitar, and on some albums I played vibes."

In 1952 Lee's father got a job with Weyerhaeuser and moved his family to Tacoma, Washington, where Lee peeked in on backyard rehearsals of a teenage band that would become the Kingsmen of "Louie, Louie" fame. His father had bought him a 1940s drum kit for $100 from a pawn shop, and Lee taught himself how to play.

"It was a huge bass drum with a big tropical scene painted on the front and it had straps on it so you could carry it down the street," says Dorman. "Some of the Kingsmen were rehearsing in my neighborhood one day, and I walked over to listen. I got to know them pretty well, and a couple of times I actually kept a beat for them during rehearsal when the drummer wasn't there."

In 1955 Lee's father took a job in Washington, D.C., and the family moved to Kensington, Maryland, where in high school Lee began playing drums for a band called the Dukes, performing top 40 rock and roll at sock hops and school dances.

Following graduation from Walter Johnson High School in Kensington, Lee attended college for two years on the Monterey Peninsula, taking general education courses. "Then fate steered me down the music highway," he says.

Learning that a robust music scene was developing in San Diego, Lee relocated there in the summer of 1964, and soon joined a foursome called the Prophets. "We played around San Diego about the same time Gary Puckett was playing the Quad Room in one of the biggest bands in the area called the Outcasts. Lee Michaels was on keyboard, and the drummer was Johnny Barbados, who wound up with the Turtles. There were a lot of really good musicians in San Diego, who were coming up like I was, and that's where I first met Ron Bushy."

In 1965, the Prophets decided to add topless girls to their act and put together a show to take to Las Vegas. "We opened a lounge show at Caesar's Palace," says Dorman. "They called the show Buddha Belly's Purple Veil Review, or something like that. We all wore tuxes and did our thing, and then the girls came out and did their thing."

Dorman's group spent two months at Caesar's, then went on to play the Riviera and the Thunderbird. "The money was good and the band received free room and board. Even today when you play casinos, that's part of the deal. If you stay away from the tables, you don't have to spend any money." When the girls decided to leave the act, Dorman and the other band members found a Vegas agent, who put them on the road performing at supper clubs. "We worked what I call the West Coast chitlins circuit, which is all of the little one-stop hoppers from San Diego as far east as El Centro, and then Vegas, Reno, Tahoe, and all the way up to Billings, Montana. And that was pretty good bread."

During their travels, the band ended up in Los Angeles, alternating two-week stints between two popular clubs both called the Mirage. One was on Van Nuys Boulevard at the Ventura Freeway in the San Fernando Valley, and the other on Santa Monica Boulevard near 10th Street in Santa Monica, where Lee renewed acquaintances with Ron Bushy.

"The Butterfly was going to audition a guy from the Spoonful. And I happened to be there," recalls Dorman. On his 25th birthday in 1967, Dorman auditioned for the Iron Butterfly and was hired as the band's bass player that night.

"Here I was on my way back to school, and music kept pulling me. I just never thought about it as a career, it just always seemed something for fun. I think being part of a band that made a record was special, and then, of course, my gosh, I had the opportunity to be part of a band that was successful. There are so many good bands that never reach that level."

Dorman's father was always behind him in anything he wanted to pursue. "Back when I was going to college I told him, 'I'm not sure what I want to do.' And he said, 'It doesn't make any difference. Try something. If you don't like it, then change. But whatever you do, try to be the best at it. If you learn to be a dentist, then wind up owning a bowling alley, so what? If somebody has a problem with their teeth there, you'll have that knowledge and you might be able to help them out. You don't lose any knowledge." Lee has always cherished the support and advice of his father, who died in 1979.

Like the pilot of a vessel, Lee weathered the demise of both the Butterfly and Captain Beyond, and remained when each band resurfaced. Lee was there when Captain Beyond was resurrected in 1977, when Warner Brothers called Dorman's attorney and said, "We'd like to have a third Captain Beyond album." So original drummer Bobby Caldwell returned and Willy Daffern joined the band as lead vocalist. Captain Beyond recorded its third and final album, *Dawn Explosion,* under the Warner Brothers label before breaking up for good in 1978.

Although none of the songs charted for Captain Beyond, Dorman says that in later years he discovered a Captain Beyond CD in Europe and two unofficial Web sites. "Many musicians have come up to me and said, 'Now that was a band's band.' It was jazz rock, and we opened in Europe and never went back. We played very little in the states, which probably contributed to the demise of the band."

Following the breakup of Captain Beyond, Dorman decided to take a break from music. "Occasionally I would get a phone call from a booking agent who wanted to know if we could get the Iron Butterfly together, and sometimes two or three of us would get together and go out and play the songs. It was maybe 30 days out of a year."

Throughout the years, several incarnations of Iron Butterfly have performed with different members. "Occasionally I worked with Mike Pinera and Erik Braunn. We would just go for a couple of weeks here and there." Ron and Lee performed as Iron Butterfly, Featuring Lee Dorman and Ron Bushy. "We had been trying to get Doug involved, and he was not ready at the time. Finally all of a sudden he called up and said, 'You know, I think it's time.'" That was in July of 1994. "Of course it's always nice when you have the real lead singer," Dorman says with a hearty laugh. "Now we've been working a lot better circuit. We've been to Europe and we're scheduled to go back again."

While in Europe, a German motion picture film company followed the band around filming a documentary of Iron Butterfly and the psychedelic era. "They were at all of our jobs with cinematic cameras and they were backstage, they were on the tour bus, they were at the whole thing," says Dorman. In October 1998, the film was in the final stages of being edited.

Lee, who has never been married, lives in the Southern California beach community of Dana Point and also shares an apartment in Burbank with his girlfriend, Linda Zimmerman, a James Beard–honored cookbook writer and a real estate agent. "Linda and I met in Chicago in 1968 and were around each other a total of 10 days at different times, but we didn't see each other again until 1996," says Dorman. Linda moved to Los Angeles in 1969 to work in the film industry, becoming an associate producer for the movie *Grease* and for other films. "Since we've been back together, she'll introduce me to somebody or I'll introduce her to somebody, and it turns out that we'd met that person a long time ago. For a long time we were within 20 miles of each other, but we didn't know it."

Lee also teaches a studio workshop and conducts demo sessions throughout Florida. "Several studio owners are friends of mine who link my name to their studios because they're small and my name gives them credibility. I really enjoy it, and it's also a paid vacation. I get to go to Florida and hang out and take on a different role in music than I usually do."

Lee describes himself as easygoing. "I'm real laid-back until I get pushed real hard. Some people say that I'm too laid back, that I could be doing more, and maybe they're right. But it just takes a lot for me to be self-lit." But Lee prides himself on his ability to organize and on his production and audio values. "I really like organizing things and seeing that they come off. There's always gonna be a slight margin for error, but I pride myself on keeping it as low as possible."

Following the third Captain Beyond album, Dorman sold everything, moved to the beach, and started doing a lot of sailing. He took some courses, got his Coast Guard license to operate 100-ton sailing vessels, and served as captain of a lightweight charter business for three years. "I took people to Santa Barbara and Catalina. And I brought a couple of boats down from San Francisco. My presence was known by all of the record companies. Here were all of these people I knew who had money and loved to go sailing," says Dorman. He skippered bay cruises and sunset cruises offering choice of cuisine, from hot dogs to lobster and caviar. "It was fun. I got to run around in shorts and a T-shirt and get paid for it." Lee didn't own a boat, but would make arrangements to rent other people's boats, depending on the size of the parties, whether it be 30-foot vessels or a 100-foot yacht.

Although Lee and Linda have no children, they share a Rottweiler, a Rhodesian ridgeback, and a cat. "We're looking for a place where they can have some room and be able to go in and out," says Dorman.

With Iron Butterfly in full flight, Lee tours regularly. "I like going places," admits Lee. "Some of it can get a little long in the tooth, but those that are long in the tooth are when you go on at 11 p.m., you have to get up at 4 in the morning to leave on a 6 o'clock plane. That's the only time. And I really like good food, so when I have the opportunity I take my little *Zagat* guide with me and go to a good restaurant, because believe me, I've had all the burgers there are, and I don't want to do any more."

Dorman admits he probably could have done more in his career had he moved more quickly on opportunities. But what better feeling is there than to know that every project in which he's been involved has ended up with a record deal. "If I just sat in a rocking chair and reflected, I would say to myself, 'Hey, I was part of something that put a notch somewhere. And it's a miracle that I was able to be in my lifetime part of something that made a difference.' And Iron Butterfly and 'In-A-Gadda-Da-Vida' made a difference to a lot of people." Dorman adds, "I'd like to do one more recording project, regardless of where it goes."

THEN AND NOW
ERIK BRAUNN

Success can be measured not only in professional achievements but also in the ability to attain inner peace, whether
through creative expression or the mental strength and
well-being derived from studying philosophy or religion.
A student of the martial arts since the late '60s, Erik Braunn
has attained success in many ways, including a spiritual
strength obtained through his involvement in four different
forms of martial arts—tae kwon do, kuk sool won, shoto-
kan, and jeet kune do. Though he prefers to practice independently, Braunn has achieved his personal goals and continues to practice
daily. Superstardom came and went for Braunn at a very early age, but he has
managed to make a comfortable living for himself by keeping music a vital part
of his existence.

For as far back as he can remember, Erik Braunn wanted to become a professional musician. When he was 4 years old his mother bought him a violin and
enrolled him in lessons at a Boston music store. "I studied violin with the chair-
person of the Boston Symphony,"
recalls Braunn, who rode the train
once a week from the suburbs to
Boston to take his lessons. After
a year and a half, Braunn was
excelling, but his mother couldn't
afford to continue paying for lessons
so the symphony accepted him into
its prodigy program and taught him
at no charge. He made his first
recording at 6 years of age, a piece
by Paganini called *Moto Perpetuo*.

Born August 11, 1950, in Pekin,
Illinois, Braunn has lived in
Anchorage and Fairbanks, Alaska,
on the edge of the Everglades in
Florida, and in Boston, Chicago,
L.A., San Francisco, and New York.
After his mother married a major
in the Air Force, sometimes the
family would move as frequently

PHOTO COURTESY OF ERIK BRAUNN.

as once a year. By the time he reached high school, his mother, a registered nurse, had settled in the San Fernando Valley where Braunn attended Cleveland and Reseda High Schools. "I pretty much raised my two younger brothers, until the time I joined Iron Butterfly at age 16 and moved away from home."

Braunn, who began playing guitar at the age of 13, studied classical guitar in the late 1980s at Los Angeles Pierce College under Dr. John Schneider. But he claims most of his knowledge has come from spending hours in libraries and studying music with some great teachers. "I studied jazz with Barney Kessel, Joe Pass, the late Duke Snider, and my first teacher, Milt Norman, who was a genius, and known for his incredibly fast chord progressions. I also studied with Ted Green, who is still recognized as one of the geniuses in the guitar world."

Braunn owns his own publishing company he playfully named Zen Dujour, which means "enlightenment of the day." He wrote or co-wrote 19 Iron Butterfly songs, including one on the *In-A-Gadda-Da Vida* album called "Termination," and three on the third album, *Ball*.

In 1974 and 1975, Braunn and Ron Bushy recorded *Scorching Beauty* and in 1976 *Sun And Steel* with MCA Records. Braunn recalls, "I had just left Iron Butterfly, and I made a tape with the L.A. Jazz All Stars, a wonderful group of jazz musicians, and I recorded with a studio band that went on to work with Linda Ronstadt." Braunn presented his tapes as a solo artist to Mike Maitlin of MCA records, which agreed to produce an album. "*Scorching Beauty* was kind of a disaster," admits Braunn. "However, I think the *Sun And Steel* album was the best-produced and best-engineered album Iron Butterfly ever made." The name was based on a book that Braunn had read by Yukio Mishima, a colonel in the Japanese army in about 1972. "Mishima was a full-blown Samurai warrior. He had his own army and tried to overthrow the government. His ideals in 'Sun and Steel' were about the refinement of the soul and spirit."

When Braunn first joined Iron Butterfly in 1967 he had turned down a scholarship to UCLA for arts and drama. In high school he had won several acting awards during competitions at the University of Southern California and UCLA. "I had a drama class the last period of every day, and we had a brilliant teacher who taught Val Kilmer and Connie Seleca. We had elaborate productions. One department built the sets, another department made all of the costumes, and, of course, there were the actors. So I was used to being on stage when I joined the band."

Following his departure from Iron Butterfly in December 1969, Braunn bought a house in Tarzana from Neil Diamond, who had built a studio in a barn on the property. "I put together a band called Flintwhistle back in '70–'71." The band included Darryl DeLoach and the late Steve Weis, brother of former Iron Butterfly guitar player Danny Weis. "We rehearsed in the studio and played around a little bit, but I decided to start recording on my own and learned production. I made about 40 or 50 recordings of songs I wrote. I'd perform with Richie Hayward, the drummer from Little Feat, and a guy named Craig Cole, who was living in my guest house at the time. He played saxophone and he was really good. I would invite these guys up and we recorded a song called 'Am I Down' and a few other songs that helped me get the MCA deal." Braunn sold the house to John Sebastian in 1973.

Like many recording artists of the 1960s Iron Butterfly had a string of bad luck with managers. "One of our managers withheld tax forms from the IRS for the one year that the band made the most money, and the IRS came and cleaned everybody out. I probably lost $3 million in property. I was 20 at the time. The best management I've ever had has been myself, and that's when I re-formed all the original members for the 40th anniversary of Atlantic Records. I managed that, and I hired the agents."

Braunn, who has been writing songs since the age of 13, has more than 300 songs in his catalog. A Doors fan, Braunn knew Jim Morrison and, for a brief time, shared the same girlfriend. Braunn recalls, "Jim and I started talking back-stage at a college date in Berkeley and our conversation turned to girlfriends. He had a girlfriend named Pam and I had a girl named Sheri. He started talking about seeing this other girl who was a waitress. And I said, 'I've been seeing another girl, and she's a waitress, too. She works down at the Image,' which was a club on Sunset Boulevard. And he said, 'So does my girlfriend. Her name is Raggy.' We were both seeing the same girl, and we both just started laughing. Neither of us ended up with her."

In 1989 Eric married the woman he had been together with since 1981, Gail Johnson. Gail is now assistant vice president of Coast Business Credit. She is also a novelist. The couple, who live in the San Fernando Valley, have three Dalmatians.

Erik, who has written in a variety of musical styles including rock and roll, hard rock, country, jazz, and folk, still hopes to get back on the road. "I like touring and performing. I still work at my guitar playing, and I think I'm up there with the good boys, but to me there was a point when I realized that you've got to write songs, and you've got to be able to write good songs. The lyrics and the melody have to be strong. I'd like to be known as a good guitar player, a good writer, a good singer, and I'd like to have my music inspire people."

Braunn finds some of the misperceptions about Iron Butterfly amusing. "Somebody once commented that they thought it was strange that I was alive because they thought I was a heroin addict, which I never have been. In fact, I don't do any drugs at all."

Braunn is quick to identify his two proudest achievements: being part of a band that recorded a historic quadruple platinum album and resurrecting the original band for Atlantic Records' 40th anniversary celebration at Madison Square Garden. "Iron Butterfly was the first band to sell more than 20 million albums, and we did it without a hit single. The platinum album was created for Iron Butterfly by Ahmet Ertegun, president of Atlantic Records. RIAA, the sanctioning body, didn't recognize platinum at the time," said Braunn. "The only other band ever to get that honor was Led Zeppelin."

A plethora of stellar artists comprising a Who's Who in Atlantic's history performed for the 40th anniversary concert, including Sam Moore (of Sam and Dave), Phil Collins, Led Zeppelin, Yes, and the Bee Gees. Iron Butterfly had 12 minutes to play and was the 12th act. "When we came on, we got an instant standing ovation—the first of the day—and we got one in the middle, and we got one at the end," recalls Braunn. "I remember being backstage and crying afterwards, because it was such an emotional thing."

Erik enjoys motorcycles and motorcycle road racing. He owns a Honda CVR 900 RR, which means "race-ready." In addition to martial arts, Braunn is a Golden Gloves–certified boxer and enjoys target shooting (but doesn't hunt), gardening, and nature. Erik and Gail have more than 24 different species of roses on their property. "Gail orders bulbs from Holland so one thing comes up and dies down and another pops up. We have a lot of birds in our neighborhood and we like to feed them."

Erik also enjoys practicing guitar and spending a couple of hours a day in the library. "I've read practically everything in the library on philosophy, psychology, novels, autobiographies, biographies, and poetry. I'm a big Edgar Allan Poe fan," he says. "I think as a songwriter all of the mistakes I've made make me who I am today. I'm concentrating mostly now on putting together the songs that I want to play and putting a band together."

Many individuals have influenced Braunn. "I have always looked for inspiration, and I've never had any trouble finding it. People who have touched my life include my first guitar teacher, Milt Norman, and my first drama teacher, Robert Carelli, as well as Jimi Hendrix and Jim Morrison."

Tim Buckley was also an inspiration to Braunn. "I had seen Buckley at the Troubadour and he sang like an angel. And I used to go down for the concerts and watch him before we went on every night that he played. He was just exceptional."

Despite the many interests that have competed for his attention over the years, Erik is unequivocal about defining the driving force in his life. "Everything's always been about the music to me," says Erik. "Music is most important for me. Music has determined how I've lived my life, and I imagine it always will."

INDEX

A

A&M Music, 243, 253
Abbott, Don, 148
Ace Records, 7
Action!, 135
Adamsville, Tenn., 192
Albin, Peter, 268
Albuquerque, N.M., 22
Alexandria, Va., 296
Allbut, Barbara, 80, 82, 87, 90, 91, 93–96
Allbut, Jiggs (Phyllis), 80, 82, 87, 90–92
Amarillo, Texas, 6, 34
American Bandstand, 53, 135, 240
Anderson, Jane, 171
Anderson, Jon, 300
Angels, 80–96
Anthony, N.M., 28
Appell, Dave, 58, 65
Apple Records, 106
April-Blackwood Music, 243, 253
Arcata, Calif., 282
Arlington, Texas, 179
Ash Grove, 266
Asher, Jane, 102
Asher, Peter, 100, 102, 104–108, 112, 114
Association, 223
Atco Records, 35
Atlantic City, N.J. 45
Atlantic Records, 174, 288, 308, 309
ATV Music, 65
Autumn Records, 132, 135, 136, 142, 147, 151, 152

B

B.T. Puppy Records, 55, 70, 74, 75
Bag O' Nails, 119
Balin, Marty, 289
Baltimore, 89, 217
Barry, Yank, 46
Barthol, Bruce, 259, 266, 267, 277–282
Beach Boys, 187
Beatles, 7, 42, 65, 100, 155, 207, 222
Beau Brummels, 132–160
Beaverton, Ore., 294
Beckett, Larry, 223
Bell Buckle, Tenn., 193
Belleville, N.J., 85
Bement, Dwight, 228, 229, 232, 235, 238–241, 248, 253
Bendett, David, 208
Bennett, Billy, 171
Berkeley, Calif., 158, 272, 278, 279, 280
Beverly Hills, Calif., 72
Bido Lito's, 287

Big Brother and the Holding Company, 273
Big Hugh Baby (WLAC), 192
Big Three, 200
Billboard magazine, 29, 135, 169, 200, 260, 293
Birmingham, Ala., 169, 220
Birmingham, England, 118
Block, Martin, 58
Bonds, Gary "U.S.," 40–48
Bono, Sonny, 135
Boone, Steve, 200, 201, 214–219
Boston, Mass., 306
Bottom Line Records, 60
Braunn, Erik, 208, 288, 290, 293, 295, 304, 306–309
Breckenridge, Colo., 186
Brentwood, Tenn., 245
Brighton Beach, N.Y., 57, 63, 64, 265
Brooklyn College, 53, 73, 272
Brooklyn, N.Y. , 52, 57, 270
Brooks, Donnie, 17, 144
Brooks, Harvey, 290
Brown, James, 170
Buckley, Tim, 222, 309
Budd, Eric, 4, 5, 11, 14, 20–22, 25, 32
Burbank, Calif., 208, 220, 304
Bushy, Ron, 288, 292, 295, 296–300, 302, 304
Butler, Joe, 200–202, 204, 211–214

C

Caldwell, Bobby, 301
California State University, Hayward, 30, 31
California State University, Long Beach, 282
Camp Lejeune, N.C., 215
Campbell, Glen, 157, 231
Campbell, Jo Ann, 94
Canadian American Records, 90
Capitol Records, 54, 280
Caprice Records, 80, 81
Capricorn Records, 301
Captain Beyond, 301, 303
Carabetta, Frank, 171
Carousel Ballroom, 147
Casady, Jack, 262
Castaic, Calif., 187
Castle, 287
Catskill Mountains, 72
Cavallo, Bob, 202, 217, 222
CBS Songs, 35
Chater, Kerry, 228, 229, 232, 235, 242–245, 252, 253, 292

Chatsworth, Calif., 294
Cher, 135
Chicago, Ill., 33, 261, 280
Chiffons, 54, 67
Christian Brothers University, 194
Church Street Five, Daddy G and, 41
Cipollina, John, 268
Circle Theater Company, 211
Circus, the 202
Clark, Dick, 41, 87, 135, 169, 170, 187, 247
Clinton, Conn., 296
Clonmel, County Tipperary, Ireland, 145
Clovis, N.M., 9, 12, 14, 19, 21, 25, 26
Club Paradise, 183
Cohen, David Bennett, 259, 270–276
Cohen, Herb, 221
Colorado Springs, 241
Columbia Records, 228–230, 235, 243
Columbus, Ohio, 229
Coney Island, 63
Connie Francis, 88
Cooder, Ry, 175
Cooke, Sam, 42
Corinth, Miss., 192
Costa, Don, 86
Country Joe and the Fish, 258–263
Cow Palace Auditorium, 134
Creatore, Luigi, 52
Crichton College, 194
Culver City, Calif., 299
Curcio, Fran, 171

D

Dallas, Texas, 173, 178, 179, 181, 293
Dana Point, Calif., 304
Dawn, Tony Orlando and, 59
Dean, Fuzzy, 148
DeLoach, Darryl, 288, 307
Denson, Ed, 259
Denver, 16
Diamond, Neil, 248, 307
Diddley, Bo, 43
Diltz, Henry, 221
Dingo Records, 167, 168
Dinosaurs, 267
Diplomat Club, 165–168
Doherty, Denny, 200, 202
Donahue, Tom, 132, 134, 135, 139, 142, 143, 147, 157, 286
Doors, 308
Dorman, Lee, 288, 289, 294, 295, 298, 301–305
Dot Records, 34, 185

Douglas, Chip, 221
Douglas, Mike, 136
Dryden, Spencer, 268
Dugan, Karol, 221
Dunhill Records, 220
Dusk, 82

E

Eastern New Mexico University, 34
Eastport, Long Island, 216
Edge, Graeme, 118
El Cajon, Calif., 242
El Paso, Texas, 21
Elektra Records, 200, 206
Elliot, Cass, 200, 202
Elliott, Ron, 132, 135, 136–140, 143, 146, 151, 153, 155, 156
Emerson, Keith, 290
Emeryville, Calif., 157
EMI, 35, 59, 101, 280
Epic Records, 249
Erlichman, Marty, 243, 253
Ertegun, Ahmet, 174, 309
Evans, Rod, 301
Even Dozen Jug Band, 200, 206, 207
Evergreen, Colo., 291
Everly Brothers, 5, 21, 68

F

Facenda, Tommy, 41
Fallon, Nev., 18
Family Dog, 261
Family Stone, Sly and the, 132
Faryar, Cyrus, 208, 221
Fillmore Auditorium, 260, 261
Fillmore West, 148, 262
Fireballs, 4–36
Fish and Chip, 268
Flash Cadillac and the Continental Kids, 240, 241, 248
Ford Ord, 21
Fordham University, 282
Forest Hills, N.Y., 275
Formerly Fat Harry, 280
Forsha, John, 221
Free Speech Movement, 258
Freed, Alan, 58
Frei Universitat, Berlin, 281
Ft. Lauderdale, Fla., 219
Fuller, Jerry, 229, 230, 248

G

Galaxy, 287
Garcia, Jerry, 273
Genero, Loraine, 171
Gentrys, 167
George Washington University, 272
George, Lowell, 217

Gerace, Tony, 171
Gibson, Paul "Butch," 164, 167, 170, 171, 192
Gilmer, Jimmy, 6, 13, 15, 22, 33–36
Glen Cove, Long Island, 212
Glendale College, Calif., 221
Golden Gate University, 282
Goodeve, Grant, 236
Gottlieb, Lou, 185
Goucher College, 85, 89
Graham, Bill, 260, 262, 281
Grateful Dead, 273
Great Neck, N.Y., 201
Green, Charlie, 288
Greenwich Village, 200, 201, 211, 212, 266, 271, 272
Grossmont College, 242
Guida, Frank, 40, 46
Guillaume, Robert, 74
Guthrie's, 179

H
Hard Times, 247
Harper, Kan., 22
Harpers Bizarre, 152
Harrison, Ark., 214, 224
Hartnell College, 30
Hatch, N.M., 28
Havens, Richie, 207
Hayward, Justin, 119
Hayward, Richie, 308
Healdsburg, Calif., 137
Hendrix, Jimi, 275, 290
Henske, Judy, 222
Hermosa Beach, Calif., 301, 302
Hi Records, 168
Hibbing, Minn., 233
Hilo, Hawaii, 223
Hirsh, Gary "Chicken," 260, 273
Hoh, Eddie, 221
Holly, Buddy 10
Hollywood, Calif., 174
Homespun Tapes, 274
Hooker, Charlie, 174
Hopkin, Mary, 106
Hullabaloo, 136, 202
Humboldt State University, 282
Hunter, Bob, 267
Hurt, Mississippi John, 202

I
Independence, Mo., 13
Ingle, Doug, 242, 243, 252, 287, 288, 290, 291–295, 298, 304
Inn Group, 221
Iron Butterfly, 243, 253, 286–309
Irving, Don, 136, 151
Irving/Almo Publishing, 243

J
J Band, John Sebastian and the, 209
Jabberwock, 259, 267, 273
Jackson, Michael, 65
Jacksonville, Fla. 44
Jacobsen, Erik, 201–203
Jacobsen, Ronnie (Spiderman), 171
James, Sonny, 5, 23, 26
Jankowski, Linda, 80
Jefferson Airplane, 262, 288
John R. (WLAC), 192
John, Robert, 59
Jones, Booker T., 186
Jones, Paul, 105
Joplin, Janis, 273, 290
Joseph And The Amazing Technicolour Dreamcoat, 110
Juilliard School, 95

K
Kama Sutra Records, 202
Kansas City, Mo., 13, 17
Kapp Records, 4
Kensington, Md., 302
Kesler, Stan, 168
Kinetic Playground, 293
King's College, London University, 101
King, B.B. , 42, 183, 188
King, Freddie, 174
Kingsboro Community College, 74
Kingsmen, 302
Kirshner, Don, 65
Klein, George, 167, 192
KMPX, 142, 260, 286
Kouha, Andrew, 171
KPFA–FM, 259
KPPC, 142
KSOL, 132
KYA, 132, 135

L
La Mesa, Calif., 242
Laine, Denny, 118
Lark, Stan, 4, 11, 13, 15–19, 21, 25
Las Cruces, N.M., 16
Las Vegas, Nev., 18
LaSalle Extension University in Chicago, 267
Laurie Records, 54
Legrand Records, 41
Lennon, John, 126, 211
Lettermen, 65
Levitt, Danny, 157
Lewis, Jerry Lee, 11, 231
Lincoln Farm Work Camp, 271
Little Black Book, 167
Little Feat, 217, 308
Lodge, John, 119
London, England, 280
Long Island University, 213
Long Island, N.Y., 200
Longview, Texas, 27

Los Angeles Pierce College, 307
Lovin' Spoonful, 200–224
Loyola College, Baltimore, 85
Lubbock, Texas, 19

M
MacNeish, Jerry, 7, 14, 32
Malibu, Calif., 124, 187
Mamas and the Papas, 201
Manfred Mann, 105
Manhattan Beach, Calif., 187
Margo, Mitch, 52–55, 64, 67–71, 74, 76
Margo, Phil, 52–55, 64, 68, 69, 72–76
Martin, David, 164–166, 169, 171, 173, 176, 178–182, 185
Massenburg, George, 217
MCA Records, 307
McCartney, Paul, 100–102, 106, 155, 156
McCormack, Keith, 7, 13, 17
McDonald, Joe, 259, 266, 267. 273
Meagher, Ron, 132, 143, 148, 151, 153, 155–160
Medicine Ball Caravan, 142
Medress, Hank, 52–55, 57–61, 64, 73, 82
Melton, Barry "The Fish," 259, 260, 264–269, 273, 278, 279
Memphis, 165–167, 175, 180, 181, 184, 186, 188, 190, 193, 194, 205
Mendocino County, Calif., 268
Mercury Records, 201
Mesa Junior College, 247
MGM Records, 169, 189, 202
Michaels, Lee, 302
Minneapolis, 17, 21, 24, 29
Mitchell, Bob, 132, 134, 135, 147
Mitchell, Mitch, 290
Modern Folk Quartet, 221
Modern Folk Quintet, 221
Modesto, Calif., 28
Monterey Peninsula, 302
Monterey Pop Festival, 261
Moody Blues, 118–128
Morningstar Ranch, 185, 190
Morrison, Jim, 308
Mugwumps, 200
Mulligan, Declan, 132, 136, 139, 143, 145–149, 151, 153, 155, 157
Murray the K, 86

N
Nashville, 31, 35, 36, 244
National City, Calif., 239

New Christy Minstrels, 221
New Mexico Institute of Mining Technologies, 11
New Mexico State University, 16
New York City Community College, 53
New York University, 207, 282
Newell, Norman, 101
Newllano, La., 165
Night Owl Cafe, 202
Norfolk, Va., 40, 45
North American School of Architectural Design and Drafting, 18
North Hollywood, Calif., 13, 265, 278
Northridge, Calif., 294

O
Oakland, Calif., 156, 279
Omaha, Neb., 291
Ono, Yoko, 211
Ontario, Calif., 240
Orange, N.J., 90, 94
Orlando, Tony, 54, 59
Orlons, 41
Oroville, Calif., 148

P
Pahrump, Nev., 18
Panama City, Fla., 169
Pandora's Box, 287
Pasadena, Calif., 152, 153, 299
Patterson, Jerry, 164, 165, 171, 183, 188
Pekin, Ill., 306
Pelican Rapids, MN, 233
Penrod, Jerry, 287
Pepper, Allan, 60
Peretti, Hugo, 52
Peter & Gordon, 100–114
Petersen, John, 132, 143, 146, 150–156
Petty, Norman, 4, 6, 7, 10, 12, 25, 26, 29
Phantasmagoria, 293
Philadelphia, Pa., 293
Phillips Records, 82
Phillips, "Daddy-O" Dewey, 184
Phoenix, Ariz., 293
Pickwick Club, 101
Pinder, Michael, 118–128
Pinera, Mike, 293, 298, 304
Placerville, Calif., 153
Platt College, 299
Playa del Rey, 186
Pomona Valley, Calif., 183
Port Angeles, Wash., 294
Portales, N.M., 18
Portland, Ore., 223
Presley, Elvis, 34, 231
Private Stock, 249
Puckett, Gary and the Union Gap, 228–254

Puckett, Gary, 228, 229, 232–237, 253, 302
Pugliese, John Sebastian, 206

Q

Quicksilver Messenger Service, 262

R

Rachell, James "Yank," 205, 209
Radio Luxembourg, 145
Raton, N.M., 4, 9, 10, 12, 14–18, 20, 21, 23–25, 29
RCA Victor Records, 52, 64
Reinhardt, Larry "Rhino", 293, 294, 298, 301
Reno, Nev., 144
Reprise Records, 209
Rhinoceros, 288
Rice, Tim, 110
Rivière International Records, 237
Roberts, Doug, 13, 15
Rockland Community College, 74
Ronstadt, Linda, 107
Rothchild, Paul A., 207
Roulette Records, 58, 73
Royster, Joe, 41
Rumore, Duke, 169
Ryan, Mark, 262

S

Sabine Pass, Texas, 175
Sacramento, Calif., 141, 143, 268
Salinas, Calif., 30
Sam the Sham and the Pharaohs, 164–196
Samudio, Domingo "Sam," 164–167, 169, 170, 172–179, 185
San Bernardino, Calif., 185
San Diego City College, 234, 297
San Diego State College, 252, 297
San Diego State University, 239, 253
San Diego, 228, 229, 234, 239, 240, 242, 243, 247–249, 252, 253, 287, 292, 295, 296, 302
San Francisco Mime Troupe, 281
San Francisco State College, 133, 266
San Francisco State University, 282
San Francisco, 137, 141, 146, 140, 150, 151, 153–155, 190, 267

San Jose, Calif., 31
San Leandro, Calif., 91
San Mateo, Calif., 133, 147
Santa Barbara, Calif., 93
Santa Cruz, Calif. , 30, 152, 153
Santa Monica, Calif., 183, 298
Santiglia, Peggy, 80, 82, 85–89
SBK, 35, 59
Sea Witch, 247, 298
Sebastian, John, 200–202, 204–210, 214, 308
Sedaka, Neil, 57
Seguin, Texas, 29
Serendipity Singers, 82
Sherman Oaks, Calif., 221, 278
Shindig, 136
Shrine Auditorium, 288
Siegel, Jay, 52–55, 58, 62–66
Silver City, N.M., 29
Simmons, Jumpin' Gene, 167, 168
Skelton, Red, 231
Slick, Grace, 289
Sly and the Family Stone, 132
Smash Records, 80
Smith, Arthur, and the Crackerjacks, 10
Smoochie's Show Bar, 168, 169
Socorro, N.M., 11
Sonic Studios, 166
Sonny and Cher, 202
Sonoma County, 282
Sony Music Entertainment, 107
Soul, Jimmy, 43
Southern Pines, N.C., 216
Spiral Starecase, 239
Springer, N.M., 12
Springfield, Mo., 13
Springsteen, Bruce, 46
St. Augustine, Fla., 216
St. Louis, Mo., 302
St. Thomas, Virgin Islands, 216
State College Pennsylvania, 278
STAX Records, 166
Steve Boone, 202–204
Stewart, Sylvester "Sly," 132, 134, 147
Stinnett, Ray, 164, 165, 170, 171, 183
Stone, Brian, 288
Stoneground, 143
String-A-Longs, 7, 13
Stuart, Dick, 142
Suffern, N.Y., 74
Sullivan, Ed, 42, 94, 102, 169, 200, 204, 206, 222, 231
Sydney, Australia, 110

T

Tacoma, Wash., 234, 302
Tarzana, Calif., 208, 307
Taylor, James, 106
Terre-Haute, Ind., 252
Texas Tech, 18
Tharp, Chuck, 4, 11, 12, 14, 15, 18, 21, 24, 25, 28–32
Thomas Edison State College, N.J., 91
Thomas, Ray, 118
Thousand Oaks, Calif., 153
Tokens, 52–76
Tomsco, George, 4, 6, 9–15, 18–22, 25, 32
Tonight Show, 75
Top Rank Records, 6, 7, 29
Toronto, Canada, 146, 242
Trammell, Dan, 4, 5, 11, 21, 23–27
Traum, Happy, 274
Tripp, Peter, 90, 94
Tupelo Records, 167
Turks, 40
Twain Harte, Calif., 153, 154
Twin Falls, Idaho, 234
Tyler, Texas, 26

U

UCLA, 288, 307
United Artists Music, 35
United Artists, 86
University College, Dublin, 146
University of California, Berkeley, 159, 258, 279
University of California, Davis, 269
University of Connecticut, 282
University of Nevada, Las Vegas, 18
University of New Mexico, 18
University of Southern California, 253
University of Texas, Arlington, 173
Upland, Calif., 187

V

Valentino, Sal, 132, 135, 141–144, 146, 151, 153, 155
Vancouver, Canada, 242
Vancouver, Wash., 31
Vanguard Records, 260
Ventura, Calif., 143
Vernon Parish, La., 165
Vilardo, Louis, 171
Village Music Hall, 202

W

Waco, Texas, 29
Waits, Tom, 223
Waller, Gordon, 100, 102, 109–114
Warner Bros. Records, 55, 107, 132, 136, 139, 150–154, 157, 208
Warwick Records, 52, 53
Warwick, Clint, 118
Washington, D.C., 296
Watertown, S.D., 233
WCOL, 229
Weinberg, 76
Weis, Danny, 243, 252, 288, 292, 307
Weiss, George, 52
Welcome Back, Kotter, 208
Westhampton, Long Island, 201, 216
Westhampton Beach, Long Island, 216
West Memphis, Ark., 193
Westminster School in London, 100
WHBQ, 184, 192
Wheatbread, Paul, 229, 232, 246–250
Where The Action Is, 247, 249
Whisky à Go Go, 287, 298
White, Stanley, 221
Wichita, Kan., 34
Wienstroer, Norman, 6
Williams, Paul, 253
Wilson, Carl, 187
Wilson, Jackie, 42
Wilson, Sonny, 166, 185
WINS, 58, 86
Winters, Jonathan, 231
Withem, Gary, 228, 229, 232, 235, 243, 251–254, 292
WLAC, 192
WMGM, 90, 94
WNEW
Wolfman Jack, 168
Woodstock Music and Art Fair, 210, 263, 289
Woodstock, N.Y., 210

X

XL Records, 168

Y

Yakima Valley, WA, 234
Yankee, N.M., 10
Yanovsky, Zal, 200–203, 220, 222
Yarrow, Peter, 201
Yes, 300
Yester, Jerry, 203, 204, 214, 220–224
Yolo County California, 264
Ysleta, Texas, 28

Z

Zuma Beach, Calif., 124